Central & South America

healthy travel ✚

Isabelle Young
revised by Tony Gherardin

Healthy Travel – Central & South America
2nd edition, July 2008

Published by
Lonely Planet Publications Pty Ltd ABN 36 005 607 983

Lonely Planet offices
Australia Locked Bag 1, Footscray, Victoria 3011
USA 150 Linden St, Oakland, CA 94607
UK 2nd Floor, 186 City Road, London EC1V 2NT

ISBN 978 1 74059 146 1

Printed through The Bookmaker International Ltd.
Printed in China.

Illustrations: Martin Harris & Kate Nolan
Production: Recapture

Contents...

| INTRODUCTION... | | 10 |

| OVERVIEW... | | 13 |

BEFORE YOU GO... — 25

Sources of Information............ 25	PreTravel Check-ups 51
Immunisations............................ 31	What to Take 55
Malaria Prevention 39	Books.. 62
Travel Health Insurance 50	

| ON THE MOVE... | | 65 |

STAYING HEALTHY... — 71

Acclimatisation................................ 71	Sex & Travel.................................... 99
Food & Water Precautions 77	Injections & Blood
Insects & Parasites........................ 89	Transfusions................................. 102
Accidents & Injury 93	Diet & Nutrition 106
Feet 97	

HELP... — 118

| How to Get Medical Help ......119 | Signs of Serious Illness............. 124 |
| Basics .... 120 | Common Signs & Symptoms .. 125 |

FEVER & HEPATITIS... — 130

Malaria.. 130	Meningococcal Meningitis 141
Dengue & Dengue	Typhoid Fever............................... 143
Haemorrhagic Fever............... 137	Tuberculosis................................. 144
Yellow Fever 140	Viral Hepatitis (Jaundice) 146

DIGESTIVE SYSTEM... — 150

| Diarrhoea.. 150 | Non-Infective Digestive |
| Intestinal Worms........................ 168 | Problems...................................... 171 |

RESPIRATORY SYSTEM... — 176

Colds 176	Glandular Fever 181
Sinusitis 176	Cold Sores 181
Hay Fever 177	Mouth Ulcers 183
Influenza 178	Cough 184
Sore Throat 179	

EARS, EYES & TEETH... 186

Ears 186
Eyes 189
Teeth 196

SKIN... 203

Rashes 203
Prickly Heat 204
Dermatitis 205
Fungal Infections 208
Bacterial Infections 209
Scabies 210
Lice 211
Bedbugs 212
Creeping Eruption 213
Jigger Flea 214

HIV/AIDS & SEXUAL HEALTH... 216

HIV / AIDS 216
Sexually-Transmitted Infections 222

RARITIES... 228

Encephalitis 228
Filariasis 228
Hansen's Disease 230
Hantavirus Pulmonary Syndrome 231
Oropouche Fever 231
Pinta 231
Viral Haemorrhagic Fever 231
Brucellosis 232
Diphtheria 233
Measles 233
Mumps 234
Rubella 235
Tetanus 235
Varicella (Chicken Pox) 235

MENTAL WELLBEING... 236

Travel Stress 236
Culture Shock & Travel Fatigue 238
Anxiety 239
Depression 241
Physical Diseases & Mind Problems 244
Doing Drugs 246

WOMEN TRAVELLERS... 248

Menstrual Problems 248
Menopausal & Post Menopausal Travellers 251
Bladder Infections 253
Vaginal Infections 254
Contraception 258
Pregnant Travellers 265

MEN TRAVELLERS... 270

Travel Health for Gay Men 272

BABIES & CHILDREN... 275

Before You Go 275
On the Move 282
Staying Healthy 284
If Your Child Falls Ill.................289

TRAVELLERS WITH SPECIAL NEEDS... 297

Older Travellers..........................300
Diabetic Travellers 308
HIV-positive Travellers 312

CLIMATE, ALTITUDE & ACTION... 314

Climate..314
Cold...320
Altitude.......................................324
Action Safety.............................332

WATER... 339

Swimming...................................339
Marine Life.................................344
Scuba Diving..............................352
Freshwater Hazards..................360

BITES & STINGS... 365

Flying Insects.............................365
Other Bloodsuckers...................372
Venomous Stings & Bites........377
Animal Bites..............................385

AFTER YOU GET BACK... 389

TRADITIONAL MEDICINE... 394

BUYING & USING MEDICINES... 410

MEDICAL SERVICES... 424

FIRST AID... 434

GLOSSARY... 453

LATIN AMERICAN TERMS... 457

INDEX... 462

EMERGENCY RESUSCITATION... 472

The Authors...

ISABELLE YOUNG

Dr Isabelle Young qualified as a doctor in Britain before deciding there must be more to life than bleeps and hospital coffee. Her travels through various parts of the world have provided her with plenty of opportunity for putting her training into practice.

TONY GHERARDIN

Dr Tony Gherardin is currently National Medical Adviser of the Travel Doctor-TMVC Group in Australia. He is a keen traveller and has spent several years living and working as a doctor overseas. When not travelling with his family, he spends most of his time providing travel health advice to travellers heading in all directions around the globe.

Medical Advisers...

To ensure that the information included in this guide is the best available and in line with current practice, a team of expert medical advisers was on hand every step of the way.

CORINNE ELSE

Help..., Coughs, Rashes & Other Common Problems, Ears, Eyes & Teeth (Ears), Mental Wellbeing, Women Travellers, First Aid (Wound Care), Buying & Using Medicines

Dr Corinne Else spends most of her time working as a general practitioner in the UK. Every now and again she manages to take time off to travel in Africa with her husband, helping him to research and write Lonely Planet guidebooks.

CHRISTOPHER VAN TILBERG

Climate & Altitude, Water Safety, First Aid

Dr Christopher Van Tilberg specialises in wilderness and emergency medicine. He is adventure sports editor for *Wilderness Medicine Letter* and active in mountain rescue and wilderness safety education in the US. He is the author of *Backcountry Snowboarding* and *Canyoneering*, both published by The Mountaineers Books.

JOHN MASON
Babies & Children, Buying & Using Medicines

Dr John Mason was a family physician for 13 years before becoming Clinical Director of the UK-based Preventative Healthcare Company. Part of his responsibility is to provide international travel care and advice to client company employees and their families, as well as managing their healthcare while abroad.

BRIAN MULHALL
HIV/AIDS & Sexual Health

Dr Brian Mulhall is a Clinical Senior Lecturer in the Department of Public Health and Community Medicine at the University of Sydney, Australia. He has travelled extensively and has written several texts on sex and travel. His contribution was sponsored by the New South Wales Health Department and the Commonwealth Department of Health as part of a sexual health promotion program for travellers.

LARRY & PAUL GOODYER
Medical Kit (Before You Go), Safe Drinking Water, Insect Bites (Staying Healthy)

Dr Larry Goodyer is Chief Pharmacist for Nomad Travel Stores & Travel Clinics, London, UK. He is also a senior lecturer in clinical pharmacy at King's College, London. His travels in India and Australia give him the first-hand experience to produce medical kits for both tropical and developing world travel. Paul Goodyer is the CEO of Nomad Travel Stores & Travel Clinics. His travels over the last 20 years include trips to Africa, Asia, South America and the Middle East. Getting ill on the road due to lack of knowledge led to the concept of a travellers' medical centre.

SPECIAL THANKS
Special thanks go to the World Health Organization for permission to reproduce the data for the maps between the first two chapters.

From the Authors...

First, a big thank you to all the medical advisers, without whom this book would not have come into existence. Thank you also to Fred Peterson MD for his helpful comments on the text of *Healthy Travel Central & South America*, many of which are incorporated in the text of this guide.

Thanks go to the following experts who contributed text to the guide: Graeme Johnson for the section on Eyes; Iain Corran for the section on Teeth; Michelle Sobel for the Diabetic Travellers section in Travellers with Special Needs; Chris Wheeler for the text on foot care and blisters (in Staying Healthy and Wilderness Health & Safety); Bernadette Saulenier for the boxed text 'Alternative First Aid for Travellers'; and Elissa Coffman for the section on Alternative Therapies.

Some of the information in this guide was drawn from Lonely Planet guides, which are researched and written by a global team of staff and authors.

Many other people helped make this guide what it is through generously providing information, constructive comments and helpful suggestions. In no particular order, thanks go to Chris Banks and Patrick Honan of Melbourne Zoo for helpful information on snakes, spiders and scorpions; Moya Tomlinson of Women's Health (London) for suggestions for the Women Travellers chapter; Dr Michael Thomas of the Blood Care Foundation and Professor Neil Boyce of the Australian Red Cross for pointers for information on blood transfusions; Dr John Putland of the Qantas Aviation Health Services Department and the British Airways Medical Service in Heathrow for providing heaps of background information on air travel for the On the Move chapter; the National Sports Information Centre (Australia) for great reference material on climatic extremes; John Nathan for helpful insights on older travellers; Roslyn Bullas of Lonely Planet's Diving & Snorkelling series and Susannah Farfor for suggestions for the scuba diving section; the staff at IAMAT for generously providing us with information on their organisation; Darren Elder of Lonely Planet's Cycling series for finding the time to come up with the safety tips for cyclists that appear in the Wilderness Health & Safety chapter; and Jenny Thorpe and Suzanne Harrison, travelling mothers extraordinaire, for invaluable insights into the rigours of travelling with children. Thanks also go to Leonie Mugavin for her helpful suggestions, book-acquiring abilities and moral support.

Finally, in time-honoured tradition, Isabelle would like to thank her partner, David Petherbridge, for his help and unfailing support throughout this project – next time we'll climb mountains instead.

From the Publisher...

This book was commissioned from Lonely Planet's Melbourne office by commissioning editor Bridget Blair and associate publisher Chris Rennie. Production was coordinated by Recapture under director Ivan Levacic, including editing by Julian Lange, design by Katrina Tan and layout by David Kemp. The cover was designed by Mik Rutt, Wayne Murphy created the maps, and Martin Harris is responsible for all the illustrations except for the cone shell illustration by Kate Nolan.

Introduction...

Lonely Planet's aim has always been to enable adventurous travellers to get out there, to explore and better understand the world. Falling ill or getting injured on your travels prevents you from getting the most out of your travelling experience, which is why we've decided to produce this *Healthy Travel* series.

Travelling can expose you to health risks you most probably would not have encountered had you stayed at home, but many of these risks are avoidable with good preparation before you go and some common-sense measures while you are away. Concern about how to cope if you do become ill far from home is natural; this guide aims to alleviate those fears by giving you the background information to make informed decisions about what action to take in a given situation. *We should point out that this guide is not intended as a substitute for seeking medical help.*

Some chapters in this guide are designed to be read through in their entirety; the rest are there for you to dip into if the need arises. Before you leave, we suggest you take a look at the Overview chapter, which summarises the potential health risks of travel in the region, and read through the Before You Go chapter, which gives you the complete low-down on preparations for the trip. Because travel medicine is an ever-changing topic, we've given you plenty of guidance on where to get up-to-the-minute advice and information.

The Staying Healthy chapter gives you detailed advice on avoiding illness and injury while you are away, and is essential reading for everyone. It's a good idea to have a quick read through the When You Get Back chapter on your return as it gives guidance on when you need a check-up and what to look out for.

The rest of the chapters are there in case you need them – and most travellers won't need them. If you do get ill, turn to the Help... chapter. This gives guidelines on how to go about finding medical help (and can be used in conjunction with the Medical Services appendix if necessary), as well as some basic measures for looking after yourself. This chapter also summarises the possible causes of various symptoms you may have. You can use this as a guide to working out what you may have or, if you think you know what the problem is, you can turn to the relevant chapter later in the book. Alternatively, you could look up your symptom in the index.

We've tried to group diseases and other medical problems into easily identifiable categories, which are reflected in the chapter names. However, it's difficult to please everyone – if something is not where you think it should be, it's always worth looking it up in the index.

To cater for the differing needs of a wide range of travellers, we've included four chapters tailored to the needs of women, men, young and special needs travellers.

Because accidents do happen, and help may not be as rapidly available as at home, we've included advice on basic first aid measures, including what to do in an emergency, although bear in mind that you shouldn't rely solely on a book to be able to do resuscitation techniques effectively. If you are going to be travelling in remote areas, it's definitely worth doing a first aid course before you go.

We hope that having this guide will ensure you have a healthy trip, and that if you do encounter problems, it gives you the confidence to deal with them.

CENTRAL & SOUTH AMERICA

0 ——————— 2000 km
0 ——————— 1000 mi

CANADA

UNITED STATES
OF AMERICA

NORTH
ATLANTIC
OCEAN

BAHAMAS

MEXICO

CARIBBEAN
ISLANDS

Caribbean
Sea

WEST
INDIES

See Enlargement

VENEZUELA

GUYANA
SURINAME
FRENCH
GUYANA

PANAMA

COLOMBIA

Galápagos
Islands
(Ecuador)

ECUADOR

PERU

BRAZIL

BOLIVIA

SOUTH
PACIFIC
OCEAN

PARAGUAY

CHILE

URUGUAY

ARGENTINA

CENTRAL AMERICA

MEXICO

BELIZE

Caribbean
Sea

GUATEMALA

HONDURAS

EL
SALVADOR

NICARAGUA

PACIFIC
OCEAN

COSTA
RICA

SOUTH
ATLANTIC
OCEAN

Falklands
Islands/
Islas Malvinas

ANTARCTICA

Overview...

Contrary to what you might expect, it's not hard to stay healthy in Latin America. True, you may encounter health hazards you would not encounter on a holiday back home, but you'd have to be pretty unlucky or just plain careless to succumb to most of these. As long as you are up to date with your immunisations and you take some basic precautions. If you expect to get a few sick days, you probably won't be disappointed, but don't bank on not needing that return ticket.

Your health risks depend on what sort of trip you're planning and where you're going. If you're on a tight budget, and are going to be travelling rough, your health risks are different from if you were planning a two week stay in a tourist resort. Activity holidays anywhere carry higher risks of injury, and in remote or rural areas, emergency medical services are generally nonexistent. The length of your trip is important – more time away means more chance of being exposed to diseases. Contrary to popular belief, you won't become immune to serious diseases like dysentery and malaria even if you have been on the road for several months.

Your destination also affects your health risks as there are differences both between and within countries in terms of which diseases occur where, insect-borne diseases, for example, are usually more common in rural areas than in urban areas. Much of middle and South America is within tropical and subtropical zones – a wide variety of tropical diseases (such as malaria and dengue fever) occur in the region and are risks to you, especially if you travel into the jungle. It's important you take precautions against getting these diseases, but in general, you're far more likely to get a bout of diarrhoea, a cold or an infected mosquito bite than something more exotic like onchocerciasis or Chagas' disease. The heat itself is a major factor to be aware of and to deal with.

There are wide environmental variations across the region, from the notoriously polluted urban areas to the clear air and high altitude of the Andes; the parchment-dry deserts of Chile, steamy rainforests of the Amazon basin and temperate regions of the Southern Cone. You need to be aware of these challenges and know how to minimise the effects on your health.

Although the dangers of natural hazards can loom large in travellers' minds, remember that you're more likely to be injured in a road traffic accident or by other people than by a wild animal. Accidents and injury, especially road traffic accidents, are the main reason why younger travellers return in a box; for older travellers it's complications from preexisting illnesses, often heart disease.

If you do fall ill and need a medical opinion, be aware that medical services may be very different to what you are used to back home. In general, however, medical services are good

WHAT TRAVELLERS ACTUALLY GET

You'll have to try very hard to get anything more interesting than diarrhoea or an infected mosquito bite on your travels in Latin America. Here are some frequently quoted and reassuring figures on the health problems travellers get, compiled by leading travel medicine experts Steffen & Lobel and published in the highly respected reference book *Manson's Tropical Diseases*.

Most common complaint:
• travellers diarrhoea (about 50% of travellers)

Less than 10% of travellers:
• malaria (in travellers to West Africa)
• coughs and colds

Less than 1% of travellers:
• hepatitis A
• gonorrhoea
• animal bites
• hospitalised abroad or had to be evacuated

in most towns and cities, except in less-developed countries (and medical assistance is generally much harder to find in rural areas). You'll need to take this into account when planning your trip, especially if you have any ongoing medical problems or special health needs. It's a good idea to know at least some relevant phrases in Spanish or Portuguese – see the Language appendix at the back of this guide.

Here's a brief summary of what health risks you might be up against and what you can do about them; for more details on all these issues, see the Before You Go and Staying Healthy chapters.

IMMUNISATIONS (p31)

These can help protect you from some infections you may be at risk of contracting on your travels in Latin America. Ideally, you should get your immunisations organised at least six weeks before you travel, although it's always worth seeking advice up to the last minute if necessary.

- You'll need to be up to date with routine immunisations like **tetanus**, **polio** and **childhood illnesses**, including measles, mumps and rubella.
- **Hepatitis A** is strongly recommended for all travellers to Latin America, as is **influenza**
- Depending on your travel plans, you may also need to be protected against some of the following: **hepatitis B**, **meningococcal meningitis**, **rabies**, **typhoid** and **yellow fever**.
- In addition, as a requirement for entry to some countries, you need to have an **immunisation certificate** for yellow fever.

MALARIA PILLS (p42)

Malaria is a serious, but potentially preventable, risk mainly in rural, jungle areas in tropical and subtropical Latin America (see map p20). If you are going to a malarial area, it is vital you get detailed and up-to-date advice on avoiding this disease, including any antimalarial drug to take, before you go.

DISEASES CARRIED BY FOOD & DRINKING WATER (p77)

Risk

Infections transmitted in this way include diarrhoea, dysentery and hepatitis A. These are the most common causes of illness in travellers. Other diseases transmitted through food and water include cholera, typhoid, polio and intestinal worms, but these are not generally common in travellers. All these diseases are more of a risk in the wet season or after a natural disaster like a hurricane.

Prevention

You can avoid getting sick by taking some basic precautions:

- take care over what you eat
- drink safe water
- wash your hands frequently, especially after you use the toilet and before you eat

DISEASES CARRIED BY INSECTS (p89)

Risk

Insect-borne diseases are important health risks in rural areas in tropical and subtropical Latin America, but are much less of a problem in temperate South America.

Malaria (carried by infected mosquitoes) is an important risk to travellers in affected areas (see map p20), and dengue fever (see map p21; also carried by mosquitoes) is becoming increasingly common in travellers as well as in the local population, although travellers are unlikely to get the more severe form of the disease, dengue haemorrhagic fever.

Filariasis and yellow fever (both spread by mosquitoes); onchocerciasis (also called river blindness and spread by blackflies); leishmaniasis (known locally as *espundia*) and bartonellosis (spread by sandflies); Chagas' disease (also called American trypanosomiasis and spread by triatomine bugs, also called assassin bugs, cone-nosed bugs and various local names); typhus and other tick fevers (spread by lice and ticks); and plague (spread by fleas) are other insect-borne diseases that occur in parts of the region. Although some of these diseases are major public health problems in the local population, they are generally low risk to you as a traveller.

Prevention

Given the number of diseases transmitted by insect bites, it's worth doing all you can to prevent insect bites while you are away, wherever you go. Currently, yellow fever is the only one of these infections that can be prevented by immunisation.

OTHER DISEASES
Risk

Schistosomiasis (p92, and see map p23) and leptospirosis (p364) are hazards associated with swimming or doing water sports in fresh water in some parts of the region. Outbreaks of meningococcal meningitis (p364) occur periodically in parts of the region, particularly during the dry season. Rabies (p385) exists throughout the region, and pretravel immunisation may be recommended in some circumstances.

Although tuberculosis (TB; p144) is a major problem worldwide, as a short-term traveller your risk is low unless you will be living in close contact with members of the local population.

Going barefoot can put you at risk of parasites such as hookworm (an intestinal parasite; p169) or jiggers (a skin parasite, also known as *bichos de pé*, p214).

Prevention

You can avoid all these risks with some basic precautions:

- in some situations, it may be appropriate to get immunised against some of these infections, such as meningitis, rabies and TB
- avoid contact with animals as far as possible
- don't walk barefoot or in sandals, especially in rural areas

INFECTIONS TRANSMITTED PERSON-TO-PERSON (p99)
Risk

You're at risk of these infections wherever you go if you don't take measures to protect yourself. HIV/AIDS is mainly transmitted through heterosexual sex in Central and South America, and it's a growing health problem in some parts of the region. The region isn't a hot spot for hepatitis B like, say, the Asian region, but it may be a risk in some situations, and it's worth taking precautions against it. Other sexually transmitted infections such as gonorrhoea and syphilis occur.

Prevention

It makes sense to take precautions to avoid acquiring these infections wherever you go:

- always use a latex condom if you have sex with a new partner
- avoid all injections and any procedure that involves skin-piercing
- avoid any unnecessary medical or dental procedures
- minimise your chance of injury in accidents
- carry an emergency kit containing sterile needles and syringes

BLOOD TRANSFUSION (p103)
Risk

As in many developing regions of the world, blood for transfusion may not be screened as thoroughly as is desirable, due to limited technical resources. Infections that can be transmitted in this way include hepatitis B, HIV and Chagas' disease.

Prevention

You can minimise your chances of needing a transfusion by taking steps to avoid injury and by not travelling if you have a condition that makes blood transfusion a possibility. If transfusion is unavoidable for medical reasons, try to find as reliable a source of blood as possible. Insurance covering evacuation is vital.

ACCIDENTS & INJURY (p93)
Risk

Accidents *do* happen, and they're a common cause of injury (and sometimes death) in travellers. Road traffic accidents, especially involving motorbikes, are a major risk in the region.

Prevention

You can do much to avoid accidents and injury by using some common sense and being aware of potential risks.

ENVIRONMENTAL HAZARDS (p314)
Risk

Sunburn is a major risk in most parts of the region, especially at altitude. Never underestimate the potential dangers of heat, especially if you are planning an activity-packed holiday. Hot, humid conditions in the tropics make infection of cuts and scratches common.

Cold and unpredictable weather are significant risks in highland areas. You need to be aware of the effects of altitude on your health if you are planning on going to the Andes or other highland areas. Other natural hazards to be aware of include erupting volcanoes, hurricanes and earthquakes.

Prevention

You can minimise the impact of environmental challenges:

- protect your skin from the effects of the sun
- remember to allow yourself time to acclimatise to the heat and take steps to avoid dehydration
- look after cuts and scratches to prevent them getting infected
- always be prepared for climatic extremes, especially if you are trekking or walking in highland areas
- learn about the effects of altitude and follow rules for safe ascent

OTHER HAZARDS

Risk

Fleas (p376), lice (p211), bedbugs (p212) and scabies (p210) are potential hazards in many places, especially if you are staying in budget accommodation, but they don't generally cause any more harm than itchy bites. Ticks and mites (p373) are a hazard if you are planning on trekking in rural areas, and can transmit diseases such as typhus. Leeches (p372) are common, especially in damp, forested areas, but they don't transmit any diseases.

Depending on where you are going, you may need to watch out for encounters with the local wildlife, including predatory mammals, crocodiles, snakes, scorpions and spiders. If you're going to be swimming in the sea or in fresh water, you need to be wary of some aquatic creatures (p344).

Prevention

You can avoid most of these hazards by taking basic precautions:

- cover up and use insect repellents
- sleep under an insect net treated with insect repellent
- look but don't touch the local wildlife

MALARIA

UNITED STATES OF AMERICA

MEXICO

BAHAMAS

CARIBBEAN ISLANDS

NORTH ATLANTIC OCEAN

Caribbean Sea

WEST INDIES

See Enlargement

PANAMA

VENEZUELA

GUYANA
SURINAME
FRENCH GUYANA

COLOMBIA

Galápagos Islands (Ecuador)

ECUADOR

PERU

BRAZIL

SOUTH PACIFIC OCEAN

BOLIVIA

PARAGUAY

CHILE

URUGUAY

ARGENTINA

SOUTH ATLANTIC OCEAN

Falklands Islands/ Islas Malvinas

0 — 2000 km
0 — 1000 mi

CENTRAL AMERICA

MEXICO

Caribbean Sea

BELIZE

GUATEMALA

HONDURAS

EL SALVADOR

NICARAGUA

PACIFIC OCEAN

COSTA RICA

Areas with malaria

Areas with no malaria

Areas not covered by this guide

Map data supplied by World Health Organization

Map data supplied by World Health Organization

YELLOW FEVER

0 —————— 2000 km
0 —————— 1000 mi

UNITED STATES
OF AMERICA

*NORTH
ATLANTIC
OCEAN*

MEXICO

BAHAMAS

CARIBBEAN
ISLANDS

*Caribbean
Sea*

WEST
INDIES

See Enlargement

PANAMA

VENEZUELA

GUYANA
SURINAME
FRENCH
GUYANA

COLOMBIA

*Galápagos
Islands
(Ecuador)*

ECUADOR

PERU

BRAZIL

*SOUTH
PACIFIC
OCEAN*

BOLIVIA

PARAGUAY

CENTRAL AMERICA

CHILE

URUGUAY

MEXICO

BELIZE

*Caribbean
Sea*

ARGENTINA

GUATEMALA

HONDURAS

EL
SALVADOR

NICARAGUA

*SOUTH
ATLANTIC
OCEAN*

*Falklands
Islands/
Islas Malvinas*

*PACIFIC
OCEAN*

COSTA
RICA

Areas with
yellow fever

Areas with no
yellow fever

Areas not covered
by this guide

Map data supplied by World Health Organization

SCHISTOSOMIASIS (BILHARZIA)

Areas with schistosomiasis

Areas with no schistosomiasis

Areas not covered by this guide

Map data supplied by World Health Organization

LYMPHATIC FILARIASIS

0 ————————— 2000 km
0 ————————— 1000 mi

UNITED STATES
OF AMERICA

NORTH
ATLANTIC
OCEAN

BAHAMAS

MEXICO

CARIBBEAN
ISLANDS

Caribbean
Sea

WEST
INDIES

See Enlargement

PANAMA

VENEZUELA

GUYANA
SURINAME
FRENCH
GUYANA

COLOMBIA

Galápagos
Islands
(Ecuador)

ECUADOR

PERU

BRAZIL

SOUTH
PACIFIC
OCEAN

BOLIVIA

PARAGUAY

CHILE

URUGUAY

ARGENTINA

SOUTH
ATLANTIC
OCEAN

Falklands
Islands/
Islas Malvinas

CENTRAL AMERICA

MEXICO

BELIZE

Caribbean
Sea

GUATEMALA

HONDURAS

EL
SALVADOR

NICARAGUA

PACIFIC
OCEAN

COSTA
RICA

■ Areas with lymphatic filariasis	■ Areas with no lymphatic filariasis	■ Areas not covered by this guide

Map data supplied by World Health Organization

Before You Go...

Staying healthy on your travels in Latin America requires a little bit of pretravel effort. It may seem like just too much trouble now, but it could save you much hassle later – much better to get it all sorted out before you leave than to have to worry about it while you are away.

It's tempting to leave all this preparatory stuff to the last minute – don't! You'll have a hundred and one other things to do just before you go, and you don't want to have to do them with a sore arm. It's best to start thinking about travel-related health issues as early as possible, and certainly at least six weeks before you go.

Even if things don't work out as planned, it's always worth visiting your doctor or travel health clinic for advice and immunisations, however late you've left it.

SOURCES OF INFORMATION & ADVICE

Part of your pretravel preparations should be to find out about the health risks of your destination, and this has never been easier. You can get up to date information and advice on your travel health risks from your family doctor, travel health clinics, and national and state health departments. Even handier, you've got a great information source at your fingertips – the internet.

Specialist travel health clinics are probably the best places for immunisations and travel health advice,. If you have an ongoing medical condition or any general health concerns, you may prefer to go to your usual doctor as well. Some travel health clinics provide specific travel health briefs (usually for a fee) by mail, phone or fax, which you can then take to your doctor.

Most clinics sell health-related traveller essentials like insect repellent, mosquito nets, and needle and syringe kits; you can also get these from travel equipment suppliers (many via mail order) or your doctor.

For more general information on a variety of travel health issues, you could try some of the many publications available – we've listed a selection under Books at the end of this chapter. There are also authoritative websites providing information on more specialist areas like diving medicine and altitude listed in the relevant sections in this book.

UK

You can get pretravel health advice and immunisations from your GP, university or college health centre, travel medicine clinic or a specialist centre. To get you started, you could try any of the following:

Department of Health (**www.doh.gov.uk**) – government travel health advice is on the Policy and Guidance page. The booklet *Health Advice for Travellers* (available on the website or phone ☎ 0870 155 54 55 to order a copy) has basic advice and details of reciprocal health care agreements.

Hospital for Tropical Diseases Travel Clinic (☎ 020-7388 9600, **www.thehtd.org/content/travel.asp**, Mortimer Market Building, Capper Street, Tottenham Court Rd, London WC1E 6AU) – it has a Healthline on ☎ 020-7950 7799 and advice by country on the Destinations page of its website.

Liverpool School of Tropical Medicine Travel Clinic (☎ 0151-708 9393, **www.liv.ac.uk**, travel health advice line ☎ 0906-110 0210), Pembroke Place, Liverpool L3 5QA) – ring the health line for advice from a qualified travel health nurse.

MASTA (Medical Advisory Services for Travellers, **www.masta-travel -health.com**, enquiries@masta.org) – provides a network of travel clinics as well as information and travel health products.

Nomad Travel Stores & Travel Clinics (☎ 020-8889 7014, Healthline ☎ 09068 633414, **www.nomadtravel.co.uk**) – has travel clinics in London, Bristol, Manchester and Southampton (immunisations, travel health advice etc) and sells a wide range of travel equipment, as well as health-related products.

USA

To find a travel health clinic in your area, you could call your state health department, or you could try one of the following:

Centers for Disease Control & Prevention (CDC, **wwwn.cdc .gov/travel**) in Atlanta, Georgia – this is the central source of travel health information in North America. The CDC has phone (☎ 877-FYI-TRIP, 877-394-8747) and fax (☎ 888-CDC-FAXX, 888-232-3299) travel health information lines; it can also advise you on travel medicine providers in your area. It publishes an excellent booklet, *Health Information for International Travel,* also known as *The Yellow Book,* which is available on the website.

American Society of Tropical Medicine & Hygiene (☎ 847-480-9592, fax 847-480-9282, **www.astmh.org**, 60 Revere Drive, Suite 500, Northbrook, IL 60062) can also provide you with a comprehensive list of travel health providers in your area.

International Society of Travel Medicine (☎ 770-736-7060, **www .istm.org**, 2386 Clower Street, Suite A-102, Snellville, GA 30078) – contact the ISTM for a list of ISTM member clinics.

The US Department of State Overseas Citizens Services website **http://travel.state.gov** has regularly updated travel advisories and health information. Remember to take the phone number (☎ 202-647-5225) with you, as staff can provide you with access to medical advice and assistance over the phone if you are in an emergency situation overseas.

CANADA

You can get information and advice from your physician, a travel medicine clinic, Health Canada or the Canadian Society for International Health. The latter two resources can provide you with a list of travel medicine clinics in your area.

Health Canada (**http://hc-sc.gc.ca/hl-vs/travel-voyage/index_e.html**) – the Travel Health section of this government department provides information on disease outbreaks, immunisations and general health advice for travellers, and more detailed information on tropical diseases, as well as information on travel medicine clinics. You can access this information via the web or through a fax service (613-941-3900).

Canadian Society for International Health (☎ 613-241-5785, fax 241-3845, **www.csih.org**, 1 Nicholas St, Suite 1105, Ottawa, ON K1N 7B7 Canada) – this is a source of basic health information for Canadian travellers, as well as a comprehensive list of travel medicine clinics in Canada.

AUSTRALIA & NEW ZEALAND

To find clinics or advice, try:

Smartraveller – the Australian Department of Foreign Affairs & Trade's travel advisory website (**www.smartraveller.gov.au**) includes a good section on general travel health advice.

The Travel Doctor-TMVC (Travellers Medical & Vaccination Centre) group has a network of clinics in most major cities – use the phone book to find your nearest clinic or check out their website (**www .traveldoctor.com.au**). They can provide an online personalised travel health report (for a fee) via their website.

GENERAL INTERNET RESOURCES

There's heaps of good, reliable information on travel health issues on the internet, and the best thing is that it's accessible while you are on the road (so long as you can find a cybercafe) as well as before you go. Two authoritative websites are the first point of call for the latest on travel health issues:

WHO (**www.who.int**) – the official site of the World Health Organization has all the information you'll ever need on the state of the world's health, including disease distribution maps and all the latest health recommendations for risks and vaccination certificates required worldwide. The section **www.who.int/csr** that's probably going to be most useful to you has disease outbreak news and health advice for travellers. WHO publishes a superb book called *International Travel and Health*, which is revised annually and is available online at no cost.

CDC (**wwwn.cdc.gov/travel**) – the official site of the US Centers for Disease Control & Prevention has loads of useful information for all travellers, including disease outbreak news and disease risks according to destination.

Other sites worth checking out include:

MASTA (**www.masta-travel-health.com**) – this highly recommended site of the Medical Advisory Services for Travellers (see earlier under UK) is easy to use and provides concise, readable information on all the important issues. It provides online, individualised briefs.

MD Travel Health (**www.mdtravelhealth.com**), provides complete travel health recommendations for every country, updated daily.

Medical College of Wisconsin Healthlink (**http://healthlink.mcw .edu**) – this site has useful information on all the usual travel health issues, and an impressively comprehensive list of links to a variety of other travel health information sites. Browse till you drop.

Shorelands (**www.tripprep.com**) – this well organised site is easy to navigate and has lots of good travel health information, as well as a comprehensive directory of travel medicine providers around the world and handy country profiles that contain US State Department travel advisory information.

Travel Doctor-TMVC (**www.traveldoctor.com.au**) – this Australian-based site has lots of useful information, including disease outbreak news and good sections on travelling while pregnant and with children.

USEFUL ORGANISATIONS

The International Association for Medical Assistance to Travelers (IAMAT) is a nonprofit foundation that can provide you with a list of English-speaking doctors worldwide, as well as travel health information. Doctors affiliated to IAMAT charge a fixed fee. Membership is free, but the foundation welcomes a donation. For more details or to join up, check out IAMAT's website **www.iamat.org**.

MedicAlert Foundation International is a nonprofit organisation providing (for a membership fee) medical identification bracelets or tags with details of any drug allergies or important medical conditions you have, plus a call collect number for MedicAlert's 24 hour Emergency Response Center. You might want to consider this if you have asthma, diabetes or severe allergy, or if you're taking steroids or blood-thinning medicine. US residents can enrol at **www.medicalert.org**, by calling ☎ 1-800-ID-ALERT (1-800-432-5378) or by email customer_service@medicalert.org. Non-US residents can contact affiliate offices locally, see **www.medicalert.com.au/ international.html** for a complete list.

International SOS (**www.internationalsos.com**) is an international medical assistance and travel insurance provider who offers 24-hour telephone advice to travellers and may be able to recommend English-speaking doctors.

LATIN AMERICA – SOURCES OF INFORMATION

For information on a wide range of topics associated with travel in Latin America, including health tips, you could try the following resources.

South American Explorers Club – this nonprofit organisation is a long-established favourite of travellers to South America and, more recently, all of Latin America. It provides members, on request, with information on just about any topic to do with travelling in this region, and publishes an informative quarterly magazine (with an 'Ask the Doctor' feature), the *South American Explorer*. To become a member or for more information, contact the US office (☎ 607-277-0488, fax 277-6122, **www.saexplorers.org**), 126 Indian Creek Rd, Ithaca, NY 14850. It also has offices in Lima (Peru) and Quito (Ecuador).

Latin American Bureau – this London-based, nonprofit organisation is a good source of information and has extensive library facilities. It can be contacted on ☎ 020-7278 2829, fax 7833 0715;(**www.lab.org .uk**); or write to Latin American Bureau, 1 Amwell St, London EC1R 1UL, UK.

IMMUNISATIONS

Immunisations can help protect you from some infections you may be at risk of getting on your travels. Unfortunately, there are many more health problems you may encounter while travelling in Latin America that cannot be prevented in this way (for example diarrhoea, malaria and dengue fever). Be wary of advice on immunisations and other health issues given to you by travel agents or embassies, especially if they say that 'no immunisations are needed'. What they mean is that you won't be asked for any vaccination certificates when you roll up at the border, not that you don't need the jabs for your own protection.

VACCINATION CERTIFICATE

Many countries in Latin America require you to have a certificate showing you've been vaccinated against yellow fever (and sometimes cholera, although this is contrary to international law) before they will let you into the country. Quite apart from this, yellow fever vaccination is also medically appropriate for countries in the yellow fever zone. See under Yellow Fever later in this section for more details.

In any case, wherever you're going, it's a good idea to make sure your immunisations are recorded on an official document – your doctor or travel health centre will usually issue you with a record. This is useful for your own information so you know what you're protected against and when you're due for a top-up; if you fall ill, you'll be able to show it to any doctor treating you.

SPECIAL CONSIDERATIONS

Bear in mind that immunisations are not suitable for everyone. If you're pregnant, for example, there are some immunisations that are best avoided – see p267 for more details. Babies and children are also a special case – this is discussed in more detail in the Immunisations section (p277) in the Babies & Children chapter.

Some special situations may mean more vaccinations are recommended, for others, less vaccinations. Considerations your doctor will take into account will include if you have had any serious reactions to immunisations in the past, or if your immunity is lowered for some reason (for example if you're taking steroids or you're HIV-positive). In this situation, some immunisations are best avoided – you should discuss this with your doctor well in advance of travelling. For more details on travelling with HIV, see the Travellers with Special Needs chapter.

TIMING

Ideally, you'll need to make the first appointment for travel health advice about six to eight weeks before you travel. This is because you usually need to wait one to two weeks after a booster or the last dose of a course before you're fully protected, and some courses may need to be given over a period of several weeks. Although there's no medical reason why you can't have all your injections together, it's a bit masochistic and may make side effects like fever or sore arm worse. Generally, if you've had a full course of an immunisation before, you should only need a booster injection now.

Don't panic if you have left it to the last minute. Immunisation schedules can be rushed if necessary and most vaccinations you'll need for Latin America can be given together two weeks, or even one week, before you go. Just bear in mind that you won't be as well protected for the first week or two of your trip as you would be if you'd had them earlier.

! Note that a full course of rabies vaccine takes a month.

WHICH ONES?

Working out which immunisations you're going to need doesn't just depend on where you're going. Your doctor will also take into account the length of your trip, whether you're going to be travelling in rural areas or sticking to resorts, which immunisations you've had in the past, any medications you're on

Vaccine	Full Course	Booster	Comments
cholera	2 doses of oral vaccine	After 2 years	Rarely used for travellers
hepatitis A vaccine	single dose	booster at six to 12 months	gives good protection for at least 12 months; with booster, it probably protects for life
hepatitis B	two doses one month apart plus a third dose six months later	not routinely required	more rapid courses are available if necessary Immunity probably lifelong
meningococcal meningitis	one dose	three years	protection lasts three years
polio	three doses given at four weekly intervals	10 years after primary course, single booster in adult life confers lifelong immunity	full course is usually given in childhood
rabies (preexposure)	three doses over one month	not routinely required	Pre-immunisation safer than postexposure treatment only
tetanus, usually given with diphtheria	three doses given at four-week intervals	every 10 years	full course is usually given in childhood
tuberculosis	single dose	limited protection for life	rarely used in travellers
typhoid	single injection OR three or four oral doses	injection: every three years oral: three to five years	oral typhoid vaccine needs to be completed one week before you start antimalarials
yellow fever	one dose	10 years	generally only given at designated yellow fever vaccination centres; certificate is valid 10 days after the injection

and any allergies you have. So while we can give you an idea of the immunisations you're *likely* to need, for a definitive list you'll need to discuss your individual requirements with your doctor.

Routine Immunisations

Whatever your travel plans, you'll need to be up to date with these (you usually have the primary courses in childhood), because the risk of these infections is generally higher in developing countries. These include:

- tetanus, usually given together with diphtheria
- polio
- measles, mumps and rubella, possibly also *Haemophilus influenzae* (HIB) and chicken pox (varicella)
- influenza

Travel-Related Immunisations

In addition, you'll need some travel-related immunisations, depending on your destination and style of trip; we've listed these in alphabetical order. For more information about the diseases themselves, see the relevant section later in this book.

Cholera

Note that immunisation against cholera is no longer recognised as necessary or effective by WHO, and is therefore not generally recommended (except in special circumstances). As a traveller you are in any case not at a significant risk of getting this diarrhoeal disease. However, some border officials in Latin America (and elsewhere) are demanding to see a certificate of immunisation before allowing travellers across the border, even though this contravenes international law.

Your best bet is to discuss this issue with your travel health clinic or doctor before you go. You may be able to get a certificate of exemption or some other form of relevant documentation to carry with you just in case.

Hepatitis A

All travellers to Latin America should be protected against this common disease. You should have the hepatitis A vaccine, which gives good protection for several years (probably forever if you have a booster). A combined hepatitis A and typhoid vaccine has recently become available, which can help to cut down the number of injections you need to have.

Hepatitis B

Although hepatitis B is not as common generally in Latin America as in some other parts of the world (such as Southeast Asia), protection against this liver infection is recommended for long-term travellers, especially if you will be living or working closely with members of the local population. Other situations in which it is usually recommended are if you're going to be working as a medic or nurse or if needle sharing or sexual contact with a local person is a possibility at your destination. This immunisation is now given routinely to children in some countries, including Australia and the USA, so you may already be protected. If you need both hepatitis A and B immunisations, a combined vaccine is available.

Meningococcal Meningitis

Outbreaks of this disease occur periodically in some parts of Latin America, such as the São Paulo area of Brazil. Vaccination is not generally recommended except in special circumstances.

Rabies

+ For advice on what to do if you get bitten by a potentially rabid animal, see p385.

Rabies occurs throughout Latin America, and is a potential risk wherever you go. With rabies, you can choose to have a course of injections before you go (called preexposure), which gives you some protection, or you can just have the injections if you get bitten (postexposure) by a suspect animal.

If you decide to get vaccinated before you go, this consists of three injections given over the course of a month, and it's one of the more expensive vaccines. This primes your system against rabies, giving you partial, but not complete, protection against the disease. If you then get bitten by a suspect animal, you will need to have two booster injections to protect you fully. The old rabies injections were given into the stomach and were extremely uncomfortable, but the modern rabies vaccine

is usually given in your arm and has few side effects. However, the older vaccine may still be used in less developed countries.

If you decide not to have the preexposure vaccination and you get bitten by a suspect animal while you are away, you will need to have the full course of rabies vaccination (five injections over a month) as well as an immediate injection of rabies antibodies (also called human rabies immunoglobulin, or RIG).

RIG can be made from horse or human blood. Human-derived RIG may be difficult to obtain in some countries in Latin America and even if it is available, it's probably best to avoid locally produced human blood products. The other consideration is cost – both types of RIG are very expensive. This is why preexposure vaccination is always considered better than postexposure only.

! To save yourself hassle, worry and a huge medical bill, take all possible precautions to avoid getting bitten.

It's worth taking time to discuss the issue with your doctor or travel health clinic, but you should consider having preexposure rabies vaccination if you're planning on travelling through Latin America for more than three months, or if you will be handling animals for some reason. Children are at particular risk of animal bites, so it may be worth getting them vaccinated even on a short trip.

Tuberculosis

This infection is widespread in Latin America, but generally poses a small risk to travellers. You may already have been protected against this as a child. If you weren't, you probably won't need it unless you're going to be living with local people (for example if you're going back to visit relatives) for three months or longer. Note that this immunisation is not given in the USA and some European countries.

! In some circumstances (eg if you're going to be living and working with local people in a high-risk area) it may be useful for you to have a skin test for TB before you go, as this can help in diagnosing TB when you get back – discuss this with your doctor if necessary.

Typhoid

You'll need to be protected against typhoid if you're travelling in Latin America for longer than a couple of weeks. Although typhoid is generally uncommon in travellers, it is relatively more common in travellers to Mexico. The new injectable vaccine causes few side effects. For those who would prefer to avoid an injection, there is an oral vaccine, although this can sometimes cause a stomach upset.

Yellow Fever

There are two things you need to be aware of with this immunisation. First, proof of immunisation against yellow fever is a statutory requirement for entry into most Latin American countries if you are coming from a yellow-fever infected country in Africa or South America. Second, regardless of whether you need a certificate as an entry requirement, you need the vaccination to protect yourself from the disease if you are planning to visit rural areas of infected countries (see map p22). In 1996, two travellers died from yellow fever thought to have been acquired in forested areas of Brazil.

Yellow fever does not exist in all parts of Latin America, but mosquitoes capable of transmitting it do. In theory, this means it could exist if travellers from infected areas bring the disease with them. Yellow fever-free countries protect themselves from this risk by requiring you to be immunised if you are coming from an infected area. Countries differ in how they define 'infected' – discuss this with your doctor before you go, or check any of the information sources listed earlier in this chapter.

The yellow fever vaccine occasionally causes low-grade fever and a sore arm. It's not recommended if you have severe hypersensitivity to eggs or are immunocompromised for some reason.

SIDE EFFECTS

Immunisations are like any other medication: they can have unwanted effects. These are generally unpleasant rather than dangerous, although occasionally, serious allergic reactions can occur. There's no evidence that immunisations damage your immune system in any way.

A HOMOEOPATHIC ALTERNATIVE?

Yes, there are homoeopathic alternatives to 'conventional' immunisations. But be aware that their effectiveness has not been fully explored, especially under travelling conditions.

In its leaflet *Homoeopathy and Foreign Travel*, the UK-based Society of Homoeopaths (☎ 0845-450 6611, **www.homeopathy-soh.org**, email info@ homeopathy-soh.org) states, 'Whilst the value of homoeopathic remedies in the treatment of disease is well established, their value in the prevention of specific disease is not well documented'

There are practical issues to consider, too: homoeopathic immunisations need to be taken regularly, as their action is short-lived, and it's easy to forget doses and perhaps put yourself at unnecessary risk. Also, because you take these remedies orally (rather than by injection), their effectiveness may be reduced if you get a bout of diarrhoea and vomiting.

Discuss these remedies with your homoeopath as well as with your doctor or a travel medicine specialist before you go, but you might want to consider them if have left your immunisations to the last minute – you could boost protection with a homoeopathic remedy for a week or so until the protective effect of the injection kicks in. Homoeopathic immunisations may be useful if you can't have the injections.

To find out more about homoeopathic immunisations, contact a registered homoeopathic practitioner or your national organisation of homoeopaths. Some of the publications on homoeopathic medicine listed under Books at the end of this chapter cover this topic.

If you tend to faint after injections, plan to sit quietly for 20 minutes or so afterwards. The most common reactions are soreness around the injection site, sometimes with redness and swelling, and maybe a slight fever or a general feeling of being unwell. Tetanus, for example, commonly gives you a sore arm, while the hepatitis A vaccine can occasionally give you a fever in the evening. These reactions generally settle quickly with painkillers and rest, while an ice pack on your arm can help soothe any soreness.

> **If you get more serious reactions that don't settle overnight, you should contact the doctor or clinic where you got your injections.**

Very occasionally, immunisations can provoke allergic reactions because of substances they may contain, such as albumin from eggs, which is why you sometimes have to stay at the clinic for observation for a little while after the injection. Allergic reactions are a possibility with any immunisation, but some (for example yellow fever) are more likely to cause this than others. These reactions are more likely if you know you are allergic to eggs or if you have multiple allergies, especially to bee stings – something you should make sure your doctor is aware of.

MALARIA PREVENTION

Malaria is on the increase worldwide, including Latin America, where it is mainly a problem in rural, jungle and coastal areas in the tropics – see the map on p20.

> **If you're going to a malarial area, it's vital you take precautions to protect yourself from this potentially fatal disease.**

To protect yourself from malaria, you need to:

- get the latest information on risks and drug resistance from a reliable information source (see following section)
- take suitable malaria preventive drugs or carry malaria treatment with you if appropriate – discuss this with your doctor or a travel health clinic before you go, and see the section on p49

MALARIA FACTS

- Malaria is spread by mosquitoes.
- Malaria is a potentially fatal disease.
- Malaria is becoming more common and more difficult to treat because of drug resistance.
- Most cases of malaria in travellers occur in people who didn't take malaria prevention medications or who didn't take them properly.
- Most malaria deaths in travellers occur because the diagnosis is delayed or missed.
- Malaria is particularly dangerous in children and pregnant women.
- Malaria can be transmitted by transfusion of blood and other blood products, by needle sharing among intravenous drug users and from mother to foetus.

■ take steps to avoid insect bites – see the section on Insect Bites (p89) in the Staying Healthy chapter; this is even more important now that malarial parasites have become resistant to many commonly used malaria prevention medications

■ make sure you know a bit about the disease before you go, including what to do if you think you have got it – see the Malaria section in the Fever chapter for more information on diagnosing and treating malaria

MALARIA INFORMATION SOURCES

Because malaria risks and antimalarial drug resistance patterns are constantly changing, it's important you get the most up-to-date information on this before you go. Detailed information on all aspects of malaria, including risks and prevention, is readily available from travel health clinics and specialist centres

ANTIMALARIALS – THE GREAT DEBATE

Which malaria pills to take, and whether to take them at all, tends to be a hot topic of conversation among travellers to malarial areas. Listen to what people have to say, but bear the following in mind:

- the risk of death or severe illness is much greater if you don't take antimalarial drugs
- if you are taking medication to prevent malaria, the disease is less severe if you do get it
- all drugs have side effects and malaria pills are no exception; get reliable information on the risk of side effects and balance this up against the risk of malaria
- if you can't, or would prefer not to, take a particular malaria prevention medication, there are other possibilities that may be better than taking nothing at all
- you can get malaria even if you're taking your malaria pills correctly (because of drug resistance or possibly inappropriate recommendations), but see the first two points before you decide not to take them because of this
- widespread use of chloroquine has resulted in malarial resistance but on an individual basis, it's difficult to see how not using malaria pills and putting yourself at risk of illness and death will help change this
- travel medicine specialists can provide up-to-date advice
- different authorities in different countries may recommend different medications, there is no global consensus, but the principles remain the same

via phone, fax or the internet – see Sources of Information & Advice earlier in this chapter for more details. For more general information on all aspects of the disease, you could try the Malaria Foundation website (**www.malaria.org**).

Because malaria prevention is such a complex and changing issue, it's best not to rely completely on advice from friends or other travellers, however well intentioned or knowledgeable they are.

MALARIA RISK

Malarial mosquitoes bite at night and tend to be more common in rural areas than urban areas (although there are exceptions). This means that if you are going to a malarial area and you are planning to spend time in rural areas at dusk and during the hours of darkness, your risk of malaria is higher than if you spend all your time in urban areas.

Mosquitoes breed in stagnant water, so the risk of malaria is seasonal to a certain extent, with a higher risk just after the rainy season. You're generally safe from malarial mosquitoes above altitudes of 2500m (for example the highland areas of Costa Rica and Guatemala are risk free).

Just be aware that areas within the same country can have different risks of malaria and different areas may have different levels of resistance to antimalarial treatment and prevention drugs.

MALARIA PREVENTION DRUGS

❚ Remember that even if you are taking malaria prevention
medication, it's just as important to take all possible precautions
● against insect bites – see p89.

These drugs work not by preventing malarial parasites from entering your body but by killing off the parasites at a stage of their development before they can cause the disease. In recent years, the use of drugs to prevent and treat malaria has got a whole lot more complicated because of the emergence of drug resistance. The malarial parasite is now resistant to many of the old drugs used to prevent and treat malaria, especially chloroquine but also proguanil, Fansidar (pyrimethamine/sulfadoxine) and even newer drugs like mefloquine.

The answer to the problem of malarial resistance currently vexes whole departments of experts, but it's generally believed to lie in controlling the mosquitoes that spread the disease. There are hopes of a malarial vaccine, but there's still a long way to go before this becomes a reality.

Currently, chloroquine is the recommended drug for most risk areas in Mexico and Central America, apart from Panama east of the Canal Zone and the San Blas Islands. In risk areas of South America, chloroquine resistance is widespread, and so mefloquine, or Doxycycline or atovaquone-proguanil combination (Malarone), are the recommended drugs except for Paraguay, Peru apart from the border areas with Ecuador and Brazil, and the limited risk areas of Argentina near the border with Bolivia. Make sure you get the latest information on recommendations before you go, as these change all the time.

You'll need to discuss with your doctor which antimalarial drugs to take, as it's not just a question of where you're going – you also need to take into account your age, any medical conditions you have, if you're pregnant, any medications you're on, any allergies you have and what your risk of malaria is likely to be.

> **!** Just to confuse the issue, note that different prescribing authorities may make different recommendations; US travellers, for example, will not be recommended to take proguanil, which is popularly used in Canada and Europe.

For some low-risk malarial areas, such as some resort areas in Mexico, you may not need to take malaria pills; instead you may be advised to carry emergency malaria treatment to use as necessary. Before you go, make sure you are clear on what to do if you think you have malaria.

Although you will probably be able to buy antimalarial drugs in most risk areas in Latin America, it's handier to take all you think you will need with you.

Doses & Timing

You need to start taking malaria pills before you leave, so that they have a chance to reach maximum protective levels in your body before you arrive at your destination. It also gives any side effects a chance to show themselves so you can change medication before you go if necessary.

- Chloroquine (with or without proguanil) needs to be started at least one week in advance.
- It's best to start mefloquine two to three weeks before you go – see the boxed text on mefloquine for more details.
- Doxycycline needs to be started two days before you enter a malarious area.
- Atovaquone-proguanil (malaone) can be started one day before entering the malaria area.

Make sure you are clear on what dose to take before you leave – some drugs need to be taken weekly and some need to be taken daily, and you don't want to get it wrong.

Drug	Adult Dose
chloroquine	500mg once weekly
proguanil	dose daily
mefloquine	250mg (one tablet) once weekly
doxycycline	dose100mg daily
atovaquone-proguanil	dose 1 tab daily

To give you the best protection, malaria prevention medication needs to be taken regularly, so try to get into a routine before you leave. It's best to take your malaria pills after food, as this makes side effects like nausea and stomach upset less likely.

LONG-HAUL TRAVELLERS

If you're planning on travelling in a malarial area for six months or more, you may be wondering what to do about malaria prevention medication. You've got two main options: you can either continue to take the usual malaria preventive pills or you can decide not to take them. If you do decide to stop them (discuss this with your doctor before you go), you need to be extremely vigilant about avoiding mosquito bites, and you need to be very clear about where your nearest doctor is and when to take emergency standby treatment. Taking malaria pills for more than six months can work out to be quite expensive, and, unless you're really conscientious, it can be easy to forget to take your pills. Note that you don't build up immunity to malaria with time, so you're still at risk of getting it, even if you've been in a risk area for a long time.

Don't be tempted to stop taking your malaria pills as soon as you leave the region, or you may get malaria from parasites you picked up in the last few days of your trip.

- Most antimalarials need to be continued for four weeks after returning home, except malarone which can be stopped seven days after the malaria area.

SIDE EFFECTS & CAUTIONS

All antimalarial drugs cause minor side effects; however, if you experience severe side effects that make you uncertain about continuing the drug, see your doctor and discuss alternatives.

Chloroquine (Aralen)
There's long experience of use of chloroquine (and proguanil), and it's a pretty safe drug if taken as recommended. Minor side

SHOULD I TAKE MEFLOQUINE?

Here's a brief rundown of the issues surrounding this controversial malaria drug.

No one doubts that mefloquine (Lariam) is currently one of the most effective drugs at preventing malaria; the issue is side effects. Mefloquine commonly causes 'minor' side effects like nausea and diarrhoea, as do the other antimalarials, but it can also have more disturbing side effects. These range from weird dreams, dizziness and anxiety to panic attacks, depression and even fits (seizures). Some travellers claim to be permanently affected by mefloquine. Equally, a large proportion of travellers take mefloquine and have no problems.

Experts disagree on how common the disabling side effects are. Figures from studies range from one in 10,000 (about the same number as for travellers taking chloroquine and proguanil) to much higher rates (one in 140 in a recent study by the London School of Hygiene & Tropical Medicine).

While serious side-effects are probably rare, the nuisance common side-effects appear to occur more frequently than with other anti-malarials and this may affect whether a traveller takes the tablets properly, or at all. As a result of the controversy, the British guidelines for the use of mefloquine were thoroughly reviewed in 1997, and it was agreed that because of the risk of side effects, mefloquine should only be used when the risk of resistant malaria is high. Mefloquine is, however, widely prescribed elsewhere, especially in the US.

We suggest you find out for yourself what different people have to say about mefloquine and then make up your own mind.

You can get information on mefloquine from any travel health clinic, your doctor, a pharmacist or any of the websites listed earlier in this chapter. For more specific information about the mefloquine issue, you could check out the Lariam Action USA website (**www.lariaminfo.org**), which has good links to other resources on mefloquine, or the excellent 'Lariam or not to Lariam' (**www.geocities.com/The Tropics/6913/lariam.htm**), which has an incredibly comprehensive list of links, including one to the manufacturer of Lariam, Hoffman LaRoche. Alternatively, contact Lariam Action USA (info@lariaminfo.org), # 64 El Pavo Real Circle, San Rafael, CA 94903-3521.

Whatever you decide, remember that malaria is a potentially fatal disease and it's vital you take precautions against it.

effects are common and include headaches, nausea, diarrhoea, indigestion, blurred vision (temporary) and itching (especially if you're dark-skinned). Prolonged use of chloroquine (usually more than five years) can cause more serious eye problems, but this tends to be of more concern for expatriates than travellers.

! Chloroquine isn't suitable for everyone: you shouldn't take it if you have epilepsy or are taking medication for epilepsy.

Proguanil
This causes few side effects, but can cause mouth ulcers. Proguanil is not available in the USA, but if you wanted to take it, it is widely available in Europe and Canada.

Mefloquine (Lariam)
Minor side effects are relatively common, and include nausea, dizziness, vivid dreams and difficulty sleeping, and gastrointestinal upset. More severe side effects have also been reported – see the boxed text for a fuller discussion of this issue.

Mefloquine is not suitable for everyone; discuss with your doctor, but you should not take it in the following situations:

- if you have epilepsy or have had a fit in the past
- if you have had severe depression or other major mind problems
- if you are on certain medicines (such as beta blockers for a heart condition)
- because of the risk of dizziness and fits, mefloquine is best avoided if you're going to be doing precision tasks like scuba diving or flying a plane, or if you are going to high altitude (it could mask signs of altitude sickness)

Doxycycline

Side effects include diarrhoea, hypersensitivity of your skin to sunlight, and vaginal thrush. It may make the oral contraceptive pill less effective, so if this might be a problem for you, get advice on this before you go. Doxycycline can cause irritation in your stomach, so you should always swallow it with plenty of water.

Atovaquone-proguanil (Malarone)

This is a relatively new combination drug with good effect at both prevention and treatment of malaria. It is taken daily, and can be started only one day before entering the malaria area, and needs to be taken for only one week after leaving a risk area.

It is suitable for children down to 5-10 kg in weight, and has no specific general contraindications, although is not recommended for pregnant women.

It is remarkably free from side-effects, occasionally causing nausea or loose motions. The big catch is cost, it is very expensive, and so is often not suitable for long travel as the cost is to high.

Pregnant Women & Children

It's vital to discuss this issue with your doctor or travel health clinic as early as possible.

✚ Note that because malaria is a much more serious disease in pregnant women and children, and some of the more effective antimalarial drugs are not suitable, travel to high-risk malarial areas is not recommended – for more details, see the Pregnant Travellers section (p267) and the Babies & Children chapter (p270).

If necessary, chloroquine (with or without proguanil) is safe in pregnancy, although you may need to take a folate supplement if you are taking proguanil. Mefloquine is best avoided in the first three months of pregnancy, although it can be taken in the final six months of pregnancy if absolutely necessary. Doxycycline is best avoided in pregnancy. Atovaquone-proguanil should be avoided in pregnancy

Chloroquine (with or without proguanil) is suitable for babies and children; mefloquine is suitable for children above five kg, and atovaquone–proguanil is licenced for children of 5-10 kg and above. Doses are based on weight. Doxycycline is not suitable for children under 12 years.

EMERGENCY STANDBY TREATMENT
For detailed guidelines on emergency treatment of malaria, see the section on p133.

If you are going to a high-risk malarial area without access to medical care, you need to take treatment doses of antimalarial medication with you for use in an emergency. Discuss this issue with your doctor or travel health clinic before you go. It's not just a question of popping the pills; you also need to be clear about when to use it and what to do if problems arise. For treatment you need to use a different medication from the one you used for prevention.

If you can get hold of one, it's a good idea to take a malaria diagnostic test kit (eg MalaQuick) with you too. These kits are fairly accurate, although not so easy to use in the field. You can get them from selected travel health clinics (including Travel Doctor-TMVC in Australia and New Zealand, and Nomad Travel Stores & Travel Clinics in the UK). You can use the kits to confirm the diagnosis if you suspect you have malaria, even if you were taking malaria prevention medication. They usually contain two tests and you'll need to try to keep them as cool as possible, as this prolongs their lifespan.

TRAVEL HEALTH INSURANCE

However lucky (or poor) you're feeling, it's vital you have adequate travel health insurance to cover your whole trip, usually as part of a general travel insurance covering loss of belongings, flight cancellations etc. Even if the costs of medical care and supplies in many countries are low, the costs of medical evacuation are always phenomenal (thousands of dollars). If you have medical insurance in your home country, remember that it may not cover you for travel in Latin America.

Travel insurance policies are available from a variety of sources related to the travel industry, including credit or charge card companies, travel agents and travel health clinics, as well as from insurance brokers. Insurance policies vary in the details of the services they provide, so shop around to find exactly what you want. Always check the small print so you're clear on exactly what the policy covers.

Many insurance providers have a 24 hour hotline you can ring for assistance in an emergency, and they can usually provide you with names of English-speaking doctors (if necessary), arrange referral to a hospital and guarantee payment if you need to pay upfront (as is usual in most Latin American countries).

Most insurance policies should cover you for medical evacuation if necessary, but it's worth checking this. Some companies provide their own air transport and emergency services, while others contract it out.

You will need to inform the insurance providers of any medical condition you have, as this may increase the premium you have to pay. Once you're over a certain age, usually 65 years, your premium automatically increases. Note that routine health problems and preexisting conditions (and sometimes pregnancy) are not usually covered by travel health insurance policies.

Check if your policy covers the following:

■ the total cost of any medical or surgical treatment you might need

■ any additional costs you might incur if you were delayed by illness or injury or had to travel when injured

- emergency evacuation – without insurance this can cost thousands of dollars, which you would need to provide upfront
- provision of safe blood supplies
- dental treatment
- travel while pregnant
- adventure sports, eg altitude, trekking or scuba diving – consider getting special insurance to cover these activities if necessary (for details about insurance for diving, see p353)

Note that you will generally have to pay cash upfront for medical treatment and be reimbursed later, so it's a good idea to have an emergency stash just in case (your insurance provider may be able to provide a guarantee of payment which may be accepted instead, but don't count on it). Always keep any receipts in case you need to present them later to be reimbursed.

If you're going somewhere remote, you may want to consider registering with a local air ambulance service in case you need to be evacuated for medical reasons.

PRETRAVEL CHECK-UPS & OTHER PREPARATIONS

MEDICAL CHECK-UP

Not everyone needs a medical check-up before going on a trip, but in some situations it's a good idea.

- If you're going to be away for more than about six months or you're going to remote areas, now is the time to get any niggling problems checked out.
- If you're going to be doing something strenuous like trekking at altitude and you're on the good side of 40, it's probably a good idea to have a fitness check before you go.
- If you need any prescription medicines from your doctor – ask your doctor for a copy of your prescription to take with you, and a letter of authorisation to keep customs officials happy.
- If you are going to be travelling to remote areas, you should discuss taking emergency treatment for diarrhoea or chest infections with you, which you will need to get on prescription.

HEALTH-RELATED DOCUMENTS

When you're travelling, try to keep the following health-related information on your person at all times, in case of emergency:

- travel insurance hotline number
- serial number of your travel insurance policy
- contact details of your nearest embassy
- US State Department's Citizen's Emergency Center number (US citizens only)
- summary of any important medical conditions you have
- contact details of your doctor back home if necessary
- copy of prescription for any medication you take regularly
- any serious allergies
- blood group
- prescription for glasses or contact lenses
- if you are a diabetic, a letter from your doctor explaining why you need syringes etc

If you're planning on doing any diving while you are away, remember to get a specific diving medical check-up before you go as, in theory at least, you'll need a certificate of fitness before any dive centre will let you dive.

Women Travellers

Travel can pose problems with certain forms of contraception (see p258) and hormone replacement therapy (see p252), so it's best to discuss this with your doctor before you go. Make sure you take a plentiful supply of any medications with you, in case your brand is not available locally. If you think you may need to start contraception, it's worth getting this sorted out well before you go, in case you need to try a few different options before you find one that suits you. For a summary of the main options and their pros and cons on the road, see p260.

It is possible to stop your periods temporarily (p249) if they're going to be a real nuisance (for example if you're going to be trekking in a remote area), but it's best to discuss this with your doctor before you go. If you know you are prone to thrush (vaginal candidiasis or yeast infections) or cystitis (bladder infections), you may want to discuss taking prescription treatment for these conditions with you.

If you're planning on travelling while you're pregnant, you'll need to discuss this with your doctor as early as possible – see the section on Pregnant Travellers (p265) for more information.

Babies & Children

If you are planning on travelling with babies or young children, it's sensible to discuss with your doctor tactics for dealing with common problems you might face while you are away, as well as getting advice on immunisations and precautions to take. We've covered these issues in more detail in the Before You Go section of the Babies & Children chapter later in this book.

DENTAL CHECK-UP

You know it makes sense… You don't want to find you need a filling when you're travelling in a remote area far from the nearest painkilling injection. It's definitely worth making time for this before you go, especially if you haven't been for a while. Your teeth can get quite a battering when you're travelling, as you often end up drinking large quantities of sweet drinks, and if water supplies are unreliable, you may have to take a break from your usual dental health routine. For guidelines on keeping your teeth healthy while you are away, see the section on Teeth in the Ears, Eyes & Teeth chapter.

EYES

If you wear contact lenses, it's probably a good idea to talk to your optometrist about hygiene and other issues on the road. It's a good idea to take a plentiful supply of any cleaning solutions you use. If you wear glasses, consider taking a replacement pair, and take a copy of your prescription with you. It will be understood in any language if you need to have a replacement pair made up while you are away. See the Eyes section of the Ears, Eyes & Teeth chapter for more details.

FIRST AID & SURVIVAL SKILLS COURSES

Although we include guidelines on basic first aid, including emergency resuscitation, in the First Aid appendix of this book, it's no substitute for hands-on training. Everyone should be familiar with basic first aid techniques, but it is even more important if you are going to places where you cannot rely on rapid response emergency services. If you're going to be spending time in remote areas more than a day or so away from medical help (for example if you're trekking in the Andes), you should consider doing at least a basic first aid course before you leave. Contact your local first aid organisation for details of courses available. Training in appropriate survival skills is generally offered by organisations or companies concerned with wilderness activities such as mountaineering and trekking. The American Red Cross also provides training in survival skills.

EXPEDITIONS

If you're planning an expedition, the Geography Outdoors centre at the Royal Geographical Society (☎ 020-7591 3000, **www.rgs.org/eac**, 1 Kensington Gore, London SW7 2AR, UK) has good information aimed at serious expeditioners.

The South American Explorer's Club (p30) can also help with planning an expedition. Some travel health clinics (for example Nomad Travel Stores & Travel Clinics – see the UK entry under Sources of Information & Advice earlier for contact details) and equipment suppliers offer medical kits designed specifically for expeditions.

WHAT TO TAKE

MEDICAL KIT

Although in most countries in Latin America you shouldn't have any trouble getting medications, which are often readily available without prescription, it's handy to take at least a small selection of familiar basics with you. In less-developed countries, medications may be in short supply and difficult to obtain. In addition, there may be concerns about the quality of medications available in some countries. Having your own supply with you also saves the hassle of having to find a supply and then possibly having to decipher instructions written in another language.

Be Prepared

Before you go, make sure you are clear about when and how to use any medication you have with you side effects are more likely if medicines are taken inappropriately or in the wrong dose. Many medicines come with an information leaflet from the manufacturers giving safety information and guidance for use, so keep this for reference.

If you take any medicine regularly (for example for a heart condition or the contraceptive pill), remember to take a record of the prescription, giving the generic name as well as the brand name and dose in case you need to replace it for any reason.

If you're allergic to any drugs (such as penicillin), you should carry this information with you at all times. You can get engraved bracelets or tags with this information from specialist companies like MedicAlert (see Useful Organisations earlier in this chapter).

Customs

Customs officials can sometimes be suspicious of medications you may be carrying (there have been a few horror stories

DRUG NAMES

This is a confusing issue for everyone, medics included. All drugs have two names: a generic (official medical) name and the brand name (chosen by the manufacturer). Because brand names vary from country to country, we've used the official medical name for all drugs mentioned in this book. This may seem a bit frustrating to you if you're reading this at home, but it means that any doctor or pharmacist anywhere in the world will be able to recognise the generic name (or at least can look it up) and should be able to suggest brands available locally.

If you want to find out the generic name of a drug, look on the packet or leaflet accompanying the drug – the generic name should be there, usually in smaller type just below the brand name – or ask a pharmacist.

You'll find more information on all aspects of buying and using medicines while you are away in the appendix at the back of this book.

along the lines of 'Innocent Traveller Arrested for Carrying Painkillers'), so it's best to keep medicines in their original packaging or container where possible, ideally with a prescription or doctor's letter showing what it is and why you need to take it. If you keep all your medications in an official-looking medical kit, you're less likely to have problems.

Sterile 'AIDS' kits containing needles and syringes are usually easily recognised as such and shouldn't cause you problems at customs, but carrying loose syringes and needles is not a good idea. If you need these for a medical condition such as diabetes, make sure you have a doctor's letter to say why you need them.

The Kit

 If you're travelling with children, turn to the Babies & Children chapter for more guidance on what to take.

What you take depends on where you're going and what you're planning to do. What products you actually take will also depend on what your favourite brands are and what's available in your country – check with your pharmacist.

You can make up your own kit, or prepacked kits are widely available from travel health clinics and other travel equipment suppliers, saving you the trouble of having to think about what you might need. Better still, you can take a prepacked kit and add your own extras to it, perhaps using a combination of 'conventional' and 'natural' supplies.

Zip-lock plastic bags are handy for keeping medical supplies, and it's probably best to keep the whole kit together in a waterproof container, such as a clear plastic box.

Try to keep medicines as cool as possible (ie in the middle of your pack) and out of direct sunlight. Remember to keep all medicines out of reach of babies and children.

Lotions, Potions & Pills

Consider including these for travel to most destinations in Latin America:

- any prescription medicines, including malaria prevention drugs if necessary
- paracetamol (acetaminophen) or aspirin for pain and fever; consider also taking a stronger painkiller like co-codamol or an anti-inflammatory like ibuprofen
- antidiarrhoeals – loperamide (probably the most useful and effective) or bismuth subsalicylate (Pepto-Bismol)
- 'indigestion' remedies such as antacid tablets or liquids
- oral rehydration sachets and measuring spoon for making up your own solution
- antihistamine tablets for hay fever and other allergies, and for itching
- sting relief spray or hydrocortisone cream for insect bites

- emergency bee sting kit containing adrenaline (epinephrine) if you are allergic to stings
- sunscreen and lip salve with sunblock
- insect repellent (DEET or plant-based) and permethrin (for treating mosquito nets and clothes)
- anti-motion sickness remedies (such as promethazine or natural remedies – see p60)
- water-purifying tablets or water filter/purifier
- over-the-counter cystitis treatment
- antifungal cream for athlete's foot, crotch rot and thrush
- calamine cream or aloe vera for sunburn and other skin rashes

In addition, you could consider taking:

- sugar-free chewing gum to keep your mouth moist in hot dry climates
- cough and cold remedies and sore throat lozenges
- eye drops for tired or dusty eyes
- multivitamins

First Aid Equipment

We don't want to weigh you down, but you'll probably be glad to have at least some of these with you:

- thermometer
- scissors
- tweezers – to remove splinters and ticks
- sticking plasters (such as Band-Aids) of various sizes
- gauze swabs and adhesive tape
- bandages and safety pins to fasten them
- nonadhesive dressings
- antiseptic powder or solution (eg povidone-iodine), antiseptic wipes
- sterile kit, including needles, syringes, suture kit, cannula for giving a drip
- wound closure strips or butterfly closures (can sometimes be used instead of stitches)

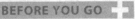

Prescription Medicines

Discuss with your doctor, if you need to take the following with you:

- emergency treatment for malaria plus malaria diagnosis kit (see p49)
- antibiotics for treating diarrhoea
- a course of antibiotics for chest, ear, skin etc infections, if you're going to be travelling off the beaten track
- antibiotics to treat cystitis
- treatment for vaginal thrush (may be available without prescription in some countries)

Remote Areas

Items you should consider taking with you if you are planning on trekking or travelling in remote or highland areas include:

- sterile kit with an intravenous-fluid giving set, blood substitute solution and other intravenous fluids
- medicines to treat altitude sickness
- antibiotic eye and ear drops
- antibiotic cream or powder
- emergency inflatable splints
- blister kit
- elasticated support bandage
- triangular bandage for making an arm sling
- dental first aid kit

And Finally...

If you have any medicines left over at the end of your trip, dispose of them carefully. You could perhaps consider giving them to a hospital or clinic, but don't be tempted to just leave them in your hotel room for the cleaner because medicines are only effective if used appropriately and can actually be harmful otherwise.

TRAVEL FIRST AID – ALTERNATIVE SUGGESTIONS

Bernadette Saulenier is a naturopath and Reiki practitioner who travels regularly between Australia and Europe. She has the following tips for travellers on homoeopathic/ naturopathic first aid. The remedies mentioned here are not likely to be available where you're going, so you will need to bring what you need with you. Remember that as a general rule, these remedies are best used for non-serious conditions and are not intended to replace medical diagnosis and treatment in serious cases.

Diarrhoea can ruin the best planned holiday and, as with anything else, prevention is better than cure. Treat water with tea tree oil, a natural antiseptic: use two drops of tea tree oil in 1L of water and let it stand overnight. Another preventive is to take slippery elm capsules orally before each meal – the powder coats and protects the delicate lining of the bowels against inflammation. If you get diarrhoea, homoeopathic remedies include arsenicum album, carbo vegetalis, podophyllum, ipecac or nux vomica – what to take depends on the characteristics of your illness. Ask your practitioner for guidance on this before you leave.

Constipation is also common when you're travelling: try pear or prune juice, or a tablespoon of linseeds / psyllium husks sprinkled on your food. Remember to drink plenty of water. If you are really desperate, you could try taking a mixture of cascara, senna and chelidonium herbs.

If you're hopping in and out of buses carrying heavy luggage, you're quite likely to get a few bruises. Arnica cream is a great remedy, applied on the bruise immediately (but avoid using it on open wounds and cuts). For bleeding wounds, take arnica 30c under your tongue.

Cocculus drops or ginger tablets are good remedies for preventing motion sickness, and homoeopathic melatonin

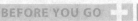

drops are excellent for jetlag. Gelsemium drops or tablets will alleviate the aches and pains of sore muscles, and taking any form of antioxidant such as grapeseed extract or vitamin A, C or E will help your body to cope with fatigue, stress and lack of fresh air – all common on a long journey.

Mosquitoes hate the smell of geranium, so avoid getting bitten by putting a few drops of geranium oil on your skin. If you get bitten in spite of all your precautions, a drop of lavender oil will soothe the itch. For other bites and stings (spiders, bees, wasps or fleas) a few drops of Ledum 30c under your tongue is beneficial.

For sunburn, try a few drops of soothing hypericum oil, which also promotes healing, or comfrey cream. If you're feeling the heat, take the tissue salt of calcium sulphate (Calc. Sulph 6x) every 15 minutes until you feel refreshed, or try Dr Bach's Rescue Remedy.

For irritant skin rashes and minor burns, try soothing calendula or comfrey cream. Lycopodium in a homeopathic form will help fungal infections at the constitutional level, but topically you may find tea-tree oil, thuja and comfrey creams helpful.

Colds and flu seem to be common wherever you go. Echinacea tablets or vitamin C will boost your immune system and help you avoid illness. If you are stricken, combination 'Q' of tissue salts will help with sinus and throat infections, and herbal tea of thyme or sage will alleviate sore throat and feverish symptoms. Gelsemium will get rid of muscular aches and pains, and allium cepa will help with a runny nose and watery eyes.

For stress or panic attacks, Dr Bach's Rescue Remedy is invaluable. A few drops under the tongue every 15 minutes works wonders. If sleep eludes you, a tincture or tablet of combined valerian, scullcap and passionflower (or any of these herbs alone) is the best cure. Hops is another herb with soothing effect. If you cannot find herbs, a good alternative is to take tissue salts of magnesium phosphate (Mag. Phos. 6x) before bed.

ALTERNATIVE TRAVEL KITS

You can make up your own travel kit with your favourite natural remedies, or you can buy a ready-made kit. Unless you're planning to take just a few familiar remedies, you should get advice from your practitioner or local homoeopathic or naturopathic pharmacy. Alternatively, we give some guidance on homoeopathic and naturopathic remedies in the boxed text 'Travel First Aid – Alternative Sugestions'. Some of the texts listed under Books have suggestions for alternative travel kits.

From England, Neal's Yard Remedies (**www.nealsyard remedies.com** or **www.nyrusa.com**, mailorder@nealsyard remedies.com, advice@nealsyardremedies.com) is a long-established supplier of natural remedies. It has a variety of mini-kits pre-packed with first aid remedies.

Also in the UK, Helios Homoeopathic Pharmacy (☎ 01892-537254, fax 01892-546850, **www.helios.co.uk**, email pharmacy@helios.co.uk) has a compact and incredibly comprehensive homoeopathic travel kit containing 36 remedies for travel-related problems (everything from drowning to fear of flying), with a helpful leaflet giving guidance on what to use when. It's probably suitable for someone with prior experience of homoeopathy.

You can order plant-based remedies like echinacea and Sweet Annie (good for digestive upsets) from Joanne Alexander at Snow Mountain Botanicals (smb@pacific.net, fax 707-743-2037); check out the website at **www.snowmountain botanicals.com**.

BOOKS

If you're looking for more information or perhaps just some bedtime reading before you go, here's a small selection of some of the many books available on travel health and related issues. Books are published in different editions by different publishers in different countries, but a bookshop or library should be able to track down the following recommendations from the author or title.

GENERAL REFERENCE

For an authoritative, comprehensive and earnest reference source, try *Travellers' Health* by Dr Richard Dawood. *Where There is No Doctor* by David Werner is an excellent 'how-to-do-it' manual for the medically naive, aimed at people going to live in remote areas of developing countries. There's a companion text (only for sadists, surely), *Where There is No Dentist*.

For a chatty, entertaining and comprehensive guide aimed at travellers and expatriates, try Dr Jane Wilson-Howarth's wonderfully titled *Bugs, Bites & Bowels*. Dr Wilson-Howarth is co-author with Dr Matthew Ellis of a similar, very detailed guide for travelling parents, *Your Child's Health Abroad*. *Staying Healthy in Asia, Africa & Latin America* by Dirk Schroeder is a something of a classic: it's a good, well organised, no-nonsense health guide for travellers. The *International Travel Health Guide* by Stuart R Rose is updated annually and is a good source of general information.

If you're looking for a first aid manual, get hold of the authorised manual of your national first aid organisation such as the Red Cross or St John Ambulance Society.

ALTERNATIVE THERAPIES

For something a bit different, try *The Traveller's Guide to Homoeopathy* by Phyllis Speight or *The World Travellers' Manual of Homoeopathy* by Dr Colin Lessel, which is incredibly comprehensive and full of fascinating detail – a work of love. *Homoeopathic Alternatives to Immunisation* by Susan Curtis makes interesting reading and is available by mail order from Neal's Yard Remedies (for contact details, see the Alternative Travel Kits section opposite).

CLIMATE, ALTITUDE & ACTION

If you're planning on trekking or doing other adventure activities in Latin America, you may want to read up on some health and safety issues before you go. For a comprehensive overview of health, safety and general outdoor survival

issues, Tim Macartney-Snape's *Being Outside* is hard to beat. *Hiking & Backpacking – A Complete Guide* is an excellent, comprehensive, easy to read and practical guide to all aspects of walking in the wilderness, with a North American slant.

If you're planning on doing some trekking in remote areas or at altitude, *Medicine for Mountaineering* (edited by J Wilkerson) is a classic reference for travellers likely to be more than 24 hours from medical care, or try the very readable *The High Altitude Medicine Handbook* by Andrew J Pollard & David R Murdoch (although it's aimed primarily at medical practitioners). There are a couple of good pocket guides for trekkers, including *Altitude Illness – Prevention & Treatment* by Stephen Bezruchka and *Mountain Sickness – Prevention, Recognition & Treatment* by Peter H Hackett.

If you want to make yourself really paranoid, try the surprisingly readable *Bites & Stings – The World of Venomous Animals* by John Nichol. You can find out all about the hazards of the deep in *Dangerous Marine Creatures* by Dr Carl Edmonds.

If you've ever wondered what to do if a volcano erupts at your feet or how to improvise a cooking pot from a length of bamboo, you'll find all the answers and much, much more in the *SAS Survival Guide*.

LATIN AMERICA-SPECIFIC PUBLICATIONS

Most guidebooks have at least some health information for travellers. Lonely Planet's travel guidebooks to Latin American destinations give country-specific details of health risks, and *Trekking in the Patagonian Andes* has good health and safety tips for trekkers in the region.

The newsletter of the South American Explorer's Club, *South American Explorer,* contains health items for travellers to Latin America – contact details are given under Useful Organisations earlier in this chapter.

On the Move...

Getting there is half the fun they say... If you don't enjoy the moving experience (and many travellers don't), you'll want to read this chapter before you leave terra firma. Or bounce over it.

FIT TO FLY?

If you're normally fit and healthy, flying shouldn't be any particular problem for you beyond the stresses involved in any form of travelling. However, there are certain situations in which you should check with your doctor before flying:

- if you've got preexisting heart or lung problems, although as a general rule you shouldn't need extra oxygen if you can climb a flight of stairs
- if you've had an operation within 10 days of flying, check with the airline if you are able to fly
- if you've had blood clots in your blood vessels in the past, as sitting immobile for long periods of time during the flight may make further clots likely
- if you're more than 36 weeks pregnant (most airlines will not let you fly after 35 weeks)
- if you have a bad cold, sinus infection or a middle ear infection, it's best to avoid flying until you're better, as you're at risk of severe ear pain and possibly a burst eardrum – see p106 for more details
- if you've been scuba diving, you shouldn't fly for 12 hours after any dive and for 24 hours after a dive requiring decompression stops; note that you will need medical clearance before you fly if you required recompression treatment

TRAVELLING WELL

If you're flying, the low cabin-air humidity is great for minimising the odoriferous effects of squashing 300 or so stressed people into a closed space for eight or more hours, but it does dry you out. You'll feel better if you drink lots of nonalcoholic fluids – avoid tea, coffee and alcohol, as they can all increase fluid loss. Mineral-water aerosol sprays and skin moisturisers can also be helpful.

FEAR OF FLYING?

If even the thought of flying reduces you to a quivering wreck, you may not be reading this book. If you are, you might like to know that help is at hand and that courses are available to cure you of your trembles. These usually involve behavioural therapy – you're exposed to various flying situations under controlled conditions, eg in a flight simulator, and in this way learn to combat your fears. Some psychologists specialise in this area.

Considerable success is reported, and improvement can last up to five years after the course. Ask your airline or travel health provider for details of courses available to you. Or you could try a virtual reality clinic – check out **www.virtuallybetter.com** for details of one US-based clinic.

At cruising altitude, the volume of enclosed gases (for example in your ears) expands by about a third, but this shouldn't cause a problem if you can pop your ears (try swallowing or holding your nose and puffing out your cheeks). You may find your abdomen swells up, though, so you might want to avoid bubbly drinks.

Aromatherapy is great for when you're on the move – try a few drops of rosemary or lavender in a tissue or handkerchief, and waft it under your nose every so often.

Sitting inactive for long periods of time on any form of transport, especially in hot climates, can give you swollen feet and ankles, and may make blood clotting in your leg veins more likely, especially if you are prone to these, or are pregnant. Known perhaps unfairly as 'economy-class syndrome', clots forming in the legs is properly called 'deep-venous thrombosis', or DVT. This is a potentially dangerous syndrome, as clots can leave the leg and go to the lungs causing severe illness.

Immobility is the key factor, and the overall risk for long-haul travellers is that DVT occurs at about 1 in 6000 people. People at higher risk of DVT include those with underlying clotting disorders, obesity, certain medications, and chronic illness.

Prevention is relatively simple. Wriggle your toes and flex your calves while you're sitting and, as often as you can, get out of your seat, stretch and walk around. All the modern carriers provide instructions for in-flight exercises. Drink plenty of water or fruit juice during the flight to avoid dehydration, and avoid putting bulky luggage at your feet so you can move your feet and legs with relative freedom. Compression socks and stockings are helpful where swelling of legs and feet is likely. If you are known to be prone to blood clotting, you may want to discuss this with your doctor before you leave, as you may need to take low-dose aspirin or an injection of a blood thinner.'

Obviously, you'll need to keep any as-needed medications (for example for asthma or angina) readily at hand during any journey, especially a long one.

JET LAG

If you're going to be flying across three or more time zones, you may experience jet lag. This term describes a syndrome that long-haul travellers will be all too familiar with: tiredness

---

FLYANA

For an incredibly comprehensive discussion of all the worries you may ever have had about flying and health, check out the website at **www.flyana.com**. If you can fight your way through the ads and glowing testimonials from grateful users, you can find out all about dehydration, use of insecticide sprays, fear of flying and much, much more. Just bear in mind that the woman behind it all, Diana Fairechild, has something of an axe to grind with the airline industry.

(but you can't sleep at the new night-time), headache, irritability, difficulty concentrating, loss of appetite and other gut disturbances (such as diarrhoea or constipation). Some of these effects are due to the physical stresses of the flight, like dehydration and immobility, but others are the result of having to reset your body clock to the new time.

Over a 24 hour period, your body shows rhythmical changes in various functions (including body temperature, levels of hormones and blood pressure), which are designed to prime you to be active during the daylight hours and to sleep during night-time. The trouble is that your internal clock takes time to adjust to a new routine. When you fly directly to a new time, there's a temporary mismatch between the time your internal clock thinks it is and the new time at your destination, which results in the set of symptoms we recognise as jet lag.

If you've crossed a few time zones on your flight, jet lag can make you feel below par for up to a week after you arrive. It tends to be more of a problem if you're flying west to east. If you're crossing many time zones, you might want to consider having a stopover, as this can help your body adjust more quickly.

Unfortunately, there's no wonder pill for jet lag and, considering how many different factors are involved in setting and maintaining body rhythms, there's unlikely to be one in the future. However, you can speed up the adjustment process by helping out the *zeitgebers* (don't you love it? It's German for 'timegivers'). These are external influences that impact on your internal rhythms, the most important ones being meal times, sleep times and exposure to bright light. Try the following strategies for reducing the impact of jet lag:

- recognise that jet lag may be a problem in the first few days and adjust your itinerary accordingly. Stopovers, if possible, can be helpful
- on the plane, set your watch to the new destination time and adjust your schedule to this time
- if it's daytime on arrival, get active and don't give yourself the chance to doze off

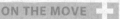

- eating is a potent time-setter, so try to take all your meals at the appropriate new destination time
- it can be torture, but try to stay awake until at least a reasonable bed time
- if you just can't keep your eyelids open, take a short nap, but beware – set your alarm or get someone to wake you
- the first night's sleep may be a bit fragile, but after that things should improve

Drug remedies you could consider to help your body clock to adjust include sleeping tablets or melatonin. Sleeping tablets can help by enabling you to sleep at the appropriate time, but they can make you feel 'hungover' the next day and are not suitable for everyone.

There's been much excitement about melatonin, a naturally occurring hormone which influences body rhythms. Although melatonin is widely available from naturopathic suppliers, you should be aware that it's not as yet officially sanctioned (which means that it hasn't been fully studied for safety and possible side effects, and the optimum dose hasn't been determined), so it's not available on a medical prescription. If you decide to try it, follow the dosing instructions on the packaging. Melatonin needs to be taken at an appropriate time before sleep (usually about 8 pm at the new time).

Other less practical options (for the desperate only, surely) include mind-bogglingly complicated fasting/food regimens (check out the regimes in *Overcoming Jetlag* by Dr Charles F Ehret & Lynne Waller Scanlon – said to be used by the US Army Rapid Deployment Forces) and bright light exposure via special light bulbs (but try carrying those in your pack).

MOTION SICKNESS

There are plenty of winding roads, diesel fumes, crowded public transport and various less than sweet odours to get you chundering when you're on the move in this part of the world, so take a good supply of motion sickness remedies if you know you're susceptible to this. Children and pregnant women are most likely to get motion sickness, but it can strike anyone.

In case you're fortunate enough not to know, early signs of an impending puke include headaches, dizziness and clammy skin. This is the time to take action. Put this book down...

If you can, fix your eyes firmly on the horizon and keep your head still (for example, brace it against a headrest). If you're below deck on a ship, lie down and close your eyes. If you can, try eating something bland, like a dry biscuit – tasting and smelling a lemon may help. Cigarette smoke is guaranteed to make you feel worse, so avoid it if you can – not always easy in non-Western countries. Place yourself in the most stable part of the vehicle if you can: between the wings on a plane, in the middle of a boat or in the front seat of a car.

You'll find a variety of anti-sickness remedies on the market. Preparations containing ginger or mint (including mint sweets) are helpful, and don't need to be taken in advance. Other remedies need to be taken before you travel. Eating lightly before the journey may also help.

Hyoscine (as tablets or skin patches) is effective for short journeys, but has side effects like dry mouth and blurred vision, and is not suitable for everyone. It's best avoided by children, older people and pregnant women. Hyoscine skin patches are known as Scopoderm in the UK and Transderm-Scop in the US.

Antihistamines (for example cinnarizine, cyclizine, dimenhydrinate or promethazine, with various brand names; see p422) are longer-lasting and have fewer side effects. They're generally available without prescription. Some antihistamines may make you drowsy, which can be an advantage on a long journey, but you should avoid driving and alcohol if you take them.

Alternatively, you could try something a bit different: special elasticated wristbands are available that work by applying pressure to acupuncture points, or there's a considerably more expensive battery-operated version.

Staying Healthy...

Only a few travel-related illnesses, and none of the common problems like sunburn, diarrhoea and infected cuts, are preventable by immunisation. Staying healthy on your travels is not just about getting the right immunisations and a supply of malaria pills, it's also about being aware of the risks and taking some basic precautions to avoid them.

+ Healthy mind, healthy body – for tips on cutting down on the mental stresses of travelling, see the Mental Wellbeing chapter.

+ Planning to let your hair down? For some safety tips on alcohol and drugs, see p246.

ACCLIMATISATION

Don't plan on hitting the ground running, especially at the start of a long trip. It's worth taking some time to allow yourself to adjust physically and mentally to your new environment and lifestyle. Factor in some time to take a breather, recover from jet lag and catch up on sleep and perhaps missed meals.

> Air pollution is a serious problem in most major cities in Latin America, and can have be a significant health risk for travellers with heart or lung problems – see the boxed text (p182) in the Respiratory System chapter for more details.

HEAT

If you've gone from a cool, temperate climate back home to a hot tropical one, give yourself a chance to get used to the heat. Your body has an amazing capacity to adjust to temperature changes, but it doesn't happen overnight. You're probably going to feel hot and easily exhausted for about a week. After this, your body will have made adjustments to cope with the heat and you'll find your capacity for activity is about back to normal. Never underestimate the dangers of the heat – for a full discussion of these, see the section on Heat in the Climate, Altitude & Action chapter.

Many people find they sweat heavily in the heat. You'll need to drink plenty of fluids to replace the amount you're sweating out – cool bottled, boiled or purified water is best, but any not-too-sweet soft drinks (it may be a challenge to find these, but try asking for a *soda* or fruit juice (undiluted or diluted with safe water) are OK. The juice from green coconuts (*pipas*) makes a refreshing, safe drink.

- Always have a supply of safe drinking water with you and remind yourself to sip from it regularly while you're out, or stop at lots of drinks stalls.

- Remember that tea, coffee and alcohol all have a diuretic effect (ie they make you lose fluid), so it's best to go easy on these.

- Avoid overexerting yourself (and this includes eating a big meal) during the hottest part of the day – it's the perfect time for a siesta or for reading that airport novel.

Physical activity generates heat, which means that your body has to work even harder to stay cool. If you're going on an activity-packed holiday, plan to take it easy during the first week, building up to maximal activity as you acclimatise.

It's probably best to leave those body-hugging lycra outfits at home for this trip, at least off the beach; loose, light-coloured (dark colours absorb the heat more) clothing made of natural fibres like cotton will help protect your skin from the sun without preventing heat loss.

Prickly heat and fungal skin infections are common in the hot, humid conditions, and can be a nuisance. You can help prevent them by washing regularly with water and carefully drying all those nooks and crannies, especially between your toes.

You'll probably find that your feet and ankles swell in the heat, especially at first, so it's a good idea to take footwear that will accommodate this. For more guidelines on looking after this vital part of your travel equipment, see the section on Feet starting on p97.

SUN

If you've come to Latin America to escape the seasonal gloom of a temperate climate, it can be hard to resist the temptation to stretch out in the sun and make that crawled-out-from-under-a-stone pallor just a distant memory. But, unless you've been in a media blackout zone for the last decade or so, you'll know that there's no such thing as a safe suntan. Before you settle in

SUNSCREEN

These products increase the length of time you can stay in the sun before you burn by reducing the amount of harmful radiation that penetrates the skin. The SPF (sun protection factor) rating is a rough guide to how long you can last without burning, but don't rely too much on it. Laboratory conditions are no match for the realities of beach life. It's probably best to start with the highest SPF you can find (ideally 30+). Check that it blocks out both UVA and UVB (usually labelled as 'broad spectrum').

A suntan is a layer of skin pigment called melanin formed in response to sunlight on your skin. It can protect against sunburn, but not against the ageing effects of the sun. It takes two to three weeks before a suntan can provide good protection against sunburn, although there is evidence that having a suntan doesn't protect you from the harmful effects of the sun's rays.

If you do decide you want to tan, make sure you allow your skin to tan slowly without burning, starting with 15 or 20 minutes exposure a day, increasing this gradually. As soon as your skin starts to feel sore or look red, head for the shade.

Remember that while freckles may be cute, they're also a sign that you've had too much sun.

THAT OZONE HOLE

Ozone is a molecule that consists of three oxygen atoms bound together. A layer of ozone particles exists about 19 to 30km above the earth's surface, and plays a vital role as a sort of global sunscreen – it helps prevent potentially damaging ultraviolet radiation from penetrating the earth's atmosphere. Without the ozone layer, humankind, not to mention other forms of life, would have long ago been killed off from the damaging effects of UV radiation.

In recent years, ozone depletion by manufactured chemicals, mainly chlorofluorocarbons (CFCs), has resulted in the formation of the ozone 'hole'. This is an area of ozone-depleted atmosphere that, for complex reasons to do with winter temperatures, exists over Antarctica, even though most ozone depleters are emitted by countries in the northern hemisphere. In the southern spring (October and November), the hole expands northwards, covering part of the South American landmass as far north as about 42° latitude, before contracting back towards Antarctica in December.

This has resulted in some alarmist reports about the effects of the ozone hole, such as flocks of sheep in Patagonia being blinded by cataracts. Medical authorities in Chile have issued dire warnings about the potential effects of the hole, and advise people to cover up and use the strongest sunscreen they can. While it is obviously sensible to take measures to avoid overexposure to the sun wherever you are, it's worth bearing in mind that the intensity of UV radiation is less the further you are from the equator.

for some serious sun worshipping, take a few steps to limit the potential for damage.

! Remember to protect yourself during any outdoor activity (especially if you're near water or at altitude, where the sun's rays are that much stronger), including sightseeing and riding in the backs of open pick-ups or lorries or on top of buses.

Sunlight or solar energy is made up of radiation of many different wavelengths. The rays in the ultraviolet (UV) part of the spectrum are the bad guys. In the short term, they can cause sunburn (and snow blindness if you're somewhere snowy). This is bad news, but the long-term effects are even scarier:

- skin ageing: wrinkles, crow's feet, liver spots, warty rough areas (solar keratoses), broken veins
- skin cancer, including malignant melanoma (the nastiest type)
- eye problems: cataracts and malignant melanoma of the back of the eye

Sun intensity is affected by many factors, including obvious things like latitude (greater around the equator), time of the year (summer) and time of the day (midday). Sun intensity is also increased at altitude and by reflection off sea, snow and buildings. You can get severely sunburnt in no time at all in highland areas in Latin America. Lake Titicaca is particularly bad for this, as in addition to being at high altitude, the sun is reflected off the water. And in South America, the state of the ozone layer, which naturally protects us from harmful rays is a big concern – see the boxed text for more details.

Stay pale and interesting by covering up with clothes and wearing a hat. These provide by far the best protection from harmful rays, much better than any sunscreen. Take all the sunscreen you think you may need with you, as high protection factor creams are less readily available, and are often expensive.

A wide-brimmed hat (or a legionnaire's cap with a neck protector – leaves a lot to be desired style-wise, but very effective) keeps damaging rays off all those easily forgotten bits:

nose, ears, back of the neck, bald patch. You could consider wearing a 'sunsuit' on the beach. These are popular in places such as Australia where skin cancer rates are among the highest in the world. They are ideal for kiddies.

You'll also need to protect your eyes. Make sure you have sunglasses that block out UV rays; these aren't necessarily the most expensive ones.

The sun is generally at its fiercest between 11 am and 3 pm, so it makes sense to spend this time resting in the shade or indoors.

Note the following traps for the unwary:

- sunscreens need to be applied 20 to 30 minutes before going into the sun and reapplied frequently after that, especially after swimming
- you can get sunburnt through water (eg if you're snorkelling), so take care to cover up with a T-shirt and use plenty of water-resistant sunscreen
- how hot it is doesn't make any difference to whether you'll burn – you can still get burnt on a cold day if the sun is shining
- you can burn on a cloudy day because clouds still let through some UV radiation; and you can burn even in the shade from reflected light, especially off water

COLD

Latin America is a land of geographical and climatic extremes. Cold and wet weather can kill if you are unprepared, especially if you are overnighting in highland areas, or even if you're on a day trip and the weather closes in unexpectedly. In fact, day trips can be more risky, as you tend to think you don't need to bother because you're just going to be out for a short time. Be prepared if you're on a bus journey that takes you over highland areas. For more details on the effects of excess cold and how to prevent them, see the section on Cold in the Climate, Altitude & Action chapter.

ALTITUDE

If you are going to any high altitude destinations in Latin America, you need to be aware of the effect on your body of the lower oxygen concentration that exists at higher altitudes, especially above about 2000m (note, for example, that Mexico City is at an altitude of 2100m and La Paz in Bolivia is nearly 4000m). Altitude sickness is a potentially dangerous condition, and a few travellers die from the effects of altitude every year – make sure this isn't you. For more details, see the Altitude section in the Climate, Altitude & Action chapter later in this book.

FOOD & WATER PRECAUTIONS

SAFE FOOD

! Staying healthy is also about eating properly, especially when you're on a long trip – for the complete lowdown on eating well, see the Diet & Nutrition section at the end of this chapter.

It's generally agreed that food, not water, is the most common source of gut troubles in travellers. Food can be contaminated with disease-causing microorganisms at many stages of the production chain, including during harvesting, transportation, handling, washing and preparation. Many forms of diarrhoea and dysentery (bloody diarrhoea) are transmitted in this way, as well as other diseases, including hepatitis A and E, typhoid (not common in travellers generally but relatively more common in travellers returning from Mexico) and polio.

You can get sick from contaminated food anywhere but it's more likely when you're travelling, for a variety of reasons. Sewage disposal systems may be inadequate in nations with poorer infrastructure and in disadvantaged sections of the population in other countries. (In many nations in Latin America there is a sharp division in terms of living standards and health care provision between those who have and those who have not.)

This, coupled with the higher existing levels of disease in parts of the population, makes it much more likely that food, cooking utensils and hands will be contaminated with disease-causing microorganisms, mainly from faeces. If, for example, a fly lands on your food back home, it probably hasn't had a chance to wipe its feet on a pile of faeces beforehand, but this may not be true in many places.

!　Bear in mind that although you can build up immunity to some diarrhoeal diseases, you can't build up immunity to many of the more serious diseases (such as dysentery or food poisoning) or to parasites (such as tapeworm).

Another thing about travelling is that it usually entails 'eating out' three meals a day for perhaps weeks on end, which means you have to rely on other people to prepare your food safely. This is always a risk, especially in countries with limited resources – after all, even in countries with supposedly high food safety standards, such as Australia, outbreaks of food poisoning occur with alarming regularity.

Although travellers have always been given advice on safe eating, travellers diarrhoea isn't yet a rare and endangered illness – rates have remained pretty constant (around 30% to 80% for travel in developing countries) over the years. Part of the reason for this has to be that the advice given is often impossibly restrictive to follow and, in some cases, borders on ludicrous. Can you really see yourself examining the cook's fingernails before you eat your meal or throwing your food away because a fly dared to land on it? Get real...

Eating safely is about taking simple precautions to minimise your risk of getting something nasty, it's not achieving a laboratory ideal. It's down to common sense, plus a little background knowledge. It may mean that sometimes you don't eat exactly what you want, but hey, what's new?

Safe to Eat

Here are some guidelines on the kinds of things that are much less likely to cause problems. Remember that microorganisms love hot, humid climates, and will multiply gleefully in food left

GOOD FOOD

To get you started, here are some suggestions for what is likely to be low-risk food.

- Tortillas – pretty reliable even if they've been left standing as bacteria tend not to multiply on dry food items.
- Tacos, tostadas, quesadillas, enchiladas – should all be safe to eat if they are hot through, but it's probably best to avoid cold fillings and garnishes.
- Guacamole – probably best avoided if you're in any doubt, as it is a cold dish and can contain potentially contaminated salad items.
- Condiments such as spicy sauces are probably best avoided if they're cold, as they often sit around on tables, getting topped up as needed, and can get contaminated.
- Tamales plus the many regional variations – should be fine as they are usually steamed for an hour or two before serving.
- Arepas – as for tortillas, should be safe to eat but avoid cold fillings.
- Soups – these are popular and usually a safe bet if they are hot; the only one to be especially wary of is *ceviche*, traditionally made with raw seafood and therefore potentially unsafe (although since the outbreak of cholera in the region, authorities in Chile have decreed that ceviche has to be cooked).
- Fruit juices – be wary of these as the equipment used can be contaminated, as can additives like water and milk.

Note that a squeeze of lemon or lime on salad or other food is no guarantee of safety, whatever you may be told. Acidity does kill off bugs, but a dribble of juice won't help much.

MILK & DAIRY PRODUCTS

The concern with milk is not so much that you may get diarrhoeal diseases from it, but if it is unpasteurised (ie straight from the udder), you can get several quite serious diseases, including tuberculosis (TB), brucellosis, listeriosis and salmonellosis. The same goes for products made from unpasteurised milk. Unpasteurised cow's milk, goat's milk and, to a lesser extent, sheep's milk can all be risky. The form of TB cows carry is a bit different from the usual human form but it still causes the same disease. Pasteurisation involves heating milk to temperatures that kill off any microorganisms. Milk and dairy products in major cities and urban areas will generally be pasteurised, but in rural areas you may be offered a drink straight from the udder. If necessary, you can boil unpasteurised milk to make it safe. Watch out for milk diluted with unsafe water or ice.

sitting around in these conditions, especially if refrigeration is unreliable or unavailable.

- Heating kills germs, so food that's served piping hot is likely to be safer than lukewarm or cold food, especially if it's been sitting around.

- Fruit and vegetables can be difficult to clean (and may be contaminated where they are grown), but they should be safe if they're peeled or cooked.

- Well cooked meat and seafood is generally OK; raw or lightly cooked meat and seafood can be a source of disease.

- Tinned food is usually safe (check 'best before' dates if necessary).

- You'll be delighted to know that all forms of bread and cakes are usually safe, although it's best to avoid cream-filled goodies, as microorganisms such as salmonella (a cause of food poisoning) love cream.

Finally, your stomach's natural defences (mainly acid) can cope with small amounts of contaminated foods – if you're not sure about something, don't pig out on it!

What to Avoid

And a few cautions to keep in mind. We can't tell you exactly what to avoid in every situation in every country because there are so many variables, but we can give you some simple guidelines to help you decide what's likely to be less safe.

- The more food has been handled (including peeling, slicing and arranging), the more likely it is to have been contaminated by unwashed hands.
- Food can be contaminated by dirty dishes, cutlery or utensils; blenders or pulpers used for fruit juices are often suspect.
- Food that looks and smells delicious can still be seething with disease-causing microorganisms.
- Hot spices don't make food safe, just more palatable.
- Salads, like other vegetables, are hard to clean and may be contaminated where they are grown – if you're in any doubt about hygiene standards, it's best to avoid salads altogether.
- Fruit juices and other drinks may be diluted with unsafe water.
- Be wary of frozen food (including ice cream) if refrigeration is questionable (because of power cuts or lack of availability); freezing doesn't kill disease-causing microorganisms.

Where to Eat

There are no hard and fast rules we can give you, but again, use your common sense. Star rating is certainly no guarantee of food safety, as food poisoning outbreaks on cruise liners regularly remind us, but in theory, standards are easier to enforce in major hotels than in a food stall in a market. Having said that, it's easy to stay healthy even if you eat at small, cheap eating places – try to pick busy, popular places that look clean, and choose freshly prepared dishes rather than ones that have been sitting out on display for hours.

Safest of all is probably to self-cater with fresh produce from the market, although be wary of meat that has been left out

STREET FOOD

Whether or not to eat 'street food' is one of those classic travellers' conundrums. Common sense tells you that most street vendors probably can't afford to buy high-quality ingredients, and many won't have access to adequate (if any) washing facilities or toilets. And you can't really expect your average street vendor to be up with the latest food hygiene practices. On the other hand…street food is a way of life in many tropical countries, and arguably very much part of the travel experience. It's definitely your call, but you can minimise the undoubted risks by careful selection, following the guidelines given in this section. Basically, choose hot, freshly cooked items, preferably that have not been touched by the vendor's hand since cooking – this is where carrying your own utensils or a paper plate comes in handy.

without refrigeration. Remember that you can contaminate your own food if you don't take care to wash your hands and any utensils you use.

DRUGS TO PREVENT DIARRHOEA

Before you get your hopes up too high, you should know this isn't an option for most travellers and is just not practical for long-term travellers. However, in some situations it may be advisable, for example if you have a preexisting condition (such as HIV infection or inflammatory bowel disease) that makes it particularly important for you to avoid illness, or if you're a businessperson on a short trip.

The two main possibilities are antibiotics or bismuth subsalicylate (Pepto-Bismol), which is not an antibiotic. Although some antibiotics have been shown to be effective in preventing diarrhoea in travellers, there are concerns that this may make antibiotic resistance more likely; there's also a risk of side effects. Bismuth subsalicylate works by reducing the amount of fluid your gut produces in response to toxins from bugs. It comes in liquid form (60ml four times daily) but tablets are more practical for most travellers (take two tablets four times daily). It's a possibility to consider (and preferably to discuss with your doctor first) if you are on a short trip, although it's not suitable for everyone – see the section on p162 for more details.

CLEAN HANDS

Before you skip over this uninspiringly titled but surprisingly important section, we're talking about washing your hands before you eat. Obvious perhaps, but in Western countries we've been able to become complacent or perhaps just lazy about this because we have efficient waste disposal systems and (usually) safe, plentiful water supplies.

Many diseases associated with poor living standards (such as dysentery, typhoid and hepatitis) are simply diseases of poor hygiene. So it's worth reminding yourself to wash your hands before you eat and always after using the toilet. This is particularly important if you're eating with your hands. Short fingernails are easier to keep clean than long ones. It's a good idea to take your own utensils (plastic cup, bowl, spoon) with you so you can use them for street food or eating meals on trains.

Try to remember to keep your hands away from your mouth and eyes, especially on public transport, as you can introduce infection in this way.

SAFE DRINKING WATER

Water, water everywhere, but not a drop to drink… You need to drink lots of water to stay healthy, especially in hot climates, but can you drink the water safely? Although contaminated food is probably the most common source of gut infections when you're travelling in Latin America, water can also be a source of illness, including diarrhoea, dysentery, hepatitis and typhoid.

In countries with good infrastructure and resources, communal water supplies are generally safe from contamination, but you can't rely on this in nations with fewer resources. Contamination of the water supply can occur at some point, usually by human or animal sewage.

! Never assume that water from rivers, streams or lakes is safe, as even in relatively unpopulated areas it can be contaminated by animals, trekkers or by chemical pollutants, even if it is very cold.

Your travel guidebook or a reliable local source will be able to give you specific information on water safety at your

HEALTH BOOSTERS

Travel can involve many stresses healthwise, leaving you vulnerable to illness at a time you could really do without it. One way to help avoid problems is by making sure you are as fit and healthy as possible before you go. Many travellers, however, take the additional precaution of boosting their body's powers to fight off infection with natural remedies. You'll probably find it helpful to consult a practitioner to get individually tailored advice, but here's a rundown of some of the options available. Follow the dosing instructions on the packaging or your practitioner's advice, and remember to take basic food and water precautions as well.

- Acidophilus – one of a number of 'probiotics', this bacteria is present in live natural yoghurt and is claimed to have a beneficial effect on the balance of bacteria in the intestine; it's popularly used by travellers to prevent diarrhoea, although some experts question whether the bacteria would survive the acid conditions in the stomach.

destination. Unless you are sure the water is safe, it's best to err on the side of caution. If you're not sure, avoid drinking tap water and don't brush your teeth in it. Ice is only as safe as the water it's made from, so it's best to avoid this too. If you're desperate for a cool drink, seal the ice in a plastic bag before putting it in your drink – but make sure the bag is clean first! Alcohol has some disinfectant properties, but at drinking strength it won't make water safe to drink. A squeeze of lemon or lime juice can help but you shouldn't rely on it to make your drink safe.

- Aloe vera – an immune enhancer when taken by mouth, this widely available plant also has antiseptic properties when applied topically.
- Cat's claw – originally from the Latin American rainforest, this herb is said to have antiinflammatory and antioxidant properties.
- Echinacea – the top-selling herb in the US, this is a good, readily available (back home at least) general immune-booster.
- Garlic – popular immune booster; often comes in combination with horseradish.
- Glutamine – this amino acid is needed for the immune system to function properly.
- Grapefruit seed extract – said to have antibacterial, antifungal and antiviral activity, this is recommended for intestinal and other infections.
- L-arginine – an amino acid involved in immune function, and promotes wound healing.
- Vitamin C – cheap and readily available in many different forms.

Bottled water is generally widely available in most parts of Latin America, especially in urban or tourist areas, or fill your own container with water from a reliable source before you set out for the day – hotels often have a supply of boiled water available for the use of guests.

A label of *agua mineral* is no guarantee of quality, though. As a general rule, it's best to stick to major brands of bottled water. Choose brands preferably with serrated tops and always check the seal carefully. If you're in any doubt, choose carbonated water (for example a plain soda), as the acidity from carbonation kills off any microorganisms.

The cost of bottled water can add up over a long trip, especially if you're travelling in hot climates, and there's a very real concern over the environmental – and aesthetic – effect of millions of discarded and unrecycled plastic bottles. If you're trekking or travelling off the beaten track, bottled water is just not practical and may not be available in any case. In these situations, you can make water safe to drink by boiling it, adding chemical disinfectants to it or by using a commercial water purifier. Which method you use depends on where you are and the type of trip you are on.

! Make sure you have more than one means of purifying water in case one method fails (eg take some iodine as well as a pump-action purifier).

Boiling

The simplest and most effective way of making water safe to drink is to boil it, which kills all disease-causing bugs. You just need to bring it to a rolling boil for a minute or two and then let it cool – prolonged boiling is not necessary. Water boils at lower temperatures at high altitude, but even at the altitudes you may reach at some Andean destinations, it'll still reach temperatures high enough to kill disease-causing microorganisms. However, if necessary, to be absolutely sure you could let it boil for about five minutes in these circumstances.

Chemical Disinfectants

If boiling doesn't sound like a practical option, it's relatively easy to disinfect clear water with chemicals. Chlorine and iodine are the chemicals most widely used, and at optimal concentrations both kill bacteria, viruses and most parasites (one exception is the recently identified parasite, *Cryptosporidium*). Iodine and chlorine are both available as tablets or liquids ('tincture' of iodine), and iodine is also available as crystals. You can usually buy them from good pharmacies or travel health clinics, or outdoor equipment suppliers.

Factors that affect the ability of these chemicals to disinfect water include concentration, how long you leave the water to stand after adding the chemical, water temperature (the colder the water, the longer it needs to be left to stand before use) and any particulate matter in the water.

Make sure you follow the manufacturer's dosage and contact time if you're using tablets, but as a rule, remember to leave the water for at least 20 minutes before drinking it. If the water is really cold, you will need to leave it for longer, sometimes an hour or two; alternatively, you could add the chemicals the night before and leave it to stand overnight. With 2% tincture of iodine, you need to add five drops to every litre of water to be purified.

Chlorine is considered less reliable in general than iodine as it is more likely to be affected by factors such as water alkalinity. Silver tablets are also available, but they are not effective against parasite cysts, so they shouldn't be used without filtering the water first.

> **|** Iodine should not be used continuously to purify water over a
> **●** long period of time (more than six weeks), as it can cause thyroid
> problems; iodine should also be avoided if you're pregnant or have
> thyroid problems, and it's not suitable for children under 12 years
> of age.

The taste of chemically treated water can be a major turn-off, but there are ways of neutralising this. Charcoal resins or a carbon filter can remove the taste and smell of chemicals, or you can add ascorbic acid (vitamin C) or flavouring. Remember only to add these after the treated water has been allowed to stand for the required length of time.

> **!** If the water is cloudy, chemicals won't be effective because organic matter tends to neutralise the chemical – you'll need to filter the water first, or add alum to precipitate it out.

Water Filters & Purifiers

No, you don't need to be a rocket scientist to understand what these devices do – it's actually pretty straightforward.

Not sure about the terminology? Simple filters are just sieves or strainers, and their effectiveness depends on how fine they are. Generally, they don't make water safe to drink without further treatment (boiling or chemicals), as they don't remove the smallest disease-causing organisms (viruses and some bacteria), although fine-pore ceramic filters are exceptions. Purifiers are dual action: they filter water and disinfect it (for example with an iodine resin) to remove viruses; often they include a final step to remove the taste of the chemical disinfectant and any other chemicals such as pesticides.

Filters and purifiers can be gravity or pump action. Pump action is probably the more realistic option unless you have plenty of time on your hands, but can be hard work. Water purifiers often contain a carbon filter to remove traces of chemicals used to disinfect the water, but note that using carbon on its own does not make water safe to drink.

It's worth having an idea beforehand of what you're looking for; here's a suggested pre-purchase checklist.

- What does it claim to remove? Does it make water totally safe to drink?

- What do you want to use it for? Some devices are suitable for occasional or emergency use, whereas others are good for continuous use over a long period of time.

- What's the flow rate like? You don't want to pump for two hours for a sip of water.

- How portable/breakable is it? Ceramic filters are very effective but need a bit of care, as they can crack.

- How often does the filter need to be replaced? Filters can get clogged and there's a risk of bacterial growth occurring in them, so they usually need to be cleaned or replaced after a while.
- How easy is it to take apart and clean if it becomes clogged?
- Is it endorsed by an independent organisation?

There are some interesting variations available, such as a filter that fits onto a tap and a straw (for reaching those inaccessible puddles…), so it's worth shopping around to find what you want. Water filters and purifiers are available from most major travel health clinics and from outdoor equipment suppliers, often by mail order. Alternatively, a search on the internet brings up a heap of possibilities.

Make sure you have more than one means of purifying water in case one method fails (eg take some iodine as well as a pump action purifier).

> **!** Even if you're using a water purifier, choose the cleanest water source possible, and never drink water from rivers, lakes or wells without purifying it first.

INSECTS & PARASITES

+ For the complete low-down on little – and large – critters that bite and sting, see the Bites & Stings chapter later in this book.

PREVENTING INSECT BITES

Small bloodsuckers tend to rate highly in the travellers 'most hated' list. The itch and discomfort from their bites is sanity-challenging enough, but to add insult to injury, a handful of insects are responsible for transmitting a variety of pretty major diseases, many of which are serious public health problems.

- mosquitoes – malaria, dengue fever, filariasis, yellow fever
- ticks – typhus, relapsing fever and other fevers
- lice – typhus
- flea – plague
- sandfly – leishmaniasis, sandfly fever, bartonellosis

- assassin bugs – American trypanosomiasis (Chagas' disease)
- blackfly – onchocerciasis (river blindness)

These diseases are much more of a problem in tropical and subtropical areas of Latin America than in the temperate countries of the Southern Cone. Although the risks of meeting a disease-carrying insect vary to a certain extent depending on where you're headed, it obviously makes sense wherever you go to make sure you don't get bitten. The only one of these diseases against which there is currently an effective immunisation is yellow fever.

! Remember: if you don't let yourself get bitten, you won't be at risk of developing any of these diseases.

The best way to prevent insect bites is to use insect repellents on your skin as well as physical barriers to bites, such as clothes, nets and insect screens. Biting insects are attracted by the most surprising things, not many of which you can do anything about directly: body heat, chemicals in your sweat, perfumes, soap and types of clothing. Most mosquitoes are night-biters, but the dengue mosquito bites mainly during the day.

Basic precautions for preventing insect bites include the following:

- cover up with long-sleeved tops and long trousers; light-coloured clothing is thought to be less attractive to mosquitoes than dark colours
- use insect repellents on any exposed areas; if you're using sunscreen or other lotions, apply insect repellent last, and reapply after swimming if necessary; note that insect repellent may reduce the protection of a sunscreen
- sleep in a screened room or, if this is not possible (quite likely), sleep under a treated mosquito net; always cover children's beds or cots with treated mosquito nets; air-conditioned rooms are usually insect-free zones
- remember day-biting mosquitoes, and avoid shady conditions in the late afternoon or taking an afternoon siesta without the protection of a mosquito net
- spray your room (or tent) with an knock-down insect spray before you retire for the night to get rid of any lurking insects

- consider using electric insecticide vaporisers or mosquito coils – you will need a power socket for a vaporiser, and both are less effective if you have a fan going

Insect Repellents

There are many insect repellent products on the market, but the most effective are those containing the compound DEET (diethyltoluamide) – check the label or ask your pharmacist to tell you which brands contain DEET. Some major brands include Autan, Doom, Jungle Formula, Off!, Repel and Rid.

DEET is very effective against mosquitoes, midges, ticks, bedbugs and leeches, and slightly less effective against flies. One application should last up to four hours, although if it's very humid or you're very sweaty, it may not last as long. Basically, the higher the concentration, the longer it will last; around 50% is optimal, although there are some longer acting formulations with lower strengths of DEET. Remember to try a test dose before you leave to check for allergy or skin irritation.

If you're worried about the safety of DEET, be reassured: it's generally agreed that safety concerns over DEET are largely unfounded. However, for children, it's probably best to err on the cautious side. Choose a lower strength long-acting cream.

 You may prefer to use one of the new lemon eucalyptus-based natural products, which have been shown to be an effective alternative to DEET, with similar action times (although DEET is probably still your best bet in high-risk areas). Other natural repellents include citronella and pyrethrum, but these tend to be less effective and to have a short action (up to an hour), making them less practical to use.

Cotton bands soaked in insect repellent can be useful to wear on your wrists and ankles (especially ankles, as these are a prime target for mosquitoes), and the repellent won't rub off as easily.

Treating Clothes & Nets

Permethrin is pyrethrum-like compound that is very effective and can be applied to clothes and mosquito nets (but not on your skin). It repels and kills mosquitoes, fleas, ticks, mites, bedbugs, cockroaches and flies. If you're planning on trekking through potentially tick-infested areas (rainforests, scrubland, pastures), consider treating your clothes, particularly trousers and socks, with permethrin before you go.

! You get the best protection against mosquitoes (and other insects) if you apply a DEET-based product on your skin, and use permethrin-treated clothes and nets.

Mosquito Nets & Screening

If you're spending some time in tropical Latin America, consider taking a mosquito net with you – they don't weigh much and don't take up much room. You can just tuck it away in your pack until you need it. Make sure you get one that has been soaked in permethrin, or you can treat your own net, if necessary.

Travel health clinics and travel-equipment or specialist outdoor equipment suppliers generally have a wide variety of mosquito nets to suit your individual needs. Free-standing nets are a great option; IAMAT (see Useful Organisations in the Before You Go chapter for more details) have a version you could check out.

Other Possibilities

Taking vitamin B1 (thiamine), garlic or brewer's yeast have all been advocated as making you less attractive to insects. They may be worth a try, but just bear in mind that they haven't been shown to work in trials. Electronic buzzing devices were a fad for a while but there is no evidence that they work.

SCHISTOSOMIASIS (BILHARZIA)

This parasitic disease is a risk to you in some parts of South America, mainly the north and east of Brazil, around Lake Valencia (and a few other areas) in Venezuela and the central part of the coastal area of Suriname, around Paramaribo – see the map on p23, and get up-to-date information on this before you go. The disease is caused by a tiny worm that lives in freshwater snails for part of its life cycle and in humans for the second part. For more details about diagnosis and treatment of the disease, see the section on p362. Schistosomiasis can be treated, but it's best not to get infected in the first place.

If you're going to a risk area, you should take precautions to avoid the disease. You get schistosomiasis through contact with fresh water. The following precautions are sensible in risk areas:

■ avoid swimming, paddling, crossing streams and water sports that involve immersion in fresh water in risk areas, whatever locals tell you

■ boil or chlorinate all drinking water, as you can get schistosomiasis through drinking affected water

■ there's no risk of schistosomiasis from sea water but you may be at risk if you swim in river estuaries

■ wear waterproof footwear to cross waterways if necessary

■ although infection is less likely, you are still at risk further offshore, eg if you swim from a boat

■ if you do get wet, dry off quickly, as the disease-causing worms can't survive long out of water

■ snail-free, chlorinated swimming pools are safe, but stagnant water is especially dangerous (such as a lake behind a dam)

■ if you're using water to wash in, either boil and chlorinate it or keep it in a snail-free container for at least two days (the worms die off in 48 hours if they don't reach a human)

ACCIDENTS & INJURY

! 'Natural' phenomena such as hurricanes and earthquakes can also be a hazard in Latin America – see the boxed text for guidelines on keeping safe in an earthquake.

It's time to mention the 'D' word. It might come as a surprise to you, but the most common cause of death in younger travellers is accidents, not nasty tropical illnesses (for older people it's preexisting illnesses like heart disease). Accidents are the main reason for needing a blood transfusion or other medical treatment, which in some areas carries infection risks.

EARTHQUAKES

Mexico, Central America and the Pacific side of South America are all in a geologically volatile zone, as evidenced by the regular volcanic eruptions and frequent earthquakes in the region. Earthquakes don't usually give any advance warning, so it's a good idea to have a contingency plan in case you suddenly feel the earth move. Most Andean construction is not noted for its earthquake durability. A good source of information on earthquake safety and preparedness is the American Red Cross (**www.redcross.org/services/disaster**), who recommend the following action in the event of an earthquake:

- drop, cover and hold; move only a few steps to a nearby safe place
- if you are indoors drop under a sturdy desk or table, hold on, and protect your eyes by pressing your face against your arm; if there's no table, choose a safe place against an inside wall where nothing can fall on you
- if you are in bed, hold on and stay there, protecting your head with a pillow
- if you are outdoors, find a clear spot away from buildings, trees and power lines, and drop to the ground
- if you are in a car, slow down, drive to a clear place, and stay in the car until the shaking stops

Remember that after shocks are common, and if you feel one, drop, cover and hold on, as described above, each time.

When you're on holiday, you tend to take all sorts of risks you probably would not dream of taking at home – it's part of what makes travelling so exciting. But remember that you're not immune from danger just because you're on holiday. Accidents are, well, just that, and they can and do happen. If they depend on your actions, they're preventable to a certain extent, especially if you're aware of the risks.

While we don't want to rain on your beach party, just be aware that alcohol and other mind-altering substances are major factors in accidents of all types in travellers, from dignity-challenging falls to life-threatening road traffic accidents.

So now that we've thoroughly depressed you, what steps can you take to ensure you come back in one piece?

> **!** Although outside the scope of this book, remember that personal injury through crime is a potential danger in some areas. Check your travel guidebook for more guidance on personal safety.

ROAD SAFETY

It may be the Latin temperament, but you'll probably find that although there are road rules, no-one pays much attention to them. As a result, road traffic accidents are a real risk, and can involve pedestrians, vehicles and, especially, motorcycle riders. Brazil, for example, has one of the highest road traffic accident rates in the world. Accidents involving public transport vehicles, especially buses, are common throughout the region, as a lack of resources and the need to make a living may take precedence over basic safety considerations. Roads in rural areas are often in poor condition.

Some basic, if obvious, safety tips include the following:

- avoid alcohol when driving, even if there are no laws to break
- use a seat belt if possible and resist the temptation to go as fast as the other lunatics
- wear a helmet and protective clothing if you're riding a bicycle, motorcycle or moped – shorts and T-shirt don't provide much protection against road rash if you come off
- check that your hire car has the minimum safety features – like brakes

- avoid travelling at night, which can be tricky in the best of conditions and can entail all sorts of unexpected hazards
- if self-driving, seek advice locally on road conditions before setting off, especially in remote areas

SWIMMING SAFETY

Hundreds of people drown every year on Latin America's beaches. Children and young adults are especially at risk. Even experienced swimmers get taken by unexpectedly strong currents. For guidelines on how to deal with strong currents, see the section on p343 in the Water chapter later. Don't expect to see lifeguards and safety notices; in many places you're on your own if you get into trouble in the water.

- Check locally for advice on currents and other swimming hazards – just because there are no warning signs doesn't necessarily mean it's safe.
- Play safe and avoid going in if you're unused to surf or you're unsure of your swimming capabilities.
- Never run and dive in the water, even if you've checked the depth before, in case it's unexpectedly shallow.
- Don't swim straight after a meal, as you are more likely to get cramps.
- Don't swim if you've had alcohol or other mind-altering substances.
- Wear shoes to protect your feet from injury.
- Check the beach for sharp objects and soft ones before you sit down – many beaches double as public toilets and general dumping grounds.
- Try not to swallow water when you are swimming or doing water sports in the sea or in pools, as it can be a source of intestinal infections.

Some marine creatures can sting or bite, so don't touch anything unless you know what it is. Water pollution is another major issue for swimmers, especially on urban beaches. For more details on both these hazards, see the Water chapter later in this book.

FIRE & FIXTURES

Fire is another obvious hazard, particularly in countries where smoking is a national pastime. Never smoke in bed, and if you're that type, work out potential escape routes before you go to sleep at night.

> **!** Balconies are a notable hazard for the unwary and the inebriated – stay well away from the edge.

FEET

Chris Wheeler, Melbourne-based podiatrist (when he's not off road-testing his own advice), has the following to say about that most vital piece of travel equipment – your feet.

To paraphrase the sage: 'while travel makes the heart grow fonder, it is true that the smile comes from the feet'. Your feet come in for a lot of wear and tear when you're travelling, and even relatively minor afflictions can make your life a misery. The good news is that with just a bit of care you can avoid most problems.

FOOTWEAR

If you're not going too far off the beaten track, your best bet is likely to be light-weight walking shoes (the next step up from running shoes). These are supportive where they need to be (around the heel), cushioned where they should be (under the base of the heel and under the ball of the foot) and allow the foot to bend where it's happiest to. Most importantly, you have a wide range of brands to choose from so you can find one that suits the shape of your foot best. Unless you're planning on trekking, it's probably best to avoid serious hiking boots because they're heavy and stiff. Open footwear such as sandals or thongs are tempting in a hot climate, but they leave your feet open to injury (and subsequent infection), and over a long period of time they can cause your skin to dry out, giving you cracked and painful heels.

FOOT HYGIENE

Try to make sure you wash your feet once a day, and dry them carefully, especially between the toes. If you're a sweaty foot person, consider wiping between the toes with methylated spirits (pre-injection swabs are available from pharmacists and won't take up much space in your medical kit).

If you wear open footwear, you can help prevent cracked heels by using a skin-softening agent (any simple moisturiser will do) and a pumice stone to remove dry skin.

Deliciously soothing foot sprays, moisturisers and balms are available for tired feet – well worth the extra weight in your pack.

BLISTERS

The scourge of hikers, blisters occur when there is repeated friction to the skin. Prevention is all-important. Make sure your footwear is well worn in before you set off sightseeing or on a hike. At the very least, wear them on a few short walks before you leave – don't plan to wear them in for the first time while you are away. Your boots should fit comfortably with enough room to move your toes, and be sure your socks fit properly. If you're going to be doing lots of walking, it's worth investing in socks specifically made for walkers. Socks made from a synthetic fibre called orlon have been shown to decrease the size and frequency of blisters. Wet and muddy socks can also cause blisters, so slip a spare pair of socks in your daypack and change your socks when necessary. Keep your toenails clipped, but not too short.

If you do feel a blister coming on, take immediate action. Apply a simple sticking plaster or preferably one of the special blister plasters which act as a second skin, and follow the instructions on the packaging for replacement. 'Second skin' products reduce the shearing forces that cause blisters. You could try stretching the offending part of the shoes or wearing a different pair of socks.

If you're planning on going on a hike and you haven't time to toughen the skin of your feet up by graduated walking,

you could consider soaking your feet in a weak solution of potassium permanganate for 20 minutes daily (add a teaspoon of crystals to 4L of warm water) to toughen the skin. In the army, new recruits were once told to urinate on their feet to toughen the skin, but this won't endear you to your travelling companions.

A blister won't get infected as long as it is intact. If the blister looks as if it is about to burst or is already broken, apply an antiseptic ointment such as chlorhexidine to reduce the risk of infection and cover it with a thick pad of sterile gauze (preferably over a nonadherent dressing like melolin). If you've got hydrodermic dressings such as Duoderm with you, apply it and leave it in place for seven days or so.

OTHER PROBLEMS

Prevent ingrowing toenails by proper toenail cutting techniques ie use nail clippers to trim the nail straight across (not curved). Gently trim the corners if they are sharp. Corns and calluses can arise from repeated irritation. A callus is where repeated irritation causes the top layer of skin to thicken. If this irritation continues, usually over a bony prominence, the callus will thicken to form a corn. Much like a blister, these are best treated by avoiding the irritation that leads to their formation. Use of a pumice stone will slow the rate of return of a callus, but corns need to be removed by a foot specialist.

SEX & TRAVEL

It seems that not even the runs, rickety beds, paper thin walls, sunburn and sand can dampen the ardour of many travellers. Maybe it's the aphrodisiac properties of the heat, or the feeling of freedom travelling can give. Or is it just the cheap beer? Maybe sex is the reason you're going travelling. Whatever the reason, it makes sense to arm yourself with the facts about your risks of getting a sexually transmitted infection (STI), as well as a pack of condoms. STIs are a worldwide problem.

A sexual encounter with a new partner anywhere carries a risk of HIV or one of the other STIs, but it can be even riskier when

THE CONSEQUENCES OF WAR

The armed conflicts of the early 1980s have left a legacy of undetonated antipersonnel mines and explosives in Central America. The figures are sobering, with Nicaragua, unsurprisingly, the worst affected with 73,000 mines remaining; between 5000 and 8000 mines and other explosives in Guatemala; 2000 mines in Honduras; and approximately 1000 mines along the Costa Rica border with Nicaragua. To make things more tricky, the locations of these mines have been affected by the devastation recently caused by Hurricane Mitch.

You can get information on risk areas from US State Department or UK Foreign Office Travel Advisories, as well as locally. You're unlikely to wander through minefields if you stick to usual tourist routes, but take extreme care if you are going off the beaten track in affected countries, especially near border areas. Bear in mind some basic guidelines:

- never touch any war relics
- never stray from well marked paths and stick to the main tourist attractions in badly affected areas
- check with reliable sources locally (eg your embassy) about the possibility of mines if you do plan to go off the usual tourist route
- if you accidentally wander into a mined area, retrace your steps if you can clearly see them; otherwise, stay where you are and call for help
- don't rush in to help a mine victim, as there may be other mines nearby; find someone who knows how to safely enter a mined area

You may be aware of several high-profile campaigns aimed at tackling this important humanitarian issue. Mines have far-reaching effects, long after the original conflict is past. They not only kill and maim innocent people, but they also have a huge social and medical cost. For more information on how you may be able to help, contact the International Committee of the Red Cross (☎ 22 734 6001, **www.icrc.org**, 19 avenue de la Paix, CH-1202 Geneva, Switzerland) or your national Red Cross branch. There are also national organisations working locally on mine removal and assistance to victims.

you're travelling. This is partly because the countries you're travelling in may have higher infection rates for HIV and STIs than your own, but also because when you're travelling you're more likely to be in contact with people who are at greater risk of being infected. More worrying still, surveys have shown that, in spite of the risks, many travellers don't take precautions to protect themselves.

It's easy to think 'it could never happen to me', but it can and does (sex *and* STIs). Anyone who's having sex can get an STI, 'nice' girls and college boys included. You may think you're safe, for example, because you're not going to have sex with someone in a high-risk group or you're only going to have sex with fellow travellers. Think again. Who has your fellow traveller had sex with before you? Can you trust them to have been as careful or as aware of the risks as you?

Traditionally high-risk groups are men who have sex with men, people who inject drugs, sex workers, anybody who's had multiple partners and anybody who's had sex with people in these groups. You'll know if you're in the first group, and perhaps you'll recognise and be able to avoid the second and third groups, but are you sure you'd know if someone was in one of the last two groups? It's difficult to be sure of your new partner's sexual history and you may just be getting the edited highlights. 'Sex worker' is a pretty vague category anyway, and starts to look even vaguer when you've included someone who has sex with travellers in return for free meals, drinks or status. You can be fairly sure that you're not going to be the first traveller they've had sex with.

In theory at least, STIs are simple to prevent – don't have sex. But…for many people, risk reduction is a more realistic option. We're not suggesting you become a celibate saint, but keep your head out of the clouds – avoid obviously risky situations (use your common sense and don't believe everything your new partner may tell you) and always use condoms if you have sex with a new partner. Check out the following safety tips:

- consider safer ways of having casual sex that don't involve intercourse
- if you have a regular partner, play fair by making sure you don't transmit an STI to them
- many STIs are passed in an alcoholic haze – try to avoid getting into situations where this might happen
- you never know when you might need a condom, so be prepared – it doesn't mean you have to have sex

If you do slip up while you're away, don't just pretend it never happened and perhaps put yourself and other partners at risk – arrange for a check-up when you get home.

INJECTIONS & BLOOD TRANSFUSIONS

INJECTIONS

Injections and other medical or dental treatment procedures can involve infection risks if the needle or equipment is not adequately sterilised. If there are traces of blood or other body fluids on the equipment, there are risks of transmission of diseases such as hepatitis B and HIV. As a general rule, it's a good idea to avoid injections and any other procedures that involve breaking the skin unless you are confident of the hygiene standards.

It's a good idea to carry a few sterile needles and syringes in your medical kit for use in an emergency, but only if you always carry them on you and are prepared to insist on them being used. Prepacked 'AIDS packs' are available from most travel health clinics and travel equipment suppliers.

> **!** Make sure you carry a note on you from your doctor saying what they are for, as officials can be very suspicious otherwise, especially in countries where drugs are a big issue.

If you do need an injection, make sure you see the sterile wrapping opened in front of you.

- You can minimise your risks of needing medical or dental procedures while you are away by having medical and dental check-ups before you go, and taking good care of yourself while away.
- Any equipment used for a medical or dental procedure can be contaminated if it is not properly sterilised.
- If you are offered an injection, ask if there is a tablet you can take instead.
- Boiling needles for 20 minutes will inactivate HIV.
- Never share needles.
- Acupuncture, tattooing and ear, nose or body piercing can all carry risks of infection.

BLOOD TRANSFUSIONS

The AIDS epidemic has brought this issue into the limelight for travellers, especially in areas where levels of HIV/AIDS are high (such as Brazil currently; for more details, see the section on HIV/AIDS in Latin America on p216). However, HIV is by no means the only risk associated with transfusions. Malaria, hepatitis, syphilis, leishmaniasis and Chagas' disease can also be transmitted in this way. Serious reactions can also occur if the blood is not matched properly.

Reliable sources of blood are currently only available in some 40 to 50 countries in the world, which is obviously a hugely unsatisfactory – and unfair – situation. Efforts are being made

LEAD

One source of lead exposure that particularly affects Latin American populations is lead-glazed ceramics. These are commonly used to prepare, store and serve food and drinks. There is concern, though, that these items are not being fired at temperatures high enough to ensure that the lead is properly bound. This means that acidic foods and drinks, such as wine, fruit juices, coffee, tomato-containing sauces and salad dressings are able to leach lead from the glaze, which is then consumed.

Lead poisoning tends to affect children primarily, and can cause learning disabilities, impaired hearing and decreased mental abilities. Worryingly high levels of lead have been found in children in some parts of Latin America, particularly in urban, polluted areas such as Mexico City. Other major sources of lead include vehicle emissions, lead paints and folk remedies, which can sometimes contain large quantities of lead (for example the Mexican remedies Azarcon and Greta are particular culprits).

There have been no studies looking at how lead exposure affects travellers. Normal water purification techniques, for example, will not remove lead from the water. Although you'd probably rather not have that extra lead knocking around your body, it's unlikely to be a major hazard, especially in short-term travellers.

to increase the provision of safe blood throughout the world, but there's a long way to go. Even when blood is screened for all the endemic diseases, there's still a risk that early infections will have been missed. In most parts of Latin America you can assume that blood available in major centres will have been adequately screened. In Brazil, for example, the AIDS crisis has prompted improvements in donor selection and screening procedures, and the blood now available is considered pretty safe (from HIV at least; Chagas' disease is harder to detect reliably).

In any case, remember that the chances you will need a blood transfusion while you are away are pretty small. One study estimated that in a two week trip, about one in 10,000 travellers would need a blood transfusion. Your risk obviously increases the longer you are away, and if you are doing 'risky' activities like rock climbing or trekking. The most important thing to remember is to make sure you have adequate medical insurance, covering emergency evacuation if necessary.

Although it's probably down to fate in the end, there's a lot you can do to minimise your risks of needing a blood transfusion:

- take steps to avoid injury, especially road traffic accidents (the most likely reason for needing a blood transfusion if you're otherwise healthy) – see the earlier Accidents & Injury section for details
- take precautionary measures against diseases such as malaria and dengue fever, which carry a risk of needing a blood transfusion
- think twice about travelling in less developed countries in the region if you have a condition that might mean that you need a blood transfusion, eg a stomach ulcer or if you are pregnant

As a general rule, blood should be transfused only when absolutely necessary, and in many cases non-blood fluids can be used safely instead in the short term. However, in practice, unless you know about these things, you'll have to rely on someone else's opinion. You could consider carrying sterile fluids for use in an emergency, although this is not likely to be a practical option unless you are in a very remote area away from medical help. If you want to find out more about this issue, there's a useful online summary of the currently accepted guidelines on blood transfusion for international travellers (www.armchair.com/info/bloodtrf.html).

If a blood transfusion is unavoidable, try to make sure it's from as reliable a source as possible – check with your embassy, your travel insurance company, clinics dealing with international travellers, the Red Cross, or the local expatriate community for safe local sources. You should be able to find a source of adequately screened blood in most major cities.

Check what arrangements your travel insurance company has for providing safe blood and other fluids in an emergency. Alternatively, you might want to consider joining the Blood Care Foundation. This charitable organisation has a global network of blood banks that claim to supply travellers with safe blood and sterile transfusion equipment within 12 hours anywhere in the world, for a membership fee. The Blood Care Foundation (☎ 01732-742 427, fax 451 199) can be contacted at 16 Lonsdale Gardens, Tunbridge Wells, Kent TN1 1NU, UK.

Your blood group	Blood types you can receive
A	A, O
B	B, O
AB	A, B, AB, O
O	O
rhesus positive	rhesus positive, rhesus negative
rhesus negative	rhesus negative

DIET & NUTRITION

Eating well is all about making sure you get enough of the right nutrients to enable you to function at your best, mentally and physically. It can also make you less vulnerable to illness. Dietary considerations can be important when you're travelling because you may be eating very differently from normal, and at the same time, a different lifestyle and new activities may mean you have different nutritional requirements. Activity (and this includes sightseeing) and stress can increase your nutritional requirements. If you fall ill or are injured, you need a good diet to give your body the best chance to recover.

Being unfamiliar with local foods may make you less likely to vary your diet and you may be uncertain about their nutritional value. You may skip good things like fresh fruit and vegetables if you're worried about possible effects on your health. If you're

IODINE & GOITRES

If you're travelling in the Andean region, you may see local people with swellings around their throats – goitres. Goitres occur when the thyroid gland swells because of a lack of iodine in the diet (the thyroid gland needs iodine to produces thyroid hormones). Iodine deficiency has very serious effects in pregnant women, causing death or profound disability in newborn babies.

Iodine deficiency occurs as a result of eating food grown in iodine-depleted soil but also because the diets of local people include foods that actively affect iodine. These include foods such as cassava, sweet potato, millet and cabbage. Bolivia, Ecuador and Peru are countries where this has traditionally been a problem. However, a simple intervention by many Latin American countries – fortification of table salt with iodine – has resulted in considerable success in combating this problem.

on the move all the time, it may be difficult not to miss meals. It can all add up to you feeling below par and being more vulnerable to infection and other illnesses.

In general, with a little bit of effort, it shouldn't be too difficult to make sure you eat a balanced diet in most parts of Latin America. The local diet tends to consist of a carbohydrate staple (rice, cornmeal and other cereals, plantains, cassava or manioc, potatoes, bread), which you eat with a protein source (beans, meat, fish or cheese) and vegetables. Fresh fruit is widely available.

However, in some places and in some situations, this might not be so easy. You may find the food unpalatable, and alternatives may be limited. And you can get the budgeting bug so badly that your diet suffers.

MUY PICANTE

Testing your pain threshold by eating hot (spicy) food is a thrill that most travellers will find hard to resist. Not that all Latin American food is hot by any means, but chillies are an important part of the diet in Mexico.

Chillies and sweet peppers are members of the capsicum family, and are indigenous to Latin America. There's plenty of evidence to suggest that chillies were cultivated for thousands of years before the Spanish arrived. Seeds from domesticated chillies dating back to 3500 BC have been found in Mexico and Peru. Chillies were used then as now to enhance the usually bland flavour of staple foods – beans, corn, cassava and potatoes in Latin America.

The Spanish and Portuguese took them back to Europe, and from there they spread to Asia and Africa, where they were enthusiastically adopted into the local cuisine. This had always been spicy, but before chillies, black pepper was used to add heat to a dish. The Habanero chilli is the hottest chilli of them all. Definitely to be treated with respect.

Chillies and sweet peppers come in many different shapes, sizes and colours – today there are over 200 varieties grown in tropical regions worldwide. Mexico is the third-largest pepper producing country in the world. The active ingredient in chillies is a substance called capsaicin, which is found mainly in the seeds and membranes, as well as the skin to a varying extent. If you prepare chillies, remember to wash your hands well after and don't touch any sensitive areas or cuts, as you'll find they sting unbearably. Salt is said to be a good treatment for burning hands.

So why do people put themselves through this torture? Well, it seems that it makes them feel good!

When capsaicin touches your mouth, you start salivating to try to get rid of the irritant, and this stimulates your taste buds. Before you know it, you'll be wanting a second bite at the chilli. Capsaicin is also claimed to increase the concentration of endorphins, natural feel-good factors, in your brain by an effect on a substance that carries pain messages to the brain.

Hot food generally comes from hot tropical climates. One reason may be that eating chillies stimulates sweating, which helps cool you down. Spicy food may be just what's needed to stimulate lethargic appetites in hot climes. If you would prefer to forgo the pain – and pleasure – of eating searingly hot food, ask for it to be 'no picante'.

So if chillies make your mouth feel like the inside of a volcano, what do they do to the rest of your guts? Surprisingly, the answer seems to be very little. Studies have shown no internal damage to intestines, and certainly there is nothing to suggest that stomach problems are more common in chilli eating populations of the world. Chillies won't make unsafe food safe, though.

If you've taken one bite of the chilli too many, or the heat has crept up on you unawares, the accepted wisdom is to reach for alcohol (a cold beer or frozen margarita is perfect), milk, yoghurt or something bland like rice or bread – but not water. Capsaicin is not water-soluble and water isn't very effective at neutralising the pain. You need to work up to hot food – what you find unbearable at the start of your trip, you'll probably be adding a pinch of chilli to liven up by the end.

Chillies are a rich source of vitamin A and C. Originally, chillies were used medicinally, as appetite stimulants, to help circulation, as hangover cures and to relieve pain. They were also used for diseases like malaria. Currently, capsaicin is marketed as a pain-relieving cream or lotion for arthritis and facial pain.

EATING THE RIGHT STUFF

Everybody needs six basics for life: water, carbohydrates, protein, fat, vitamins and minerals. Foods aren't a pure source of just of one type of nutrient – they contain various elements in different quantities, so the best way to make sure you get enough of the right things is to eat a varied diet.

You need to eat a variety of foods from each of five core groups:

■ bread, other cereals (rice, cornmeal, quinoa etc), potatoes, cassava (manioc) and other tubers – eat lots of these, as they provide carbohydrate, fibre, some calcium and iron, and B vitamins

■ fruit and vegetables – eat lots of these, they give you vitamin C, carotenes (vitamin A), folates, fibre and some carbohydrate

■ milk & dairy products – eat moderate amounts for calcium, zinc, protein, vitamin B12, vitamin B2, vitamin A and vitamin D

■ meat, fish; nuts, beans and pulses (lentils) – these provide iron, protein, B vitamins (especially B12; meat only), zinc and magnesium; eat from this group in moderation

■ fat and sugar-containing foods (butter, oil, margarine, cakes, biscuits, sweets, soft drinks etc) – eat sparingly from this group, which mainly provides fat (including essential fatty acids), some vitamins and salt

If you're ill, your requirements change, for example you may need to eat more foods containing protein, vitamins and minerals.

Vitamins & Minerals

These nutrients are needed in small amounts for many of the processes carried out in your body and are essential for health. In many developed countries, foods like bread and breakfast cereals are usually fortified with vitamins, but this isn't necessarily the case elsewhere. Cooking vegetables tends to decrease their vitamin content.

Although most nutritionists would agree that it's best to get what you need by varying your diet, when you're travelling there are some situations when it may be a good idea to take multivitamin and mineral supplements. Many vitamins and

QUINOA

This cereal is unique to the Andean region, and is a traditional food crop in many countries in the area. Quinoa is a little bit like rice or oatmeal, and is prepared in a similar way. It's used in soups or ground and used as flour to make bread. It's thought to have been cultivated in the Andean highlands since 3000 BC. Although you may find it is something of an acquired taste, there's no doubt that it is extremely nutritious, more so than other cereals such as rice or maize. It is high in protein, minerals and vitamins, and is similar to milk solids in its protein content. In particular, it has more calcium and iron than most other cereals. It's also a good source of magnesium, zinc, copper, vitamin B6, folate and biotin. Traditionally, the juice extracted by pressing quinoa seeds was used as an antiseptic for skin injuries.

minerals come from fresh fruit and vegetables, so supplements are a good idea if you think you'll be missing out on them for any reason (for example if you're on a long trek or you're travelling somewhere where they are likely to be in short supply). Tinned foods are generally a poor nutritional substitute for fresh items.

If you have heavy menstrual periods, especially if you've cut out animal products from your diet, you may need to take multivitamin supplements containing iron to prevent anaemia. If you don't eat any foods of animal origin, you will need to take a vitamin B12 supplement.

Finally, if you're recovering from illness, taking multivitamin supplements may give your body a helping hand.

Energy & Protein

All the starchy staples (or complex carbohydrates) that make up such a big part of the Latin American diet are good sources of food energy. Sugary foods are good as instant energy suppliers, but complex carbohydrates are better for providing more sustained energy, as they are broken down more slowly in the body. If you don't have enough carbs in your diet, more protein is used instead, making less available for growth and repair.

You shouldn't have any trouble finding sugary foods: good sources of sugar include fruit (drying fruit concentrates the sugar), jam, honey and milk. If your blood sugar gets low, you may start to feel weak, wobbly and headachy, signalling that it's time for that chocolate fix.

Protein is an important component of your diet, but healthy adults only need a small amount of protein daily. Protein is important for growth and repair, so it's vital that growing children get sufficient quantities. Protein can also help with wound healing, so try to increase the amount you are eating if you have been sick.

Good sources of animal protein include meat, fish, poultry, eggs and dairy foods (milk, cheese etc). Non-animal sources include cereals (bread, rice, oats etc), nuts, seeds and pulses (beans, lentils etc).

Fat is the most concentrated source of energy, providing, weight for weight, just over twice as much as carbohydrate or protein. Foods rich in fat include all the obvious things like oil, butter, and any foods cooked in these; meat; egg yolks and many processed and fast foods. Less obvious foods rich in fat include coconut milk, avocado and nuts. Palm oil and coconut milk are rare plant sources of saturated fats. Dare we tell you that alcohol provides nearly as much energy as fat?

FADING AWAY?

You may find you lose weight while you're travelling, especially if you're on a long trip. There are lots of reasons for this, including falling ill, having a change in diet and perhaps being more active.

You may have a bit of padding to spare, but keep an eye on how much weight you're losing. Don't allow yourself to lose too much, as this may put you at risk of illness as well as draining you of energy. If you find you're losing weight and you're eating a vegetarian diet, remember that you generally have to eat larger quantities of plant foods to get the same amount of energy. Increase your quota of energy-giving foods, including fats, and consider taking multivitamin supplements. If you have ongoing diarrhoea, you may not be absorbing nutrients properly. If you're ill, get medical advice on this.

We should point out that probably an equal number of travellers find they put on weight, so don't rely on a holiday to shed those extra pounds.

VEGGING OUT

If you've somehow managed to close your eyes to the realities of meat production back home, you may find that wandering through a few markets brings it up close and personal. Or you simply may get bored of *bifstek* and grilled chicken. Disease-causing organisms love meat, so you may decide to avoid the risk and go veg.

Meat and fish are an integral part of the Latin American diet in greater or lesser quantities. Depending on how strict a vegetarian you are and where you're travelling, you shouldn't find it too hard to have a reasonably healthy vegetarian diet in Latin America – although beans and rice can get a bit monotonous.

If you've just turned vegetarian, be aware that your body takes a bit of time to adjust to getting some nutrients from plant sources, so take a bit of care with your diet. Getting enough protein isn't generally a problem, as beans are ubiquitous, and especially if you eat cheese and eggs. Nuts are also easy to find and a good, if fattening, source of protein.

Proteins from plant sources are often deficient in one or more amino acids (the building blocks of protein). Most traditionally vegetarian diets have dealt with this by basing meals around a combination of protein sources so that deficiencies are complemented. Examples of combinations include beans and rice, pulses and cereal (beans and tortillas) and nuts and cereal (nut butter on bread).

BEANS

There are several contenders, including potatoes, tomatoes and chillies, but beans are arguably the New World's greatest contribution to the global cuisine. Latin Americans themselves are great bean consumers; together with grains or tubers, beans form the staple diet for the majority of the population. The variety of bean dishes on offer across the region is phenomenal, and you'd be very unlucky not to find a bean dish on the menu.

The kidney (or haricot) bean is the most common bean used, in various incarnations: white, red, pink, pinto (speckled) or black. Lima beans (or butter beans) originated in South America, while newer arrivals from the Old World include broad beans *(fava)* and chickpeas *(garbanzo)*. Soya beans have recently gained ground, and soy-based dishes are often found in vegetarian restaurants. Brazil is said to be the largest bean-producing country in the world.

Beans are nutritious, satisfyingly filling and cheap – which makes them a great option for travellers on a tight budget. Beans are usually an important component of most vegetarian diets. Nutritionally, beans are a good source of protein, carbohydrate and B complex vitamins. They are also one of the best sources of dietary fibre – something of a mixed blessing, as the gas-producing potential of beans is legendary, and this potentially antisocial by-product is often the reason they are avoided in spite of their healthful properties!

When any fibre is fermented by bacteria in your gut, it increases the amount of gas produced, and beans have a lot of fibre. They also contain substances called oligosaccharides, which are gas producers par excellence. Humans don't have the right enzymes to digest these complex sugars but bacteria do, producing heaps of carbon dioxide. Soaking dried beans in water overnight helps reduce the amount of oligosaccharides left in the beans.

Although researchers are feverishly working to produce a gas-free bean, and thus earn themselves a small fortune, it hasn't materialised yet. In the meantime, if you're concerned about the potentially ozone-depleting effect of suddenly eating beans for every meal, introducing beans gradually allows your gut to acclimatise. Although this won't reduce the total amount of gas produced, your gut will be better able to cope with it and less likely to embarrass you socially. If the beans still have their outer skin on, eating it is supposed to help, as the skin contains minerals that bind some of the gas-producing substances.

And in case you're wondering, yes, human methane is likely to have the same effect on the environment as animal methane, which is said to contribute to greenhouse gases and global warming. However, in terms of quantity produced, even bean-eating humans just can't compete with animals. It would certainly be a cruel irony if human flatus threatened our survival in the future!

Because iron from plant sources is less well absorbed than iron from meat, iron deficiency anaemia is a risk if you aren't careful, especially in menstrual-age women. You can improve absorption of iron from food by having a source of vitamin C (for example fruit, fruit juice or vegetables) at the same time; conversely tea, coffee, and phytate and oxalates from plants reduces the absorption of iron.

Vitamin B12 is another micronutrient you need to be careful about, as it is only derived from animal sources. If you cut out all animal foods from your diet, you'll need to take a B12 supplement to make up for this.

Good plant sources of nutrients include:

- protein – beans, lentils, bread, grains, seeds, potatoes, nuts
- calcium (for healthy bones) – seeds, green leafy vegetables, nuts, bread, dried fruit
- iron – pulses, green vegetables, dried fruits, nuts, plain chocolate

FOOD FOR ACTION

Food is fuel, and if you're active you need lots of it. For example, you can use up to 4000Cal (16,400kJ) a day if you're active in a temperate climate. You need more energy to keep warm in a cold climate, when you might need up to 5000Cal (20,500kJ) a day.

If you are going trekking in a remote area, you can't rely on getting supplies along the way (and it wouldn't be fair on local people to expect this). This means taking all you need with you (although you may be able to top up on perishables along the way), so it's a question of balancing up the weight, bulk and energy-giving properties of food items available locally. Bearing in mind the limited culinary (and fuel) possibilities of a portable cooker, you will want to take lightweight food that can be quickly prepared. If you're going on a long-ish hike, you'll also want to have some variety (and vitamins) in your diet.

Most trekkers plan on taking enough for three main meals a day: a hot breakfast and evening meal plus a pre-prepared (or at least easily prepared) cold midday meal. In addition, take plenty of between-meal snack food. Always take more supplies with you than you think you will need, just in case.

What you take depends on what's available locally. Dehydrated meals are a camping stalwart, if not exactly a favourite, but may not be available in some areas. Some suggestions for good camp and trekking food are as follows:

- instant cereals or *harina tostada* (toasted wheat flour) – these are widely available, nutritious, light to carry and easy to prepare
- muesli – light, nutritious and doesn't need cooking
- bread, in any of its endless local variations

- packet soups, instant pasta and rice – good camping stalwarts
- nuts – walnuts, peanuts (groundnuts), brazil nuts
- *dulce de leche* – a South American speciality of caramelised condensed milk; spread on bread or biscuits
- dried fruits and fruit cake
- chocolate, sweet biscuits – widely available, good quality; great for instant energy and morale boosting

Sources of protein include dehydrated meals, cereals, dried mushrooms, cheese (hard cheese or processed varieties will survive best), nuts, beans and, if you're not carrying them too far, tinned meats and fish.

Although wild foods such as berries may be an option in some areas, it's best not to rely on these to supplement your diet. If you do decide to try wild food, make sure you know what you are doing.

Help...

✚ Remember that it's always best to seek help as soon as possible if a child is ill – see the Babies & Children chapter for more advice.

✚ First aid is covered in the appendix starting on p434.

Being ill far from home is miserable, but it's even worse when you don't speak the language and the medical system is unfamiliar and possibly less reliable than you are used to. Scarier still is the thought of all those nasty tropical diseases that everyone's been talking about and that you now think you must have.

Take heart: you're generally at pretty low risk of most 'tropical' diseases – you're much more likely to get diarrhoea, an infected insect bite or a cold. Don't forget that your body has an enormous potential to fight off infection, and most minor illnesses respond to simple, nondrug treatments.

Travel medicine clinics have medical kits containing various prescription and non-prescription medications for common travel illnesses. As a general rule, you should only self-medicate if there is no alternative (usually because you're in a remote area far from medical help) and you are confident you know what you are doing. The treatment guidelines we give in this book are to help you make decisions about what to do in a given situation; they are not intended as a substitute for getting medical advice.

❗ You must see a doctor if you're seriously ill or you've tried all the simple measures without any effect or there's no improvement in your condition after a day or two.

If you're concerned about getting medical help while travelling, remember that doctors in touristed areas will be used to treating common travellers ailments. Also, doctors who work in tropical countries will have substantial experience in diagnosing and treating tropical diseases (such as malaria) – much more than your doctor back home is likely to have.

> ! It's best to avoid treating fellow travellers unless you know what you're doing, as you probably won't be doing them any favours.

HOW TO GET MEDICAL HELP

If you need medical assistance, your embassy should be able to provide you with a list of local doctors. Otherwise, you could try some of the following options.

- Ring your travel insurance hotline – they should be able to recommend a local doctor. Make sure you always carry the number on you while you are away.

- If you are a member of IAMAT (see Useful Organisations in the Before You Go chapter for details), they will supply you with the names of local doctors – again, make sure you carry this information on you at all times.

- Upmarket hotels can often recommend a doctor and usually have a doctor attached to the staff.

- In an emergency, US citizens could try contacting the State Department's Citizen's Emergency Center (see p27) for advice.

- You could try asking other travellers, members of the expat community or members of international aid organisations for the names of reliable doctors.

- Some key hospitals are listed at the end of this book in the Medical Services appendix, or you could try the telephone book or check your guidebook.

- Remember, you could always try contacting your doctor back home for advice, especially for exacerbations or complications arising from preexisting conditions.

See the Medical Services appendix for more details about the availability of medical services at your destination. You should have no trouble finding doctors and hospitals in all major towns. If you are in more remote areas, missionary hospitals or hospitals run by international organisations are a good bet. In rural areas, healthworkers can usually provide basic medical advice.

Pharmacists and drugstore owners are a source of basic health advice for a large section of the local population. Bear in mind, though, that they are generally not medically qualified and their advice is no substitute for a proper medical consultation. They may recommend dangerously inappropriate treatment (for example tuberculosis treatment for a simple cough), with potentially disastrous effects.

BASICS

WORKING OUT WHAT'S WRONG

Try to decide what your main problem is: do you feel feverish, have you got a headache, diarrhoea, a skin rash or a cough? If you think you know what's wrong, turn to the appropriate chapter later in this book (look up your symptom in the index); otherwise, ask yourself some simple questions.

- What diseases am I at risk for? See the summary at the beginning of this book and the maps; if you're outside the danger zone, then these diseases are very unlikely.

- Am I in a malarious area? (See map p20 and check locally.) If the answer is yes, read the section on malaria and seek medical advice as soon as possible (within 8 hours). Remember you can get malaria even if you are taking malaria prevention medication but that it's unlikely less than a week after you first arrive in a malarial area.

- Did I complete my vaccination courses properly before leaving? If yes, then these diseases are very unlikely.

- Have I been in any specific risk situations recently? Have I been bitten by insects (malaria, dengue fever etc), ticks (typhus, relapsing fever), had contact with animals (rabies), had any injections or transfusions (HIV, hepatitis B) or swum in rivers or lakes (schistosomiasis)?

- Have any of my travelling companions been ill? If yes, you may be suffering from the same illness.

- Is a sexually transmitted infection a possibility?

BASIC MEASURES

If you're ill, there are some simple things you can do to give your body the best chance to get better.

- Stop travelling and rest up for a while.
- Make sure you're as comfortable as the circumstances allow: get a room with a fan if it's hot or extra blankets if it's cold. It's probably worth spending a bit more on a decent room, as you'll be surprised at the difference cheerful surroundings can make.
- Drink plenty of fluids (safe water, weak tea or herbal teas), especially if it's hot or you have a temperature.
- If necessary, give yourself a break from alcohol, tobacco and strong tea or coffee.

If you are ill, it is always a good idea to take your temperature (see following section) and possibly get someone to take your pulse.

! Seek medical help if you don't improve after 48 hours (or before then if you get a lot worse).

TEMPERATURE

Take your temperature at regular intervals (for example four times a day) while you're ill, as this can give you an idea of how quickly you are improving or whether you need to try something different – see the section on Fever later in this chapter for more guidelines.

There are three main types of thermometer: mercury, digital and liquid crystal ('fever strip'). Mercury ones are the most accurate, but they're also the most delicate and you can't take them with you in the cabin on a plane. Liquid crystal thermometers are the least accurate, but they're very convenient – follow the instructions on the packaging. The following instructions are for mercury and digital thermometers:

- wipe the thermometer with a small amount of antiseptic solution to make sure it's clean
- shake the thermometer so that the mercury is down in the bulb
- place the thermometer under the tongue; if there is a chance it may be bitten (for example a young child or if the person is very sick) place it in the armpit or (for young babies) grease it slightly and slip it in the rectum

- leave the thermometer in place for two to three minutes (or follow the instructions on the packet), then remove it
- read and make a note of the temperature; temperatures are usually read in degrees Celsius, but may also be read in degrees Fahrenheit

PULSE & BREATHING RATE

Feeling the pulse and measuring the breathing rate is an important part of any medical assessment. Both can provide a great deal of useful information, but only if you know what to look for and how these clues fit in with the rest of the picture. They're probably not going to be that useful in most common situations when you feel ill, although they are important to note in an emergency situation. For more guidance on how to deal with an emergency, see the inside back cover.

Pulse

To take your pulse, put two fingers on the inside of the wrist at the base of the thumb, and count how many beats there are to the minute; don't use your thumb because this has a pulse of its own that may confuse things. In an emergency situation, if you can't feel a pulse in the wrist, try feeling the side of the neck beside the voice box (the Adam's apple in men) – see the illustrations on p446 for more guidance.

As well as counting the pulse, think about what it feels like: is it strong or weak? Is it regular or irregular? Some abnormalities you may notice, and what they may mean if you are ill, are as follows. You need to seek medical advice urgently in all these situations:

- regular fast pulse (eg up to 120 or 140 beats/min, or bpm) – associated with high fever and serious illness
- weak, rapid pulse – shock (severe illness, major trauma etc); see inside back cover for guidelines on emergency resuscitation
- irregular, very slow or very rapid pulse – heart problems
- slow pulse in spite of fever – could be typhoid (see p143)

WHAT'S NORMAL?

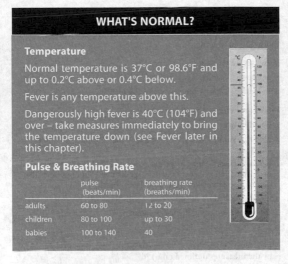

Temperature

Normal temperature is 37°C or 98.6°F and up to 0.2°C above or 0.4°C below.

Fever is any temperature above this.

Dangerously high fever is 40°C (104°F) and over – take measures immediately to bring the temperature down (see Fever later in this chapter).

Pulse & Breathing Rate

	pulse (beats/min)	breathing rate (breaths/min)
adults	60 to 80	12 to 20
children	80 to 100	up to 30
babies	100 to 140	40

Breathing Rate

Count the number of breaths per minute (get someone else to do this, as it's impossible to get an accurate count on yourself). The breathing rate can be increased in many different situations, including lung problems (such as a chest infection) and fever.

OTHER SIGNS

Other things you should check for and note include:

- any rashes, wounds, lumps or bumps
- yellow colour of the skin and whites of the eyes – jaundice
- pale lips and nails, pale inside of eye – anaemia
- blueness of the lips – may indicate a serious lung or heart problem
- unequal or otherwise abnormal pupils of the eyes
- abnormal drowsiness and/or confusion – this always indicates serious illness

SIGNS OF SERIOUS ILLNESS

You must seek medical attention if you experience any of the following problems.

- any severe blood loss
- any severe continuous pain
- more than a day without passing any urine

Blood anywhere it shouldn't be:

- blood in urine
- blood in vomit – this may look like 'coffee grounds'; it won't always look bright red
- blood in faeces – may be bright red, more likely to be browny red and mixed in, or faeces may be black like tar (but remember that taking iron tablets can turn your faeces black)
- blood coughed up in spit
- any vaginal bleeding during pregnancy

Fever:

- high fever (more than 40°C or 104°F) that can't be brought down by the measures outlined on p126
- any fever without obvious cause that lasts more than two to three days

Problems with your digestive system:

- severe diarrhoea and vomiting lasting more than a day (see p156 for more guidance)
- abdominal pain and vomiting without being able to defecate
- severe vomiting that means you can't take any fluids for more than a day
- severe weight loss (usually more than a tenth of your normal body weight)

'Head' problems:

- convulsions
- severe headache with neck stiffness and sensitivity to light
- dizziness or extreme weakness, especially on standing

Lumps, bumps etc:

- any sores that won't go away
- any lumps that appear and grow
- any mole that bleeds or changes shape

COMMON SIGNS & SYMPTOMS

FEVER

✚ Note that children can get very high temperatures very quickly and this can be dangerous if it causes fits (convulsions). See the section on p292 for more details.

The term 'fever' means having a temperature higher than normal (see p123). It always means that there is a disease process going on, and in travellers it's most likely to be a sign of infection. Producing a fever is thought to help the body's natural defences to fight infection.

Having a fever usually makes you feel pretty rough. You may feel intermittently hot and cold, with 'goose bumps' or shivering, and you usually feel completely drained of energy. The fever process itself causes aches and pains (often backache) in your muscles and joints and headache.

You can feel hot without having a temperature above normal and sometimes you can feel cold even though your temperature is raised, so it's always worth taking your temperature with a thermometer to be sure. (Trying to decide if you have a temperature by touching your forehead with the back of your hand is notoriously unreliable.) Take your temperature at regular intervals – four times a day – and note what it is so that you can keep track of any improvement or changes, and also to give you an idea of the pattern of the fever.

❗ Although the pattern of the fever can sometimes be helpful in determining the cause, in practice many diseases don't show the textbook fever patterns, especially in travellers, so it's best not to rely on this.

If you have a really high temperature, you may experience rigors – unpleasant episodes of violent shivering and drenching sweating. They are always a sign of very serious illness, and you should seek medical advice as soon as possible, and immediately try simple measures to lower your temperature.

If you have a fever:

- take paracetamol (acetaminophen) to lower your temperature and relieve any aches and pains
- dehydration is a risk with any fever, especially in hot climates, so drink plenty of fluids
- help your body to cool down – take cool showers or use wet cloths or sponges and a fan
- make sure you don't get cold (although piling the blankets on to 'sweat it out' is not helpful)

Having a fever increases your metabolic rate and can make you lose weight – this is just the fever part of the illness, if you have diarrhoea and vomiting as well, this will exacerbate the problem. Because of this, it's important to try to maintain a basic intake of food while you are ill and to make up for this as you start feeling better and your appetite increases. See the Diet & Nutrition section at the end of the Staying Healthy chapter for more guidelines.

These measures all treat the symptoms of the fever, not the underlying cause. You'll also need to work out what's causing the fever.

Causes

Many fevers, as at home, are caused by viral illnesses, such as colds and flu (see the Respiratory System chapter) which can start suddenly and rarely last more than about three to five days. With any fever, always check for any obvious causes:

- runny nose – cold (p176)
- cough – bronchitis, pneumonia (p184)
- sore throat – tonsillitis, glandular fever (p179)
- earache – ear infection (p187)

Disease	Page	Associated Symptoms/Other Clues
flu	p178	may cause generalised aches and pains without any other symptoms
diarrhoea (various causes)	p150	see the Digestive System chapter later in the book for guidelines on diagnosing and treating diarrhoea
heatstroke	p318	headache, weakness, muscle cramps; more likely if you've been very active in unaccustomed heat
malaria	p130	fever often intermittent, joint aches, chills, headache; also possibly cough, abdominal pain, diarrhoea and jaundice*
dengue fever	p137	fever may seem to go, but comes back after a few days; headache, severe aches and pains, rash (possibly)
glandular fever-like illnesses	p181	sore throat, swollen neck glands, no energy
hepatitis	p146	nausea, vomiting, jaundice, dark urine, light faeces
meningitis	p141	fever, headache followed by neck stiffness, vomiting, sensitivity to light
schistosomiasis (bilharzia)	p362	itching, wheezy cough and diarrhoea, but often no symptoms
amoebic liver abscess	p166	pain in right upper part of abdomen
typhoid (and related illnesses)	p143	often causes a persistent fever; diarrhoea may be a late symptom
tuberculosis	p144	recurrent evening or night fever, usually with cough
typhus	p375	red rash, distinctive sore at site of tick bite, more likely if you've been trekking in rural areas
Chagas' disease	p369	symptoms rare early in the disease; follows bite by a bedbug-like insect

*jaundice = yellowing of the skin and whites of the eyes

- facial or sinus pain – acute sinusitis (p176)
- abdominal pain – see following section
- bladder symptoms (p253)
- pelvic infection (p254)
- skin infection (p208)
- toothache – dental abscess (p199)

If you've ruled out all these, then you can start thinking about some other causes of fever, which we've summarised in the table.

ABDOMINAL PAIN

It can be notoriously difficult to work out what's causing this – if the pain is severe, it's safer to seek medical advice as soon as possible. To give you some guidance, we've listed a few of the more common scenarios:

- often occurs with diarrhoea, when it's usually crampy; comes in waves and may be relieved by passing wind or faeces; you may have a fever
- constipation is often associated with spasms of pain in the lower abdomen
- central lower abdomen – bladder infection, period pains, pelvic infection
- upper abdomen, just under rib cage, burning, worse after meals – heart burn, indigestion
- upper right abdomen, just under ribs – hepatitis (sometimes), liver abscess, gall stones
- appendicitis – see p174
- severe, colicky (comes and goes) pain that makes you writhe around and may go down into your pelvis (or testicles in men); could be a kidney stone – see p173

NAUSEA AND VOMITING

When you're travelling you often get short episodes of nausea, sometimes with vomiting. They usually settle within a day without any specific treatment. They're usually due to viral infections, but there are many other causes:

- medicines, eg malaria pills, antibiotics
- motion sickness (p69)
- food poisoning (p153)
- diarrhoeal illnesses (p150)
- dehydration or heatstroke (p318)
- meningitis (p141)
- migraine headache (p196)
- pregnancy (p265)

HEADACHE

Most fevers cause headache. Other possibilities are:

- dehydration, heatstroke (p318)
- migraine (p196)
- stress headache
- trapped nerve (sharp stabbing pains, intermittent)
- neck problems (eg arthritis)
- malaria (p130)
- dengue fever (p137)
- meningococcal meningitis (p141)
- altitude illness (p329)
- typhoid fever (p143)

RASH

There are many causes of rashes. See the section on p203 for a more detailed discussion of skin problems, but causes include:

- viral illnesses
- measles & other childhood illnesses (p233)
- fungal infections (p208)
- allergic reactions, dermatitis (p205)
- dengue fever (p137)
- typhus (p375)
- haemorrhagic fevers (p231)
- cutaneous leishmaniasis (p366)
- schistosomiasis (p362)

Fever & Hepatitis...

In this chapter we've grouped some important infections that usually have fever as their main symptom – for a full summary of the (many) possible causes of fever, see p126.

➕ For guidance on how to take a temperature see p121.

MALARIA

➕ This section gives you guidelines on diagnosing and treating malaria. For detailed guidelines on preventing malaria (antimalarial medication and insect bite avoidance), see that section in the Before You Go chapter earlier in this book.

About a million new cases of malaria occur every year in malarial zones of Latin America (see map p20). About half these cases are in Brazil, and about one-third are in Bolivia, Colombia, Ecuador, Peru and Venezuela. Malaria does not exist in highland areas above about 2000m.

Malaria is caused by a parasite called *Plasmodium*, which is carried by a type of night-biting mosquito present in most lowland tropical and subtropical areas. When an infected female mosquito bites you, malarial parasites are injected into your bloodstream and get carried to your liver, where they multiply. During this phase you don't get any symptoms.

Symptoms appear when the malarial parasites enter your bloodstream again, which occurs after a variable length of time depending on the type of malaria (usually about one to three weeks, but sometimes up to a year). The malarial parasites enter and multiply in red blood cells, eventually destroying them. This can have effects on many organs in your body, including your guts (causing vomiting and diarrhoea), kidneys (causing kidney failure) and brain (cerebral malaria).

There are four types of *Plasmodium* parasites, but the one of most concern is *P. falciparum*, which causes the most severe disease and is responsible for most malaria deaths worldwide. The other types, *P. vivax* (common worldwide and the main type found in Central America), *P. ovale* (uncommon) and *P. malariae* (uncommon), are less likely to cause severe complications so rapidly, but infection with any of them still needs to be treated promptly. *P. vivax* and *P. ovale* can remain inactive in the liver for some time and can cause disease several weeks or months after you've left a risk area.

> **!** You can't tell the different forms of malaria apart on the basis of the early symptoms, so you have to assume that any malaria is due to *P. falciparum* unless proved otherwise (by a blood test).

Malaria can be effectively treated with drugs and the symptoms quickly disappear as the parasites are cleared from the blood. If malaria is treated appropriately, it doesn't recur.

> **!** Malaria can progress rapidly to severe complications (sometimes within 24 hours), so it's extremely important to seek medical help urgently if you get a fever in a malarial area.

Symptoms

Unfortunately, the symptoms of malaria are very variable and rather nonspecific, making it notoriously difficult to diagnose. The most important sign of malaria is having a fever (38°C 100.5°F or higher)

In theory at least, you should notice three stages: a cold stage when you shiver and your temperature rockets up; followed by a hot stage when you feel hot, flushed and have a high temperature (this lasts for several hours); finally you get a wet stage when you become drenched in sweat and your temperature falls. This is the textbook scenario – in reality the picture is likely to be much more vague, especially if you were taking malaria pills.

Suspect malaria if you have a fever – it may just feel like an attack of flu – with or without any of the following symptoms:

- headache and aching muscles and joints
- nausea and vomiting, or diarrhoea (especially in children)
- cough
- abdominal discomfort and jaundice (yellowing of the skin and whites of the eyes)
- confusion, leading to coma (cerebral malaria)

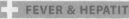
Remember that you can still get malaria even if you are taking malaria prevention pills.

Diagnosis & Treatment

> Note that it takes at least a week for the disease to appear after an infective bite, so a fever within the first week of your arrival in a malarial area is very unlikely to be malaria (unless you've come from a malarial area).

Malaria can be quickly and simply diagnosed from a sample of your blood, usually taken by pricking your finger. The test may need to be repeated if it's initially negative and you know malaria is likely. Most doctors and clinics in malarial areas will have facilities for doing a malaria blood test, or you can do a test yourself if you have a kit with you. You may be able to buy kits locally in some countries.

If you think you may have malaria:

- rest and take steps to bring down the fever – see p126 for guidelines on general measures
- drink plenty of fluids
- seek medical help as soon as possible for a blood test to confirm the diagnosis
- once the diagnosis is confirmed, take the doctor's advice on treatment, as they are likely to be experienced in treating malaria and will know what the most appropriate treatment is for the area you are in

If your symptoms recur or continue despite treatment, seek medical advice, as you will need further treatment; or it may not be malaria, and you may have another illness that needs treating.

Don't forget that you will still need to take malaria prevention medication after you recover – get medical advice on what would be most appropriate in your situation.

> Malaria can appear after you've left the malaria risk zone – if you get a fever in the weeks or months after you were in a malarial risk area, seek medical help urgently and be sure to tell your doctor where you've been and what malaria pills (if any) you were taking.

Emergency Self-treatment

Self-treatment of any serious disease, including malaria, is not something to be undertaken lightly, but it may be appropriate in certain situations.

- You should only consider self-treatment in an emergency, ie if you do not have access to medical care within 24 hours of the start of symptoms.

- Emergency self-treatment is a first aid measure only – you still need to get yourself to medical help as soon as possible.

As discussed under Symptoms earlier, it can be difficult to know when to self-treat, but use the following rule of thumb.

> **!** If you are in a risk area, you must suspect malaria if you have an otherwise unexplained fever (over 38°C) that lasts more than eight hours without responding to simple fever-reducing measures (see p126).

Fortunately, the new malaria diagnosis kits mean that diagnosing malaria in yourself is less of the hit-and-miss affair it used to be

Malaria Treatment Drugs

Although we give currently accepted guidelines here, recommendations change as resistance patterns vary and new facts come to light, so it's best to get the most up-to-date advice from your doctor or travel health clinic before you go, or to seek reliable local advice if necessary. As a general rule:

- you need to take an antimalarial that is different from the one that you were taking as prevention

- because of drug resistance, you need to be sure you are taking the appropriate treatment for the area you are in; inadequately treated malaria can recur later

The reason you need to take a different antimalarial drug for treatment is because the strain of malaria may be resistant to the antimalarial you were taking. In addition, you are more likely to experience side effects if you take the same antimalarial for treatment as you were taking for prevention.

MALARIA DRUG RESISTANCE

Drug resistance patterns change all the time, so you should get the most up-to-date information before you go. At the time of writing, areas with little or absent chloroquine resistance included most of Mexico and Central America north of the Panama canal, Argentina, Paraguay and much of Peru. Chloroquine-resistant malaria existed in most malarial areas of tropical South America, (Amazonia)

The main treatment options currently include:

- chloroquine – if you were not taking any prevention, and you're in a chloroquine-sensitive area (see boxed text)
- sulphadoxine/pyrimethamine (Fansidar) – if you were not taking any preventive medication or you were taking chloroquine (with or without proguanil)
- atovaquone-proguanil (Malarone) – this is good if you were taking mefloquine or doxycycline for prevention
- quinine sulphate – although an effective treatment, because of problems this drug is not usually recommended for emergency standby treatment in travellers
- mefloquine – can be used if you were taking doxycycline as prevention
- artemether-lumefantrine (Riamet) – highly effective combination treatment for those twelve years or older

Other treatments may come on the market in the near future as malaria experts struggle to cope with the spread of drug resistance worldwide. In particular, you may hear talk of artesunate or artemether in connection with the treatment of malaria. Riamet is an example of one of these drugs that has been brought to commercial reality. These compounds are related to artemisinin, or qinghaosu, which has been used for over two millennia in traditional medical practice in China. They appear to be safe and effective in the treatment (but not prevention) of severe malaria, but because of fears of the emergence of resistance, use is restricted to some highly drug resistant areas.

> **!** Note that the antimalarial drug halofantrine is now known to cause heart rhythm problems in susceptible people, and these effects are more likely if you have been taking chloroquine, mefloquine or quinine. It is therefore no longer recommended for standby treatment. However, it may still be available in some areas and is better than nothing in an emergency.

Side Effects & Cautions

✚ Mefloquine and chloroquine are dealt with in the section on Preventing Malaria in the Before You go chapter.

Atovaquone plus proguanil (Malarone) is highly effective against multidrug resistant strains of malaria. It's also safe and unlikely to cause you any adverse effects.

Sulphadoxine/pyrimethamine (Fansidar) has been widely used to treat malaria. Resistance has emerged in some parts of the world, mainly in Asia. It's generally safe and effective at the doses used for treatment, although it is no longer recommended for use as a preventive agent. This is because serious skin reactions have occurred when it was used as a weekly dose.

> **!** You shouldn't take Fansidar if you are allergic to sulphonamide drugs.

Be aware that side effects with mefloquine are common at the doses used for treatment, and include lightheadedness, nausea, dizziness and vertigo; more serious side effects occur in about one in 100 people at this dose.

Quinine is the most effective drug against chloroquine-resistant malaria, but it's quite a toxic drug, so it is not usually recommended for use as emergency standby treatment. It needs to be given with another agent, usually sulphadoxine/pyrimethamine (Fansidar), doxycycline or tetracycline.

MALARIA STANDBY TREATMENT – DOSES & SCHEDULES

Although we have done our best to ensure that these doses are correct at the time of going to print, there are many variables to take into account, so you should check these with your doctor before you leave, most notably the resistance in various parts of the world. Note that although we give doses for children here, we do not recommend that you take children to high risk malarial areas.

Treatment	Adult	Child (by weight)
atovaquone-proguanil (Malarone)	four tablets once daily for three days	11 to 20kg one tablet once daily; 21 to 30kg two tablets once daily; 31 to 40kg three tablets once daily; over 40kg, as for adult
sulphadoxine/ pyrimethamine (Fansidar)	single dose of three tablets	5 to 10kg half tablet; 11 to 20kg one tablet; 21 to 30kg 1.5 tablets; 31 to 45kg two tablets; over 45kg three tablets
quinine sulphate PLUS sulphadoxine/ pyrimethamine (Fansidar)	two 300mg tablets three times daily for seven days	10mg/kg three times daily for seven days
	dose above	dose above
OR PLUS doxycycline	100mg once daily	over 8 years: 2mg/kg twice daily for seven days
OR PLUS tetracycline	250mg four times daily for seven days	over 8 years: 5mg/kg four times daily for seven days
mefloquine	two 250mg tablets and a further two six hours later	child 15kg or over: 15mg/kg single dose
chloroquine	4 tablets (150mg base) each on days 1 and 2, & 2 on day 3 (ie total of 10 tablets)	25mg base/kg over three days
artemether-lumefantrine (Riamet)	4 tabs together at 0, 8, 24, 36, 48 and 60 hrs	12 years and older: as for adult, not used for children under12 years

Side effects of quinine are common, and include ringing in the ears, muffled hearing and sometimes dizziness, usually on the second or third day of treatment. These side effects usually go away once you stop taking it.

Quinine can cause heart problems, so you need medical supervision if you are on any heart medications, and these problems are more likely if you have been taking mefloquine for prevention. It can also cause your blood sugar to drop.

> **!** Be aware that quinine is very toxic if taken at more than the recommended dose, and you should always keep it well out of reach of children.

Artemether-lumefantrine (Riamet) combination is a highly effective treatment, is fast-acting and has few side-effects.

DENGUE & DENGUE HAEMORRHAGIC FEVER

This viral disease (see map p21) is transmitted to humans via the bite of an infected mosquito. Dengue fever has spread rapidly in the last decade and is now one of the top public health problems in the tropical world. There has been a marked increase in cases of dengue in tropical and subtropical areas of Latin America over the last decade, and travellers to risk areas have been infected. The number of cases is expected to continue to rise in the future.

There is no vaccine against dengue, with none likely in the near future. You can avoid dengue fever by taking steps to prevent mosquito bites, bearing in mind that the dengue mosquito bites mainly during the day. Dengue is seasonal to a certain extent, but outbreaks can occur at any time – get the latest information before you go from your doctor or any of the information sources listed in the Before You Go chapter.

Prevention

There is currently no vaccine for dengue fever and no specific treatment if you get ill. If you're going to risk areas, it's vital to take precautions to avoid getting bitten by day-biting mosquitoes. See p89 for more details on measures you can take. If necessary, you can apply sunscreen over insect repellent. Cover up, and if you take a daytime nap, remember to use a mosquito net, or rest in a well screened or air-conditioned room.

Symptoms

The illness usually starts quite suddenly with fever, nausea and vomiting, headache and joint and muscle pains. The aches and pains can be severe, hence the old name 'breakbone fever'. The fever sometimes appears to settle after a few days, only to reappear a few days later (known as 'saddleback fever'). Typically, you get a fine red rash, often around the third to fifth day, which signals the second phase of the disease, and recovery usually follows soon after.

The illness can last anything from three to about 10 days, settling spontaneously without any specific treatment. However, many travellers report experiencing extreme tiredness with muscle wasting and lack of energy for several weeks or months after, which can be debilitating and may be a good reason to cut your trip short. On the other hand, the symptoms can be mild and you may not realise that you've had it.

THE RISE & RISE OF DENGUE

In the late 1940s, the mosquito responsible for transmitting dengue (and yellow fever) was nearly eradicated from the Americas. Now, however, nearly every country in the Americas has been reinfested, and dengue fever has returned with a vengeance, with large outbreaks reported in many countries of the region in the last few years. Dengue haemorrhagic fever is also on the rise.

There are many reasons for this, including lack of resources for control programs and increasing resistance of the mosquito to commonly used insecticides. Poor living conditions and the rise in urban settlements with concomitant deforestation

Rarely, you can get a more severe, potentially fatal form of dengue called dengue haemorrhagic fever (DHF), which is associated with uncontrolled bleeding and shock from loss of blood. Although DHF receives a lot of publicity and is frightening, it is very rare in travellers. DHF is thought to be due to infection with a second strain of the dengue virus within a certain period of time. You can get minor bleeding – nose bleeds, bleeding gums, bruising – with simple dengue, so it doesn't necessarily mean that you've got DHF.

Diagnosis & Treatment

There's no specific treatment, but if you think you might have dengue fever:

- seek medical advice as soon as possible so that the diagnosis can be confirmed and other diagnoses, including malaria, can be ruled out
- rest and drink plenty of fluids
- take simple painkillers if necessary but avoid aspirin, as this can increase the likelihood of bleeding problems

in many parts of tropical Latin America have encouraged the spread of dengue fever. Water supplies are often stored in containers at home, which provide ideal breeding grounds for the mosquito. Dengue mosquitoes are much less common in rural areas and are rarely found at altitudes above about 2000m.

At the same time, population migration and international air travel has encouraged the spread of the disease throughout the tropics. Although mosquito control programs are being stepped up in some parts of Latin America, on a global scale, prevention of dengue fever depends on eradication of mosquito breeding grounds, improving urban living conditions and widespread use of insecticides – so don't hold your breath.

DENGUE AGAIN?

There are four different strains of the dengue virus. If you get dengue, you develop immunity against the infecting strain, but you'll still be vulnerable to the three remaining strains, so you could get it again. You're more likely to get a severe form of the disease second time around so if you've had dengue in the past, you should discuss the risks with your doctor before you go, and be very careful to avoid mosquito bites at all times.

A blood test can help to diagnose dengue fever. You need to keep a look-out for signs of DHF. Seek medical help urgently if you have any of the following (if they do occur, it's usually around the third day of illness):

■ any worsening of your condition, especially if associated with any of the following symptoms

■ spontaneous bruising of the skin, nose bleeds, bleeding from the gums, vomiting blood or abdominal pain

■ signs of blood loss – thin, rapid pulse, restlessness, pale face and cold fingers and toes; see the first aid section p434 for dealing with shock

You should seek medical advice for any fever that develops within two weeks of leaving a dengue risk area.

YELLOW FEVER

This viral disease (see map p22) is related to dengue fever and is transmitted through the bite of an infected, day-biting mosquito. Yellow fever is mainly a problem in forested areas of the Amazon, Orinoco and Magdalena river basins. In normal circumstances it is mainly a disease of monkeys and some rodents, but humans get infected when they enter these areas. Urban epidemics can occur when infected humans return to the cities, where it is spread by the mosquito responsible for transmitting dengue.

In recent years there has been a sharp increase in yellow fever cases in Latin America. This is thought to be a result of a combination of factors, including the phenomenal spread of the mosquito that transmits the disease, and increasing visits to and urbanisation of forest areas. Many countries have vaccination programs in place, including Brazil, where yellow fever vaccination has been made routine for children in risk areas. However, movement of unvaccinated people through risk areas helps to spread the disease. Travellers on trips into the rainforest have been infected, and in recent years, two travellers are known to have died from yellow fever after visiting Brazil.

Although the risk to most travellers is generally low, if you're going on a tour into a high-risk area, vaccination is recommended. The yellow fever vaccine appears to be 100% effective. If you're just travelling in urban areas, you're at very low risk of the disease, unless an epidemic is occurring. Note that yellow fever vaccination is mandatory for entry into some countries, regardless of risk – see the Immunisations section in the Before You Go chapter for more details.

! Prevention of yellow fever is through vaccination if necessary, and by taking measures to prevent mosquito bites at all times.

Symptoms of yellow fever range from a mild fever that resolves over a few days to more serious forms with fever, headache, muscle pains, abdominal pain and vomiting. This can progress to bleeding, shock and liver and kidney failure. The liver failure causes jaundice, or yellowing of your skin and the whites of your eyes – hence the name.

There's no specific treatment but you should seek medical help urgently if you think you have yellow fever.

MENINGOCOCCAL MENINGITIS

✚ Not every headache is likely to be meningitis – see p129 for a list of common causes of headache.

Meningococcal infections occur worldwide, with epidemics occurring sporadically in many countries. Outbreaks occur every few years in Brazil, mainly in the São Paulo area, for

MENINGITIS

Meningitis is any infection of the lining of the brain and spinal cord. Lots of different infectious agents can cause meningitis, including bacteria and viruses. Viral meningitis usually settles without any treatment, whereas bacterial meningitis can rapidly cause death and is the one you're most likely to have heard of.

example. Different strains of the bacteria responsible for the disease are recognised, and vaccines are available against strains A and C. Strain B is the type most commonly found in the Americas and Europe.

The disease is spread by breathing in droplets coughed or sneezed into the air by an infected person (often healthy carriers of the bacteria) or by direct contact with their nasal secretions. The disease is most common in poor, overcrowded areas, in winter and spring. It can occur at any age, although young children are at particular risk.

> **!** Meningococcal meningitis is an extremely serious disease that can cause death within a few hours of you first feeling unwell.
> ● Seek medical help without delay if you have any of the symptoms listed.

Symptoms of meningitis include:

- fever and chills
- severe headache
- neck stiffness – bending your head forward is difficult and causes pain
- nausea and vomiting
- sensitivity to light – you prefer lying in a darkened room
- with meningococcal meningitis, a widespread, blotchy purple rash can appear early in the illness

Treatment is with large doses of penicillin (for example 1.2g of benzylpenicillin in adults, 600mg for children up to 10 years) given directly into the bloodstream or, if that's not possible, intramuscularly. If you're allergic to penicillin, an intramuscular injection of cefotaxime or chloramphenicol are suitable alternatives.

If you've been in close contact with a sufferer, seek medical advice, as you can protect yourself from infection by taking antibiotics, usually rifampicin 500mg twice daily for two days (child 10mg/kg, child under one year 5mg/kg) or ciprofloxacin 500mg single dose (not suitable for children).

TYPHOID FEVER

Also known as enteric fever, typhoid is widespread in Latin America. This bacterial disease (it's caused by a type of salmonella bacteria, *Salmonella typhi*) is common where sewage disposal is inadequate and water supplies are likely to be contaminated. Occasional large outbreaks occur. Paratyphoid is a similar but milder disease.

Typhoid is transmitted via contaminated food and water, and symptomless carriers, especially when they're working as foodhandlers, are an important source of infection.

Although it's generally uncommon in travellers, most cases brought to the USA originate in Mexico, partly because of the large number of US travellers visiting Mexico.

Symptoms

These are variable, but you almost always get a fever and headache to start with, initially very similar to flu, with aches and pains, loss of appetite and generally feeling unwell. Typhoid may be confused with malaria.

The fever gradually rises during a week. Characteristically your pulse is relatively slow compared with the fever (for example 80 beats/min for an adult instead of perhaps 100) – but this is something a medic will pick up better than you, so don't agonise over it too much. Other symptoms you may have are constipation or diarrhoea and stomach pains.

You may feel worse in the second week, with a constant fever and sometimes a red skin rash. Serious complications occur in about one in 10 cases, including, most commonly, damage to the gut wall with subsequent leakage of the gut contents into the abdominal cavity. Sometimes this is the first indication of an infection. Other symptoms you may have are severe headache, sore throat and jaundice (yellowing of your skin and the whites of your eyes).

Diagnosis & Treatment

Diagnosis is by blood test, and the earlier typhoid is diagnosed the better. Seek medical help for any fever (38°C and higher) that does not improve after 48 hours. Typhoid is a serious disease and is not something you should consider self-treating.

Rehydration therapy is important if diarrhoea has been a feature of the illness, but antibiotics are the mainstay of treatment. Antibiotic resistance is common.

TUBERCULOSIS (TB)

Called consumption in the old days because people just wasted away with it, TB is making a comeback globally, and Latin America is no exception. One reason is that drug resistance is on the increase worldwide.

TB is a bacterial disease. Only about 15% of people who become infected go on to develop the disease, as the TB bacteria can lie dormant for years. If your immunity is lowered for some reason, for example due to poor nutrition or another disease like HIV/AIDS, the disease can appear.

TB is transmitted by breathing in droplets expelled through coughing, talking or sneezing. Only people ill with pulmonary (lung) TB are infectious. Your risk of being infected increases the closer you are to the person and the longer you are exposed to them. You can also get a form of TB through drinking unpasteurised milk from an infected cow.

TB is rarely seen in short-term travellers, as you need close contact with a sufferer with active disease to catch it. It is a risk if you are planning to live or work closely with members of the local population or you are planning to stay for more than a few months in Latin America.

REEMERGENCE OF TB

If you thought TB was on the way out, you'd be wrong. It appears set to be one of the biggest health threats of the 21st century – currently it kills more people worldwide than malaria and HIV combined. WHO is so alarmed at the re-emergence of this age-old killer that it declared TB a global health emergency. It estimates that a third of the world's population is infected with TB, and although Asia is currently worst affected, economic uncertainties, the rise of HIV/AIDS and devastating natural disasters are threats to the situation in Latin America. HIV infection weakens the immune system, making TB infection more likely to emerge.

The biggest worry currently is the emergence of treatment-resistant TB, now found in all countries in Latin America and elsewhere. Until 50 years ago, TB was incurable but drugs were discovered in the middle of the 20th century that were very effective at treating it. It takes several months of drug treatment to get rid of TB, even though people start to feel better after a few weeks. People stop taking their treatment too early, either because they feel better or they can't afford to pay for treatment, and this has resulted in the rise of drug-resistant TB. So once again we are faced with the prospect of untreatable TB.

Find out all about TB before you go from WHO's TB web page (**www.who.int/gtb**).

Prevention
It is possible to be immunised against TB, and you may already have had a routine TB vaccination as a teenager, although not in North America.

If you think you may be at risk, avoid prolonged exposure to circumstances that make transmission more likely, such as sleeping in crowded communal dormitories or travelling on crowded public transport.

You're more likely to get infected if your resistance is low, for example through ill health or poor nutrition, so it makes sense to look after yourself while on the road. Never drink unpasteurised milk (or anything made with unpasteurised milk) – if you're in any doubt, boil it first.

Symptoms

TB doesn't cause an immediate life-threatening illness like, say, malaria or dengue, but it can cause more chronic problems. TB classically affects the lungs but it can affect almost any other part of the body, including your joints, bones, brain and gut. Pulmonary TB is the most common way in which TB shows itself in adults.

Symptoms develop slowly, often over the course of several months, and include weight loss, fever, night sweats and a cough with blood-stained spit. Diagnosis is by a laboratory test of your spit. Sometimes the disease can be much more severe, especially in children, presenting symptoms of meningitis (headache, neck stiffness, sensitivity to light) and leading to coma.

Diagnosis & Treatment

TB is not something you're going to be self-treating, so seek specialist advice if you think you may be infected. Treatment is with a combination of antibiotics over a prolonged period of time (six to eight months, but sometimes up to a year). Multidrug-resistant TB is common in Latin America and is obviously a major headache to treat but it is possible, although treatment is expensive.

VIRAL HEPATITIS (JAUNDICE)

This infection of the liver can be caused by at least five different viruses: hepatitis A, B, C, D and E. All five viruses cause a similar short-term disease but three (B, C and D) can cause persistent infection in a proportion of sufferers, resulting in long-term liver problems. The different viruses are transmitted in different ways: A and E are spread via contaminated food and water, whereas B, C and D are spread via blood or sexual contact. In children, hepatitis B can be transmitted by prolonged contact with a carrier. A blood test can diagnose which type you have, but you'll probably have a good idea anyway.

Hepatitis A is extremely common in all parts of Latin America (and elsewhere) and is a real risk to all travellers. Hepatitis E occurs in parts of Latin America, and is a particular threat to pregnant women.

Unlike hepatitis A and E, infection with hepatitis B can persist in about 5% to 10% of people, and these carriers are important sources of infection. Latin America is not a particular hot spot for hepatitis B, although carrier rates in some parts of the Amazon region are high. Hepatitis C is a major cause of blood transfusion-related hepatitis in the West and appears to be a growing problem worldwide, but is not going to be a major worry for you as a traveller. Hepatitis D only occurs in conjunction with hepatitis B infection.

SYMPTOMS

Hepatitis starts with vague flu-like symptoms, including fever, chills, headache, and joint aches and pains. You usually feel drained of energy; you have no appetite, and smokers often report being turned off cigarettes. These nonspecific symptoms can go on for two to three days, when you get nausea, vomiting, diarrhoea (possibly) and pain in the upper right-hand side of your abdomen. A day or so later you may notice that you're passing dark urine and your faeces are a lighter colour than normal. The whites of your eyes turn yellow, and later your skin starts to look yellow. This yellowing is called jaundice, and occurs because your liver can't clear the bile chemicals properly.

! Hepatitis is a much more serious disease in pregnancy, so you must seek medical help urgently in this situation.

Although these are the classic symptoms, hepatitis can be a mild illness without jaundice in many people, especially children, although older people are often more severely affected.

You usually find that you start to feel better as the jaundice appears. Hepatitis can leave you feeling very washed out and weak for some time after – about six weeks on average but sometimes up to three months, so be prepared. It might be one reason to come home early if you're on a long trip.

Rarely, you can get serious complications, as a result of overwhelming liver failure. Seek medical help urgently if you get suddenly worse or if you have any of the following:

- severe vomiting and dehydration
- bruising for no reason
- bleeding from your gums or nosebleeds
- blood in your urine or faeces
- confusion and drowsiness

TREATMENT

There's no specific treatment for hepatitis A and E apart from rest and tender loving care. However, you should seek medical advice as soon as possible to have the diagnosis confirmed. You probably won't feel like doing much for a while, so make sure you've got somewhere comfortable to stay. There's no particular need to stay in bed; just do as much or as little as you feel up to.

- Drink plenty of fluids, especially if you don't feel like eating because of the nausea.
- If you feel like eating, try to stick to a low-fat (the liver has to work harder to deal with fatty foods), high carbohydrate diet.
- Avoid anything that might damage your liver further, such as alcohol and medications (including aspirin and paracetamol (acetaminophen).

In fact, it's a good idea to avoid any medications if possible while you have hepatitis, because drugs won't be disposed of as efficiently as normal and can have unpredictable effects.

If you're using the oral contraceptive pill, you'll need to stop taking it until the illness settles.

Infection with hepatitis B causes a similar illness to type A, but the symptoms can be more severe and there's a higher risk of liver failure. Note that the illness can take up to six months to appear after infection. Persistent infection carries the risk of long-term liver damage, and liver cancer in a minority of cases.

> **!** If you think you may have been exposed to hepatitis B, a protective shot of antibody can help protect against it; alternatively you could start a course of the usual hepatitis B vaccination – discuss this with your doctor.

PREVENTION

Effective vaccines are available against hepatitis A and B; there are no vaccines against the other types of hepatitis. In many countries (including Australia and the USA), hepatitis B vaccination is becoming routine and you may have been immunised at school. For more details, see the Immunisations section of the Before You Go chapter.

In addition, it's advisable to take basic food and water precautions to protect yourself against hepatitis A and E. Shellfish are particularly risky, so are worth avoiding for this reason. Avoid swimming in polluted water.

Protect yourself against hepatitis B infection by avoiding risk situations:

■ always use a condom if you have sex with a new partner

■ avoid blood transfusions and other medical (or dental) procedures where possible

■ never share needles

■ avoid risk situations like getting your ears or other body parts pierced, having a tattoo or being shaved with a re-used cut-throat razor

Digestive System...

We've devoted quite a bit of space to this topic, in recognition of its importance to travellers.

DIARRHOEA

✚ See also the section on diarrhoea in babies and children (p293).

Although it's not inevitable that you will get diarrhoea (commonly known as 'turista', 'Montezuma's revenge' etc) while you are away, it is pretty likely. Digestive upsets are the most common travel-related illnesses, affecting about a half to a third of travellers to tropical destinations, so you may as well be prepared. Just in case anybody out there is not sure what we're talking about, by diarrhoea we mean passing loose, frequent faeces, often associated with vomiting.

Although there are other causes of travellers diarrhoea (see the boxed text), your risk of getting ill mainly depends on how likely it is that the food and drink you are consuming is

---

CAUSES OF TRAVELLERS DIARRHOEA

About one third of cases, usually mild, are due to nonspecific causes including:

- stress
- jet lag
- new foods and a change in eating habits

The rest are divided up as follows:

- bacteria, the commonest cause
- viruses ('gastric flu')
- parasites (including *Giardia* and amoeba)
- food poisoning (eg from a toxin, often bacterial, in the food)

contaminated with disease-causing microorganisms. If you're roughing it, and eating from small stalls and restaurants where hygiene is more likely to be a problem, you're more likely to catch something. If you are away on a long trip, there's a higher chance you will get ill at some stage.

Not surprisingly, you'll find diarrhoea a hot topic of conversation among travellers, and it can be hard to separate fact from fiction at times. Just remember:

- travellers diarrhoea is generally a short, mild illness lasting on average about three to five days
- because of this, you don't usually need to get medical advice or have a laboratory test
- replacing lost fluids and salts is the most important part of treating any watery diarrhoea, whatever the cause
- you don't usually need antibiotic treatment for mild to moderate diarrhoea
- there are certain situations when antibiotics need to be used – in these situations it's best to get medical advice rather than to try and treat yourself

AVOIDING DIARRHOEA

Although we don't want to deprive you of a fascinating talking point during your travels, it's obviously best to avoid getting diarrhoea in the first place. Unhygienic food preparation practices and contaminated water are common causes of travellers diarrhoea. It sounds gross, but basically you get diarrhoea by eating other people's faeces, through contaminated food, water and eating utensils. Hands used to prepare food may not have been washed thoroughly after toilet duty. Flies carry dirt and microorganisms on their feet. In dusty, urban areas, tonnes of dry faecal matter floats around in the atmosphere, and this can land on food left sitting around.

➕ For detailed guidelines on choosing safe food and water, see Food & Water Precautions in the Staying Healthy chapter.

You can also get diarrhoea from direct contact with an infected person (if you touch hands etc that haven't been washed adequately) or from swimming in contaminated water (by swallowing small amounts). Some infective agents such as *Giardia* can survive even in chlorinated water, and rivers and oceans may be contaminated with sewage – see the section on on Water Pollution in the Water chapter for more details.

TYPES OF DIARRHOEA

Different microorganisms cause different types of diarrhoeal illnesses, which may need to be treated in different ways. In this section we've described the three most common types, although in practice it's often not as clear-cut as this makes it seem. The most important things to look out for are: high temperature, blood in your faeces and how severe the diarrhoea is, ie how often you have to go to the toilet. Full treatment details, including advice on what to eat and drink while you are ill, are given in the section following, starting on p160.

Watery Diarrhoea

This is the type of diarrhoea you're most likely to get when you are away. The cause varies with your destination, but it's usually bacterial, often a strain of a bacteria called *Escherichia coli*. Relatives of this microbe are normal residents of your gut, but this is a strain that has turned nasty.

The usual scenario is that the illness starts a few days after you arrive, and involves up to six episodes of loose faeces a day. You may feel sorry for yourself, but it doesn't usually make you feel particularly unwell. If you get a fever with it, it's usually low (less than 38°C). Nausea and vomiting are common, especially at the start, but it's not a major feature of the illness (compare this with food poisoning – see Vomiting & Diarrhoea later in this section). Stomach cramps, bloating and frequent gas are also common. If you notice blood in your faeces, you've got dysentery – see the following section.

The illness generally resolves itself in a few days (on average three to five). It rarely causes severe dehydration, although the potential is always there and is more of a risk in children and older travellers.

Don't panic and start stuffing yourself with medications – you don't usually need antibiotics for this type of diarrhoea, and 'stoppers' are usually best avoided too (see p162 for more on this type of medication). The most important treatment measure is to avoid dehydration by replacing lost fluids and salts, which you should start doing straight away.

Bloody Diarrhoea (Dysentery)

Dysentery is any diarrhoea with blood in it. It can be more severe and protracted than the more common watery diarrhoea described earlier, and usually needs antibiotic treatment. Out of every 10 travellers who get diarrhoea, only about one in will have dysentery. The most common cause is one of a number of bacteria, including various shigella and salmonella species, but amoebiasis (p166) is a less common cause.

Dysentery usually begins with nonspecific flu-like symptoms, and you often feel really rough, with headache, high fever (38°C and above), and aches and pains all over. To start with, the diarrhoea is often watery and in large quantities; later it gets less and you start to notice blood and mucus (slime) mixed in your faeces. Painful stomach cramps are often a feature of the illness, usually heralding a dash to the little room.

Get medical advice if you have dysentery, as you'll need a laboratory test and a course of antibiotics (see p161). In the meantime, rest and make sure you drink plenty of fluids.

> ! If you have dysentery, you should avoid antidiarrhoeal medications such as loperamide that 'stop you up' because there is a risk of serious complications occurring, including dilation and bursting of the colon.

Vomiting & Diarrhoea

✚ See p128 for a full summary of the many causes of vomiting.

If you suddenly get an attack of nausea and profuse vomiting soon after eating, it's probably due to food poisoning. This is a worldwide problem that is more likely when you're eating food

DIARRHOEA AT A GLANCE

Some characteristics of various diarrhoeal illnesses are summarised here, with their treatments, but remember that diarrhoeal illnesses are notoriously difficult to diagnose on the basis of symptoms alone. The only way to be sure of the diagnosis is through a laboratory test.

Illness	Incubation period	Characteristics
food poisoning	usually comes on soon after eating	symptoms come on rapidly after eating the bad food; tends to cause vomiting predominantly; usually over in 24 to 48 hours
bacterial watery diarrhoea	usually strikes about the third day after you arrive	diarrhoea tends to be watery, less bloating and less flatulence than with giardiasis
shigella	two to three days	high temperature, blood in diarrhoea, abdominal cramps can be severe
giardiasis	two to six weeks	symptoms are variable but usually sudden onset explosive diarrhoea, associated typically with abdominal distension, cramps and flatulence
amoeba	minimum one week, may be as long as several weeks	bloody diarrhoea (not profuse like bacterial diarrhoea causes), cramps, tends to be prolonged
Cyclospora	two days to two weeks	prolonged diarrhoea with weight loss
irritable bowel syndrome	may start for the first time after an acute attack	may have alternating diarrhoea and constipation, abdominal pains, but no weight loss
tropical sprue	usually develops after an acute attack of diarrhoea	prolonged watery diarrhoea, usually associated with profound weight loss

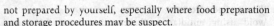

not prepared by yourself, especially where food preparation and storage procedures may be suspect.

Vomiting is the main symptom, often with stomach cramps and some watery diarrhoea later. You may have a suspicion that you've eaten something that wasn't fresh (such as seafood); another clue is if everyone who ate the same thing comes down with the same illness.

No specific treatment is needed as a rule. You should rest, sip fluids if possible, and wait for it to settle down, which it should start doing in about 12 to 24 hours. Generally, it's best to avoid anti-vomiting medication, as vomiting is your body's way of getting rid of the bad stuff.

> **!** You should seek medical help urgently if the illness doesn't settle down within 24 hours, if it gets much worse, if there's any blood in the vomit or diarrhoea, if you have a high fever or if you have very severe stomach pains or a severe headache.

DEALING WITH DIARRHOEA

If diarrhoea strikes, you don't necessarily need to reach for your medical kit for 'stoppers' and antibiotics; there are some simple measures it's worth taking:

- rest – this gives your body the best chance to fight whatever is making you ill; in any case, being on the move with diarrhoea presents a few logistical problems

- drink plenty of fluids – see What to Drink in this section for more guidance on what and how much

- take your temperature and note what it is; repeat this to see how the illness is progressing

- examine what's coming out of your guts to check for blood or mucus (slime)

- be aware of how often you're passing urine and what colour it is, so you can check you're not getting dehydrated

- note any other symptoms you may have – diarrhoea can occur in many other illnesses, including malaria and hepatitis

- remember that diarrhoea is contagious so be scrupulous about washing your hands after you use the toilet

When to See a Doctor

Avoid using antidiarrhoeal remedies (apart from oral rehydration salts) and get medical help if you experience any of the following:

- you can't keep any fluids down because of vomiting for more than 24 hours (less for a child; for example, a couple of hours if they really can't take any fluids)
- the diarrhoea is coming out of you in a watery torrent
- your temperature is 38°C or over
- there's blood or slime in your faeces
- the diarrhoea doesn't clear up after four or five days, or more than a day in a child with moderate to severe diarrhoea
- you think you may have malaria (see p130)
- if you're jaundiced (your skin and the whites of your eyes are yellow; see p146)

✚ Remember that children very quickly become dehydrated with diarrhoea or vomiting, so you need to seek help more readily for them. See the section on diarrhoea (p293) in the Babies & Children chapter for more details.

What to Drink

You need to replace what's being lost through the diarrhoea and any vomiting: mainly salts (sodium, potassium and chloride) and water. Sachets of oral rehydration salts (ORS) are readily available throughout Latin America and contain optimum amounts of glucose and salts. Glucose (sugar) is necessary because it encourages the absorption of sodium and water, and it makes you feel better by boosting your energy levels. Follow the instructions and make up the ORS in the specified quantity of purified or bottled water. There's no magic ingredient in ORS, but the relative quantities of salt and sugar are important.

❗ You can make up your own solution if necessary by adding six teaspoons of sugar (or honey) and half a teaspoon of table salt to 1L of boiled water. Make it more palatable by adding any flavour you like, for example lemon, ginger or orange juice.

IF YOU GET DIARRHOEA

Take basic measures: rest, drink plenty of fluids (ORS essential for children and older travellers) and avoid antidiarrhoeals

↓

More than six times in 24 hours? — YES → See a doctor OR take a single dose of ciprofloxacin 500mg

NO ↓

↓ No better after 24 to 48 hours?

Temperature 38°C or more? — YES → ↓

NO ↓

Passing blood in the diarrhoea? — YES → See a doctor OR if no doctor, take ciprofloxacin 500mg twice daily for five days OR norfloxacin 400mg twice daily for three days

NO ↓

↓ No improvement after taking antibiotics?

Can't keep any fluids down because of vomiting? ↓

NO ↓

See a doctor OR if no doctor consider taking metronidazole 250mg three times daily for five to 10 days OR tinidazole 2g single dose (will treat giardiasis and amoebiasis)

Drink lots of fluids; wait for diarrhoea to settle

↓

Persistent diarrhoea (ie more than about seven days) →

Although ORS is essential in children and elderly travellers, if you're a normally fit and healthy adult and the diarrhoea is mild (up to six bursts a day) you can make do without ORS. Instead, make sure you drink plenty of fluids, including soup (contains salt) and fruit juices (contain glucose and potassium), and eat starchy foods (see following section).

Other liquids you could drink include weak black tea with a small amount of sugar added, purified water or, if nothing else is available, soft drinks allowed to go flat and diluted with purified water (but avoid colas if possible). A good alternative are herbal teas, which are widely available in Latin America.

!● Alcohol, strong tea, coffee and other caffeine-containing drinks (such as colas) are all best avoided because they can irritate the gut and promote fluid loss.

!● It's best to steer clear of dairy products while you have diarrhoea – you can get an intolerance to the sugar in milk when you have diarrhoea, which then exacerbates the problem.

What to Eat

It's easy to get hung up about what, if anything, to eat when you have diarrhoea. But relax, use your common sense and try to tune in to what your body is telling you – if you feel like eating, go ahead. Starchy foods like tortillas (not oily), bread, rice, potato or salty crackers (and any other local variations on these) are recommended because they encourage absorption of fluids, sodium and glucose in your gut.

Although eating may increase the bulk of your faeces, it shouldn't worsen the illness, so there's no need to starve yourself deliberately. But if you don't feel like eating, don't force yourself to. Unless you've been travelling hard for some time, you're going to be basically well nourished and able to withstand a couple of days with little or no food. It may make you feel a bit wobbly, so add a bit of sugar or honey to your drinks.

Your overworked guts will appreciate small amounts of food at regular intervals rather than great big meals, and this may

FLUID BALANCE

If you're vomiting or feeling sick, try taking small sips of fluid regularly rather than forcing yourself to down a whole glass in one go. You need to drink the equivalent of two average-sized glasses of fluid every time you have diarrhoea. You should aim for a total fluid replacement of at least 3L over 24 hours, or more if you're not eating anything at all.

Use how much urine you're passing as a rough guide to your fluid balance. Small amounts of dark urine suggest you need to increase your fluid intake. Passing reasonable quantities of light yellow urine indicates that you've got the balance about right. As a rough guide, aim to produce a reasonable quantity of light-coloured urine every three to four hours while you're awake.

help make you feel less nauseated, too. You may find that eating brings on stomach cramps and you have to dash to the toilet. This is because of a natural reflex whereby eating increases the activity of the gut, which can get exaggerated in a diarrhoeal illness. It doesn't make you a great dinner companion, but you'll probably find that once you've answered the call of nature you can return to finish your meal! (But remember to wash your hands very thoroughly.)

It goes without saying that it's best to stick to a bland diet while you have diarrhoea and as you recover, and to go easy on fibre providers like fruit, vegetables and nuts. Ripe bananas are good, as they tend to stop you up and are a source of potassium and glucose. As the diarrhoea clears up and you start to get your appetite back, add in more foods gradually until you're back to normal – this can take some time, up to a week, but if you feel otherwise well, there's no need to worry.

FIT TO EAT

While you have diarrhoea, it's good to eat:

- boiled potatoes
- plain rice
- plain bread or tortillas
- any of the other Latin American starchy staples, so long as they are not too oily
- dry biscuits, salty or not too sweet
- bananas

If possible, it's best to avoid:

- fruit and vegetables, except bananas
- dairy products, including yoghurt
- spicy foods
- greasy foods

Antidiarrhoeal Remedies

There are remedies you can take to stop you up if you get diarrhoea, but as a general rule, you're better off allowing the illness to run its course.

Antimotility drugs (ie 'stoppers') like loperamide, diphenoxylate (with atropine) and codeine phosphate slow down your guts, reducing the number of times you have to visit the little room. These are sold under a wide variety of brand names and are usually available without prescription.

Stoppers can be useful if you have to travel on a toilet-less mode of transport or attend an important meeting, but you should treat them with a bit of respect. If you do need to take them, be careful not to take more than the recommended dose.

It's usually best not to take stoppers for more than 24 hours because of the risk of side effects (swelling and bursting of the intestine and constipation). Another reason not to take them for longer is that diarrhoea is nature's way of flushing out microbes and their poisons, and stopping this may prevent the illness from settling.

! Note that these drugs should be avoided in children because of the risk of side effects, and you shouldn't take them if you have a high fever or are passing blood or mucus (slime) in your faeces.

Bismuth subsalicylate (Pepto-Bismol) can be useful in treating diarrhoea, although it is less effective than the antimotility drugs. Bismuth shouldn't be taken if you have asthma or if you are taking aspirin, are sensitive to aspirin or have been told to avoid aspirin for any reason. It can cause ringing in your ears and blackening of your tongue. It's not recommended to take large amounts over a prolonged period of time (maximum three weeks).

 Alternatively, peppermint oil is an antispasmodic that may be helpful if you're experiencing abdominal cramps. It has no serious side effects. Homoeopathic remedies for treating diarrhoea include carbo vegetalis and nux vomic (see p60), although these are unlikely to be available locally. Some herbal teas available locally may be helpful for soothing stomach cramps.

Antibiotics

If you are seriously ill or the diarrhoea just won't go away, you'll probably need antibiotic treatment. In this situation, you should seek medical advice on the most appropriate treatment and you may need a laboratory test to determine the cause of your illness.

! Remember that most cases of travellers diarrhoea do not need treatment with antibiotics, and will clear up on their own in a few days.

Whether or not to treat simple watery diarrhoea with antibiotics is much less clear-cut, and it's an issue the experts can't agree on. There's plenty of evidence to show that taking a dose of an antibiotic (such as ciprofloxacin 500mg, single dose) with loperamide (an antimotility drug) can reduce the

A WORD OF WARNING

You'll probably find many antidiarrhoeal remedies on sale in pharmacies throughout Latin America. In general (apart from rehydration salts), it's best to avoid them. They are unlikely to be helpful and may be harmful. In particular, avoid any containing the following:

- tincture of opium or morphine
- clioquinol, which may be marketed as Enterovioform – this is associated with severe side effects and should be avoided
- combinations of remedies (eg an antimotility medication with an antibiotic)

Two remedies that are not thought to have any effect in the treatment of acute diarrhoea are kaopectate and acidophilus (also known as lactobacillus, found in yoghurt), although studies have indicated that acidophilus may have a limited role in preventing diarrhoea in the first place.

length of a diarrhoeal illness quite dramatically. Because of this, some doctors will advise you to carry a treatment dose of an antibiotic to take as soon as you develop diarrhoea. Others, however, argue that the benefits are not offset by the risks (including possible side effects of the antibiotic and the emergence of bacterial resistance) and that in any case diarrhoea in travellers is usually a mild illness that will clear up quickly enough on its own.

It's best to discuss this issue with your doctor before you go, as it depends on the length of your trip, how disruptive an episode of diarrhoea would be, and your normal state of health. On balance, it's probably worth having a course of antibiotics with you, but keep it for a bad attack of watery diarrhoea (dashing to the toilet more than about six times a day).

If you're travelling in remote areas without access to medical care, you may need to self-treat your diarrhoea with antibiotics. It is notoriously difficult to make an accurate diagnosis on the basis of symptoms alone, but in this situation, you could consider the following treatment:

- severe watery diarrhoea or bacterial dysentery (p153) – take a course of ciprofloxacin (500mg twice daily for five days) or norfloxacin (400mg twice daily for three days); children can be given a suitable dose (based on weight) of co-trimoxazole
- amoebiasis or giardiasis (p164), – take metronidazole (250mg three times daily for five to 10 days) or tinidazole (2g single dose)

Don't take any antibiotic you are allergic to; for more guidance on antibiotics, see p418 in the Buying & Using Medicines appendix.

PERSISTENT DIARRHOEA

You may find that, often after an acute attack, the diarrhoea comes and goes and doesn't clear up. You'll need to get this checked out by a doctor. You'll need a laboratory test to clarify what's causing it so that the appropriate treatment can be prescribed. Use your common sense, but as a rough guide 'persistent' diarrhoea is anything lasting longer than about a week. Infections causing persistent diarrhoea include:

- giardiasis
- amoebiasis
- bacteria (eg salmonella or campylobacter)
- cyclospora (a recently identified parasite)
- tropical sprue
- intestinal worms
- tuberculosis

Noninfectious causes include:

- post-infectious irritable bowel (see the boxed text 'Irritable Bowel Syndrome')
- inflammatory bowel disease
- temporary intolerance to lactose, the sugar in milk

Tropical sprue is an uncommon condition thought to be due to persisting infection, agent unknown, of your small intestine (the top part), causing you to be unable to absorb nutrients properly. It can be very debilitating, with persistent diarrhoea and weight loss. It can be diagnosed by a laboratory test on a sample of your gut, and is effectively treated with an antibiotic (such as tetracycline with folic acid).

Giardiasis

This illness is caused by a single-celled parasite, *Giardia lamblia*, which you acquire when you ingest food or water contaminated by the hardy cysts of the parasite. *Giardia* can also infect animals, and may be found in streams and other water sources in rural areas, especially on trekking routes. The illness usually appears about a week after you have been exposed to the parasite. Sometimes you get just a short episode of typical 'travellers diarrhoea', but it can cause gradual, intermittent diarrhoea.

> **!** You often get noticeable weight loss with giardiasis, as this infection prevents food from being absorbed properly in the upper part of your gut.

Giardiasis can start quite suddenly, with explosive, watery diarrhoea (without blood). More often you get loose, bulky, foul-smelling faeces that are hard to flush away (assuming you have the luxury of flushing, of course), with lots of gas, bloating, stomach gurgling and cramps. You can sometimes get a mild fever and often feel nauseated, with little or no appetite, 'indigestion' and rotten egg burps. Although all these symptoms commonly occur in giardiasis, they are nonspecific symptoms and can occur in other types of diarrhoea too – don't assume you've got giardiasis just because you've got rotten egg burps.

It's best to seek medical advice if possible, but if you are in a remote area away from medical help, you could start a course of antibiotics: either metronidazole 250mg three times daily for five to 10 days or tinidazole 2g single dose (tinidazole is not currently available in the USA). You should be able to find one or other of these drugs locally if necessary.

IRRITABLE BOWEL SYNDROME

This is a very common condition resulting from bowel dysfunction. You probably won't get it for the first time while you are travelling, but a change in diet and increased stress may make symptoms more likely. There is also some evidence to suggest you're more likely to get it following an episode of food poisoning or travellers diarrhoea. Although the symptoms can be troublesome, they aren't life threatening. The symptoms are variable in nature and severity but may include:

- abdominal pain and spasm (often in the left lower abdomen), relieved by passing wind or faeces
- abdominal bloating (due to trapped wind)
- diarrhoea or constipation
- passing ribbon-like or pellet-like faeces

Symptoms may last only a few days or can persist for a weeks; they often recur. Different people respond differently to treatment. If constipation is the major factor, an increase in dietary fibre will help. If bowel spasm and pain is the main problem, an antispasmodic such as mebeverine 135mg three times daily or peppermint oil capsules may help. Use your common sense and avoid any foods that make the symptoms worse.

If you are not sure of the diagnosis, the symptoms don't fit the pattern described, you have pain that is new or severe or you are unwell in any other way, you should seek medical advice.

Corinne Else

Amoebic Dysentery

It's worth knowing about amoebic dysentery because, although it's less common than giardiasis, it can cause problems outside the gut and it won't clear up without antibiotic treatment. It's caused by a single-celled parasite called *Entamoeba histolytica*, which you get by eating food and water contaminated by the parasite cysts (sounds familiar?). It causes dysentery, ie you get blood and mucus in your faeces. The diarrhoea is often relatively mild and tends to come on gradually. Associated symptoms like fever, vomiting and stomach cramps are much less likely than with giardiasis or bacterial causes of dysentery, although they can occur.

Complications can occur if the amoeba migrate to your liver or brain, where they can form abscesses, sometimes without a warning episode of diarrhoea beforehand.

> **Suspect an amoebic liver abscess if you have a fever and pain in the right upper abdomen (which may feel tender to pressure), especially if you have been having diarrhoea for a while.**

You will need to seek medical advice if you think you have amoebic dysentery, especially if you think you may have an amoebic liver abscess. Treatment is with specific antibiotics, as for giardiasis (see earlier).

CHOLERA

This diarrhoeal disease is caused by a bacterium. It's transmitted via contaminated food (especially seafood, including crustaceans and shellfish which get infected via sewage) and water. Less commonly, it can be transmitted from person to person (often via healthy carriers of the disease). Cholera has been reported in Mexico, all countries in Central America and most countries in South America.

> **The risk of most travellers acquiring cholera is thought to be very low, so long as you take some basic precautions with food and water. There is an oral vaccine available but it is not usually recommended because the risk to travellers of this disease is extremely remote.**

CHOLERA IN LATIN AMERICA

Cholera made an appearance in Latin America in 1991 in Peru – for the first time for over a century. Since then it has spread throughout the region, becoming established in several countries, and causing hundreds of thousands of cases in total in the region. By 1997, the epidemic showed signs of ebbing, but extreme weather conditions in 1998 as a result of El Nino resulted in several countries reporting outbreaks. Cholera is a very low risk for most travellers – see the main text for more details.

Many Latin American countries have responded with prevention and control measures, including banning sales of street food in affected areas and education campaigns encouraging people to wash their hands before handling foods and to avoid raw seafood. In Chile, where seafood is a major component of the diet, all shellfish must be served thoroughly cooked, and even *ceviche*, traditionally made from marinated raw fish or shellfish, must be cooked.

Cholera exists where standards of environmental and personal hygiene are low, and is of greatest risk to the poorest of the poor. Natural disasters such as hurricanes and flooding can lead to epidemics through contamination of the normal water supplies.

Cholera is likely to be around in Latin America for the foreseeable future. Elimination of the disease depends on major improvements in the supply of drinking water and sewage treatment systems (the spread of cholera has been linked to the use of raw sewage in irrigation of salad vegetables, which are eaten uncooked). Education in proper food preparation and hygiene is also vital, with street food thought to play a major role in the continuing spread of the disease.

Although in many cases cholera just causes a mild diarrhoea, about one in 10 sufferers get a severe form of the disease. In this form, the diarrhoea starts suddenly, and pours out. It's characteristically described as 'ricewater' because what comes out is watery and flecked with white mucus. Vomiting and muscle cramps are usual, but fever is rare. In the worst-case scenario, cholera causes a massive outpouring of fluid (up to 20L a day). Mild cholera is a self-limiting illness, meaning that it will end in about a week without any specific treatment.

Cholera can usually be treated effectively by fluid replacement, although some more severe cases may require antibiotic treatment (usually tetracyclines, although drug resistance is a growing problem).

If you think you may have cholera, or if you develop diarrhoea within five days of returning from an area where cholera occurs (this includes most countries in Latin America), you should seek medical help immediately. In the meantime, start rehydration therapy immediately with oral rehydration salts.

INTESTINAL WORMS

Worldwide, infection with intestinal worms affects about one-third of the population, mainly in developing countries, particularly tropical countries. In Latin America, they are thought to affect between one-fifth and one-third of the general population, although some areas are worse affected than others. In general they are related to poor standards of hygiene and social deprivation. In many parts of the region, children are treated regularly with anti-worm medicine in an effort to control this problem. In general, travellers are unlikely to be affected, but if you are on a long trip, especially if you've been roughing it or spending time in rural, tropical areas, it's possible you could pick up a light infection along the way. Worm infestations generally cause few symptoms, unless the infestation is very heavy (unlikely in travellers).

Roundworms and threadworms are acquired through eating contaminated food or water (unwashed vegetables are common culprits), or can be passed directly from person to person. A light infection with roundworms rarely causes any symptoms, but should be treated because the worms can sometimes get caught in narrow openings internally and cause blockages. Threadworms cause intense anal itching, especially at night – you may have had an infection in childhood. They are small, white and thread-like, and you may notice them wriggling in your faeces or on toilet paper.

Other worms, such as hookworms and strongyloides, develop in the soil and can penetrate the skin of bare feet. Both types of worm find their way to the gut, sometimes causing a cough as they pass through the lungs. Untreated, they can live in your gut for years. Hookworms suck blood, so if the infection is heavy, it can cause anaemia.

Treatment of worm infestation is with special anti-worm medicines, such as mebendazole, albendazole or piperazine (for threadworm). Note that mebendazole is not suitable in pregnancy or in children under two years of age.

TAPEWORMS

Tapeworms have a very high yuk value; worse still, they have the potential to make you seriously ill. You acquire tapeworms by eating raw or lightly cooked infected meat – sausages and smoked meat are especially suspect. Pork and beef tapeworms are common in South America, and beef tapeworm is common in Mexico.

Tapeworms don't usually cause any symptoms, although occasionally you can get abdominal discomfort, diarrhoea and weight loss. (Strange but true: in times gone by, tapeworms were used as an ingenious weight loss device.) Segments of tapeworm can sometimes wriggle their way out of your anus. Pork tapeworm is altogether a more serious disease, as sometimes the larvae penetrate the gut wall, and form cysts in the muscles and brain. This condition is called cysticercosis, and symptoms depending on what part of your body is affected. If the brain is affected, fits may occur.

HYDATID DISEASE

This disease is caused by a tapeworm and occurs worldwide. It is common in sheep and cattle raising areas of South America, for example Argentina and Patagonia. It is mainly a disease of domestic animals (sheep, cattle, pigs and horses mainly) and dogs. Humans can get infected accidentally by touching dogs (tapeworm eggs stick to your fingers and get transferred to your mouth in this way) or by eating food (such as unwashed vegetables) contaminated with infected dog faeces. Dogs become infected by eating the flesh of infected domestic animals. In badly affected areas, there are programs under way to educate farmers not to allow dogs into the slaughter yards.

Once inside you, the eggs hatch into larvae that form cysts (fluid-filled sacs) in different parts of your body, mainly the liver and lungs. Symptoms are not common, and cysts can take a long time to develop. Treatment can be difficult (it usually involves surgery to remove the cysts), so prevention by taking food and water precautions and avoiding contact with dogs is important, especially if you are trekking through sheep or cattle country.

Treatment of tapeworm infection is with specific drugs (niclosamide or praziquantel), although surgery is required to treat cysticercosis.

PREVENTION

With all intestinal worms, prevention is the main aim:

- don't walk barefoot in rural areas
- take basic food and water precautions and wash your hands before eating

- avoid undercooked meat and fish
- steer clear of dogs
- If you have been on a long trip, spending time in rural, tropical areas, it's probably a good idea to get a laboratory test done on your faeces when you return to check for worms.

NON-INFECTIVE DIGESTIVE PROBLEMS

It's not all diarrhoea and parasites when you're travelling. All the digestive problems like constipation and indigestion that are common at home are also common on the road.

CONSTIPATION

Far less has been written about travellers constipation, but it is at least as common as travellers diarrhoea. Plenty of factors conspire to stop you up while you're travelling, including immobility if you're stuck on a bus, plane or train for hours on end, not drinking enough fluids, disruption to your normal routine, jet lag and a change of diet. A lack of privacy and time to relax can be enough to bring on constipation if you have a shy bowel, or you may find it difficult to get used to squatting (although this is supposed to be a more 'natural' way of defecating). Drugs such as antidiarrhoeals can cause relatively intractable constipation.

The end result is being unable to defecate as often as normal, which can make you feel bloated and uncomfortable, with no appetite and no energy. If you have piles, being constipated can worsen them.

If you know you are prone to constipation, consider bringing your own supply of bran with you or a reliable remedy you know. Otherwise, try a few simple measures before diving into the nearest pharmacy or your medical kit:

- make sure you drink plenty of fluids, especially if the climate is hotter than you're used to
- increase the fibre in your diet by eating more fruit (peeled), vegetables (cooked and peeled), beans and grains but avoid bananas, which can stop you up; porridge, pulses, nuts and dried fruit are

also good fibre providers; prune juice is an old favourite, if you can find it

■ a cup of hot, strong coffee can get things moving, especially first thing in the morning, while a large meal can have the same effect (remember that if you're not eating much for any reason, there's not going to be much coming out either)

■ alcohol has a laxative effect, if you need an excuse

■ finding a decent toilet may help – you could consider changing hotels

■ exercise has many benefits, including stimulating your guts

Finally, if you feel like going, don't be tempted to hang on or the moment will pass, unlike your constipation.

If simple measures fail, you could consider taking something fairly gentle like lactulose syrup (15mL twice daily, takes about 48 hours to work) or senna, a gut stimulant (two to four tablets at night, works in eight to 12 hours).

PILES & OTHER ANAL PROBLEMS

Piles (haemorrhoids) are swollen veins around the anus, either on the outside (external) or inside, occasionally popping out (internal) when you strain. Constipation (because of straining), diarrhoea, or carrying heavy packs, especially up a mountain, can be contributory factors. External piles can be excruciatingly painful. The pain can be relieved by cutting them open (still with us?) but this needs to be done by a medic, ideally under sterile conditions. Otherwise, you may need to take painkillers and hotfoot it down the mountain.

Internal piles can be uncomfortable, with a feeling of something popping out when you strain and may cause itchiness around the anus. Local anaesthetic creams (ie ones containing an ingredient like lignocaine) can help.

If you get excruciating pain when you pass faeces, especially if you've been constipated, often with bright red blood on the toilet paper, you probably have an anal fissure, a small split in the anus. It can be very painful, but there's no specific treatment apart from taking care to keep the area clean and dealing with any constipation you may have.

KIDNEY STONE

Dehydration (and other conditions) can cause chemicals in the urine to harden and form small stones in the kidney. A stone can become stuck in the tube leading from the kidney to the bladder and, if it does, you experience excruciating pain. The pain usually starts suddenly on one side, in the back just below the ribcage, spreading round to the groin in the front. Characteristically, the pain is gripey (ie it comes and goes in waves) and you can't stay still with it. It can be so severe that it makes you vomit.

Most (95%) kidney stones eventually work their way down to the bladder and get passed out within about a day or so. However, you should seek medical help if possible, as you will probably need a strong painkilling injection.

- If you have a fever, this indicates that the kidney is infected, which is a medical emergency.

If the pain subsides and has not returned after 12 hours or so, this means that you've probably passed the stone, but it's a good idea to get this checked out as soon as possible, or when you get back if you're on a short trip. Make sure you drink plenty of fluids to prevent further problems.

Anal itching may be caused by threadworms, chafing and poor hygiene. Check your faeces carefully for worms or, if you really have to know, you can put a piece of tape across your anus at night and examine it for worms in the morning. Treatment of threadworm is with an anti-worm medicine, as described in Intestinal Worms earlier in this chapter.

INDIGESTION

A change in diet, stress, anxiety and spicy foods can all make 'indigestion' (burning pains in your upper abdomen) and heartburn (burning in your gullet, often with an acid taste in your mouth) more likely when you're travelling. The discomfort is often worse when you're hungry and just after meals. Smoking and alcohol exacerbate it.

> **!** If you have a gastric or duodenal ulcer, or are taking treatment for one, this may make you more susceptible to gut infections, so it's best to discuss this with your doctor before you go, as you may be able to change to a different anti-ulcer medicine.

Simple measures to ease symptoms of indigestion include eating small, regular meals (for example, don't eat a huge meal just before you go to bed). Consider stopping smoking and cutting back on alcohol or at least giving yourself a break for a few days. It can be difficult in some places, but try to avoid spicy foods. Milk and yoghurt can be soothing, as can eating plain, starchy foods like bananas, bread, plain tortillas or rice.

You could try antacids (available without prescription; take them between meals and at night), although stomach acid has a protective effect against infective agents, so in theory this may make you more vulnerable to gut infections.

> **!** You need to seek medical help urgently in the following situations: if the pain is severe and not relieved by any of these measures; if it wakes you at night; if it seems to go through to your back; if you have had a stomach or duodenal ulcer in the past or if you vomit blood.

APPENDICITIS

If you've still got your appendix, acute appendicitis is a possible cause of severe abdominal pain. It's reasonably common in both adults and children, and you should consider it if you've got abdominal pain that's colicky or constant, and increases in severity over a short period of time (12 to 24 hours). Symptoms can vary, but typically they're as follows:

- central abdominal pain that may be colicky (comes and goes) or constant, and which moves to the right lower abdomen after a few hours, becoming constant
- nausea, loss of appetite and sometimes vomiting
- mild fever but not usually very high
- diarrhoea in some cases, but it's not usually very severe
- the right lower abdomen is tender when you press on it

Seek medical help urgently if you think appendicitis may be a possibility, as you'll need surgery if the diagnosis is confirmed. It's potentially extremely dangerous if it's not treated quickly.

Respiratory System...

Coughs and colds can be troublesome when you're travelling and can sometimes lead to worse problems, so make sure you recognise the symptoms and don't let complications get a hold.

COLDS

It's not just the culture that's different and exciting, the viruses are too. The common cold is common the world over. Because colds are spread by droplets (eg sneezing) and close personal contact, you're more likely to get them in crowded urban environments, by travelling on crowded public transport or by eating in crowded restaurants. Air pollution in big cities, and hawking and spitting compound the problem.

As for symptoms, you know the score – slightly raised or normal temperature, runny nose, sore throat and maybe cough. Colds usually go away in a few days without any special treatment, but when you're travelling you're more vulnerable to complications like sinusitis, bronchitis and ear infection.

Recognise the symptoms of a cold as a sign to take it easy for a day or two. Unless you get complications, antibiotics are no use because colds are caused by viruses, not bacteria. Drink plenty of fluids, treat yourself to some good meals and take simple painkillers if necessary for any aches or pains. You can make your own cold remedy by adding honey or sugar to lemon or lime juice and top up with boiled water.

 If you've got homoeopathic remedies with you, try taking gelsemium or allium cepa. Helpful naturopathic remedies include Combi Q tissue salts, thyme and sage tea or, perhaps most popular of all, echinacea tincture or tablets with or without zinc.

SINUSITIS

This usually follows a cold, and can be a pain – literally. The sinuses are air-filled cavities in the skull above the eyes and on either side of the nose, designed to make our heads lighter so that they don't drag on the ground. If the lining of the cavities becomes infected and the normally empty spaces fill with mucus or pus, it causes you pain.

Symptoms are headache (usually over your forehead) or face pain, which is worse when you strain or bend over. Your forehead or cheeks may feel tender when you press them, and you feel something dripping down the back of your throat. Typically the pain isn't there when you get up, but comes on during the morning, reaching a crescendo about lunch time before gradually receding. It's possible to be quite ill, with a fever and aches and pains.

Try inhalations of steam, menthol, tiger balm or eucalyptus or tea tree oil as a first measure, together with simple painkillers. If this doesn't help, you could try taking a nasal decongestant like pseudoephedrine hydrochloride 60mg four times daily (though not if you have high blood pressure). Antihistamines may also help.

If you have a fever and you feel rough, you'll probably need a course of antibiotics – see a doctor if possible. If not, suitable antibiotics are co-amoxiclav 250mg three times daily OR cefaclor 250mg three times daily.

> **!** Flying can make the pain worse, so start taking a nasal decongestant the day before you fly or use a nasal decongestant spray. Underwater diving also makes it worse, so avoid diving until you feel better.

HAY FEVER (ALLERGIC RHINITIS)

This common condition is usually due to an allergy to something in the air you're breathing, such as pollen. It can often be difficult to decide whether your symptoms are because of a cold or an allergy, although if they persist and you otherwise feel reasonably well, it's probably hay fever.

Hay fever involves lots of nose blowing. Other symptoms include sneezing, and itchy eyes, roof of the mouth and (sometimes) ears. Your chest may feel tight as you can get asthma with it (see the section on Cough later in this chapter).

INHALATIONS – HOW TO DO IT

In case you don't know, here's how:

- get hold of a washing up basin, bucket or bowl, or use a washbasin (you'll need that universal plug)
- fill it with boiling water
- optional – add a few drops of menthol (which should be widely available), tiger balm, eucalyptus or tea tree oil
- once the heat is bearable, put your face in the steam rising from the bowl and drape a towel over your head
- stay like this for as long as you can bear it or until it has stopped steaming

If you know you're susceptible to hay fever, it's a good idea to bring all your usual remedies with you. If it's being a real nuisance, try antihistamine tablets to start with (see the Buying & Using Medicines appendix for more details), but if this doesn't control it, you could try a nasal spray containing steroids (the amount used won't cause any general problems) such as beclomethasone dipropionate spray. It needs to be taken regularly to have the best chance of working.

INFLUENZA

Influenza is often called flu, and with other similar viral illnesses is spread in the same way as colds and, for the same reasons, infection is more likely when you're travelling. Although we tend to think of colds and flu as the same thing, they actually have very different symptoms. Influenza is a more severe disease. Flu tends to start quite suddenly, often with a high temperature, and it can make you feel pretty dreadful, with headache and generalised aches and pains. You may have a runny nose and sore throat with it, and often a dry cough that can last for several weeks. Although the illness usually lasts a few days, it can leave you feeling tired and out of energy for some time. The good news is that there's a vaccine against flu which is recommended for travellers. It is new each year, and contrary to popular belief, cannot give you flu.

There's no specific treatment for flu but, as for colds, complications such as a chest infection may be more likely when travelling, so it's worth taking care of yourself. You probably won't feel like doing much for a day or two anyway, so rest up. Simple painkillers (but avoid aspirin if you're in a dengue fever zone – see map p21) can help lower the fever and relieve aches and pains, and any of the remedies discussed under Colds may help your symptoms. Drink plenty of fluids because it's easy to get dehydrated with a fever, and once the fever is down, step up the food as you start to feel better. As flu is a viral illness, antibiotics won't do you any good unless you get complications.

The trouble with flu is that the symptoms are so nonspecific that lots of diseases can mimic it, and it can be hard to tell if it's flu or something more serious like malaria. To give you some guidelines, you need to see a doctor if:

- your temperature is over 39°C (102°F) and it can't be lowered by any of the measures suggested on p126
- you try all of these measures, but you don't feel better after two days – it may not be flu after all
- you feel breathless, start to cough up green spit or have chest pain – this may indicate a chest infection
- you think it could be malaria or dengue fever (check maps p20-1) – the symptoms can be identical
- you have a severe headache, neck stiffness and hypersensitivity to light – you may have meningitis

SORE THROAT

You can get an uncomfortable throat if you're travelling in dry and dusty situations, if you're mouth-breathing because

CAUSES OF SORE THROAT

- heat and dust
- viral infections, colds and flu
- bacterial infections ('strep' sore throat)
- glandular fever (infectious mononucleosis)
- toxoplasmosis
- sexually transmitted infections (eg gonorrhoea)
- diphtheria (p233)

your nose is blocked or you're doing strenuous exercise. Drink plenty of fluids, eat moist foods like fruit and vegetables, and consider chewing sugar-free gum if you can get hold of it. Your lips can get very dry under these conditions and cracked lips are uncomfortable (and an infection risk). The tender skin of your lips is also very sensitive to the sun, so use a lip salve with sunblock, and reapply it regularly throughout the day. Keep 'em luscious by using a lip balm or plain paraffin jelly at night.

Sore throats can also be caused by infection, usually viral, often with a viral eye infection (conjunctivitis – see p192) as well. They can occur on their own or as part of other illnesses like colds, flu and glandular fever (see that section in this chapter). They usually clear up on their own after a few days without any special treatment. Simple measures for treating sore throats are to gargle regularly with salty water (buy some table salt and put a few spoonfuls into a glass of purified water) or a solution of soluble aspirin or paracetamol (acetaminophen). Having lots of warm drinks will also help: add some grated ginger, lime juice and sugar (honey is better if you can get it) to a cup of hot water.

About a third of sore throats are caused by a bacterial infection. The reason this matters is that some bacterial throat infections can occasionally lead to serious complications, especially in children. Unfortunately, the only sure way to tell bacterial and viral sore throats apart is by a laboratory test, but as a rule of thumb, you need to seek medical advice for severe (eg if you can't swallow solids) or persistent (more than five days without any improvement) sore throats, as they will need to be treated with antibiotics. Suitable antibiotics are co-amoxiclav 250mg three times a day OR cefaclor 250mg three times a day.

> Note that if you've been having oral sex, especially with a new partner, gonorrhoea can cause a sore throat. If you think this is a possibility you should seek medical advice to get it checked out, as you'll need a course of antibiotics.

GLANDULAR FEVER

Glandular fever (infectious mononucleosis), also known as the 'kissing disease' because it can be passed by saliva, causes a severe sore throat. Suspect this viral disease if you have a severe sore throat that doesn't settle with antibiotics.

Symptoms include a sore throat, swollen glands (lumps in your neck, armpits and groins) and fever. You may also notice that you're jaundiced (yellowed skin and whites of the eyes). Very occasionally, it can lead to a serious complication – bursting of the spleen (one of your internal abdominal organs). If you have glandular fever and you develop abdominal pain, particularly in the left upper part of the abdomen, you need to seek medical advice urgently.

Glandular fever can only be confirmed by a blood test; there's no specific treatment. It can leave you feeling weak and washed out weeks, sometimes months, afterwards. Other viral infections can cause similar symptoms.

COLD SORES

Cold sores are caused by a herpes virus infection which recurs periodically. If you've had these before, the stresses of travel are quite likely to make them recur. Other factors that make recurrences more likely include sunlight, fever

AIR POLLUTION

This is a worldwide issue but it is particularly severe in many of Latin America's major cities. Mexico City is perhaps the most notorious – it's said to have the worst air pollution in the world – but none of the capital cities is immune. Santiago (Chile), for example, is situated in a basin between two mountain ranges, which ensures that pollution emanating from the growing number of private vehicles in the city centre, diesel buses and emissions from industrial sources collects and hangs over the city as a cloud of smog. In Mexico City, severe pollution from industry and traffic is intensified by the city's altitude and its position surrounded by mountains.

The effect of air pollution depends on the type of pollutant present, how bad the pollution is, how much you are exposed to it and any existing health problems you have. Air pollution can aggravate coughs, colds and sinus problems and cause eye irritation. Older travellers and travellers with heart or lung conditions are more susceptible to the effects of pollution. Children are also more sensitive to it, because they tend to breathe faster and spend more time outdoors. Air pollution can aggravate existing heart and lung problems, resulting in greater use of medication and possibly admission to hospital.

and menstruation. You usually know when one is coming on because you'll feel a burning sensation on the edge of your lip followed by a blister, usually the next day. They take about a week to clear up. Acyclovir cream (5%) can be effective if you apply it as soon as you feel the burning starting, but it may be difficult to get hold of locally, so take a tube with you. Using a lip salve with sunblock can help prevent recurrence.

In Mexico City air pollution is combined with the effects of altitude (ie less oxygen in the air), which can make you feel breathless, tired and headachy. If you exercise outside in the presence of air pollution, you will breathe in more pollutants as you breathe more deeply. The long-term effects of breathing severely polluted air for a relatively brief period of time are uncertain, but it is likely to be similar to the effects of passive smoking.

Governments and municipal authorities differ in their response to the problem. In Mexico City, for example, efforts are being made to reduce traffic congestion by banning each car from driving in the city one day a week, and all new cars must have catalytic converters. There's been little effect so far, however.

If you suffer from respiratory problems (such as asthma) or heart disease, air pollution is likely to affect you more severely. Discuss this with your doctor before you leave, or arrange to spend more time in less polluted parts of the country. Alternatively, you could invest in a surgical mask or air filter – the latter are sold in specialist cyclist shops.

Useful air pollution reports for Mexico City can be found at **www.sma.df.gob.mx/imecaweb/mapas/mapdat/pronos.php** – although not in English, the graphical presentation is pretty clear.

Secondary bacterial infection is a risk, so try to avoid touching the sore with your fingers. This is good practice anyway, as you can introduce infection in your eye if you then rub your eyes.

MOUTH ULCERS
These are more likely to occur if you're stressed or if you're taking proguanil as an antimalarial; otherwise, they're a bit of

a mystery. Regularly swishing your mouth out with salty water or an antiseptic mouthwash (eg chlorhexidine), or even just applying a small amount of toothpaste to the ulcer can help, although all these measures will sting at first.

COUGH

Lots of things can make you cough in this part of the world, including physical hazards like dust, smoke and air pollution, as well as infections like colds and flu, chest infection (bronchitis), asthma and even malaria (p130). There are some much rarer causes of cough which you don't need to worry unduly about, including lung flukes (p363), hydatid disease (p170) and various worm infestations (p168).

Many chest infections are caused by viruses, unless you've got a chronic lung condition or it follows another illness like flu. We know you know, but it should be pointed out that all chest infections are more common in cigarette smokers.

Bronchitis usually begins with an irritating, dry cough and a feeling of tightness in the chest. You may have a mild fever. After a day or so, you start coughing up yellow or greenish gunk. It usually clears up on its own in about five to seven days.

Antibiotics aren't usually needed (they don't work against viral infections), but there are some situations when you do need to see a doctor:

- you're pretty sick, with a high fever – it may be malaria or a more serious chest infection
- you're still coughing a week later
- you're feeling increasingly short of breath
- you have pain in your chest on coughing or taking a deep breath
- you cough up blood

If you do need antibiotics, appropriate treatment would be amoxycillin 250mg three times a day OR, if you're allergic to penicillin, erythromycin 250mg four times a day.

If you're asthmatic, you'll probably know about it before you go travelling, and you should take a plentiful supply of your usual medicines with you. Symptoms include a cough, wheeze, chest tightness and shortness of breath, which may be worse at night or brought on by exercise.

It is possible that asthma may start for the first time while you are travelling, especially if you are travelling in polluted urban areas. It's very common in children and young adults, and appears to be a disease of 'Westernisation'. Some drugs can make it worse and should be avoided, the most common one being aspirin.

If you're worried, seek medical advice so that appropriate medication can be prescribed if necessary. If you are very short of breath or wheezy, you should seek help urgently.

Ears, Eyes & Teeth...

Grouped here are three parts of the body you probably wouldn't normally give much thought to. However, they can be troublesome if they go wrong, and some aspects of travelling can make this more likely.

EARS

FLYING

Cabin pressure is normally kept at levels equivalent to those at altitudes of 1800 to 2400m (6000 to 8000ft). At these pressures, gas in body cavities (like your ears) expands by about 30%. Normally, this isn't a problem because you can equalise the pressure between the cabin and your ears by swallowing, yawning or sucking on a sweet. However, if your ear is blocked for any reason (eg if you've got a cold or hay fever), you can get a pressure build-up which is very painful, and sometimes your eardrum can burst.

It's best not to fly if you've got a cold or severe hay fever, and you shouldn't fly at all if you've got a middle ear infection. If you have to fly with a cold, the following measures should help:

- take a decongestant, such as pseudoephedrine hydrochloride 60mg four times daily (but not if you have high blood pressure), starting the day before you fly

- take an antihistamine before and during the flight (follow the dose instructions on the packet)

- try a nasal decongestant spray – use it an hour before the expected time of arrival, and every 20 minutes after this

- during the descent, pinch your nose firmly and blow hard down it – this should force the pressure to equalise, and you should feel your ears pop; do this as often as necessary

If these measures don't work, your eardrum may burst. You'll get a gradual build-up of severe pain, followed by sudden relief. You may notice a bit of bleeding from the ear.

If this happens, ideally see a doctor to get it checked out. If it has burst, it'll take about six weeks to heal up. During this time, you should avoid getting water in the ear – use ear plugs or a cottonwool ball covered in petroleum jelly when you shower or wash your hair. It's best to avoid swimming altogether until it's healed, and you should definitely avoid swimming underwater. If you do swim, take care to protect your ear with earplugs. If possible, you should get your ear looked at again in about six weeks. If you have any persistent symptoms (eg discharge from the ear), you should seek medical advice before this.

EARACHE

The most common cause of earache is fluid build-up behind the eardrum during or just after a cold. This will respond to simple painkillers and doesn't need antibiotic treatment.

Sometimes earache is due to infection, either in the outer ear (the bit you can stick your finger into) or in the middle ear (the bit behind the eardrum). The causes and treatment differ depending on where the infection is. You can tell them apart by pulling on your ear lobe – if the pain increases, it's a problem in the outer ear; if there is no pain, it's a middle ear problem.

Outer Ear Infection

This is very common in swimmers, and is sometimes called 'swimmer's ear' or 'tropical ear'. It's caused by swimming in dirty water, especially in hot, humid conditions. Bugs thrive in these conditions, and you can get an infection even if you haven't been swimming in dirty water.

'Tropical ear' is very itchy, and you may notice a discharge, as well as earache. If it's very painful, it may indicate that you have a boil in the ear canal.

Simple painkillers will help relieve the discomfort. Warmth also helps – you could try putting a water bottle filled with warm water and wrapped in a towel against your ear. If you can get hold of some eardrops, appropriate treatment is either aluminium acetate drops (this helps to toughen the skin) OR antibiotic drops, usually combined with a steroid and ideally with an antifungal too (eg neomycin with hydrocortisone and polymyxin B sulphate).

Note that antibiotic eardrops shouldn't be used for longer than a week because long term use can lead to secondary fungal infection. If your symptoms haven't settled in a week, seek medical advice, since you may need a change of antibiotic or treatment to clean out your ear canal.

> **!** To give the infection a chance to get better, make sure you don't get water in your ear for at least two weeks; use earplugs if you're washing your hair, taking a shower or swimming, and avoid swimming underwater.

Allergic reactions, eg to eardrops or swimming pool water, can also cause itching. If so, try to keep your ears dry and think about stopping the eardrops.

> **!** It's tempting, but avoid cleaning your ears out with the corner of a towel, a cotton bud or anything else, as this makes infection much more likely.

Middle Ear Infection

Typically, you get this during or just after a cold. It starts as a blocked feeling in the ear and progresses to pain, often with a fever. Later, you may notice a discharge from the ear (eg on your pillow) if your eardrum bursts, followed by relief from the pain.

If it doesn't start to get better in 48 hours, seek medical advice, as you'll probably need a course of antibiotics (usually amoxycillin). In the meantime, simple painkillers will help the discomfort and to bring any fever down. Warmth against your ear may help. You should avoid putting eardrops or getting water in your ear in case your eardrum has burst. See the previous section for guidance on this.

Note that earache in both ears is unlikely to be due to infection. It's more likely to be due to blockage by mucus, and it may respond to decongestants (eg pseudoephedrine) or antihistamines.

Earache sometimes isn't to do with your ears. Problems outside the ear – such as in the jaw, throat or teeth – can sometimes cause earache and may be the reason why the treatments described earlier don't work.

> Diving into the water when you've got a cold may push germs into your ears and make infection more likely, so it's best avoided.

DEAFNESS WITHOUT PAIN

This is usually due to wax. Don't attempt to poke anything in your ear, as this makes infection more likely. Try wax-dissolving eardrops (eg Cerumol), or warm almond or olive oil. If this doesn't work, your ears may need to be syringed out, but you might want to wait until you get home before getting this done.

EYES

This section was compiled by Graeme Johnson, an ophthalmic surgeon based in Sydney, Australia.

If you use regular medications for a preexisting eye condition like glaucoma or diabetes, remember to make sure you take plenty of supplies with you, as well as a letter from your doctor saying why you need to carry them, to avoid any problems at customs.

If you have had recent eye surgery, get advice from your eye doctor on what you can and cannot do (eg diving into swimming pools is not advisable for some time after surgery).

When you're travelling it can be hard to keep your hands clean, and general environmental cleanliness can be far from ideal in many countries, so take care to touch your eyes as little as possible, especially when you're out and about. Don't wipe your eyes with cloths or towels that could be dirty – if necessary, use a clean tissue.

SPECTACLES

If you wear glasses, remember to take a spare pair with you and consider having a pair tinted as sunglasses. Optical prescriptions are understood in all languages, so if you take a copy, you can always have a new pair made. You could consider carrying one of those miniature screwdrivers which will tighten the screws in glasses frames; these always work loose at the most inopportune times.

CONTACT LENSES

If you wear contact lenses, you will know what to take – remember that the various solutions and cleaners can take up a fair bit of luggage space. It's a good idea to take back-up glasses. Maintaining your usual hygiene standards could be difficult, especially if you're roughing it. If necessary, you can use boiled and cooled water in place of your usual cleansers. Take extra care to wash your hands with soap and water before handling the lenses.

If your eye becomes red or irritated, remove the lens, clean and sterilise it and leave it out until your eye is better. Bathing your eye in clean salty water may help. If your eye hasn't improved after 48 hours, you should seek medical advice, as it may indicate an infection that needs to be treated appropriately.

ANTIMALARIALS

If you're taking chloroquine, you may notice some blurring of vision – this doesn't indicate any permanent damage. A more serious, but rare, complication is permanent damage to the retina (the back of the eye), but this is only likely to occur if you take chloroquine in high doses for a long time (usually for more than three years).

SUN

Sunlight can damage your eyes, so make sure you take good (but not necessarily expensive) sunglasses, and wear them. Sunglasses that block out light from the sides (ie wraparound ones, or ones with side pieces) are best. Sunlight is reflected off water and snow. If you're going to be trekking in snowy conditions, ski goggles may be better. Snow blindness, or sunburn of the surface of the eyes, can be excruciatingly painful and may take a couple of days to resolve. It doesn't have any lasting effects.

DRY OR ITCHY EYES

Air conditioning, especially in aircraft, can exacerbate dry eyes and allergic eye conditions. Take lubricant drops with you (available without prescription from pharmacies) and use them frequently. Note that anti-allergy drops containing a decongestant ingredient shouldn't be used more than every few days – these are eyedrops that usually claim to make red, tired eyes look white.

SOMETHING IN THE EYE

Dust, particles of sand and insects can get blown into your eyes. If you need to, get a travel companion to wash the particle

BATHING YOUR EYES

If you've got an eye bath, this is obviously designed for the purpose, but good substitutes include any small container or glass, or an egg cup. If you have a ready-made saline (salt) solution, you can use that; or you can make up your own by dissolving a level teaspoon of salt in about 600ml (a pint) of boiled and cooled water or by adding a pinch of salt to a cup of water.

Fill the eye bath or container, bend your head over it with your eye open and blink rapidly in the water. You could get someone to pour the water into your eye if you prefer, but you'll get pretty wet. Alternatively, get someone to soak a tissue or a clean cloth in the water and squeeze it into your eye from a height of a few inches while you are lying down.

out with copious amounts of water – see the boxed text for guidance on how to do this. Salty water is better in theory, but clean water is fine if nothing else is available.

If a particle can be seen on the white of the eye or under the upper eyelid (turn the eyelid over a match or a small key), it can be gently removed with the corner of a tissue or (even more gently) a cotton bud. The clear central part of the eye is too sensitive for you to be able to do this. If you can't wash the particle away, you'll need to go to a doctor, who may be able to remove it after anaesthetising the eye.

RED EYE

If your eye is red and sticky, with a discharge, you've probably got an infection (conjunctivitis). Another cause of red eye is a haemorrhage on the surface of the white of the eye. It can look fairly spectacular, but if your sight is unaffected and you don't have any pain, there's nothing to worry about. You don't need any specific treatment and it will clear up in a week or so.

Conjunctivitis

This eye infection is quite common, especially in children. When you're travelling, it can be difficult to keep your hands clean, which is a source of infection if you then put them up to your eyes. You can also get conjunctivitis by swimming in crowded pools or dirty rivers, or through flies landing on your eyes (although you usually have a reflex blink that prevents flies landing).

Conjunctivitis can be caused by bacteria or viruses. Bacterial conjunctivitis usually quickly affects both eyes, whereas viral conjunctivitis is more likely to affect one eye only, and you don't usually get such a copious discharge. Viral conjunctivitis often comes with flu or a cold.

In addition to looking red, your eye may feel very irritated, as though there's something in it. If you have a bad infection, your eye can be quite uncomfortable, and you'll find bright light difficult to tolerate.

Treatment

If you've got a red, sticky eye, bathe it frequently in clean (boiled and cooled) plain or salty water. Try not to touch or rub your eye, as this makes the infection more likely to spread to your other eye – or to other people.

If the redness doesn't clear up in a couple of days or you've got ready access to medical care, see a doctor, as you will probably need a course of antibiotic eyedrops or ointment.

A common and effective antibiotic for eye infections is chloramphenicol (eyedrops or ointment); other commonly used antibiotic eyedrops and ointments that may be available include neomycin, gentamicin or sulphonamides. Start by putting one drop in every two hours, decreasing this as the redness and irritation improve. If you've got an ointment as well, apply the ointment at night before you go to sleep. If you've got ointment alone, apply it three to four times daily.

Ointment should be put directly into the eye, as follows: hold out the lower eyelid and squeeze about 1cm of cream into the pouch made behind the lid, then close the eye on it.

Bacterial conjunctivitis usually improves (ie the redness clears up) in two to three days, but you need to continue using the drops or ointment for three more days to make sure. If you don't notice any improvement within 48 hours of using the antibiotic, it may be that the cause is not bacterial. Viral conjunctivitis won't respond to antibiotics – it will clear up on its own, although it may take a week or two.

> As a rule, you should avoid using eyedrops containing a combination of an antibiotic and steroids (the names of these usually end in '-sone' like betamethasone), as this can sometimes cause a serious problem if the infection is not bacterial.

Trachoma

This type of conjunctivitis, spread by flies, is most common in dry, rural areas of Latin America, as well as in other parts of the world. Untreated and repeated infection results in serious damage to the eyes, and it is a major cause of blindness worldwide. Before you get too alarmed, it's not likely to be a big problem for you as a traveller in the region, as you'll generally wave off any flies that approach your eyes. Treatment is with antibiotic eyedrops (chlortetracycline) or tablets (eg a single dose of azithromycin).

STYE

If you develop a painful red lump on the edge of your eyelid, it's probably a stye. This is a bit like a pimple anywhere else. It usually clears up in a couple of days without any special treatment. Try putting a clean cloth soaked in clean hot water (not scalding) on your closed eyelid, and do this several times a day.

If it doesn't go away, it might be something called a chalazion. This is a blocked and infected gland in the eyelid, and you'll need to see a doctor about it.

BLACK EYE

If you receive a blow to the eye, you may get a black eye. This is due to bruising around and behind the eye, usually with swelling of the eyelids, but your sight is not usually affected (unless your eyelids are so swollen, that you can't open them, of course). If your sight is not normal, then you need to get medical advice as soon as possible. Minimise the bruising by putting an ice pack (or anything cold, including snow) on your closed eye.

OTHER EYE INJURIES

You can get a scratch on the eye if the branch of a bush or tree whips back in your face after the person in front passes it and bends it forward. You usually get pain straight away, which may become worse after an hour or two. If you put a pad on the eye, this makes it more comfortable, although if you're trying to walk on rough ground, this is not easy with one eye! Keep the pad on for a few hours or even a couple of days if the pain persists, although you might find it's more trouble than it's worth.

If you've got a tube of antibiotic eye ointment (such as chloramphenicol), you could use that. If the abrasion is not too deep, it should heal in one or two days.

SIGNS OF SERIOUS EYE PROBLEMS

If you experience any of the following symptoms, you should seek medical advice urgently:

- any blurred vision or loss of vision that can't be improved by blinking or washing your eye
- sudden loss of vision
- painful eye, especially if it is also unusually sensitive to light
- double vision
- eye injury followed by loss of vision or blood in the eye

A blow to the eye can cause bleeding inside the eye, which your travel companion may see as a fluid level of blood in the iris (the coloured part of the eye). This is a potentially dangerous situation – seek medical help urgently; in the meantime, rest in bed with the eye covered.

LOSS OF VISION &/OR PAIN IN THE EYE

! If you lose your sight, partially or totally in one or both eyes, you need to seek medical help urgently.

If you suddenly lose your sight (from blurring to total loss) without any pain, it could be due to a haemorrhage inside the eye or detachment of the retina (the back of the eye). You may notice a curtain obstructing part of the vision in one eye, which may be preceded by seeing lightning flashes on one side of the vision. Retinal detachment can also follow injury.

If you have blurring or loss of vision associated with intolerance to light and severe aching pain in the eye, it could be due to inflammation inside the eye (iritis) or glaucoma (where the pressure inside the eye is abnormally high). Glaucoma is

MIGRAINE

Bear in mind that migraine headaches can be associated with flashing lights or other eye symptoms like tunnel vision. The visual symptoms usually last about 20 minutes, and may or may not be followed by a headache. If you have had it before, you will know what it is, but if it is the first time, it can be frightening.

All sorts of factors can trigger migraines when you're travelling: tiredness, movement, stress and sunlight. Try taking simple painkillers as early as possible to prevent the attack worsening. Natural remedies like feverfew can be helpful (although you will need to have a supply with you).

more likely to occur in older people. Both of these conditions need urgent medical attention.

Partial loss of vision associated with giddiness (especially if you experience weakness in an arm or leg) is likely to be a stroke – a blockage of the blood vessels in the brain. This is also more likely to occur in older people.

TEETH

UK-based dentist Iain Corran gives you the low-down on staying out of the dentist's chair while you're away.

There are lots of reasons why dental problems are more likely when you're travelling. You tend to consume sugary drinks (soft drinks or sweet tea or coffee) in much larger quantities than you would at home, while practical difficulties with water supplies – or simply the lack of a washbasin – may mean that you take a break in your usual dental hygiene routine just when it's needed most. You'll probably want to avoid having to get dental treatment while you are away because it may be unreliable, expensive and could carry a risk of hepatitis B or HIV if instruments are not properly sterilised.

BEFORE YOU GO

It's a good idea to have a dental check-up about four to six weeks before you plan to travel, as this allows time for you to have any necessary treatment. Let the dentist know you're going away so you can have a really thorough examination. If you wear a brace, be sure to get it checked before you leave, and let your dentist know how long you are going to be away so any necessary alterations can be made.

DENTAL KIT

Consider taking a dental kit with you, or ask your dentist to provide you with a small tube of temporary filling material (which is a bit like chewing gum) or even a plastic filling tool (a spatula thing to help you put the filling in), but make sure you're clear about when and how to use these. Commercial dental kits are available from many travel health clinics, and usually include a dental mirror and temporary filling material, as well as instructions on how to use them. They tend to be quite expensive, but are probably worth considering if you're planning to be away for a long time or trekking in remote areas. Other useful items for dental emergencies include painkillers (eg co-codamol), a course of antibiotics (discuss this with your doctor) and oil of cloves (for toothache).

If you have been advised to have antibiotic cover for any dental treatment, eg because you have heart valve disease, then remember to carry the necessary medication with you (ie amoxicillin 3g sachet, or erythromycin if allergic to penicillin).

AVOIDING DENTAL PROBLEMS

The two main preventable causes of dental problems are tooth decay and gum disease. Tooth decay arises when refined sugars are turned into acid by bacteria in the mouth. The acid erodes the outer layer of the tooth, called enamel, eventually resulting in a cavity. Gum disease is caused by a build-up of plaque (a layer of bacteria and food gunk) on the tooth surface near the gum margin. This can cause sensitivity, particularly to hot and cold foods, and you may notice bleeding from the gums, especially when you brush your teeth.

As a general rule, try to avoid sweet sugary foods and drinks, especially carbonated soft drinks and local-style tea (which is often extremely sweet), and rinse your mouth out with clean water after you eat. In hot climates, you may find your mouth gets really dry. Keeping your mouth moist, eg by chewing on a sugar-free gum, helps reduce the risk of tooth decay, as the saliva neutralises the acid by bacteria in the mouth.

Avoid plaque build-up by brushing your teeth, ideally with a fluoride toothpaste, at least once a day. Remember to take generous supplies of your favourite toothpaste with you, as it may not be available locally. If you run out of toothpaste and you can't get any more, you can use a small amount of salt instead on a moist brush. If you're on a long trip, remember to pack a spare toothbrush. However, if you can't get a replacement, you can use your finger as a toothbrush, possibly with a small piece of clean cloth around it.

! In some places making a toothbrush from a piece of wood, by splitting the end to make bristles, is quite common, but beware of splinters in the gums.

It's also a good idea to use dental floss or tape to clean the areas between your teeth where the toothbrush doesn't reach. If you run out of floss, toothpicks can do the same job, and are widely available. Dental floss can come in handy for a multitude of minor repairs, so is well worth tucking into your pack.

! Remember that you need to use clean (bottled or purified) water for brushing your teeth or flossing – it's obvious, but surprisingly easy to forget!

If you wear a brace, it's particularly important to avoid sticky or hard foods which may damage it, as specialist treatment may be required to fix it.

DENTAL PROBLEMS

In spite of your best efforts, you may experience some teeth problems while you're away.

Broken or Lost Fillings

This can happen if you bite on something hard such as nuts or the ubiquitous crunch in a rice dish. You may feel a sudden pain, a gap where the filling was, and pieces of the filling in your mouth. As an immediate measure, rinse your mouth out with some warm salty water (add a couple of teaspoons of salt to a glass of boiled and cooled water) to clear any debris from your mouth.

If you have some temporary filling material (from your dentist or a commercial kit), you can use it to plug the hole up or you can use a piece of sugar-free chewing gum. It's important to plug it up so that the hole doesn't get filled with food, which can cause more problems. You'll need to get dental treatment for a permanent filling as soon as possible. If you're on a short trip, and it's just a small surface filling, it could wait for a week or so until you get back.

If the filling has cracked rather than fallen out, you may notice that it's sensitive to hot/cold/sugary foods and drinks. A cracked filling can lead to toothache, so try to get a permanent filling placed in the tooth as soon as is convenient.

As a general rule, avoid sugary, hot and cold foods in all these situations.

Toothache

There are lots of causes of this most unpleasant of symptoms: an injury to a tooth, a filling breaking or falling out, or tooth decay can lead to a tooth abscess.

Unless it settles quickly, you're going to need to find a dentist or doctor. In the meantime, take painkillers (eg co-codamol) regularly. Note that you shouldn't put aspirin directly on a painful tooth, as this can cause a sore patch on the gum. If you have oil of cloves with you, it can help relieve the pain when applied to the offending tooth on a clean cotton bud, although applying it may be uncomfortable.

Wash out your mouth regularly (after meals) with warm salty water. Try to avoid sugary foods, hard foods (ie nuts) and hot and cold foods. It goes without saying that you should avoid biting on the tooth.

If the pain is severe and unrelieved, perhaps with a bad taste in your mouth, you've probably got a tooth abscess, and you may need to have the tooth extracted eventually, although root treatment may save the tooth (but you'll need a good dentist). Seek medical or dental help urgently, but if you're in a remote area away from help, start taking a course of antibiotics, for example amoxycillin OR erythromycin OR metronidazole, or whatever you have with you (so long as you're not allergic to it).

! If your face becomes swollen or you develop a fever, you must seek medical help as soon as possible, as it means that the infection is spreading. In the meantime, drink plenty of fluids and start a course of antibiotics.

Another cause of pain in the mouth is a gum abscess, which can occur around a partially erupted wisdom tooth or when the gum has receded around a tooth, but hopefully both of these will have been picked up by your dentist before you left. Treatment is the same as for a tooth abscess.

Chipped Teeth

This can be caused by a fall, or a direct blow to the tooth. It can cause toothache immediately or after a delay, and an abscess can develop. You need to seek treatment as soon as possible, as you may need root canal treatment or extraction of the tooth. In the meantime, take painkillers if necessary.

Crowns & Veneers

If a crown comes out, stick it back in and then find a dentist to glue it back on. If a crown breaks (usually front porcelain ones), it's unlikely that you'll be able to get a new one made, but you should be able to find a dentist to put on a temporary crown, which should last you till you get home.

If a veneer cracks, chips or breaks off, you probably don't need to get dental treatment until you get home, as it's not likely to cause any damage to the tooth if it is not replaced in the short term. A rough edge may initially cause some irritation.

If a Tooth is Knocked Out

If you can find the tooth, wash it in milk (better) or clean water and, if practical, place it back in the socket to reimplant it. Get dental help as soon as possible. If it's in a child, remember that milk teeth won't need to be replaced.

If it is not practical to attempt to reimplant it (eg if it's chipped or broken or you've got other injuries in your mouth), keep the tooth in milk, and try to get a doctor/dentist to attempt to reimplant it.

Reimplantation may not be successful, but it is worth trying. If more than two hours have passed between the tooth being knocked out and reimplantation, the chance of success is slim.

If you are left with an open socket, rinse your mouth out with warm salty water. Don't rinse too vigorously, as this may dislodge the clot forming in the socket. Avoid strenuous exercise for a few hours.

If there is persistent bleeding from the socket, place a clean piece of cloth across the top of the socket and bite onto it for 20 to 30 minutes. If bleeding persists, seek expert advice as soon as possible, as the socket may need stitching. Make sure you know what type of stitches have been put in, and whether or not you need to go back to have them removed.

Sometimes the socket can become infected and very painful. Use warm salty water mouthwashes and take painkillers as an immediate measure. Seek treatment as soon as possible for specialist treatment and possibly a course of antibiotics.

GETTING DENTAL TREATMENT

The same rules apply to finding dental treatment as for medical treatment, and a personal recommendation from a reliable source is probably the best way to go. Five-star hotels, the local expatriate community and embassies may be able to point you in the right direction. If possible, try to find a dental teaching hospital – most capital cities should have one. Charges for treatment vary, but it's probably best to negotiate the price before treatment starts.

A major concern when receiving any dental treatment is the risk of contracting infections like HIV or hepatitis B from the dentist or the instruments being used, but there are some basic precautions you can take. Check that the dentist is wearing a clean pair of dental gloves, and make sure they wash their gloved hands if there's any doubt in your mind. Ideally, they should put on a new pair for each patient, but this may not be possible in some areas. You should consider taking a pair of disposable surgical gloves in your medical kit. If you need an injection, make sure the dentist uses a new, sterile needle.

Always tell anyone who is going to give you dental treatment about any existing medical condition or medication you may be on, before they start treatment.

Skin...

➕ For details on the effects of the sun on the skin, see p314

➕ See the First Aid appendix for treatment of cuts, burns and scalds

➕ For bites and stings, see p365

➕ For information on looking after your feet, see p97

The skin is your body's first line of defence against the outside world. When you're travelling it's subjected to assaults from all directions: physical hazards like the sun, wind and cold; insects and parasites of all shapes and forms which attack it with glee; and bacterial and fungal infections which thrive in hot and humid conditions. Although there's a great line-up of weird and wonderful 'tropical' skin diseases, your skin problems are likely to be much more prosaic: sunburn, bacterial infections and allergic rashes are the most common afflictions.

RASHES

Skin rashes can occur as part of a more generalised disease. In this case it will usually be obvious, because you'll usually have a fever and other symptoms such as sore throat or nausea, as well as vomiting. Some diseases that are associated with a skin rash include:

■ the 'childhood' illnesses (which can occur at any age if you haven't had them before) – measles, rubella and chicken pox (p233)

■ glandular fever and other viral infections (p181)

■ food poisoning or allergies (p153)

■ dengue fever and other viral haemorrhagic fevers (p231)

■ meningococcal meningitis (p141)

■ tick-transmitted fevers (p373)

■ schistosomiasis (p362)

■ worm infestations of the gut (p168)

■ Chagas' disease (p369)

PRICKLY HEAT

This uncomfortable rash is caused by blockage of the sweat ducts. It's called 'prickly heat' because as sweating tries to occur in the blocked glands, you get an uncomfortable prickling sensation. Common in hot, humid conditions, it can strike you when you first arrive or further down the track. It's very common in babies and children.

! Nappy rash can be a big problem in hot climates – see the Babies & Children chapter for more guidance on dealing with this.

At its mildest, prickly heat consists of a rash of painless clear blisters without any redness. These usually burst quickly and don't cause any other problems. The next step up is prickly heat proper. You get itchy areas of redness, with spots and small blisters, usually in covered, sweaty areas like around your waist, chest or back, under your breasts or in the groin. You may get it on the backs of your knees or in the elbow creases. Babies and young children commonly get it on their heads.

Because the problem is the build-up of sweat in blocked ducts, treatment is aimed at preventing sweating:

- stay cool – rest and use fans, cool showers, cover yourself with damp cloths or move to an airconditioned hotel
- wear loose cotton clothing
- wash with water – overuse of soap may destroy the skin's natural oils and defences and is thought to be a contributory factor
- calamine, calendula or comfrey cream on the rash can be soothing
- antihistamine tablets will help stop the itching
- watch for signs of secondary infection (see p347)

Prickly heat usually clears up in a few days. Rarely, the rash refuses to go away and becomes widespread. Because your sweat ducts are blocked all over, this affects your heat controlling mechanisms and you can get heatstroke because of it. This type of heatstroke is more likely after you've been in a hot climate for several months.

ITCHY SKIN RASH – CAUSES

- dermatitis (allergic or irritant reactions) – often on hands or other exposed areas
- prickly heat (p204) – armpits, waist, groin, head (in babies and children)
- fungal infections (p208) – sweaty areas: armpits, groin, under breasts, between toes
- insect bites (p365) – any exposed area
- scabies (p210) – intense itchiness, especially at night
- reaction to medicines – rash all over
- swimmer's itch (p363) – anywhere that was in contact with water
- creeping eruption (cutaneous larva migrans, p213) – moving red tracks, usually on feet and legs

DERMATITIS

Dermatitis is a general term for an itchy skin rash. It's very common worldwide and can be caused by a whole range of factors, from simple chemical irritation to reactions to plants and insects. It may be an in-built tendency in some people, when it can occur without any obvious cause. In this situation it's known as atopic dermatitis or eczema, and may be associated with asthma or hay fever. Most people with eczema will have had it for some time, often since childhood, and it is unlikely to develop for the first time on your travels.

Itching is the main feature of any dermatitis, which appears as thickened, red and often cracked skin. There may be some blistering, particularly if it has been caused by contact with a plant. Where you get it depends on what's causing it: eczema usually affects your hands, inside of the wrists and backs of the

CONTACT IRRITATION

Many tropical plants cause blistering or itching on contact. Members of the poison ivy family, including poison ivy, poison oak, mango trees, cashew trees and gingko are notorious for producing skin irritation and inflammation. Other irritant plants include members of the philodendron family. If you're walking through heavily vegetated areas, you may brush against one of these plants or their fruit, although it can be hard to identify the cause.

Contact with some little critters can produce skin irritation. Blister beetles are found worldwide, especially in warm, dry climates. They're about an inch long, with slender bodies encased in shiny green or blue wing cases. If you touch one or one gets crushed on your skin (or blown into your eye), it causes a burning sensation like a nettle sting and later a blister. Calamine cream can help soothe the irritation, which usually clears up in a matter of hours. Cantharidin, the irritant substance produced by the beetles, was used as a medicine for over 2000 years to treat various ailments, including bladder troubles, warts and impotence. It's extremely poisonous if taken internally.

Fuzzy caterpillars are best avoided as they can cause an irritant rash with swelling and blistering. If you do get stung, try to remove all hairs by using a piece of sticky tape. Ice may help to soothe the irritation. If the hairs get in your eyes, they can cause conjunctivitis.

knees; while contact dermatitis, caused by something you've touched, will appear wherever contact was made.

If you haven't had dermatitis before and it suddenly appears when you're travelling, it's most likely to be due to contact with something…the question is what. It may be a chemical irritant, eg soaps or detergents, or something that you are allergic to, eg an ingredient in a new skin lotion or a plant you've touched or brushed past.

Some unlucky people can get dermatitis, often with blistering, as a result of mild to moderate sun exposure – consider this possibility if it only occurs on parts of your body that have been exposed to the sun. Alternatively it could be a reaction to the sunscreen you're using, or it could just be sunburn.

It's not always easy to work these things out, but a bit of common sense and a certain amount of trial and error can help. For example in this case, you could see if covering up or changing sunscreen helps. Don't forget that you can develop a sensitivity or allergy to something you have used without problems in the past.

Treatment

Most contact dermatitis will gradually settle once the irritant or allergy-causing substance is removed. If you can work out what the culprit is, avoid it! Otherwise, finding the cause only really matters if it doesn't go away.

If the rash is mild, try liberally covering it with a simple moisturiser (like aqueous cream or white soft paraffin). The trouble with 'cosmetic' moisturisers is that they can contain ingredients that may exacerbate the rash, but if you've got nothing else, it may be worth giving them a try.

 Calendula or comfrey cream may help to soothe an itchy rash.

If this doesn't work, a weak steroid cream can help, such as hydrocortisone 1% cream or ointment, and is quite safe to use for a short period of time. You may find that if the skin is thick, eg on the palm of your hand, a stronger steroid cream is needed, such as betamethasone 0.025% or 0.1% cream.

If the skin is cracked and weeping, it's likely to be infected and an antibiotic cream will be helpful.

Note that all steroid creams should be used as sparingly as possible, twice a day. Don't use anything stronger than hydrocortisone 1% on the face or genital area. If you're using these creams for the first time, discuss it with a doctor or pharmacist if possible.

! If a steroid cream makes a rash worse, stop using it – you've probably got the diagnosis wrong! Steroid cream on its own will make ● fungal and bacterial infections much worse.

FUNGAL INFECTIONS

These are common diseases worldwide, but are even more common in hot, humid conditions. (A piece of bread in a plastic bag quickly goes mouldy in the heat, and it's the same principle with your skin and fungal infections.) If you've already got a fungal infection before you leave, you'll probably find it gets worse when you're travelling.

Fungal infections can affect different parts of your body, but the basic principles for preventing them are the same:

■ wear loose fitting, cotton clothing
■ wash regularly and dry yourself carefully, especially between the toes, around the groin area and under the breasts

You can get fungal infections from other people, animals or the soil, and they can affect different parts of your body.

Treatment of these rashes is generally with an antifungal cream – there are many different creams available (eg clotrimazole, ketoconazole, miconazole, nystatin, terbinafine and amorolfine) but all need to be applied daily or twice daily and used for at least a couple of weeks.

Scalp

Ringworm of the scalp (tinea capitis) gives you flaky, round lesions and is more common in children. Treatment is with antifungal tablets, such as fluconazole 50mg daily for two to four weeks OR griseofulvin 500mg (10mg/kg/day in children) daily for six to 12 weeks (avoid in pregnancy).

Body

Ringworm on the body appears as flaky, red areas which spread outwards, leaving a clear patch in the middle. Treatment is with antifungal cream.

Another fungal infection that is common in the tropics is tinea (also called pityriasis) versicolor. It often affects young adults and can be difficult to get rid of. You get round slightly scaly, itchy patches which may be lighter or darker than the surrounding skin, usually over your shoulders, chest and back. Seek medical advice, but treatment options include selenium sulphide shampoo OR an antifungal cream OR itraconazole 200mg daily for seven days OR fluconazole 50mg daily for two to four weeks for persistent problems.

Crotch

Tinea cruris, or 'jock itch', appears as a red, flaky rash in the groin crease, especially in men; there's often a fungal infection of the feet too. Treatment is with antifungal cream.

Feet

Athlete's foot is extremely common in hot, humid climates. You get a flaky rash between the toes, which can progress to splitting of the skin. Dry carefully between your toes and use an antifungal cream or powder, or calendula tincture.

BACTERIAL INFECTIONS

✚ For more guidelines on preventing and treating bacterial skin infections, see the First Aid chapter (p434).

Warmth, humidity, dirt and dust make bacterial infections of the skin very common when you're travelling. They're extremely common in local populations too, occurring in one-tenth of adults and up to one-third of children in the tropics. Bacterial infections usually have pus as their main feature. Any break in the skin, however small and insignificant it may seem at first, can get infected if you don't take steps to prevent it. If the infection spreads, it can make you seriously ill with blood poisoning. Boils and abscesses (collections of pus under the skin which form hot red swellings, often with a head of pus) are also more common. Folliculitis, a rash of pimples caused by infection of the hair follicles, is more common in hot, humid climates, especially if you swim in dirty water.

! Surfing abrasions and cuts should be treated quickly with iodine antiseptic as the germs in corals can cause serious infections if left alone.

Impetigo is an extremely common bacterial skin infection, especially in hot, humid climates. It typically affects children but is common in adult travellers too. It usually starts on the face, often around the mouth or from a mosquito bite. The first sign of this infection is the appearance of blisters on the face, looking a bit like a cold sore at first. These then burst, forming golden, crusty sores, which can spread quickly to different areas of the skin. Impetigo is very contagious, and can easily be spread by fingers and towels or face cloths. Treat impetigo as follows:

- wash the crusty sores regularly (eg twice a day) with soap and water or an antiseptic solution like povidone-iodine
- apply an antibiotic cream (eg fusidic acid three times daily for five to seven days) on the sores after washing the crusts off
- take a course of antibiotics (eg flucloxacillin OR erythromycin if penicillin-allergic) if it's very severe or doesn't respond quickly to treatment

SCABIES

You're not that likely to get this infestation unless you're planning on intimate, prolonged contact with a sufferer. The villain is the scabies mite, which burrows into your skin, usually between the fingers, the wrists and genital areas, where it lays its eggs.

It causes intense itching, which is much worse at night, and has a high risk of secondary bacterial infection. The itching isn't actually due to the mites themselves but is a sensitivity reaction they produce in you six to eight weeks after you've been infected. It can persist even when the mites have gone.

SKIN LESIONS

Skin lesions, especially wound infections, are extremely common in the tropics and can be a nuisance. Some causes of sores include the following:
- bacterial infection
- insect bite
- tropical ulcer
- leishmaniasis (p366)
- Buruli ulcer (pX)
- guinea worm ulcer (p228)
- cutaneous diphtheria (p233)

You may see typical burrows between the fingers. It's not a tropical disease as such but is encouraged by poor personal hygiene, eg when water isn't readily available for washing.

Treatment is with malathion or permethrin lotion (preferably); benzyl benzoate lotion may still be available locally but should be avoided in children. You need to cover your whole body apart from your head (except in young children) and leave it ideally for 24 hours, but overnight treatment (10 to 12 hours) is probably adequate.

Itchiness may persist for 10 to 12 days even after successful treatment of the mite, so try to soothe it with calamine lotion or antihistamine tablets. You need to wash all your clothes and anything you've been sleeping in (eg your sleeping bag and liner) to prevent reinfection. Anybody who has shared a bed with you will also need to be treated. It's not very pleasant but at least scabies mites are not known to transmit any diseases.

LICE

Contact with lice is a definite possibility in many countries, especially if you're roughing it. There are three types of lice which infest different areas: head, body and pubic areas (crab louse). They all cause itching due to bites. You may not see the lice themselves, as they're transparent, but they lay eggs that look like white grains attached to hairs. Lice are passed by close contact between people (sexual intercourse for pubic lice) and via infected bedding or clothing for body lice.

Head lice can be treated with carbaryl, malathion, permethrin or phenothrin lotions – apply the lotion to your head and wash it off after 12 hours. Alternatively, use any hair conditioner and get a (good) friend to comb through your hair – the lice just slip off. You'll need to repeat this every three days or so for two weeks after the last louse was spotted. Treat anyone you share a bed with as well. The empty egg cases can stick around after the lice themselves have gone.

Treat body lice by getting rid of them: wash all bedding and clothing in hot water, which kills the lice. Body (clothing) lice can, rarely, transmit typhus via their faeces.

Pubic lice should be treated by applying malathion OR carbaryl lotion all over your body (not just the pubic area) and leaving it overnight. You'll need a second treatment after seven days to zap any lice appearing from surviving eggs.

BEDBUGS

You're very likely to get acquainted with these, especially if you're on a shoestring budget. Bedbugs are 3mm x 4mm oval insects that live in mattresses, cracks in the walls etc, but not on you. They merely visit you when it's dark for a meal. Bites, which can be itchy, are usually in a line of two or three on your face, arms, buttocks or ankles: anything accessible. If bites are itchy, try some calamine lotion.

The best way to get rid of them is to spray furniture and wall cracks with an insecticide, or to use a permethrin-impregnated mosquito net. Better still, find another hotel.

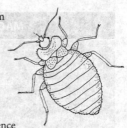

There's been much debate about whether bedbugs can transmit HIV – in theory at least it's a possibility but there is no evidence to suggest they do.

CREEPING ERUPTION

This moving rash (also called cutaneous larva migrans, because it migrates, or geography worm) is caused by the larvae of various worms, usually the dog or cat hookworm, which are passed in their faeces. It occurs worldwide, but it's much more common in hot, humid environments which encourage development of the larvae. You're at risk anywhere contaminated with dog and cat faeces, usually by walking barefoot or sitting on sandy beaches (you should always wear thongs or sandals).

You can get mild itching and a rash when the larvae first enter your skin, but the real fun begins when they start to migrate a few days later. They produce intensely itchy red tracks that advance slowly day by day. They're desperately hoping you're a cat or dog, as they can't live in humans and will die after a few weeks.

You could just wait for them to die naturally, but you're probably not going to want to leave it that long. Treatment is by freezing the head of the track with ethyl chloride spray or applying an anti-worm medicine like thiabendazole (made up into a 10% solution) directly to the track. Alternatively, albendazole 400mg twice a day for five days is very effective. As with any skin condition in the tropics, look out for secondary infection.

A similar rash can be caused by intestinal worms (see the Digestive System chapter), but they tend to be much speedier.

MAGGOT BOILS

Yup, these are as horrible as they sound, but you'd be fairly unlucky to get one. You have to admire the ingenious way in which they are caused, by a type of fly called a botfly. This fly catches other biting insects in mid-air such as mosquitoes and deposits its eggs on their body. When the insect bites you, the eggs hatch and the larvae sneak through the puncture wound, where they stay, forming a boil. Boils usually occur on the head, and have a central pore (the breathing hole of the larvae). Sufferers often report a feeling of movement in the boil.

Getting rid of the larva can require a bit of ingenuity itself. Blocking the breathing hole with something like petroleum jelly may make the larva come up for air, at which stage you can grab hold of it. Alternatively, there are those who advocate tempting it out by waving a piece of bacon over the hole.

A more conventional option is to have minor surgery to open up the hole so that the larva can be extracted with forceps. Alternatively, you can apply a small bandage over the boil to suffocate the boil's inhabitant (leave it in place for three to four days to be sure), then remove it and the larva. It's important to remove the larva intact as, apart from any aesthetic considerations, half a worm can cause an intensely irritant reaction.

JIGGER FLEA (TUNGIASIS)

These fleas are known by a variety of names. *Tunga penetrans*, sand flea, chigoe (not to be confused with chiggers, which are mites), *bichos de pé*, and other local variations. They live in sandy soil and infest pigs, humans and other mammals. They occur throughout tropical Latin America and they're fairly common in travellers who go barefoot and wear open sandals in these areas.

The flea burrows into your skin, commonly the soles of your feet or on your toes, under the toenails. It forms a swelling the size of a pea with a central black spot (the back end of the flea).

Treatment is aimed at getting rid of the flea and preventing any secondary bacterial infection. Textbooks talk of microsurgery but it is possible to dig it out relatively painlessly using a sterilised needle and plenty of antiseptic solution. You should make sure you remove it whole and take care to keep the open wound clean afterwards.

HIV/AIDS & Sexual Health...

✚ For a general discussion about sex and travel, including how to avoid sexually related health problems, see the section on Sex & Travel in the Staying Healthy chapter earlier in this book.

HIV/AIDS

AIDS stands for acquired immunodeficiency syndrome, and it describes the collection of diseases that result from suppression of the body's immune system by infection with the human immunodeficiency virus (HIV). HIV targets cells in the blood that are an important part of your immune system, which protects you from infections. At present, although there are effective (but toxic) treatments that can keep AIDS at bay for a period of time, there is no known cure.

TRANSMISSION

In Latin America, as elsewhere in the world, there has been a shift from transmission of HIV mainly in men who have sex with men towards transmission through heterosexual sex. HIV can be transmitted through vaginal, anal or oral sexual intercourse between men and women or between men.

HIV infection can also be transmitted through blood or blood products, and a major risk factor is the sharing of needles for drug use. Other risk situations include inadequate sterilisation or reusing of needles, syringes and other equipment in medical and dental procedures, as well as tattooing, ear and body piercing, and using cut-throat razors. Transmission through infected blood transfusions in many countries in the region has fallen as better screening procedures have been put in place (see the section on Blood Transfusions in the Staying Healthy chapter for more details). HIV can also be transmitted during pregnancy from mother to unborn child.

FACT OR FICTION?

It can be confusing trying to separate fact from fiction with HIV, but here's the current wisdom on it:

- a vaccine against HIV is looking promising, but there's a long way to go, so don't throw away those condoms just yet
- worldwide, most HIV infections are acquired through heterosexual sex
- the more sexual partners you have, the more at risk you are for HIV/AIDS
- you can be perfectly healthy for 10 years or more after infection before any signs of the disease show up
- you can't tell by looking at a person if they are infected or not
- HIV can be transmitted through infected blood transfusions
- HIV is not thought to be transmitted by saliva
- acupuncture, tattooing, ear and body piercing, injections and other medical and dental procedures with unsterilised equipment can all transmit HIV infection
- HIV is a sensitive little virus and needs pretty intimate contact to be transmitted – it's not transmitted by hugging, social kissing, using the same toilet seat or sharing a cup
- it's not passed in swimming pools
- insects like bedbugs and mosquitoes do not transmit HIV

RISKS

The risk of acquiring HIV per exposure varies enormously, from one in 20 to one in 1000 for different types of sexual intercourse, one in 20 for needle sharing, to near certainty for a contaminated blood transfusion. In general, it's twice as easy to transmit HIV from men to women than the other way round, and receptive anal intercourse is especially risky. Many other factors can affect the risk, including the stage of infection (early and late are the most risky), the strain of HIV and whether you have another STI. Having another STI increases your risk of getting HIV, and if you are already infected, it increases the chance of you passing it on.

HIV INFECTION & AIDS

There aren't any immediate signs of infection, although you may get a glandular-fever-like illness a few weeks after infection, with fever, aches and pains, a skin rash and swollen glands. After this you may have no more symptoms for 10 years or more, although this time of being HIV-positive is very variable. This is the danger period in terms of passing the infection to others, because you're healthy and you may not realise that you've got HIV. Eventually, your immune system starts to show signs of strain, and the syndrome of AIDS starts.

A blood test can show if you're infected or not, but it won't show positive for about three months after you may have been exposed to HIV.

HIV & YOU

While you are away, you could put yourself at risk of HIV infection if you:

- have sexual intercourse with an infected person
- receive an infected blood transfusion or injection
- share needles with HIV-infected injecting drug users

You're obviously going to want to take steps to avoid these risk situations – always practise safer sex; avoid getting into situations where you might need a blood transfusion; and never share needles with other injecting drug users.

If you're worried that you may have put yourself at risk of HIV infection:

- don't sit and brood on it – phone an AIDS helpline as soon as possible to talk about your concerns; either wait until you get back home if you're on a short trip, or check your guidebook or a phone book for the local number
- protect any subsequent sexual partners by always using a condom
- make an appointment with your doctor or a sexual health clinic when you get back to discuss what to do next

Remember that an HIV test won't be able to tell you either way for about three months after the risk situation; in the meantime you will need to practise safer sex.

You may have heard about a 'morning after' treatment for HIV, called postexposure prophylaxis. It's a cocktail of antiviral drugs that, in theory, stops HIV infection getting a hold after you've been exposed to it. Although it may be of value for health workers who accidentally get jabbed by contaminated needles, its use after sexual exposure is very controversial. It's not guaranteed to work, and there are enormous practical problems associated with its use – it's extremely expensive, several different drugs have to be taken every day for at least

WHAT IS SAFER SEX?

Using a latex (rather than natural membrane) condom is extremely effective at preventing transmission of HIV and other STIs. Use only water-based lubricants, as petroleum or oil-based lubricants can damage rubber.

Condoms are generally widely available from pharmacies in Latin America. Ask for a 'camisinha' or 'camiseta de Venus' in Brazil, or 'los preservativos' or 'condones' in Spanish-speaking countries.

You may feel awkward about discussing condoms because of cultural differences or a worry that you might be seen as 'forward' or as having planned it, but it's a small price to pay for peace of mind and your good health.

Your local health centre, any travel health clinic and any sexual health clinic will be able to provide you with more information on safer sex or, if you have access to the web, you could check out the UCSF safer sex site (**hivinsite.ucsf.edu/InSite?page=kb-07-02-02#**) for more info. The Terrence Higgins Trust website (**www.tht.org.uk/index.htm**) also has loads of information on all aspects of preventing and living with HIV/AIDS.

HIV/AIDS IN BRAZIL

This is worth highlighting, if only so you are not bowled over by the hysteria that generally surrounds the issue in Brazil. Brazil currently has one of the highest rates of HIV infection in the world, with an estimated 600,000 HIV cases. As in many affected countries, HIV infection is not evenly distributed here, and a large proportion of affected people are concentrated in urban areas.

There are lots of reasons for the pattern of the epidemic in Brazil, including the popularity (and acceptability) of bisexuality in men, a more relaxed attitude towards sex of all kinds, and the sharing of needles among injecting drug users. While infection among injecting drug users and bisexual men is high, AIDS is also one the leading causes of death among women of reproductive age.

There are high-profile public education campaigns to tackle the high level of fear and misunderstanding about the infection and how it is transmitted, and these are having some success. For over a decade, Brazil has provided free antiretroviral medicine to

six weeks and it can cause unpleasant side effects. For most travellers, this isn't an option, and you shouldn't rely on it.

AIDS IN LATIN AMERICA

Compared with other regions of the world, the HIV epidemic has been fairly limited so far in Latin America. Of the total number of people living with HIV/AIDS worldwide, 5% are in Latin America and the Caribbean. Overall, there is a relatively low level of infection in the general population, and at present infection is mainly concentrated in high risk populations, especially in the most socially and economically vulnerable citizens unable to pay for it, and has become one of the leaders among developing countries in treating its AIDS victims. One of the biggest threats to the program, though, is the rising cost of new drugs (essential for patients resistant to old antiretroviral treatments). In 2007, following a breakdown in negotiations with the large pharmaceutical company Merck, Brazil announced it would bypass Merck's patent and reproduce the drugs inexpensively – a move that even the WTO accepts in the event of national emergencies. It has also had a great deal of success with prevention schemes, educating youth about the dangers of unprotected sex, and distributing free condoms on a massive scale (25 million are distributed nation-wide over Carnaval). Health officials have even developed a working partnership with Brazil's prostitutes, a move that has angered church officials.

This is not intended to put you off visiting affected areas in Brazil (and elsewhere), it just highlights the importance of taking sensible precautions to avoid exposing yourself to risk. It's easy to get carried away in the excitement of the Carnaval, so be prepared, and carry a pack of condoms with you just in case.

groups, however, the incidence of infection is expected to grow. As elsewhere in the developing world, HIV mainly affects young people, with the highest rates of infection in people between the ages of 20 and 44 years.

Different countries have been affected differently by the HIV epidemic, and social and economic factors have resulted in different patterns of infection. Although there is a general shift towards transmission via heterosexual sex, in some places, including Mexico and the Andean region, men who have sex with men are still the most commonly affected group. In Central America, where the epidemic started relatively late, heterosexual contact is the main transmission route, with the epidemic being more established in Honduras and Belize than other countries in the subregion.

HIV infection is generally concentrated in urban areas (capital and major cities), although it is spreading to rural areas through migration. Commercial sex plays an important role in urban areas, with infection rates in sex workers on the rise in many places.

SEXUALLY-TRANSMITTED INFECTIONS

Although some of the 'traditional' STIs like syphilis and gonorrhoea have faded from the picture somewhat in developed countries, they're alive and kicking in most other parts of the world, including Latin America.

Why do you care? Because travellers tend regularly roll up at STI clinics back home with infections they've acquired while they were away. There's a long history of an association between itinerant populations (sailors, soldiers and long-distance truck drivers) and the spread of STIs. Most famously, Christopher Columbus and his crew have been accused of initiating an epidemic of syphilis that spread through Europe in the 16th century. The two world wars were both associated with epidemics of STIs and, more recently, the spread of HIV through Africa can be directly related to long-distance truck routes.

Many STIs (including gonorrhoea and syphilis) can be simply and effectively treated with antibiotics if they're caught early. However, others (including chlamydia and gonorrhoea) can make you seriously ill and may have long-term effects – especially if they are not treated early – such as infertility, liver disease (eg hepatitis) and an increased risk of cervical cancer (eg genital warts).

! Note that hepatitis B is the only sexually transmitted infection for which there is an effective vaccine. Discuss with your doctor, but consider getting vaccinated against hepatitis B if you think you're at high risk of infection (see p35 for more details).

Some STIs cause no symptoms or only mild symptoms that may go unnoticed; sometimes fertility problems are the first sign you have an infection. If STIs do cause symptoms, these are usually an abnormal vaginal or penile discharge, pain or irritation during intercourse or when you urinate, and any blisters, lumps, itches, rashes or other irritation on/around your genitals or anus.

! Because STIs can go unnoticed, it's best to get a check-up when you get home if you had unprotected intercourse while you were away.

If you notice any symptoms, it's best to get expert help as soon as possible. You can't tell accurately from your symptoms what infection you're likely to have, and you can often have more than one STI at the same time. Taking the wrong treatment or inadequate treatment leaves you at risk of future complications like infertility, or you may think you're cured when you're not. Try to find a reputable doctor or STI clinic for a thorough examination and laboratory tests, and see your doctor when you get back so they can confirm that the infection is gone and there are no other problems.

If you think you may have an STI:

- seek medical advice for investigation and treatment
- remember that self medication is best avoided, as it can be disastrous
- your partner will need treatment too
- avoid intercourse (assuming you still feel like having sex) until you have finished a course of treatment
- play fair, and don't spread it around

Bear in mind that STI clinics are probably not going to be called this in most parts of Latin America. Instead, they are likely to be called by the bad old names like venereo-dermatology (VD) clinic. Alternatively, you could try a family planning clinic.

In the following section we've summarised a few details about some of the STIs you may be at risk of acquiring. We haven't included specific antibiotic treatments because the sensitivity of infections to antibiotics varies from region to region and with time, and it's near impossible to diagnose STIs without a laboratory test. In any event, you always have time to find medical help.

Trichomoniasis is another STI that women may be at risk for – we've covered this in the Women Travellers chapter (p248).

Gonorrhoea

Caused by a bacterium, this STI occurs worldwide, affecting hundreds of millions of people. It usually causes a penile or vaginal discharge and burning on urination. You can also be infected in the throat or rectum. It can lead to serious complications like pelvic inflammatory disease and infertility if it's not treated promptly.

Gonorrhoea used to be effectively treated with high-dose penicillin, but multiple antibiotic resistance is a major problem worldwide, and treatment is now usually with one of the newer antibiotics. You'll need a couple of check-ups to make sure it has gone completely.

Syphilis

This ancient disease occurs in three stages, and can cause serious complications in a proportion of sufferers if it's not treated early. Initially it causes a painless ulcer (on your genitals, rectum or throat) and a rash. Later you may get a feverish illness with painful ulcers and rashes, and later still (up to 50 years) you can get problems involving major blood vessels or the brain. Diagnosis is by a blood test.

Treatment needs to be administered and monitored by an expert, and usually involves multiple injections of penicillin.

Chlamydia

Known as the silent STI because it often causes mild or no symptoms, this infection is extremely common worldwide. It's also known as NSU, and if symptoms are present they're similar to gonorrhoea but milder. It's a major cause of pelvic inflammatory disease and infertility in women. Antibiotic treatment is effective at treating this condition.

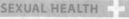

CONDOMS

What condoms won't protect you against:

- genital herpes
- genital warts
- pubic lice
- scabies

Condoms do help protect against STIs transmitted through the exchange of body fluids. These infections include:

- HIV
- hepatitis B and C
- gonorrhoea
- chlamydia
- syphilis

Genital Herpes

This is a very common cause of genital ulceration. Ulcers can be very painful, occur in clusters and may recur. It's caused by a similar virus to the one that causes cold sores on your lips, and if your partner has a cold sore, it can be transmitted to your genitals by oral sex.

The initial infection is usually the worst, and can last about three weeks. You can feel quite miserable with it, with a fever, aches and pains, and swollen glands. Once you have herpes, you are liable to have recurrences, but subsequent attacks are usually less severe, and you may recognise and be able to avoid triggers like stress or being rundown. Note that any genital ulcers make transmission of HIV more likely.

Treatment is with simple painkillers and bathing the ulcers in salty water or a mild antiseptic solution; a local anaesthetic jelly applied to the ulcers may help. Antiviral drugs (eg acyclovir 200mg five times daily for seven days) can help shorten the length of an attack and reduce the severity, but they are expensive and only moderately effective.

> **!** It's best to avoid any sexual contact while you have an attack of herpes or if you notice a sore or ulcer on your genitals.

Genital Warts

These are usually painless, and can appear on the vulva, vagina, penis or anus. Warts can be painted with an acid solution that makes them dry up and fall off, or you sometimes need to have them removed in hospital, where they can be frozen or burnt off. Occasionally they may need to be surgically removed. They can recur and often there's no obvious trigger, although smoking and stress are sometimes thought to be factors.

Fortunately, genital warts usually disappear completely, but in women they are associated with cancerous changes in the cervix, so it's important to have regular cervical smear tests if you have been infected.

Chancroid

This highly infectious STI occurs in tropical and subtropical areas, where it is the most common cause of genital ulcers. Worldwide, it's more common than syphilis. The ulcers are painful (and can get secondarily infected) and you often get swelling of the glands in the groin. It is much more common in men than in women, and it often occurs with syphilis. Antibiotics are effective against chancroid.

Lymphogranuloma Venerum

This is caused by types of chlamydia (see earlier in this section) and occurs worldwide, including South America. Symptoms are variable, but you may notice a blister or small painless ulcer or, more commonly, tender swelling of the lymph glands with fever and general aches and pains. Late problems, if it's not treated, include bladder and rectal problems and swelling of the

GENITAL ULCERS

Causes of these lesions include:

- chancroid (common in tropical regions)
- genital herpes
- syphilis
- lymphogranuloma venerum
- granuloma inguinale (donovanosis)

Genital ulcers make transmission of HIV infection more likely.

genitals (genital elephantiasis). Antibiotic treatment is effective in the early stages.

Donovanosis (Granuloma Inguinale)

You probably don't need to worry about this one as it's pretty rare, but hot spots in Latin America include the Caribbean coast. It causes a persistent genital ulcer. Antibiotic treatment is effective, but may need to be prolonged over several weeks.

Other infections

Just be aware of some other infections that can be transmitted through sexual intercourse:

- viral hepatitis (p146)
- pubic lice (p212)
- scabies (p210)
- intestinal infections (p150)

Rarities...

Grouped here are some infections you're generally going to be at very low risk of getting, except under special circumstances or, in the case of the 'childhood' infections, if you are not up to date with your immunisations. We've listed these infections in alphabetical order. If you think you might have one of these diseases, see a doctor.

EXOTIC INFECTIONS

If you get one of these, you're either exceptionally unlucky, or you were just in the wrong place at the wrong time.

ENCEPHALITIS

This brain infection can be caused by many different viruses. In Latin America, Eastern equine encephalitis and Venezuelan encephalitis may be transmitted by the bite of certain mosquitoes. These diseases are primarily diseases of wild birds or rodents that occasionally spill over into the human and horse populations. They occur in Mexico, Panama, Brazil, Argentina, Guyana and Venezuela, as well as some parts of the USA. The disease comes on with fever and headache, and can rarely cause permanent damage to the brain.

LYMPHATIC FILARIASIS

Worldwide, this parasitic disease affects about 120 million people. It occurs in parts of South America (mainly Brazil – see map p24) but is most widespread in Southeast Asia and Africa. It is caused by infection with parasitic worms which are transmitted via mosquito bites.

It is caused by blockage of the lymph channels by long, thread-like worms (filaria). Some forms (eg, elephantiasis, in which male sufferers may develop grossly enlarged testicles) are transmitted by the bite of several varieties of mosquito; others (eg, onchocerciasis or river blindness) may be transmitted by the bite of black fly, while guinea worm is transmitted by ingesting a specific infected water flea. Elephantiasis can affect the arms,

ELIMINATING FILARIASIS

Filariasis is an important cause of permanent and long-term disability worldwide, but the outlook is more optimistic than it seems at first. Recent advances in treatment and diagnosis of the disease have suddenly made eradication of the disease look like a real possibility. Strengthening this possibility further, in 1998 the pharmaceutical company SmithKline Beecham announced that it would donate one of the drugs used against filariasis (albendazole) free of charge for as long as it takes to eliminate the disease. Given that the criticism most often levelled at major pharmaceutical companies is that they don't do enough to address the problem of tropical diseases, this is a promising start.

legs, breasts or scrotum, and there is usually an associated thickening and wrinkling of the skin, which is supposed to resemble elephant skin, hence the name 'elephantiasis'.

However, not all infections lead to elephantiasis. There may be no symptoms at all with light infections, or you may get fever, painful swellings of the lymph glands (such as in your armpits, groin or elbows) and, for male travellers, swelling of the testes, with scrotal pain and tenderness. Symptoms usually develop about six months after infection.

Filariasis is extremely rare in travellers, as it takes prolonged (three to six months at least) and intense exposure to the parasite for infection to become established. There's no vaccine available against lymphatic filariasis and it makes sense to take measures to avoid insect bites wherever you are, but especially in risk areas.

Infection can be diagnosed with a blood test, and effective drug treatments are available.

HANSEN'S DISEASE (LEPROSY)

This ancient disease occurs in most parts of the world, but especially in the tropics, and you may see sufferers while on your travels. Because of the social stigma attached to the name 'leprosy', it's now officially known as Hansen's disease, after the person who first identified the causative organism in 1873.

Hansen's disease was well known to the ancient world (although supposed references to 'lepers' in the Old Testament may in fact have been a translation error). It used to be widespread in Europe in the Middle Ages, and crusaders returned with it from the Middle East. It's now estimated to affect 15 million people worldwide.

Hansen's disease is an important cause of permanent and progressive disability. It's caused by a bacterium, Mycobacterium leprae, which attacks nerves. This deadens feeling in the extremities, so sufferers damage themselves without realising it. Secondary infection of wounds due to poor hygiene causes further damage. Although the stereotypical image of a sufferer is of someone with deformities and weeping sores, in reality infection can cause a wide spectrum of disease, from simple depigmented patches of skin to characteristic deformities like claw hand.

You won't catch the disease by touching a sufferer. Prolonged contact with a sufferer (for example living in the same house) is needed for the disease to spread (possibly by droplets from the nose and mouth). Socio-economic conditions are thought to play a big part in determining spread – for example malnutrition can increase susceptibility to the disease.

Specific treatments are available and, if started early, the disease can be halted before deformities occur. The problem is that diagnosis is often delayed because of fear of the disease and its social stigma. Over the centuries sufferers have been stigmatised to an extraordinary degree – they have been shunned by society and banished into ghettoes.

HANTAVIRUS PULMONARY SYNDROME

This newly identified rare viral disease is primarily an infection of rodents. It occurs in limited areas of Brazil, Paraguay, Bolivia, Argentina and Chile. Humans are infected through living in domestic surroundings contaminated by rat urine or occasionally via a rat bite. It's generally a mild infection, occurring two to three weeks after you've been exposed to the infective agent. Symptoms are usually fever with headache and muscle pains, followed by the appearance of a red rash over the body.

OROPOUCHE FEVER

This viral disease occurs mainly in the Amazon region of Brazil. It is transmitted to humans initially through contact with forest animals (including the three-toed sloth), and then between humans by mosquitoes. Occasional large outbreaks occur in urban areas. Symptoms come on suddenly, with a high fever, headache and joint and muscle aches.

PINTA

This rare skin lesion is endemic in underprivileged, rural populations of Central and South America. It occurs mainly in children and young adults, and is transmitted by person-to-person contact. It is caused by a relative of the microorganism that causes syphilis. There are various stages of the disease. In the early stage, red, scaly lesions occur on exposed skin (including the face, arms and legs), gradually enlarging. Later, more scaly lesions appear and turn very dark, later losing all pigment and appearing white.

VIRAL HAEMORRHAGIC FEVERS

These fevers occur in different guises in different countries of the world, and include dengue fever, currently a major public health problem in tropical and subtropical regions of the world. For details on dengue fever, see the main section in the Fever chapter earlier in this book. Other less common viral haemorrhagic fevers can occasionally cause large outbreaks in local populations, but they are extremely unlikely to affect travellers. They are often restricted to quite specific geographical areas, usually indicated by their names.

In Latin America, the three main viral haemorrhagic fevers are Argentinian (caused by the junin virus), Bolivian (caused by the machupo virus) and Venezuelan (caused by the guanarito virus) haemorrhagic fevers. Argentinian haemorrhagic fever occurs mainly in an area of the pampas northwest of Buenos Aires. The Bolivian variety occurs in rural areas in north-east Bolivia.

Haemorrhagic means bleeding, which is what characterises these diseases. As a result of infection, small blood vessels in all parts of the body become leaky, allowing blood to escape. Uncontrolled bleeding occurs, resulting in shock and, sometimes, death.

These viruses primarily cause a disease in rodents, but direct contact with rodents by humans or through eating food contaminated by rodents, can pass the infection to humans. Once humans are infected, the disease may be transmitted directly from person to person by contact with body fluids.

GLOBALLY-OCCURRING INFECTIONS

Grouped in this section are some diseases that aren't confined to any particular area but occur worldwide. Immunisation programs and generally high living standards have made many of these infections rare in developed countries, but you may be at more risk of them when you're travelling in less-developed countries where immunisation programs may be less comprehensive and levels of disease higher.

✚ For details about immunisations where relevant, see the Immunisations section of the Before You Go chapter.

BRUCELLOSIS

This infection, also known as undulant fever, occurs worldwide. It is transmitted by ingesting unpasteurised milk and dairy products or through contact with meat from infected animals, mainly cows, pigs and goats. Symptoms include headache, fever, chills, sweating and abdominal pain. The fever comes and goes, with night sweats and morning chills. Sometimes the illness comes on more gradually, with weakness and exhaustion being the main symptoms. Untreated, the infection can last months or even years. It's rarely fatal, and can be effectively treated with antibiotics. It's one more reason for avoiding unpasteurised milk on your travels.

DIPHTHERIA

Vaccination against this serious bacterial disease is very effective, so you don't need to worry if you are up to date with your shots.

Diphtheria occurs worldwide, but has been controlled by vaccination in most developed countries. It mainly affects children and causes a cold-like illness, which is associated with a severe sore throat. A thick white membrane forms at the back of the throat, which can suffocate you, but what makes this a really nasty disease is that the diphtheria bug produces a very powerful poison that can cause paralysis and affect the heart. Otherwise healthy people can carry the disease-causing microorganism in their throats, and it's transmitted by sneezing and coughing.

It can also cause a skin ulcer known as a veldt sore, and vaccination protects against this form too.

Treatment is with penicillin and a diphtheria antitoxin, if necessary.

INFLUENZA

The commonest vaccine-preventable disease, influenza is a very common travellers ailment. While mostly a nuisance spoiling one to two weeks of any trip, it occasionally causes serious complications. The annual vaccine protects against circulating strains and is recommended for travellers every year.

MEASLES

Measles starts a bit like a cold, and then appears to get worse, and a fever develops. At about the third or fourth day, a rash appears on the skin, starting on the face and moving down. The rash is

POLIO

This viral disease is something of a success story in the Americas. Since the early 1990s, as a result of immunisation campaigns, polio has been eradicated from the region, although you may still see people with paralysed limbs as a result of polio in childhood. Elsewhere in the developing world, polio remains an important cause of disability. Polio is a disease of poor living standards and public hygiene; it's spread from person to person by coughing and sneezing, and through contaminated food and water. Although it causes a flu-like illness and sometimes diarrhoea, paralysis of a limb or the respiratory muscles due to damage to nerves can develop in a proportion of sufferers. Polio can be diagnosed by a blood test. Prevention is through immunisation and food and water precautions.

red, raised and tends to conglomerate together. It starts to fade after about five days. You can get ear and chest infections with measles, and also diarrhoea. Occasionally, severe complications (affecting the brain) can occur, which is why you should seek medical advice if you think you may have measles. Although it's often thought of as a childhood illness, measles can occur in adults and tends to be much more severe when it does.

MUMPS

Mumps is a viral infection of the salivary glands. You feel generally unwell and you may notice swelling around the jaw, extending towards the ear and associated with pain (especially when eating). It usually resolves after about a week without any special treatment. There is a risk of infection affecting the testicles in adult men who get mumps, although not in children.

RUBELLA

Rubella (German measles) is generally a very mild illness, a bit like a mild cold, associated with a pink, non-raised rash that starts on the face and spreads downwards. It can, however, cause severe problems in unborn children, so it is extremely important that you are immunised if you are a woman of child-bearing age.

TETANUS

You probably know that you have to be up to date with this vaccination, but do you know what you're being protected against? Spores of the tetanus bacterium are widespread in soil and some animal faeces, and occur worldwide. They can be introduced into your body through injury, for example through a puncture wound (even a very trivial one), a burn or an animal bite. The tetanus bacteria produce a toxin in your body that causes severe, painful muscular contractions and spasm leading to death through spasm of the respiratory muscles. Its old name is 'lockjaw' because of the spasms of the jaw muscles.

Tetanus needs specialist treatment in hospital, but don't worry: you shouldn't get it if your vaccination is up to date.

Clean any wound immediately and thoroughly with soap and water or antiseptic and, if you haven't been vaccinated against tetanus within the last 10 years or the wound is particularly dirty, get medical advice on having a booster dose of the tetanus vaccination as soon as possible (you may need a booster even if your vaccination is up to date).

VARICELLA (CHICKEN POX)

Another disease of childhood, usually less serious than measles can be prevented by vaccination. Antibody tests can measure immunity – usually acquired during childhood, and two doses of vaccine can be offered to non-immune travellers.

Mental Wellbeing...

If you're jetting off to an exotic destination, you probably don't expect stress or other mind problems to be high on the travel health agenda. Then again, heat, unfamiliar surroundings and lifestyle, and perhaps a lack of home comforts can mean that your holiday falls short of the stress-free nirvana you anticipated.

TRAVEL STRESS

Everything that makes travelling good can also make it stressful. You have to cope with a different physical environment as well as a new lifestyle; your normal points of reference are absent, and you're cut off from your usual support network of family and friends. Language difficulties, together with unfamiliar social and cultural cues can make communication problematic, even on a basic level.

Often the lead-up to the trip has been less than relaxing, as you rush around trying to get things done before you leave, and you often have jet lag to contend with on top of this. And then you're expected to enjoy yourself...

Unless you're on a short trip, you may find it helpful to factor in some time (and emotional space) for adjusting to your new situation. Remember:

- high levels of stress can make you less able to cope, with even minor difficulties and setbacks seeming like insurmountable hurdles

- you may feel frustrated and angry, taking your frustrations out on your travelling companions and other people you have to deal with

- stress can make you feel anxious or depressed, irritable, tired, unable to relax, and you may have difficulty sleeping (although this is often due to external causes)

- because you don't feel 100%, you may think you are physically ill, especially as the physical manifestations of anxiety can easily be mistaken for illness

- stress affects your immune system, making you more vulnerable to infections. Conversely, being physically ill affects you emotionally, often making you feel low and less able to cope

STRESS EFFECTS

Stress is thought to play a significant part in some conditions, including the following:

- tension headaches (by definition!)
- migraine
- asthma
- eczema
- irritable bowel syndrome
- premenstrual tension

- if you know you're sensitive to stress, or you've had emotional problems before (you may even have come away to escape them), you may find that, in the short term anyway, travelling can exacerbate your problems

Half the battle is recognising that the way you're feeling is because of stress rather than some worrisome tropical disease you've caught. An acute stress reaction is to be expected to some degree at the start of your travels and will probably ease by itself over the course of a few days, but you might want to activate some damage-control measures:

- take some time off to unwind: quit the tourist trail for a few days and do something completely different
- rest and try to catch up on any missed sleep (as a result of jet lag, overnight bus journeys, noisy hotel rooms etc)
- on the other hand, exercise is a great de-stresser, and worth a try if you've been stuck in trains or buses, or you're on an overland tour
- catch up on missed meals – stress is very energy-consuming
- try a de-stressing routine like aromatherapy, massage, yoga, meditation or just lying on a beach
- talk with fellow travellers, who may be experiencing similar emotions

CULTURE SHOCK & TRAVEL FATIGUE

People experience a well recognised set of emotional reactions following any major life event; when this occurs as a result of living (or travelling) for an extended period of time in a culture very different from your own, it's called culture shock. The culture shock syndrome is a well known hazard of living overseas for any length of time. It's unlikely to strike hard on a short trip, but you may notice it if you're on a long trip, especially if it is compounded by travel fatigue.

Culture shock can be thought of as a sort of psychological disorientation resulting from a conflict between your deeply ingrained cultural values and the different cultural cues and behaviours of the society you have relocated into. However broad-minded you may hope you are, deep down we all have a fundamental assumption that our own culture is right.

Culture shock doesn't happen all of a sudden – it progresses slowly, and affects some personalities more than others. Sometimes it doesn't progress, and you may get stuck at one stage. If you've been travelling a while, you'll probably recognise some of the stages and symptoms, as identified by Myron Loss in *Culture Shock – Dealing with Stress in Cross-Cultural Living*:

- euphoria, when everything is new and exciting
- hostility as the novelty wears off and the differences start to irritate – you may feel critical of your host country, stereotyping local people; you may feel weepy, irritable, defensive, homesick, lonely and isolated, perhaps worried about your physical health
- adjustment is when you start to feel more comfortable in your new lifestyle and with the new culture
- adaptation occurs when you lose that 'us and them' feeling

Here are some strategies you could try for minimising the impact of culture shock on yourself as well as on people you may come into contact with:

- accept that everyone experiences some degree of culture shock, and be prepared to recognise the symptoms as such

- find out about the country, people and culture before you go and when you're away – surprisingly, it doesn't have a huge effect but there are other good reasons for doing it

- look after your physical health – it's easier to feel positive if you feel well

- friendships and keeping in touch with home can help you feel less isolated

- you don't achieve anything by succumbing to the temptation of disparaging everything local

- having a sense of humour can help you keep your head above water – just think what good stories you'll be able to tell later

Travel fatigue is bound to affect you after you've been on the road for many months. It's a combination of culture shock, homesickness and generally feeling fed up with the hassles and inconveniences of life on the road.

ANXIETY

A certain degree of anxiety is a natural reaction to a change in lifestyle and environment, and you'll probably accept it as such. But there are situations when anxiety is a worry, either because it's over the top or because you misread the symptoms as something else.

Anxiety can take a number of forms, any of which can strike you for the first time when you're away, especially if you're a

STRANGE EXPERIENCES

Some serious illnesses like schizophrenia could theoretically be kick-started by the stress of travelling. If someone you are with starts experiencing signs like visual or auditory hallucinations, and delusions, they may need urgent medical help. They may not recognise that they are ill, which can make it frightening and confusing.

FEELING ANXIOUS?

Anxiety is the body's way of preparing for an emergency: the so-called fight or flight reaction. Symptoms are a result of physiological changes that take place, and include:

- palpitations, missed heartbeat or discomfort in chest
- over-breathing, shortness of breath
- dry mouth and difficulty swallowing
- stomach-ache, bloating and wind, diarrhoea
- needing to pass urine frequently
- periods stop
- premenstrual tension
- tremor and aching muscles
- pricking sensations
- headache
- dizziness and ringing in the ears

worrier by nature. If you have any preexisting anxiety-related problems, travel may exacerbate them.

If you recognise that anxiety is a problem, try some of the suggested short-term strategies for coping; you'll probably want to discuss longer-term methods of anxiety reduction with your doctor when you get home, especially if the problem is new or persistent. This is important because some physical diseases like thyroid and diabetic problems can cause anxiety symptoms, and your doctor may want to test for these.

Generalised anxiety often affects worriers; you feel restless, irritable and tired, stretched to the limit, with tension headaches and sleep problems. Any of the strategies for stress reduction listed at the beginning of the chapter may help; you could also try cutting out coffee and strong tea, both of which make tension symptoms worse. Drug treatment is usually only indicated if your symptoms are very severe and disabling.

> **!** Remember that alcohol withdrawal, perhaps after a binge or if you're a habitually heavy drinker, can be a cause of acute anxiety; it's best to avoid binges in the first place, and if you are a heavy drinker, it's best to cut down gradually.

Panic attacks can occur without warning and can be terrifying. They're marked by frightening physical symptoms as well as thoughts, and there's rarely a recognisable trigger. You feel like you're suffocating, you can't get enough air, and have palpitations, light-headedness, faintness and pins and needles. Often you have a feeling of being outside yourself, and everything seems unreal.

You'll probably recognise the symptoms if you've had an attack before, but if it's the first time, you may think you're dying. Sounds silly, but breathing in a controlled way in and out of a paper bag for a short time can help the symptoms of a panic attack. This is because when you panic, you start to over-breathe, and this causes you to feel light-headed and gives you pins and needles.

The main thing is to recognise what's happening, and to be reassured that you're not having a heart attack, and that it will pass eventually. Some general stress reduction is probably a good idea in the short term.

DEPRESSION

The blues can strike any time, even when you're on holiday. Stress, anxiety, disappointment, isolation and poor physical health can all make an attack of the blues likely. You know you've got it bad when you feel teary, listless and tired; you can't be bothered to do anything and nothing is enjoyable any more. You lose interest in sex and food (although sometimes you over-eat instead), you may have trouble sleeping and you just want to withdraw from the world.

Any physical illness can make you feel low, but some diseases are known for causing depression and fatigue, often for prolonged periods of time. Some notable culprits are viral diseases like flu, glandular fever, hepatitis and dengue fever; malaria is another. Other causes are anaemia and low thyroid function.

If it's just a simple case of the blues, you'll probably find that you bounce back in a few days, especially if you can identify and deal with the cause.

- Try any or all of the de-stress strategies listed on p237 and reassure yourself that it will pass.

- If you know you suffer from depression, try anything that has worked in the past.

- Exercise is known to stimulate the production of endorphins, which are natural feel-good factors.

CAFFEINE FIX

If you're feeling jittery, could it be that you've had one 'export quality' coffee too many? Caffeine, found in coffee, tea, cocoa, chocolate, cola drinks and even some medicines, is the most commonly used drug in the world. Latin America produces some excellent coffee, especially in Colombia and Brazil, and is the home of cacao, the source of chocolate.

Tea usually contains less caffeine than coffee, although this depends on the strength of your cuppa. A strong cup of coffee can contain up to about 120mg of caffeine, although a cup of normal-strength instant coffee probably contains about half this. A cup of average-strength tea contains about 50mg of caffeine, drinking cocoa contains about 20mg and cola drinks contain anything from 35 to 55mg. In addition to caffeine, coffee and tea contain weaker stimulants, including theobromine and theophylline.

- Maybe it's time to stop and re-think what you're doing, and perhaps to head home.

If your depression is a follow-on from a physical illness, it may be reassuring to recognise that this is the reason you are feeling low. It's also worth seeking medical advice, as antidepressant drug treatments may be helpful in this situation.

- If you think you may be depressed and things haven't improved over a couple of weeks, you should think about getting medical help. Depression is an illness, and it can be successfully treated with medication ('conventional' antidepressants or the herbal remedy St John's wort) or counselling. Severe depression can be very frightening and if it's not treated, you're at risk of suicide.

Caffeine has a stimulating effect on the brain, as well as effects on the heart and kidneys. Although small amounts of caffeine are undoubtedly beneficial in most people, too much caffeine is not. Caffeine excess can make you feel jittery and irritable, giving you palpitations, indigestion and insomnia. Through an effect on the kidney, caffeine increases the output of urine. Some people are more sensitive to the effects of caffeine than others, but most people are able to build up a tolerance. There may be a psychological effect at play too, as people often won't drink coffee at night-time but will drink cocoa or tea. Children are often very sensitive to caffeine, and their main source tends to be cola drinks and chocolate.

Caffeine is mildly addictive, and if you reduce or stop your intake suddenly, you can get withdrawal symptoms. These include headache, general irritability, tiredness, and, possibly, muscle aches.

PHYSICAL DISEASES & MIND PROBLEMS

✚ Depression and tiredness can follow several diseases, as discussed earlier under Depression.

Any serious physical illness, but especially infections, can cause delirium. This shows itself as confusion, restlessness, disorientation, sometimes hallucinations, and it can be difficult to persuade someone who is delirious to stay in bed or to take treatment. Treatment of the underlying illness will settle it. If you or someone you are with is this ill, seek medical attention urgently; in the meantime, take steps to bring down the fever and make sure the person doesn't hurt themselves.

Alcohol withdrawal is a specific form of delirium, and strikes people who are habitually heavy drinkers who suddenly stop (as can happen if they're ill and miss their usual alcohol intake). It's a serious, life-threatening condition, which needs medical advice urgently.

Some therapeutic drugs can cause problems with your mind. You may be aware that the antimalarial mefloquine (see p48) can cause a variety of symptoms, from abnormal dreams to panic attacks, depression and hallucinations. They're all more likely if you've had psychological problems in the past, and your doctor will usually have recommended an alternative drug in this case. If you're taking mefloquine, it will probably have been prescribed well before you leave, and you'll have had a chance to deal with any potential problems before you go. However, if you do experience problems while you're away, stop taking it and seek medical advice about alternative protection. Since mefloquine is only taken once weekly, you should be able to organise an alternative antimalarial (see Malaria Prevention in the Before You Go chapter) without any break in protection.

Some diseases affect the brain and can cause changes in behaviour or level of consciousness, such as concussion following a head injury (p446) or meningitis (p141).

DRINKS

Latin America is a great place for drinking – there's such a variety of alcoholic and nonalcoholic drinks available that it is hard to know where to start. Beer is very popular, usually available bottled or draught, while Chile and Argentina produce South America's best wine. Two favourite South American fermented brews include *pulque* (made from the sap of agave) and *chicha* (made from corn). To take the top of your head off, there's one of the many sugar-cane spirits, called variously *aguardiente*, *pinga* and *cachaca*.

It's probably a good idea to be wary of some local brews, especially distilled spirits, as they can contain additives you might not want to treat your system to. They can also contain methanol, a highly toxic form of alcohol, which has the potential to cause permanent blindness, among other things. Watch out for drinks diluted with unsafe water – alcohol won't necessarily make them safe to drink.

It's not just a question of what these drinks can do to you, however, it's also what they make you do to yourself. Before you begin a session, assess the potential risks – how are you going to get back to your hotel, for example. You're much more likely to have an accident while under the influence of alcohol or other drugs, and you're more likely to take unnecessary risks that you might regret later.

And if you wake up regretting that last tequila, remember that dehydration, especially in hot climates, causes many of the symptoms of a hangover. Drink lots of water before you go to sleep and if you wake up in the night (quite likely after all that fluid), make yourself drink another glass or two of water.

DELIBERATE DRUGGING

There are plenty of stories of travellers (and residents) who have been drugged and then robbed, sometimes worse. Several different drugs are used, including in Colombia a substance called *burundanga*, derived from the leaves of the borrachero tree, but the most infamous is probably the so-called 'date rape' drug, Rohypnol or flunitrazepam.

Flunitrazepam is a benzodiazepine drug, a family of sedatives that includes Valium (diazepam). Flunitrazepam is illegal in the US, but it is produced and sold in Latin America and Europe. The drug's effects begin about 30 minutes after taking it, and can persist for up to eight hours. It produces sedation (drowsiness), dizziness, memory impairment and confusion. It's not likely to kill you (although it is possible if you take it with in combination with other drugs and alcohol), sedation can be profound, and there have been reports of women being raped after they were drugged.

The manufacturer of Rohypnol, Roche, has produced a newer formulation that turns a dark blue colour when it is added to drinks, but the older colourless formulation may still be available. Be extremely wary of accepting drinks, food or even cigarettes from strangers.

DOING DRUGS

In many parts of Latin America, drugs of all varieties are easy to come by. If you do decide to take drugs, make sure you are aware of the legal and health consequences first. You can find out the legal status of different drugs at your destination from your travel guidebook, embassies and other sources of information. The health effects of doing drugs are widely publicised, but here's a brief summary of the main problems. See the Traditional Medicine chapter later in this book for a warning about trying *ayahuasca*, a local hallucinogenic.

By definition, these substances affect your mental state – this is after all the reason for taking them – but they can have unwanted or unexpected effects, especially if you're taking them for the first time.

- Acute anxiety or panic attacks are common with marijuana (and also LSD or mescaline), and are more likely if you're taking it in a stressful situation or for the first time.
- Acute paranoia ('persecution complex') can occur after taking cocaine, crack, amphetamines or ecstasy, and can be extremely frightening.
- Overdose can be fatal anywhere, but especially where you can't rely on the emergency services.
- If you're injecting drugs, never share needles with other users – for more details, see the section on Injections & Blood Transfusion in the Staying Healthy chapter.

Anxiety attacks or acute paranoia are likely to resolve without any specific treatment, although they may be pretty unpleasant at the time.

Just be aware that there's no quality control on the drugs you buy, and locally available substances can be unexpectedly strong or may be mixed with other harmful substances. You're at the mercy of sellers when it comes to quality of ingredients, and their main concern is unlikely to be your good health.

- Because unexpected reactions – including accidental overdose – can occur any time, you should never take drugs when you are alone.

Women Travellers...

Travelling can present some particular problems for women, and some women's health issues are a bit trickier to cope with on the road.

MENSTRUAL PROBLEMS

PRACTICALITIES

Although you shouldn't have a problem finding tampons and sanitary pads, especially in urban areas, it's probably best to take all you think you'll need with you. Disposal of used tampons and sanitary towels can be a major concern (and not just when you are travelling), especially in remote or environmentally sensitive areas. So what do you do?

- You could burn them; this is environmentally the best option, but it's hardly practical.

- If you're in the wilderness, you could bury them, but you will need to dig a decent-sized hole and cover it well.

- You could carry them out with you and dispose of them somewhere more convenient later.

- Reusable items are available from specialist shops selling environmentally friendly products, but they do rely on you having access to adequate water and washing facilities.

- Some women travellers recommend using a rubber cap device, worn in the vagina and similar to an upside-down diaphragm. It has to be removed every six to 12 hours to be rinsed and emptied then replaced. Between periods you carry it in a cotton bag in your luggage. The Keeper is one brand, and (wouldn't you know it) there's a website (**www.keeper.com**) where you can find out more.

Cleanliness is obviously even more important when you're travelling; wash your hands carefully before and after changing tampons, and change them regularly.

MENSTRUAL-FREE TRAVEL

If all this sounds too daunting for words, it is possible to take measures to temporarily prevent menstruation, for example if you're going on a trek in a remote area. Discuss this with your doctor before you go, but some options include the following.

- If you're taking the combined oral contraceptive pill, you could carry on taking the pill without the usual break (or skip the seven days of inactive pills), although it's not advisable for more than three cycles at a time and, if you're unlucky, you may have some breakthrough bleeding.

- For a short trip, norethisterone (a progesterone) can be used to postpone a period. You need to start taking it three days or so before menstruation is due to begin and continue until the end of the holiday (for up to two to three weeks); menstruation occurs again two to three days after stopping. The dose is 5mg three times daily and side effects are rare, but it's not suitable for long term use. It's not a contraceptive.

- An injected progesterone contraceptive produces light, infrequent periods or none at all in most women – great for when you're travelling. However, you need to have injections every eight to 12 weeks and the effect on menstruation is initially unpredictable.

PREMENSTRUAL SYNDROME

If you normally get period pains and premenstrual bloating, you may find these are worse while you are travelling, for a variety of reasons – physical and psychological stresses, unaccustomed heat and prolonged immobility (on long bus or plane journeys). If you think this could be a problem, take a good supply of a painkiller or any other remedies that you know work for you. Alternatively, you could consider starting the oral contraceptive pill before you leave, but it's best to sort this out in plenty of time before you go.

 Remedies that may be helpful include evening primrose oil, which can be taken in capsule form or as the oil, and vitamin B6, magnesium or calcium supplements. Or you could try the delightfully named Chaste tree (Vitex agnus castus) or dong quai, a herbal treatment widely used in Asia for 'women's problems'.

LIGHT OR ABSENT PERIODS

You often find that your periods disappear or become irregular when you're on the road, probably because of the mental and physical stresses of travel and the change to your usual routine. Other causes are pregnancy, drastic weight loss and hormonal contraceptive problems. Obviously the most important cause to exclude is pregnancy – see the section 'Am I Pregnant?' later in this chapter for more guidelines.

There's usually nothing to worry about, although if you don't have a period at all for more than about three or four months, it's a good idea to get a check-up. Periods usually get back to normal once you have finished your travels.

! New, severe period pains can be a result of a vaginal infection or a tubal pregnancy (if there's a chance you may be pregnant), so seek urgent medical advice in this case.

HEAVY PERIODS

Light or absent periods are great, but you can find that your periods become heavier or more frequent while travelling, so be prepared for either possibility!

! If your periods are heavier than usual, you may develop a mild anaemia; boost your diet with fresh fruit and green vegetables, or consider taking a multivitamin and iron supplement.

Heavy bleeding is often due to hormonal problems. If you suffer heavy persistent bleeding for more than seven days which shows no sign of lessening and you are in a remote area and unable to get medical advice, you could try taking norethisterone (a progesterone tablet) 5mg three times daily for 10 days (if you can find it). If you're prone to unpredictable bleeding, you might want to discuss taking a supply of norethisterone with you before you go.

Bleeding should stop by the end of the course and you should expect to have a period after about seven days of finishing the course. If the bleeding does not stop, you will need to seek medical advice urgently.

Note that this is only for emergencies, and you should not take it if there is any chance you may be pregnant, or if you have a history of gynaecological problems or are otherwise unwell – you must seek medical advice in all these cases.

! Abnormally heavy periods can be an indication of problems with the cervix or womb (such as pelvic inflammatory disease, fibroids, miscarriage), so you should try to find a doctor to get it checked out as soon as possible.

MENOPAUSAL & POSTMENOPAUSAL TRAVELLERS

Hot flushes can be worse while you are travelling, as hot weather, spicy meals and any sort of emotional upset can trigger them. It's probably worth discussing this with your doctor before you go so you can work out ways of dealing with it. If you're not taking hormonal replacement therapy, this could be an option to consider. Try simple measures to keep cool, such as wearing loose cotton clothing, not overexerting yourself, resting during the heat of the day and, if evening flushes are a problem, it may be worth making sure you have a room with a fan or air-conditioning. Cool drinks and eating small, frequent meals may also help.

 Many natural remedies can be helpful for menopausal symptoms, including the herb dong quai (for flushes), St John's wort (Hypericum perforatum, for depression), ginseng (to reduce sweating) and Bach flower remedies, so check these out with your practitioner before you go, and take a good supply with you.

Dry, itchy skin can be a problem at and after menopause. The physical hazards of travelling can exacerbate this, so take care to protect your skin from the sun and wind by using sunscreen and moisturisers.

Cystitis (see that section later in this chapter) can occur at any age but is very common after menopause, and travelling can make an attack more likely.

> ❗ If you're postmenopausal, and you're not on HRT, you need to seek medical advice for any vaginal spotting or bleeding that occurs, although if you're on a short trip, this can probably wait until you get back.

HRT & TRAVEL

As for any medication, it's best to take all you'll think you'll need with you. If you have an implant, will it be due for renewal while you are away? If you're going to be travelling in the heat, sweating and swimming may mean your patches stick less well, so you might want to consider changing to a tablet or gel preparation before you go.

If you're taking a preparation that induces bleeding, it may be possible to change to a different one that induces periods every three months instead of every month if a period is going to be inconvenient while you're travelling. Periods can be postponed by manipulating your progestogen dose, but this can sometimes lead to heavy bleeding, so it's best to discuss this with your doctor before leaving.

HRT makes you slightly more prone to thrombosis (blood clots) in your leg veins, especially if you're immobile for long periods of time, for example on a long flight or bus journey. A few things to try:

- take regular walks
- when you're sitting, wriggle your toes and flex your calf muscles
- support stockings or tights are an option but not a very attractive one in a hot climate
- drink plenty, as dehydration makes clotting more likely

If you're going to be at high altitude for any length of time, discuss this with your doctor before you go because you may be at greater risk of blood clots.

If you have been on HRT for some time and you develop heavy or irregular bleeding while you are away, it could indicate a problem with the lining of your womb (such as thickenings called polyps or even early cancer), and you should seek medical advice as soon as possible.

BLADDER INFECTION

Also called cystitis, the main symptom is having to empty your bladder frequently – great when you're travelling! Although you have to go more frequently, you only pass small quantities of urine, often with pain or a burning feeling and sometimes an ache in your lower abdomen.

Cystitis is often due to infection by bacteria that normally live in the bowel. It's very common in women. The reason for this is that, compared with men (who relatively rarely get cystitis), the tube leading to the bladder in women is short, making it easy for bacteria to enter the bladder. This is also why bladder infections often occur after sexual intercourse, and are more likely if you use the diaphragm for contraception.

If you think you've got cystitis:

- drink plenty of fluids to help flush the infection out; citrus fruit juice or cranberry juice (if you can find it) can help relieve symptoms
- take a non-prescription cystitis remedy (these usually contain an alkalinising agent like potassium citrate, sodium bicarbonate or sodium citrate) to help relieve the discomfort; alternatively, add a teaspoon of bicarbonate of soda to a glass of water
- if there's no improvement after 24 hours despite these measures, you may need a course of antibiotics

Get medical advice, but there are several antibiotic options for cystitis, including single dose treatment with trimethoprim 600mg, norfloxacin 800mg or ciprofloxacin 500mg (avoid all three in pregnancy). Other antibiotics (suitable in pregnancy) include amoxycillin (take two 3g doses 12 hours apart) or nalidixic acid (1g four times daily for seven days). Avoid any antibiotic you are allergic to – see p406 for more details.

> **!** If you have the symptoms described earlier, you almost certainly have cystitis, and it will almost certainly respond to a course of recommended antibiotics. If it doesn't, or if the symptoms recur quickly, you should seek medical advice so a urine test can be done to clarify what's causing your symptoms.

If cystitis is left untreated, there's a risk of the infection spreading to the kidneys, which causes a much more serious illness.

! Symptoms of a kidney infection include a high temperature, vomiting (sometimes) and pain in the lower back – you should seek medical attention in this case.

Just to confuse the issue, about a third of women with symptoms of cystitis don't have an infection at all (it may be a sort of 'irritable bladder' syndrome), so it's definitely worth trying some simple non-antibiotic measures first. It's worth bearing in mind that 'cystitis' can be caused by a sexually transmitted infection, so you should get this checked out if you are concerned, especially if you have any other symptoms such as an abnormal vaginal discharge.

! Help prevent cystitis by drinking plenty of fluids and making sure you don't hang on too long – empty your bladder at regular intervals. If you know that you are prone to cystitis, arrange to take a couple of courses of treatment with you in your medical kit.

VAGINAL INFECTIONS

If you've got a vaginal discharge that is not normal for you (more copious, abnormal colour, smelly) with or without any other symptoms, you've probably got an infection.

■ If you've had thrush before and you think you may have it again, it's worth self-treating for this (see following section).

■ get medical advice as you will need a laboratory test and an appropriate course of treatment.

■ It's best not to self-medicate with antibiotics because there are many causes of vaginal discharge, which can only be differentiated with a laboratory test.

Although candidiasis ('yeast' infection) is probably the best known cause of vaginal problems, and the one women are most likely to self-diagnose, it's worth remembering that it probably accounts for only 20% to 30% of all vaginal infections, which is a relatively small proportion. Sexually transmitted infections (such as gonorrhoea) are an important cause of vaginal discharge.

THRUSH (VAGINAL CANDIDIASIS)

If you don't already know, symptoms of this common yeast infection are itching and discomfort in the genital area, often in association with a thick white vaginal discharge (said to resemble cottage cheese). It's due to an overgrowth of the vaginal yeasts, usually the species called *Candida albicans*, which are present normally in the vagina and on the skin.

Many factors, including diet, pregnancy and medications, can trigger this infection, which is normally kept at bay by the acid conditions in the vagina and the normal balance of organisms. Heat, the oral contraceptive pill and antibiotics can all make an attack more likely, so it's no surprise that it's even more common when you're travelling.

Although candidiasis is not a sexually transmitted infection as such, it makes sense to treat your regular partner with an antifungal cream on the genital area for five days.

You can help prevent thrush by wearing cotton underwear and loose-fitting trousers or a skirt; it's a good idea to wash regularly but some soap and bath salts can make vaginal irritation and candidiasis more likely, so are best avoided.

If you have thrush, a single dose of an antifungal pessary (vaginal tablet), such as clotrimazole 500mg is an effective and convenient treatment. Short courses of three to 14 days are also available but are less convenient. Alternatively, you can use an antifungal cream (eg clotrimazole 1% or econazole nitrate 1%) inserted high in the vagina (on a tampon) instead of a pessary. The treatment can be used even if you're on a period. Antifungal cream can be used in addition to a pessary to relieve vulval itching. A vaginal acidifying gel may help prevent recurrences.

If you know you are prone to thrush, take a supply of pessaries or cream with you in your medical kit.

HEALTH TIPS FOR LESBIANS

Lesbians around the world have created some of the many resources that are now available to make your trip easier – it's worth the effort to do some research before leaving home. Wondering what to do miles from home when symptoms are already presenting is definitely a situation to be avoided.

If you can, make sure you are as healthy as possible before leaving home. Improving your fitness and general wellbeing can provide a buffer to the demands of travel and the health challenges in front of you. You might want to check out a lesbian health guide like *Caring for Ourselves – The Lesbian Health Book* (Jocelyn C White & Marissa C Martinez, eds) or any general women's health guides.

Enjoy your travel experience, but remember that simple safe sex precautions are even more vital when you don't know your partner's medical history. Lesbian sex is low risk, but this doesn't mean that it's no risk.

Avoid touching or tasting blood or body fluids. Use gloves and dental dams or another latex barrier with plenty of wet stuff and your favourite water-based lubricant. Note that extremes of heat can melt dental dams in their packaging.

Depending on where you are travelling, you may need to be creative, but never be careless. Don't share sex toys without washing them between each use; alternatively, cover them with condoms. Travelling into some countries with your toys on board can be a bit embarrassing, but let's face it, if tampons are in short supply, other womanly essentials will be totally out of stock. So plan ahead if you intend to play around.

> If you need further guidance on what women safely do together, then call your gay and lesbian switchboard for a local clinic, or visit any good gay and lesbian bookstore before you leave.
>
> And a final warning…beware the dreaded love bug. The authors of this section, one European and one Australian, met in North America, fell in love and have never recovered…
>
> Leonie Englefield & Caz Price

If you're stuck in a remote area without medication, you could use natural yoghurt (applied directly to the vulva or on a tampon and inserted in the vagina) to soothe and help restore the normal balance of organisms in the vagina. Sitting in or washing with a weak solution of vinegar or sodium bicarbonate may also help. If thrush is really being a nuisance, some nonspecific strategies you could try are cutting down on sugar and alcohol, and eating more plain live yoghurt.

BACTERIAL VAGINOSIS

Also known as nonspecific vaginitis or *Gardnerella* vaginitis, bacterial vaginosis is the most common cause of abnormal vaginal discharge. It can cause a range of symptoms, but the most common are odour (fishy) and discharge (white-grey).

Although it is more likely if you are sexually active, there's no evidence that it is transmitted by intercourse. It's not caused by any one organism – instead there's a general change in the whole vaginal environment, with the good guys, the lactobacilli that normally keep the vagina healthy, being replaced by a variety of bad guys.

Treatment is with an antibiotic, usually metronidazole 500mg twice a day for seven days.

SEXUALLY TRANSMITTED INFECTIONS

+ For a more detailed discussion of STIs, see the HIV/AIDS & Sexual Health chapter earlier in this book.

Prevention is definitely the aim with sexually transmitted infections (STIs). Symptoms include sores in the genital area, an abnormal vaginal discharge and sometimes cystitis symptoms.

- Signs of an STI are usually an abnormal vaginal discharge or sores in the genital area; sometimes it can cause symptoms of cystitis (see earlier in this chapter).
- Casual intercourse is risky anywhere in the world; asking your partner to use a latex condom helps prevent transmission of STIs, but is not 100% effective.
- Having an STI can make you more vulnerable to HIV infection.
- STIs need to be diagnosed and treated properly, as they can cause chronic pelvic inflammatory disease (in women) or infertility (women or men) later, so it's worth finding a doctor or clinic to get it checked out.
- It's important that your partner is treated for the STI as well.
- You may have an STI even if you have no symptoms – if you think you may have put yourself at risk, get a full check-up when you get home.

Trichomoniasis

This sexually transmitted infection often occurs together with other STIs. Symptoms include vaginal discharge (thick yellow), itchiness and sometimes discomfort on passing urine. About 50% of women with the infection don't have any symptoms. Men rarely have any symptoms, but partners must be treated to prevent reinfection. Treatment is with an antibiotic, usually metronidazole either in a single dose of 2g or 250mg three times daily for seven days.

CONTRACEPTION

It makes sense to discuss your contraceptive needs with your doctor or a specialist family planning clinic well in advance of travelling. Even if you're planning on celibacy, it's always worth being prepared for the unexpected.

There's a whole range of options available to you, so if one method doesn't suit, there's plenty more to choose from. Seek

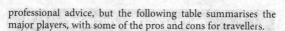

professional advice, but the following table summarises the major players, with some of the pros and cons for travellers.

> **!** New sexual partner? Go 'double Dutch' – use a barrier method in addition to a non-barrier method to protect yourself against HIV and STIs (and babies).

Contraceptives (including condoms) are generally widely available, but it's best to take your own supplies, as you may not be able to find exactly what you want when you want it. If you need contraceptive advice while you're away, you could try a local doctor, hospital or family planning clinic. If you do have to see a doctor, use common sense and choose someone you can trust. If you can't find a reputable female doctor, insist on having a chaperone present if you need to be examined.

ORAL CONTRACEPTIVE PILL

As for any medication, take enough (and some more) to last the entire trip, as your brand may not be available locally. If you are crossing time zones, or travelling at night, it can be easy to forget to take a pill:

- combined oral contraceptive (COCP) – make sure that you do not leave more than 24 hours before taking the next pill; take it earlier rather than later
- progesterone-only pill (POP) – the timing needs to be much more precise with this; if you're more than three hours late, you'll need to take additional contraceptive precautions for the next seven days

Vomiting or diarrhoea can mean the hormones are not absorbed properly and therefore that you are not protected. For either the COCP or POP:

- if you vomit or have severe diarrhoea less than three hours after taking the pill, take another pill
- if more than three hours, or if vomiting and diarrhoea persists, take the pill as normal, but take additional contraceptive precautions for the rest of the cycle

You should stop taking either the COCP or POP and use an alternative method of contraception if you get hepatitis

CONTRACEPTION OPTIONS

Method	Advantages on the Road
combined oral contraceptive pill	effective and reliable; periods may be lighter and PMT less
progestogen-only pill	useful for a selected group of women (eg older women, heavy smokers, migraine sufferers); not affected by antibiotics
Hormonal implants	effective and reliable; nothing to remember or lose; not affected by diarrhoea and vomiting or antibiotics; periods usually lighter and may disappear altogether; injection lasts eight or 12 weeks
intrauterine copper devices ('the coil')	convenient – nothing to remember or lose; reliable
Intrauterine progestogen	convenient and reliable; period pains are improved and periods are usually lighter and may disappear; STIs less likely to cause problems than with the coil and there's less risk of tubal pregnancy
diaphragm or cap	no hormonal side effects
female condom	available over the counter; less likely to rupture than male condoms
male condom	readily available; no mess – important if washing facilities are in limited supply; can be carried just in case

Disadvantages on the Road	Protects Against HIV, Hepatitis B & STIs?
only effective as long as you remember to take it! diarrhoea and vomiting, and some antibiotics, can reduce effectiveness; fluid retention side effect may be worse in hot climates	No
effectiveness reduced by diarrhoea and vomiting; small margin for error if you forget to take it	No
irregular bleeding can be a problem, especially at first; if you're going to be away on a long trip you will need to arrange when and where to have the next injection	No
STIs more likely to cause long term problems, so this method is not advisable if casual sex is likely; tubal pregnancy may be more likely	No
periods may be unpredictable at first	No
hygiene may be a problem when travelling; difficult to replace if lost; you need a refit (diaphragm) if you lose a lot of weight (4kg)	protects against some STIs, but not HIV
useability could be improved, but sense of humour may help	Yes
can split or leak – needs to be used correctly to be effective	Yes

MISSED A PILL?

If you miss a pill (either the combined oral contraceptive or progestogen-only pill), take the missed pill straight away, and take the next pill on time, even if it is the same day.

You'll need to use a different form of contraception for the next seven days in the following situations:

- progestogen-only pill: if you took it more than three hours late
- combined pill: if you took it 12 or more hours late

In addition, for the combined pill, if the seven days extend into the pill-free gap (or into the inactive pill interval), you should start the next course straight away without the usual break.

(jaundice), as the jaundice can interfere with the usual way in which the body deals with the pill.

Some common broad-spectrum antibiotics (such as ampicillin) can reduce the effectiveness of the COCP (but not POP); the UK Family Planning Association advises you should use additional contraceptive methods during a short course of these antibiotics and for seven days afterwards (the leaflet accompanying the pill packet will give you more guidance on which drugs to be careful with, but if in doubt, take extra precautions anyway). If you get to the end of the pill packet during the week after finishing the antibiotics, you should start the next packet straight away and take additional precautions.

At high altitude you get an increase in circulating red blood cells so there's a theoretical risk that side effects of the COCP like blood clots in the leg veins or lungs may be more likely. If you think this may be a problem for you, it's a good idea to discuss the issue with your doctor before you go.

INTRAUTERINE DEVICES (IUD)

If you can't feel the strings, you should assume you are not protected and use an alternative contraceptive method until you can get it checked out by a doctor.

! You should seek medical advice urgently if you develop low abdominal pain, especially with a fever and vaginal discharge; if you miss a period; or if you develop unusually heavy or painful bleeding.

BARRIER METHODS

See also Contraception in the Men Travellers chapter for more details on condoms. A couple of points to bear in mind:

- heat can cause rubber to perish so check your diaphragm for holes periodically, and try to keep it in a cool place
- consider taking a second diaphragm with you, especially if you are going to be away for a prolonged period of time

EMERGENCY CONTRACEPTION

In an emergency, you can try to prevent pregnancy following unprotected intercourse by taking a couple of high doses of oestrogen, which helps prevent the fertilised egg from settling in the lining of the womb.

Ideally, you should see a doctor who can prescribe the so-called 'morning-after' pill. You need to take two doses 12 hours apart, and you need to take the first dose as soon as possible within 72 hours of unprotected intercourse. The high dose of oestrogen may cause nausea and vomiting. If you vomit within two hours of either dose, the dose should be repeated. You should not take the morning-after pill if you are suffering from a severe migraine at the same time. Your next period may be either early or late. If you are taking the oral contraceptive pill, continue taking it as normal.

! The morning-after pill is not 100% foolproof; it's for emergencies only not for use as a regular method of contraception.

The morning-after pill usually prescribed contains ethinyloestradiol 50 micrograms and levonorgestrol 250 micrograms. The dose is two tablets followed by another two 12 hours later. The important ingredient is oestrogen (usually in the form of ethinyloestradiol). If it's not practical to seek medical advice, then see if you can buy a pill containing the same dose of oestrogen (check the packet or ask the pharmacist to tell you), and treat yourself as indicated in the previous paragraph. If you can't find a high-strength pill, you could use a 'normal' contraceptive pill, as follows:

- if the pill contains 20 micrograms of oestrogen, take five pills and then another five 12 hours later
- if the pill contains 30 micrograms of oestrogen, take three pills and another three 12 hours later

Another method of preventing pregnancy is to have an intrauterine contraceptive device inserted within five days, but you'd want a reliable doctor for this.

AM I PREGNANT?

If you have reason to be concerned about pregnancy, be suspicious if you miss a period (or have an unusually light one); other signs are enlarged, tender breasts and, although this is usually a later sign, nausea ('morning sickness'). So what do you do if you think you may be pregnant?

It's probably best to continue (or start) using a reliable contraceptive method (there is no evidence that the contraceptive pill harms the foetus, for example, so it's probably best to continue taking it until you know for certain that you are pregnant, especially if you are still sexually active).

Get a pregnancy test as soon as possible so that you have plenty of time to make arrangements – you may be able to buy a kit from a pharmacist in some big cities; otherwise, go to a doctor, clinic or hospital and ask for a pregnancy test to be done (note that a pregnancy test won't show positive before the first missed period). If it's negative, but you still think pregnancy is a possibility, wait two weeks and then repeat it.

If you're happy to be pregnant, you should see a doctor as soon as possible for blood tests and advice on optimising the outcome for you and the foetus. Some medications you may be taking (such as antimalarials) are known to be harmful to the foetus, also some diseases (including malaria and hepatitis A and E) may be more serious in pregnancy. For more details on travelling while pregnant, see that section later in this chapter.

If you decide you want to terminate the pregnancy, timing could be important: abortions are best done before (and in many Western countries can be difficult or impossible to obtain after) the 12th week of pregnancy (counting day one of pregnancy as the first day of your last menstrual period). In many developed countries, abortion is effectively available 'on demand' but this is not the case in many parts of the world, including in Latin America. In addition to social and ethical constraints, it may also actually be against the law of the country, so you should check this as soon as possible.

In addition, consider carefully where you would want to have the procedure done; it may be worth changing your travel plans to accommodate this. Remember that any surgical procedure carries a risk of HIV or hepatitis B transmission in a country with less developed medical services. In less competent hands, abortion carries significant risks of infection, blood loss and permanent infertility.

> You should avoid a 'back street' abortion at all costs – these are notoriously dangerous, and can result in long-term problems or even death.

PREGNANT TRAVELLERS

The days of seeing pregnancy as an 'indisposition' are long gone, and many women either choose or end up having to travel while they are pregnant, without any adverse effects on mother or foetus. However, there are some important considerations to bear in mind if you are planning to travel while you're pregnant, and these are summarised in this section. We should stress that this is to give you an idea of the issues that may be involved – you should seek expert medical advice well before you plan to go on any trip.

! If you've had complicated pregnancies before, or you're expecting twins, it would be best to postpone your trip.

WHEN?

Most doctors would suggest that the best time to travel in pregnancy is during the middle 12 weeks, when the risk of complications is less, the pregnancy is relatively well established and your energy levels are getting back to normal.

Before the 12th week, there is a relatively high risk of miscarriage (which could require surgical treatment like a scrape of the womb lining or even a blood transfusion) or a tubal pregnancy, which occurs in about one in 200 pregnancies and nearly always requires surgical treatment; it is an emergency situation. In addition, many women experience morning sickness in the first three months (sometimes for longer), which could make travelling less than enjoyable. Occasionally, it can be severe enough to require treatment in hospital. More mundane, but just as incapacitating for travelling, is needing to empty your bladder more frequently as the enlarging womb takes up more room in the pelvis and presses on the bladder.

! Note that most airlines prohibit flying after the 35th week of pregnancy (sometimes this can be waived if you have a doctor's certificate to say that there are no complications) – this is because they don't want to risk a woman going into premature labour on a flight, not because there's thought to be any intrinsic danger to the pregnancy.

In the last three months, major complications such as premature labour, blood pressure problems and problems with the placenta can all occur, so you would probably not want to risk a trip of any length during this time.

WHERE?

! It's best to avoid travelling to a high-risk malarial area if you're pregnant because malaria is very much more serious in pregnant women, and can have disastrous effects on the foetus. Some of the more effective antimalarial drugs are not suitable to take in pregnancy, which makes it even riskier.

You need to take into account the standard of medical facilities and the safety of blood for transfusion, in case any complications occur while you are away. For the same reason, it's probably not a good idea to plan a trip to remote areas while pregnant, in case complications occur that need to be treated urgently. High altitude trekking or scuba diving, assuming you'd want to do either of these activities in mid-pregnancy, are not advisable either.

IMMUNISATIONS & MALARIA PREVENTION

Your best bet is to make sure you're up to date with all your vaccinations before you get pregnant. Generally, it's best to avoid all vaccinations in the first 12 weeks of pregnancy, as there's a theoretical risk of harm to the foetus and miscarriage. In addition, 'live' vaccines ideally should be avoided at any time during pregnancy. Live vaccines include yellow fever and oral typhoid. You may be able to get a certificate of exemption for yellow fever if necessary. Hepatitis A is a much more serious illness in pregnancy, so it's important to be protected against it with the hepatitis A vaccine, and to take food and water precautions. An inactivated polio vaccine can be used instead of the usual oral live vaccine in pregnant women if necessary. A tetanus booster can be given safely in pregnancy, and tetanus protection is conferred to the newborn.

Travel to malarial areas is not recommended but if necessary, preventive medication is considered safer than risking the disease in pregnancy. Chloroquine and proguanil are considered safe in pregnancy, although you may need a folic acid supplement with proguanil, and this combination is not highly protective as resistance has increased. Mefloquine can be used in the last 24 weeks of pregnancy, although it should be avoided if possible for emergency treatment. If prevention fails, quinine is known to be safe in pregnancy for emergency treatment (for more details, see Malaria in the Fever chapter earlier in this book).

SPECIAL CONSIDERATIONS

All the predeparture preparations discussed in the Before You Go chapter apply if you're pregnant, but there are some special considerations for pregnant travellers. Be prepared, especially if this is your first pregnancy. It's a good idea to read up on pregnancy before you go so you have an idea of what to expect (such as tiredness, heartburn etc) and are familiar with any minor problems that may arise. Discuss these with your doctor, and work out strategies for coping in advance.

! Make sure you are clear on what your travel health insurance covers you for during pregnancy.

As a general rule, you should avoid unnecessary medications when you are pregnant. Don't take any medications while you are away unless you know they are safe in pregnancy (read the information leaflet or packaging, or ask a reliable doctor or pharmacist). It's a good idea to take a well stocked medical kit with you, with suitable medications for common problems, so that you are clear on what you should and shouldn't take while you are away.

Long flights or bus rides increase the risk of blood clots in the legs, so if possible try to get up and walk around, drink plenty of water and consider wearing support stockings to reduce this risk on a long flight.

Every traveller should take steps to avoid illness, but it's even more important in pregnancy, when illnesses can have more severe effects both on your health and your baby's. Prevent insect bites, take food and water precautions, and avoid risk situations for accidents.

During pregnancy, your immunity is lower; infections, such as cystitis and chest infections, can be more severe and should be treated with antibiotics early – get medical advice. In the tropics you may be less tolerant of the heat. Rest, drink plenty of fluids and give yourself lots of time to adjust.

It's a good idea to make sure you eat a well balanced, nutritionally sound diet during the trip. Avoid potential problem foods like raw or partially cooked eggs, peanuts and peanut products, and soft cheeses. You can get toxoplasmosis by eating undercooked meat in many countries in the region. It can cause a mild flu-like syndrome in adults, but can result in birth defects in unborn children.

And all the general advice about not smoking and being careful with alcohol obviously holds true wherever you are.

Men Travellers...

There are some conditions that only men travellers are in line for...besides, we didn't want you to feel left out.

JOCK ITCH (CROTCH ROT)

Hot, humid climates, tight underwear and infrequent washing all make this fungal infection more likely while you're travelling. It can occur in women, but it more usually affects men...as you might have guessed from these affectionate terms.

It produces itching and soreness in the groin area and inner thighs. Inspection reveals a red, flaky rash, sometimes with blisters.

Keep the area clean and dry, but do not over wash with soap, as this may increase the irritation. Wearing cotton shorts rather than close-fitting underpants can also help. An antifungal powder or cream (such as clotrimazole, econazole or miconozole) should be applied twice a day for at least seven days.

PAINFUL TESTICLE

You should seek medical advice urgently if you develop a sore testicle. If the pain started suddenly, and the testicle is swollen and red, it may be due to torsion. This is when the testicle gets twisted, which cuts off its blood supply – with the risk of irreversible damage. This is an emergency situation, as you may need surgery to fix the problem. While not specific to travellers, it demands attention if it occurs.

If the pain has come on more gradually, it may be due to an infection, often a sexually transmitted one like chlamydia (common) or gonorrhoea (less common). You may have noticed other symptoms, such as a discharge from the penis, and the testicle will feel hot and tender. You may have a fever. You will probably need a course of antibiotics to treat the infection, so it's best to seek medical advice.

Pain in the testicle can be due to a problem elsewhere, eg stones in the urinary tract (see p173), when the testicle will look and feel normal to the touch.

LUMP ON TESTICLE

Feeling your testicles for lumps is a good habit to get into, although travelling may not provide the ideal environment for doing it in – it's usually best in a hot bath or shower. If you do feel a lump, or you think one of your testicles has changed in shape or feel (eg it feels harder), you should get this checked out as soon as possible. Testicular cancer, although uncommon, tends to strike younger men. If diagnosed and treated early, it often has a very good outlook. Note that it's normal for one testicle to be larger than the other, so you should be looking for any change in either testicle.

CONTRACEPTION FOR MEN

If you're planning on being sexually active with a new partner (or even if you're not), you'll probably want to make some preparations in this department. Your choices are limited, admittedly, and probably boil down to condoms, which are sensible anyway, as you will need to protect yourself from STIs and HIV. Condoms are generally widely available throughout the region, although they may be difficult to obtain in rural areas.

Some points to bear in mind about condoms include:

- rubber condoms can disintegrate in the heat – try to keep them cool if possible and check them carefully before use
- if buying locally, check expiry dates and buy only items that are likely to have been stored properly (out of direct sunlight)
- local brands may be less reliable than international brands, and sizes can vary, so you may want to take a supply with you
- many commonly available lubricants cause rubber to perish, so be careful with what you use

SEXUALLY TRANSMITTED INFECTIONS (STIS)

These infections can cause genital sores, discharge from the penis and/or burning when you pass urine, but be aware that you can have an infection even if you don't have any symptoms. You need to seek medical advice if you notice any of these symptoms, so that the most appropriate antibiotic treatment can be given. For more information on STIs, including HIV/AIDS, see the HIV/AIDS & Sexual Health chapter earlier in this book, or visit your local sexual health clinic before you go.

PROSTATE PROBLEMS

While there's no reason why you shouldn't travel if you've got symptoms of prostate enlargement, it's probably a good idea to discuss this with your doctor in advance, especially if you are going to be travelling in remote areas. That way, you can work out strategies for dealing with any problems that might arise while you're away. The main concern is if you become unable to pass urine at all; in this scenario you will need to have a tube (catheter) inserted up the penis into the bladder to drain it manually. It's not something that you can accurately predict, so in certain situations it might be appropriate to take a sterile catheter set with you.

! If you are unable to pass any urine at all for more than 24 hours (you'll probably feel very uncomfortable before this) seek medical advice urgently.

TRAVEL HEALTH FOR GAY MEN

Glen Monks, UK-based Health Promotion Specialist for gay men and drugs, has the following tips for gay men.

BEFORE YOU GO

Try to get hold of the telephone number of a gay advice/support agency in the country(ies) you are visiting and also the number of an HIV/AIDS advice/support service or helpline. Try your travel guidebook or *Spartacus*, the international gay guide, which has listings for each country. Your local service at home should also have listings.

If you're HIV-positive, it's a good idea to consult your specialist for advice on possible risks before you travel as vaccination advice (eg Yellow Fever vaccine) can be more complex.

✚-For more information on travelling with HIV, see the Travellers
with Special Needs chapter.

CONDOM CARE

Extra-strong condoms and water-based lubricant form the
essential safer sex toolkit for gay men. You need to protect
yourself from HIV and other sexually transmitted infections
(STIs) even more when travelling than you do when you're
at home.

For more information about condom availability and care,
see that section in this chapter. Note that in some countries it is
impossible to find extra-strong condoms and water-based lube,
so it's best to take a plentiful supply with you.

IMMUNISATIONS

See the section on Immunisations in the Before You Go chapter
for general recommendations on this, but note that hepatitis
A and B can both be transmitted through sex and are fairly
common among gay men. Hepatitis A is passed on through
human faeces, so sex or even handling used condoms may
present a risk.

GAY ABANDON

Everyone, no matter their sexuality, tends to be less inhibited
away from home. Letting you hair down and having some fun
is fine, so long as you don't put yourself and others at risk.

Personal safety is paramount. If you're the new boy in town
and agree to go back to some other guy's place, are you getting
into a vulnerable position? Is there someone else who knows
where you'll be? How will you get home?

Remember that the law on sex between men varies greatly
around the world, as does the policing of public sex venues
and cruising sites. Public attitudes differ too, so find out about
this before you go – try your travel guidebook or gay groups at
home for information on this.

Be prepared: some people will be very upfront about safer
sex and others very coy. The key thing, whatever your cultural

disposition, is to avoid getting or passing on HIV and other STIs. To do this, however awkward it might feel and however many language barriers there seem to be, you will need to raise the subject of condoms and lubricant and make sure that you use them. Remember, you're the one on vacation, not HIV.

AFTER THE FUN
Few of us are saints all the time. If you have any concerns at all, it's a good idea to pay a visit to your sexual health or HIV clinic when you get back home.

Babies & Children...

The whole of this book applies as much to children as it does to adults (except where we've indicated otherwise), but in this chapter we've highlighted some of the health issues that are especially relevant when you're travelling with babies or young children. Children can be surprisingly adaptable to climate and time changes, but you need to bear in mind that they are more susceptible to disease and accidents, and to take appropriate precautions to protect them. Children also change very quickly – they can deteriorate or improve within a matter of hours – so it's important to be vigilant, especially with young children.

BEFORE YOU GO

Good preparation is the key to a successful trip with babies or children, so it's worth putting a bit of effort into this before you go.

SPECIAL CONSIDERATIONS

Some issues to consider when you are planning your trip are the age of your children and what type of holiday is likely to suit you and them best, as well as the specific health risks of your destination and what medical facilities are available locally. Latin American society is very family-oriented and people generally think the world of children, which makes it a great place to come with a family. Health-wise, some countries obviously present more hazards than others; generally the less-developed, tropical countries in the region are likely to be more problematic. Bear in mind that travel in some Andean countries (such as Bolivia) involves high altitude and exposure to climatic extremes.

As far as age is concerned, it's mainly to do with diet and ease of transportation, as well as the potential for boredom. Babies are easy to feed (if they are exclusively breastfed), they're relatively easy to carry around in a sling and you don't need to worry about them getting bored by sightseeing. On the other hand, they are a concern if they get sick, they can quickly become dehydrated and are very sensitive to heat and sun. Toddlers are more complicated to feed, transport around and to keep amused and safe, particularly around water. Obviously it's best to avoid travelling during toilet training.

Staying in a resort is probably going to be easier than a backpacking-type holiday involving lots of long journeys, although this may depend on your children's temperament and ages. It's worth researching exactly what is available for the children before you go.

Health risks depend as much on the type of holiday you're planning as on the location. Backpacking through remote areas exposes you to more risks than staying in an upmarket hotel in a resort area. Don't assume that international-type hotels will necessarily have the standards of water quality and general cleanliness that you are used to. It's a good idea to find out about medical services at your destination, especially if your child has an ongoing condition like asthma, diabetes or epilepsy that may need treatment while you are away.

SOURCES OF INFORMATION

See the Before You Go chapter earlier in this book for contact details of travel health clinics and other information sources. Some travel health providers and other commercial health-related organisations have good leaflets and information sheets for travelling parents, including Nomad Travel Stores & Travel Clinics (listed under Sources of Information & Advice in the Before You Go chapter) and the UK-based chain of pharmacies, Boots the Chemist.

Many of the travel health websites listed in the Before You Go chapter have items on travelling with children, some more informative than others. Try the Travel Doctor-TMVC website for a good, helpful summary written from personal experience.

If your child has an ongoing condition (such as diabetes or asthma), contact your national organisation or support group, as they often have good information for travellers – for more details, see the section on Travellers with Special Needs in the Before You Go chapter.

An excellent, comprehensive guide for parents is *Your Child's Health Abroad* by Dr Jane Wilson-Howarth & Dr Matthew Ellis. For a useful insight into travelling with children of various ages, Lonely Planet's *Travel With Children* has loads of practical suggestions.

DOCTOR & DENTIST

It's a good idea to make sure your child is as healthy as possible before you go. When you see your doctor to discuss any immunisations and malaria preventives your child may need, take the opportunity to discuss basic preventive strategies and to work out a plan of action for problems that are likely to occur, like diarrhoea or fever.

If your child has an ongoing condition like eczema, diabetes or asthma, it's best to be clear about what to do if the condition worsens while you are away, and to make sure you have a plentiful supply of any medications they normally take.

It's worth making sure your children have a dental check-up before going away, but remember to leave enough time for any treatment to be carried out if necessary.

IMMUNISATIONS

It's just as important for children to be protected against diseases through immunisation as it is for you. They should be up to date for all routine childhood immunisations and, in addition, they'll need the same travel-related vaccines as you – see the Immunisations section in the Before You Go chapter for more guidance on this. This is especially important if your child is going to be in close contact with local children while you are away.

Most fully immunised school-age children won't need further doses of routine immunisations, but babies and younger children who haven't completed their normal childhood immunisations may need to complete the schedules earlier than normal. You should discuss this with your doctor when you start planning your trip.

Note that some vaccines have age limits or are best avoided in childhood – discuss this with your doctor. For example:

- diphtheria and tetanus (usually with pertussis, as DTP) – the first dose can be given at six weeks of age if necessary
- polio can be given at six weeks if necessary
- measles can be given at six months of age if necessary (it's normally given as part of the MMR vaccine at 15 months of age) – measles is common in many Latin American countries and can be a serious illness; mumps and rubella are less of a worry

Travel-related vaccines that your child may need include the following:

- hepatitis A vaccine can be given from the age of one year (two years in the US
- typhoid and meningococcal meningitis vaccinations aren't normally given below two years of age; young children may be more susceptible to meningitis
- rabies (preexposure) vaccine isn't normally given before the age of one year; you should be aware that children are more at risk of rabies because they tend to want to pat animals and they may not tell you if they have been bitten; also they're more likely to get bites to the head and neck, which carry a greater risk of rabies
- yellow fever can be given from nine months, usually after twelve months
- tuberculosis (not used in the US) and hepatitis B vaccines have no lower age limit
- influenza vaccine can be given to children from six months of age

If your child is going to have a reaction to an immunisation, this will usually occur about 48 hours after the injection and generally settles with a dose or two of paracetamol (acetaminophen) syrup or suppositories. Note that children can go on to have further reactions and sometimes develop rashes 10 days after the immunisation, so the earlier you get this organised, the better.

MALARIA PREVENTION

For more general information on malaria risk and prevention, see the Preventing Malaria section of the Before You Go chapter earlier in this book.

! **Malaria is very dangerous in children, and you should think very carefully before taking children to malaria risk zones in Latin America – discuss this fully with your doctor or travel health clinic.**

If you do take children into a malarial area, it's absolutely vital to protect them by taking steps to avoid mosquito bites and giving them antimalarial drugs. Chloroquine, proguanil and quinine are known to be safe in children of all ages, and mefloquine can be given to babies over three months. Mefloquine should be avoided if your child has any history of seizures. Doxycycline should not be given to children under 12 years because of potential side effects (may stain teeth and retard growth).

Note that if you are taking malaria prevention medication yourself and you are breast feeding your child, you will still need to give your child antimalarials.

! **Be careful to keep antimalarials out of reach of children – even a few tablets overdose of chloroquine can be fatal in small children.**

Getting your children to take their malaria pills can be a real challenge, as only chloroquine is available in suspension form (in some countries). You may have to resort to crushing the tablets into a powder and disguising them in a small amount of food or drink.

! **If it's a battle to persuade your child to take the medication, it can be tempting to stop as soon as possible; however, it's very important your child carries on taking antimalarials for four weeks after leaving a malarial area – otherwise, they are at risk of getting malaria.**

EMERGENCY TREATMENT FOR MALARIA

If you are going to a malarial area (not advisable – see the cautions in the previous section), it may be necessary to carry a dose of malaria treatment for your child. You need to discuss this fully with your doctor or travel health clinic before you go. Make sure you are clear about when you might need to use it.

NAPPIES, FORMULA FEED & BABY FOOD

It's worth taking a plentiful supply of nappies (diapers) with you. Washable nappies and liners tend to take up less luggage space than disposable nappies and are more eco-friendly. If you need them, you should be able to find disposable nappies in most towns and tourist centres in Latin America, although they are less easy to find in rural areas. It's the same story for tins of baby food, although formula feed is widely available.

Disposing of nappies can be a headache as well as an environmental nightmare, especially in countries where waste disposal systems are less than ideal (most of Latin America). Washable nappies (worn with a liner) rely on you having access to water and washing facilities, but are a good alternative. You could burn disposable nappies (not a very practical option); otherwise, it's probably best to take a supply of large plastic bags or nappy sacks with you and to dispose of them as thoughtfully as you can.

MEDICAL KIT & MEDICATIONS

It's a good idea to take a child-specific medical kit in addition to your own basic medical kit (for detailed suggestions on what to include for yourself, see the What to Take section in the Before You Go chapter). If your child takes any medications regularly (for asthma, eczema or diabetes, for example), remember to take a good supply of these with you.

You'll need to include something for pain and fever, for example paracetamol (acetaminophen) syrup or suppositories for little ones, Junior paracetamol (acetaminophen) for older children or ibuprofen paediatric syrup.

Consider taking a course of antibiotics with you for treating common ailments like ear infections or coughs, especially if

MEDICATIONS TO AVOID

Some drugs you might be prescribed if you get ill should be avoided in children under the age of 12 years because of the possibility of side effects. Drugs to avoid in children include:

- for pain and fever – aspirin and aspirin-like drugs
- antibiotics – ciprofloxacin and doxycycline
- antidiarrhoeals – loperamide, diphenoxylate, bismuth
- antimalarials and malaria treatment – mefloquine before the age of three months; doxycycline in children below 8 years

If you are at all uncertain about the dose or whether the medicine is suitable for children, check with a doctor before giving it.

you are planning on going to remote areas in less developed countries, where you may not have ready access to medical care or supplies.

Discuss your individual needs with your doctor, but some suitable antibiotics include co-amoxiclav, cephalexin or clarithromycin (if your child is allergic to penicillin). See the section on Antibiotics in the appendix on Buying & Using Medicines for more details.

Take a plentiful supply of oral rehydration salt sachets, barrier cream for nappy rash, calamine cream or aloe vera gel for heat rash and sunburn, motion sickness remedies, sunscreen, antiseptic wipes and antiseptic liquid or spray. Sterilising tablets are a good idea for cleaning feeding utensils, or you might want to consider taking a sterilising unit with you.

If you do need to give your child medication, remember they will generally need a child-sized dose, and not all medications are suitable for children. Follow the dosing instructions given by your doctor or on the packet. Doses are generally worked out from how much your child weighs, so it's a good idea to have a rough idea of this before you go away.

It's a good idea to carry plastic spoons (5mL and 2.5mL) with you for measuring out doses of liquid medications. A plastic syringe (5mL or 10mL) can be handy for giving medicine (and fluids) to a reluctant patient.

ON THE MOVE

Long journeys aren't always going to be a bundle of fun with children, so be prepared! Consider arranging your itinerary to minimise the number of long journeys you have to do, or consider alternative means of getting around (such as flying instead of taking a two day bus journey). For toddlers or older children, travelling at night may be one solution, although it might be exhausting for you. Take plenty of travel games, puzzle books, reading books, colouring books and electronic games. A new toy might just provide enough interest to last a journey.

Trains tend to have more scope for running around than buses. It might be worth checking on the toilet situation for any mode of transport you choose, although most bus drivers are likely to be sympathetic to the vagaries of children's bladders. It's always worth checking the seating arrangements for young children, as you may be expected to keep your child on your knees for the journey.

On flights, air pressure changes can cause ear pain in babies and young children – for more details, see the section on Ears in the Ears, Eyes & Teeth chapter earlier. Older children can be encouraged to blow their noses, which should help their ears to pop. Younger children and babies can be given decongestant nose drops if necessary (get these from your doctor or pharmacist before you go) as well as paracetamol (acetaminophen) syrup to ease the pain. Give the syrup approximately one and a half hours before landing. If you are

COPING WITH JET LAG

Travelling eastwards is potentially the most difficult for your child to cope with. Allow your child to get plenty of sleep. You could consider using a mild sedative, eg an antihistamine like promethazine. When you arrive, slot your child into their new routine immediately. Serve their meals at the correct time and put them to bed at the local time. Also spend plenty of time outside because light (particularly sunlight) and physical activity in the first half of the day will help the body clock to adjust faster.

Be aware that our body temperature falls during the night and initially this will occur in the middle of your new day. Even though you may have travelled to a warmer climate, your child may require warmer clothes for a few days before their body clock adjusts.

John Mason

bottle feeding during the flight, try to sit the baby or toddler upright as far as possible, as feeding can sometimes increase the ear discomfort. Note that if your child has an ear infection or a bad cold, you should postpone flying until it is better.

Motion sickness is extremely common in children – if you know yours is prone to it, consider using an anti-sickness remedy like promethazine (follow the dosing guidelines, and note that it's not recommended for children under two years) or ginger. Promethazine has the added advantage that it often makes your child sleepy – possibly sanity-saving on a long journey – although the effects are very variable. A naturopathic soothing alternative is chamomile.

Bear in mind that children (and adults) can get thirsty and hungry on journeys very quickly, which is one preventable reason for bad temper. You might want to make up some milk beforehand if you're bottle feeding, although it will only keep for a limited amount of time, or you can get bottles with powder and water which you can mix up when you need. It's always a good idea to take a few snacks and cartons of drink for giving out to little ones on the journey. A change of clothing and plenty of wipes and tissues are always a good idea to have on hand for the inevitable spills.

STAYING HEALTHY

FOOD, WATER & CLEANLINESS

For most destinations in Latin America, you need to be more careful about food, water and general cleanliness than you would be normally. If possible, breastfeed babies and young toddlers, as this reduces their risks of getting diarrhoea through ingesting contaminated food and water. If you give babies and children water, use only boiled water (allowed to cool) or bottled water, and if you are bottle feeding, remember to use only boiled or bottled water to make up the formula. Iodone is best avoided in children under 12 years, although chlorine tablets are an alternative. You'll probably want to avoid giving children carbonated and other soft drinks, but packet fruit juices and UHT milk are usually available and make safe substitutes.

If you can, try to prepare any food for babies yourself, making sure that the utensils you use are sterile (take sterilising tablets with you). For more details on food to avoid, see Food & Water Precautions in the Staying Healthy chapter earlier.

Children who are crawling or just walking are particularly at risk of diseases spread via dirt, so take care to wash hands and faces frequently throughout the day, especially if you're travelling on public transport, and discourage wandering hands in the mouth, eyes and nose as far as possible. A supply of wet wipes can be invaluable, especially on long journeys.

If you get sick with diarrhoea yourself, be extremely careful to wash your hands after using the toilet to avoid passing diarrhoea to your child. However, it works both ways: be careful with nappies and other sources of contamination if your child has diarrhoea to prevent it passing to you.

DIET & NUTRITION

There are lots of reasons why your child may not want to eat while you are away. New foods can induce surprise and a reflex refusal, stress and new surroundings can distract children from eating and the heat can often reduce even the healthiest of appetites. Try to introduce new foods gradually, perhaps starting before you leave, and consider taking a supply of familiar dry foods with you to provide an element of continuity. If the local cuisine is not proving a hit, Western-style dishes are often available, especially in touristed areas.

If you're on a long trip, try to make sure your child has as balanced a diet as possible, including a source of protein (beans, meat or fish), fresh fruit (peeled) and vegetables (peeled and cooked). Even if your child isn't inclined to eat, fluids are a must, especially if it's hot.

INSECT BITES

Biting insects carry a number of serious diseases, including malaria, so it's extremely important to protect your child from this hazard. For more details, see the section on Preventing Insect Bites in the Staying Healthy chapter, but the main messages are to make sure your child is covered up with clothes, socks and shoes, and to use insect repellents on exposed areas – either DEET-containing repellents or the new natural repellents containing lemon eucalyptus. Permethrin-soaked mosquito nets are very effective at preventing bites at night and during daytime naps (the mosquito that spreads dengue fever bites during the daytime).

Try to discourage scratching of bites if they do occur, as this often leads to infection. Keep fingernails cut short and use calamine cream or a sting relief spray to ease irritation.

ACCIDENTS & OTHER HAZARDS

Children tend to be accident-prone at the best of times, but the hazards are even greater when you're travelling, so you need to be even more vigilant than normal. Road traffic is often chaotic and unpredictable, and pavements (sidewalks) nonexistent. If you're travelling in a motor vehicle, seat belts and child safety seats are often absent. Most hotel rooms and restaurants are not built with children in mind and may have a nightmare-inducing lack of safety features, particularly where windows and balconies are concerned. Some precautions:

- be on the look out for potential risk situations and unsafe features
- keep all medications in child-proof containers and out of reach of prying fingers
- try to be aware of what your child is doing at all times, especially if they're playing outside
- consider using a harness for toddlers when you're travelling or walking in crowded places
- make sure your child has some form of identification on them at all times, including details of where you are staying
- never let your child touch any domestic or other animals
- if you're planning to travel by car, consider taking a child safety seat with you
- drowning is surprisingly common – be particularly vigilant around swimming pools or at the beach, and remember that drowning can occur in shallow water as well as deeper water
- check new beaches for debris, discarded hypodermics, glass and tins, as well as various offerings left by people and animals

In addition, children's natural curiosity and fascination with all creatures great and small make them more vulnerable to insect and scorpion stings, snake bites and animal bites. For more details on these hazards, see the Bites & Stings chapter later in this book.

POISONOUS PLANTS

Small children are attracted like magnets to plants, particularly if they are colourful and look appetising. Toddlers will eat almost anything, regardless of taste. Children need to be supervised, especially if they are somewhere outdoors with access to plants and bushes. Contact with some plants and grasses may go unnoticed until a reaction occurs.

Some plants and grasses can cause toxic or allergic reactions when they come into contact with bare skin, so it's best to make sure your child is covered up if they are playing in grassland. This will help protect them from insect bites too.

If you catch your child eating a plant, keep a sample for identification. Watch for any symptoms, and encourage your child to drink plenty of fluids to help dilute any potential toxic effects. If possible, seek expert advice. If this is not available, you can induce vomiting by giving your child ipecacunha syrup (if you can find it) – but be aware that some experts believe children should never be given ipecacunha. This is usually only effective within four hours of eating a suspect plant, but it may be worth trying while you find medical help.

John Mason

CUTS & SCRATCHES

This is something to be particularly vigilant about, as it can be difficult to keep children clean, especially if they are running or crawling around. Any break in the skin can rapidly become infected in warm, humid climates – wash any break in the skin carefully with soap and water or antiseptic solution (or an antiseptic wipe if you haven't got access to water) and keep it covered with a sterile, non-adherent, non-fluffy dressing (a sticking plaster is fine if the wound is small). It's probably worth checking your child carefully at the end of each day for cuts, scratches and potentially problematic bites. Itchy insect bites are a common source of infection – another reason for making a strenuous effort to avoid them in the first place.

SUN

Anyone can get sunburnt but little ones are especially vulnerable and need to be protected as much as possible from the sun's harmful rays. Keep them covered up (for example with a long-sleeved T shirt and long trousers or skirt and hat, or an all-over sunsuit – popular in Australia and available elsewhere). Apply liberal amounts of the highest factor sunscreen you can find on any exposed skin and re-apply it frequently. Avoid the sun during the middle of the day when it is at its fiercest. Beware of the strong reflections of the sun from sand and water. Not only is sunburn miserably painful for your child, it's thought to be a major risk factor for skin cancer in later life.

HEAT & COLD

If your child is not used to a hot climate, they will need time to acclimatise. Children tend to acclimatise relatively easily, but young children (with their greater surface area relative to their body mass) can lose fluid through sweating very rapidly and become dehydrated and vulnerable to heatstroke (see p318). Babies and young children may not be able to tell you how hot they're feeling, so if you're feeling the heat, check to see how your child is coping, and in particular whether they are dressed appropriately. Discourage mobile youngsters from rushing around in the heat of the day.

Because babies and children can become dehydrated relatively easily, they require a significant increase in their fluid intake. As a general rule you can double their fluid intake. Consider sprinkling a little extra salt on their food, as salt can be lost through sweating, especially to start with. You could also encourage them to eat lots of juicy fruit and vegetables.

Keep an eye on how much urine they are passing – small amounts of dark urine or dark urine-stained nappies in babies mean you need to increase their fluid intake.

> ❗ If you're carrying a child in a baby-carrier backpack, remember that they are exposed to the elements, and protect them against sunburn, heat exhaustion and the cold.

Children are also susceptible to the cold as they lose heat very rapidly, especially if they are immobile in a carrier, so always wrap them up well and check them regularly for signs of cold. Give them plenty to eat and drink as they can use up their energy reserves quickly and this makes them more vulnerable to the cold. Appropriate clothes and layers are vital.

ALTITUDE
Children are as susceptible to the effects of altitude (which means less oxygen to breathe) as adults, and they may not be able to tell you if they have symptoms. The symptoms of altitude illness (headache, nausea, vomiting) may be nonspecific, mimicking other childhood illnesses, so it is particularly important for you to be aware of the possibility, and to be confident you can recognise these symptoms in your child.

Read the section on Altitude in the Climate, Altitude & Action chapter later for more details.

INSECT STINGS
Children seem to attract bees and wasps like the proverbial honey pot, so be prepared with sting relief spray and lots of sympathy. Take plenty of insect repellent and sting relief sprays and cream. If you know your child is allergic to bee stings, discuss this with your doctor before you leave.

IF YOUR CHILD FALLS ILL

Children are at risk of the same diseases as you are when you are away, so unless otherwise indicated, you can follow the guidelines given in the main text (but remember that children need different doses and possibly different drugs – see the

Medical Kit & Medications section earlier in this chapter for more details). Because children can't always tell you what's wrong and in many cases don't show typical symptoms of diseases, it's even more important to seek medical help at the earliest opportunity, and always seek medical help urgently if you have any concerns about their condition. Local doctors and health workers will be very experienced in dealing with all common childhood problems, so getting reliable medical assistance shouldn't be a problem even in less-touristed areas.

IS MY BABY/CHILD UNWELL?

Children can quickly change from being well and active to becoming ill, sometimes seriously ill. In young children especially, the signs can be quite subtle and difficult to interpret, which can be a worry.

As the parent, you will know your child best of all and any change in their behaviour should be taken seriously – listen to your sixth sense. This is particularly true of young children. Babies up to six months may become quieter than usual, miserable and crying. They may not want to feed or drink or they may develop more specific signs, such as diarrhoea, a cough, vomiting or a rash.

Don't rely on a child's skin temperature as an indication of whether they have a raised temperature or not. Always carry and use a thermometer, preferably a digital one, or a fever strip. It is important to have an actual reading of the temperature. A cold child to touch may have a raging temperature and the other way round.

Older babies and toddlers may just not 'perform' as well as you are used to. They may stop walking, stop sitting up and stop feeding themselves or being as generally developed as you are used to. Children of this age are unable to tell you what's wrong and this may be the only sign before a rash or a cough appears. If you have any cause for concern, check the temperature and make sure your child is taking at least enough fluids to pass urine twice a day, even if they have gone off their food.

FEVER

This is very common in children wherever they are, and is always a cause for concern. In addition, a high temperature can sometimes cause a convulsion in babies and young children. Skin temperature is a confusing and unreliable sign – see the previous entry. If you think your child has a fever, eg if she's flushed and irritable and obviously unwell:

- take her temperature (see p123 for how to do this) and take it again 30 minutes later as a check
- put your child to bed, remove most of her clothing (perhaps covering her up with a cotton sheet) and make her comfortable (under a mosquito net if necessary)
- wipe her face and body with a sponge or cloth soaked in tepid (not cold) water or place her in a tepid bath to help lower the temperature
- giving paracetamol (acetaminophen) syrup or tablets every four to six hours will also help to lower the temperature
- prevent dehydration by giving small amounts of fluid often – make up oral rehydration salts with bottled or boiled water, or packet or fresh fruit juice diluted half and half with safe water; give 5mL every 15 minutes for the first hour

Remember that conditions like viral infections, colds, ear infections, urine infections and diarrhoea occur commonly, but always bear in mind the possibility of malaria if you've been travelling in risk areas.

Take steps to lower the temperature and seek medical help urgently in the following situations:

- if the temperature is over 37.7°C (100°F) in a baby of less than six months
- if the temperature is over 39°C (104°F) in any infant or child
- if your child has had fits in the past
- if it could be malaria; malaria should be suspected with ANY high fever if you are in a malarial area
- if the fever shows no sign of improving after 24 hours (take your child's temperature regularly to show you if it's going up or down)

FEBRILE CONVULSION

If your child's temperature quickly rises high, she may have a fit, whatever the cause of the fever. This generally occurs in young children up to five years of age.

- try not to panic
- don't try to restrain your child's movements, but do remove any sharp objects from the area to prevent her injuring herself
- don't put anything in her mouth
- when the movements subside, roll her onto her side so that she can breathe freely
- comfort her when it has stopped, then take measures to cool her – fans, tepid sponging, tepid baths, paracetamol
- seek medical help

MALARIA

✚ For the low-down on malaria, including emergency treatment, see the section on Malaria in the Fever chapter earlier.

Children can rapidly become very ill with malaria – which is why it is not advisable to travel with children to malarial areas – and it's easy to miss the diagnosis because the symptoms can be very vague. You need to suspect malaria if your child develops a fever with or without flu-like symptoms that persists for more than eight hours if you are in or have visited a malarial area within the last few months. Seek medical help urgently for a blood test and treatment. If you are in a remote area without access to medical help, you'll need to give your child emergency standby treatment while you seek medical help – make sure you discuss this with your doctor before you go.

DIARRHOEA

Children, especially young children and babies, are more likely than adults to get diarrhoea when they are away. They also tend to get more severe symptoms, and or longer. It's partly because children tend to be indiscriminate about what they put in their mouths and it's hard to keep them clean, but it may also be because they have less immunity to disease-causing bugs.

Babies and children can become rapidly dehydrated through diarrhoea and vomiting, and it can be difficult to make sure they drink enough. The best fluids to give children are oral rehydration salts (ORS). You need to start giving them ORS as soon as diarrhoea or vomiting appears – you can make them more palatable by adding flavours (such as the juice of an orange), or different flavoured sachets may be available. Avoid food if they are actively vomiting.

You don't need to give your child ORS if you're breastfeeding, but make sure you're taking in enough fluid yourself. If your child is being fed a milk based formula, you need to replace this with ORS until the diarrhoea is better. As the diarrhoea improves, introduce diluted milk feeds, then solids.

For older children, follow the same dietary guidelines as for adults, avoiding milk and milk-based products until your child is on the mend. The World Health Organization gives the following guidelines for the quantity of fluid replacement:

under two years	one half to one quarter cup per loose stool
two to 10 years	one half to one cup per loose stool
over 10 years	as for adults (see p159 for more details)

If children are vomiting, allow the stomach to rest (eg for an hour) before trying to give fluids, then reintroduce fluids very slowly – 5ml every 15 minutes for the first hour, and building up from there. If your child is refusing to drink, try giving small amounts by teaspoon or syringe every few minutes.

Seek medical help earlier rather than later, especially if you notice any of the following symptoms developing:

■ prolonged vomiting and diarrhoea
■ refusal to take fluids
■ listlessness
■ fever
■ blood or mucus in the diarrhoea

Faeces in children may take 10 to 14 days to return to normal, sometimes longer following an episode of diarrhoea. As long as the faeces are not too frequent, parents should not worry about slightly loose faeces in an otherwise fit and recovered child.

Note that symptomatic antidiarrhoeal medications ('stoppers') are not generally recommended in children and should be avoided. If your child is ill enough to need antibiotics, you should seek medical advice; if you are in a remote area away from medical assistance, co-trimoxazole is a suitable antibiotic options (see p418 for more on antibiotics and diarrhoea).

! As a general rule, avoid giving your child any antidiarrhoeal remedies (apart from ORS and the antibiotics recommended in the diarrhoea section).

TUMMY ACHE

This is a very common complaint, as it is in adults. The causes are many and varied, some serious – see p128 for more details. If your child is prone to tummy aches, the stress of travelling may make them more likely while you are away. Otherwise, situations when you should seek medical help include:

■ any tummy ache with a fever – could be malaria, typhoid, bladder infection etc
■ severe tummy ache that is continuous for more than three hours – could be appendicitis
■ tummy ache with profuse vomiting and diarrhoea – the danger is dehydration

■ tummy ache that's not normal for your child, especially if he's
generally unwell

COLDS, COUGHS & EARACHE

Children are particularly likely to succumb to new germs
in new places, so be prepared! Asthma (cough, wheezing)
may occur for the first time while you are away, and can be
frightening especially if you or your child have not experienced
it before. You should seek medical advice if your child is having
difficulty breathing, especially if you notice that their ribs are
being drawn in with each breath.

Swimming can make ear infections more likely – see p187
for more details. Remember that if your child has grommets in
their ears, they shouldn't swim.

PRICKLY HEAT & NAPPY RASH

Prickly heat tends to be more of a problem in children than
in adults. Calamine cream can soothe the irritation, and
you can help prevent the rash by dressing children in loose
cotton clothing, bathing them often and drying them carefully,
especially any skin folds and under their arms.

Nappy rash can be a lot worse in the heat. Take a good supply
of barrier creams (such as petroleum jelly or zinc and castor oil
cream or Sudocrem), and avoid plastic overpants. Wash the
area with water after they poo, dry it well, apply barrier cream
and try to keep the nappy off as much as possible.

If it's red and painful and doesn't go away with simple
treatment, it may be due to a fungal infection. In this case, try
applying an antifungal cream (options include clotrimazole, or
Canesten; or an antifungal with hydrocortisone if it is very red
and painful) applied twice daily. Check their mouth, as they
may have a fungal infection (thrush) there as well, indicated
by white patches that are difficult to remove. Treatment is
with antifungal drops (such as nystatin). Remember to change
rubber teats and feeding utensils as soon as treatment is started
and halfway through.

AFTER YOU GET BACK

Consider getting a check-up for yourself and your children if you've been on a long trip or have been travelling rough. Children are more likely to pick up intestinal parasites such as worms, so a test for this is a good idea when you get back. This is a simple test done on a faeces sample, and can be arranged easily by your family doctor. If there's any chance your child may have swum in bilharzia-infected water, you'll need to get this checked out. Remember the possibility of malaria if your child gets an unexplained fever after you get back, particularly within the first month or so, but up to a year after. Tell your doctor if you have been travelling and where.

Travellers with Special Needs...

You don't have to be able bodied or in perfect health to travel, but make sure you know what to expect and are prepared for it. A short trip to a tourist centre or urban area with well developed medical services may not present any major difficulties, but you may want to think more carefully about longer trips, especially to remote areas. It's not all bad news, however – being in a hot climate may improve conditions like arthritis and lung problems.

- Medical advice – get advice from your doctor or specialist on health problems you could encounter when you're travelling and what to do about them.
- Documentation – take with you a written summary from your doctor of your medical problems and any treatment you are currently on or have received in the past.
- Travel insurance – important for all travellers, but particularly if you have special needs (check that it covers you for preexisting illnesses); a policy that provides a 24-hour hotline is handy.
- Medical facilities – services in rural areas in many parts of Latin America are extremely limited and emergency services may be nonexistent.
- Practical difficulties – travellers with disabilities will probably find that facilities in Latin America generally lag well behind those in most Western countries.
- Medicines – although you may be able to replace some medicines while you are away, it's best to take a plentiful supply with you, as well as any equipment you need, like syringes, needles, blood or urine tests, and any arthritis aids or inhalant devices.
- Bracelets or tags engraved with your medical conditions, medications and any drug allergies – see Useful Organisations in the Before You Go chapter for contact details of one company.
- Flying – make sure you let the airline know well in advance about any special requirements you have. Your doctor or the medical department of the airline you're travelling with will be able to give

you advice on potential health hazards of flying. For example, the lower oxygen availability in aircraft cabins may be a problem if you suffer from severe heart or lung problems.

! Travelling can be very physically demanding, so your itinerary needs to be realistic and to have the flexibility to allow for rest days, sick days and any unexpected difficulties.

MEDICAL CONDITIONS & TRAVEL

Some medical conditions may make you less able to cope with the physical and environmental challenges of travelling; for example, if you have a heart or lung condition you may find the heat more difficult to cope with. Some medical conditions can make you more vulnerable to infection, and you may need to take additional preventive measures to counteract this. Common travel-related ailments such as diarrhoea and vomiting can be more of a problem if you have ongoing medical conditions, especially as they can affect the absorption of medicines. It's not all bad news, however – being in a hot climate may improve conditions like arthritis and lung problems.

If you have an ongoing medical condition, it's worth seeing your specialist physician before you go for advice on any special hazards travel may pose for you. It's also worth getting in touch with your local support group or a national disease foundation, as they may be able to provide you with specific advice and contact details of similar organisations where you are going. Some useful organisations are listed in the following section.

Check what medical facilities are available locally in case you need to call on them. Your doctor or travel health clinic or any of the information sources listed in the Before You Go chapter should be able to give you information on this; in addition, a brief run-down is given in the Medical Services appendix of this book. If you are on a cruise or an organised tour, find out what provisions they have for dealing with medical problems.

SUPPORT GROUPS & INFORMATION SOURCES

If you have any special health needs, most major national or state disease foundations or support groups should be able to provide you with information and advice on travel-related health issues. In this section we've listed some recommended resources to get you started; you could also try your doctor, specialist physician or a travel health clinic.

Arthritis – the Arthritis Foundation (☎ 800-542-0295 or 206-547-2707) produces an excellent, extremely comprehensive guide *Travel and Arthritis*; you can also access it online (www.orthop.washington.edu).

Heart conditions – for general information, US travellers could try the American Heart Association (☎ 1-800-242-8721, 7272 Greenville Avenue, Dallas, TX 75231, www.americanheart.org); in the UK you could try the British Heart Foundation (☎ 020-7935 0185, fax 7486 5820, www.bhf.org.uk), at 14 Fitzharding St, London W1H 4DH; and in Australia, you could ring the Heartline information service on ☎ 1300 362 787 (www.heartfoundation.org.au/).

Global Dialysis (☎ 44 121 242 7699), at PO Box 12821, Solihull, B91 9BT, UK produces a directory of dialysis centres worldwide; it also has a website (www.globaldialysis.com).

US-based travellers with disabilities could contact one of the following organisations:

Access Foundation (☎ 516-887-5798); PO Box 356, Malverne, NY 11565

Mobility International USA (☎ 541-343-1284), PO Box 10767, Eugene, OR 97440; website www.miusa.org

Society for the Advancement of Travel for the Handicapped (SATH, ☎ 718-858-5483), at 26 Court St, Brooklyn, NY 11242; website www.sath.org

American Association of Retired Persons (☎ 202-434-2277, 800-424-3410), 601 E St NW, Washington DC 20049, USA

In the UK, the Royal Association for Disability & Rehabilitation (RADAR, ☎ 020-7250 3222, fax 250 0212, www.radar.org.uk), at 12 City Forum, 250 City Rd, London EC1V 8AF, produces three holiday fact packs (UK£2 each), which cover planning, insurance and useful organisations; transport and equipment; and specialised accommodation.

Australians and New Zealanders can contact the National Information Communication Awareness Network (NICAN, ☎ 02-6285 3713, fax 6285 3714), at PO Box 407, Curtin, ACT 2605; its web address is www.nican.com.au.

The Global Access website (www.globalaccessnews.com) has lots of information for travellers with disabilities, as well as links to related sites.

OLDER TRAVELLERS

We hardly need to tell you that age is no barrier to travelling. When you're older (we're taking this to mean 60 plus) you have the time, sometimes the money and often the inclination to travel, as evidenced by the ever-increasing numbers of seniors who are going out there and exploring the world.

AGE, MEDICAL CONDITIONS & TRAVEL

Age itself is not a problem when you're travelling, and, statistically, older travellers are less likely to fall ill than younger ones (possibly because you tend to have more common sense). However, as you get older, you're more likely to have ongoing medical conditions, and these can be more tricky to deal with on the road. Ongoing conditions, especially cardiovascular disease, account for the higher death rate in older travellers compared with your younger counterparts.

Some medical conditions may make you less able to cope with the physical and environmental challenges of travelling; for example, if you have a heart or lung condition you may find the heat more difficult to cope with. Common travel-related ailments such as diarrhoea and vomiting can be more of a problem if you have ongoing medical conditions, especially as they can affect the absorption of medicines.

If you have an ongoing medical condition – such as heart or lung disorder, arthritis, diabetes or kidney dialysis – it's worth seeing your specialist physician before you go for advice on any special hazards travel may pose for you. It's also worth getting in touch with your local support group or a national disease foundation, as they may be able to provide you with specific advice and contact details of similar organisations where you are going. Some useful organisations are listed in the Travellers with Special Needs section in the Before You Go chapter.

It's particularly important to find out what the medical facilities are like at your destination, in case you have an exacerbation of your condition while you are away. Check with your doctor or travel health clinic or any of the information sources listed in the Before You Go chapter; in addition, some basic details are given in the Medical Services appendix of this book. If you are on a cruise or an organised tour or trek, find out what provisions they have for dealing with medical problems.

IMMUNISATIONS & MALARIA PREVENTION

Being older doesn't mean you're immune! Immunisations are just as important as for younger travellers, and perhaps more so, as immunity wanes with age. It's a good idea to get this checked out as early as possible, in case you need the full course of an immunisations which can take a few weeks. For more details of the travel-related immunisations you may need for your trip, see the Immunisations section of the Before You Go chapter. In addition to these, if you are over 65, it's a good idea to be immunised against flu and possibly pneumococcal disease, before you travel. You may be more at risk of the flu and pneumonia when you're travelling, and you don't want to waste your trip being ill.

If you need to take malaria prevention medication, be aware that some antimalarials may interact with your regular medications (for example, mefloquine can interact with beta blockers, a heart medicine), so it's a good idea to check this with your doctor.

PREEXISTING MEDICAL CONDITIONS

As we get older, over 65 years, our immune system also slows a little. This is a consideration in older travellers, who also are more likely to have an ongoing medical condition. In fact, although older travellers are less likely than their younger counterparts to get sick when travelling, the outcome is more likely to be serious. For older travellers, the most common cause of death is from preexisting conditions like heart disease.

Some medical conditions can affect your ability to cope with the physical and environmental challenges that travelling may involve; eg travellers with heart or lung conditions may find the heat more difficult to cope with.

It also means that you are more likely to be taking medications regularly. Travel-related diseases like diarrhoea and vomiting can affect the absorption of medications, and taking multiple medications makes side effects more likely to occur.

It's important to find out before you go what the medical facilities are like at your destination. If you are on an organised tour or trek, find out what provisions it has for dealing with medical problems.

MEDICAL CHECK-UP

As well as getting travel health advice, it's worth having a medical check-up before you go, especially if you are planning on doing anything strenuous like trekking, visiting very hot or cold climates or spending time at altitude. If you have any medical conditions or you've recently had surgical treatment, check with your doctor that you are fit to travel. If you are, it's a good opportunity to discuss any potential problems you may encounter while you are away and to clarify what to do about them if they do occur.

If you intend to go scuba diving, you will need to have a medical performed by a specialist diving doctor. This is particularly important, as older divers and those with preexisting medical conditions are more likely to suffer serious problems. See the section on diving in the Water chapter later in this book for more details.

DENTAL CHECK-UP

This is a always a good idea, particularly if you are going away for more than a couple of weeks. If you wear dentures, have them checked before you leave home, and make sure you wear in a new pair of dentures before you go, in case adjustments need to be made to make them comfortable. Consider taking a spare pair with you; if you have an old pair, your dentist may be able to modify them to make them useable in an emergency. Getting a new set of dentures while you're away could be a major problem. However, simple temporary repairs may be carried out by a dentist, or you can make a simple repair yourself like sticking a tooth back on or sticking a broken denture back together using glue. If you use an epoxy glue, be careful not to put them back in your mouth before the glue has set…

EYES

If you wear glasses, remember to take a spare pair with you, as well as the prescription in case you need to replace them. Take a plentiful supply of any eyedrops you use, although eyedrops that need to be kept refrigerated can be a bit problematic – keep them in the middle of your luggage, and investigate whether there is a fridge you can have access to at your accommodation.

FITNESS PREPARATION

You might want to consider starting a gentle exercise program well before you go, especially if you're out of the habit of doing much exercise. Travelling can involve a lot of standing around and lifting luggage on and off luggage racks, while negotiating

FIT TO TRAVEL

Travelling can involve a lot of standing around and lifting luggage on and off luggage racks, while negotiating your way around large airports and other transport terminals often involves a lot of walking, perhaps carrying heavy luggage. Sightseeing can also be surprisingly exhausting. If you're out of the habit of doing much exercise, it's probably a good idea to start a gentle exercise program before you go. If you're planning a trek or other strenuous exercise, it is essential to start training in advance. You can avoid activity-related injuries by warming up and stretching properly before you start and when you finish.

Finally, don't be overambitious with your travel itinerary – it's better to do less comfortably than to push yourself too hard and perhaps regret it.

your way around large airports and other transport terminals often involves a lot of walking, perhaps carrying heavy luggage. Sightseeing can also be surprisingly exhausting.

Obviously, if you're planning a trek or other strenuous exercise, you will want to prepare well in advance.

Avoid activity-related injuries by warming up and stretching properly before you start and when you finish.

Finally, don't be overambitious with your travel itinerary – it's better to do less comfortably than to push yourself too hard and perhaps regret it.

TRAVEL INSURANCE

It's important for travellers of all ages to have travel health insurance, but it's particularly important if you have an ongoing medical condition. See the main section on Travel Insurance in the Before You Go chapter for more details, but always check the small print carefully to see what the policy covers you for. A policy that provides a 24-hour hotline is handy.

MEDICAL KIT & MEDICATIONS

It's sensible to take a well stocked medical kit, including a plentiful supply of any regular medications plus a bit extra. You don't want to run out at an inopportune moment, and it may be hard to find suitable replacements. Always keep a supply of your medications on you, as well as a backup supply in your luggage, in case your luggage goes walkies.

The What to Take section in the Before You Go chapter gives detailed guidance on what you could consider taking with you. In addition, if you suffer from severe prostate trouble, you could consider taking a sterile catheter set with you – discuss this with your doctor if necessary.

You could consider getting bracelets or tags engraved with any medical conditions, medications and drug allergies to carry on you. MedicAlert is an organisation that provides these, together with a toll-free number to call in emergencies – see Useful Organisations in the Before You Go chapter for contact details.

MEDICINES

If you're on any regular medications, remember that these can interact with any medicines you may be prescribed for a travel-related problem:

- some medications can make you very sensitive to the effects of the sun – see p46 for more details
- pseudoephedrine hydrochloride (decongestant) – don't take if you have raised blood pressure
- hyoscine (for travel sickness) – best avoided if you have glaucoma or prostate problems
- antimalarials and some drugs for heart problems

ON THE MOVE

Keep any regular or as-needed medications (for angina, for example) in your hand luggage so you can access them readily during the journey if necessary.

Sitting for long periods of time, especially in the heat, can make your feet and ankles swell. Also, when you're older, you're at greater risk of developing blood clots in your leg veins if you sit immobile through a long journey; some medical conditions can also make this more likely. This is known as 'deep-venous thrombosis', or DVT; for more information see p306. Discuss this with your doctor but try the following strategies:

- wriggle your toes, flex your calves while you are sitting down
- get up and move around periodically if you can
- drink plenty of fluids (nonalcoholic) to prevent dehydration, which makes your blood more likely to clot
- your doctor may advise you to take low dose aspirin (75mg) for three days before, during and after the flight; alternatively, some doctors may suggest an injection of a blood thinning agent like heparin

➕ If you're crossing lots of time zones, jet lag can be a problem – for guidelines on minimising the impact of jet lag, see the On the Move chapter at the beginning of this book.

STAYING HEALTHY

All the general, common-sense measures suggested in the Staying Healthy chapter earlier in this book are just as relevant to older travellers.

With increasing age, you have fewer sweat glands and they work less efficiently. This means that you are likely to feel the heat more and be more vulnerable to problems like heat exhaustion and heatstroke (see p318). Take time to acclimatise, avoid strenuous exercise in the heat, especially when you first arrive, and drink plenty of fluids. With age, your blood vessels get stiffer and less reactive, making you more likely to faint in the heat. Being in a hot climate makes you sweat more, and

JUST CRUISIN' ALONG

A cruise can seem like the perfect holiday – restful, comfortable, safe from the culinary hazards of shorelife and luxurious. However, be warned that the reality doesn't always match up with the expectation. In a few cases, the cruise ship may not be quite as luxurious as you may have been led to believe. Steep staircases, lack of elevators, narrow corridors and ship to shore transfers can prove challenging if you are less than fully fit. Hygiene standards on board the ship may fall short of ideal, and outbreaks of intestinal infections are not uncommon on cruise liners. Seasickness can affect anyone, but may have more serious consequences if you have an ongoing medical condition. Shore trips can be strenuous.

Before you book that trip, check that you know what it entails and what facilities are like on board.

it's easy to become dehydrated, especially if you are taking medications to promote fluid loss, such as diuretics for a heart condition. Discuss this with your doctor before you leave, as you may need to adjust your medications while you are away. If you are overweight or have a medical condition such as heart or lung problems or diabetes, you will be more vulnerable to the effects of the heat.

Several studies have shown that older travellers are less likely to suffer from diarrhoea while travelling, perhaps because you are more discerning about where and what to eat than younger travellers. If you do get diarrhoea and/or vomiting, follow the guidelines given in the Digestive System chapter, and remember that this may mean your usual medications are absorbed less well. You're also at more risk of dehydration, so seek medical help earlier rather than later.

Constipation is a common complaint even when you are travelling – see the section on constipation in the Digestive System chapter for more details. Eat lots of fresh fruit (peeled) and vegetables (cooked) and keep up your fluid intake. If you are prone to constipation, take a supply of a remedy you know works for you.

As you get older, wounds are slower to heal. The hot, humid conditions of tropical America exacerbate this, and make infection more likely, so it's worth taking particular care to avoid insect bites and injury. If you do get a cut or scratch, take good care of it to save you trouble later.

Air pollution is a major issue in many of Latin America's cities, and can be worse at specific times of the year. Consider altering your travel itinerary if you think this may be a problem, especially if you suffer from a heart or lung condition.

Many of the popular tourist routes in South America involve exposure to significant altitude. If you're reasonably fit, altitude shouldn't pose any particular problems, although you may experience more severe problems if you suffer from breathing difficulties or a heart condition. You should allow plenty of time to acclimatise – see the Altitude section of the Climate, Altitude & Outdoors chapter for more details.

> If you fall ill, seek medical advice as soon as possible, and remember that the more drugs you are taking, the more likely they are to interact and cause unwanted effects. Always tell any doctor treating you of any conditions you have and any medications you are on. Have good insurance!

DIABETIC TRAVELLERS

This section was written by Michelle Sobel, a Type 1 diabetic who has never let her condition get in the way of her travels.

Preventive self-care is your aim, wherever you travel. Prepared and in good diabetic control, you're in the best position to enjoy your experiences abroad. Before you go, discuss with your doctor or specialist what to do if you get sick, as well as dosage adjustments, immunisations and other general travel-related health issues.

The level and type of care offered to diabetics varies from country to country. Find out before you go what to expect at your destination. National diabetic associations are usually the best source of information on local diabetic care, and national diabetes organisations at home often have information for travellers. You could try contacting any of the following:

International Diabetes Federation Ave Emile De Mot 19, B-1000 Brussels, Belgium; website **www.idf.org** – maintains a listing of diabetic associations in different countries around the world, as well as other information on diabetes.

www.childrenwithdiabetes.com/d_09_800.htm – has a list of diabetic organisations worldwide, although it is not specifically aimed at diabetic travellers.

Mexican Diabetes Federation, (☎ 5255-5511 4200) Pomona No. 15, Col. Roma, 06700 Mexico City, D.F.Mexico; website **www.fmd iabetes.org**.

South & Central American Regional Office (☎ 598 2 709 5457) Gerente Oficina Regional SACA, José Benito Lamas 2980, 11.300 Montevideo, Uruguay.

American Diabetes Association (☎ 1-800-342-2383) 1701 North Beauregard Street, Alexandria, VA 22311; website **www.diabetes.org.**

British Diabetic Association (Careline ☎ 0845 120 2960) Macleod House, 10 Parkway, London NW1 7AA; website **www.diabetes.org.uk** – produces a useful leaflet on travel with diabetes, as well as a number of country guides for diabetics.

Diabetes Australia (☎ 1300 136 588) 5th Floor, 39 London Circuit, Canberra City ACT 2601; website **www.diabetesaustralia.com.au.**

Alternatively, check out this website: **www.diabetictraveler .com**. A useful publication you could consider getting is the *Diabetic Traveller's Companion* by Nerlda Nichol.

Insulin & Other Diabetic Supplies

> Note that having syringes and meters on your person can sometimes prompt questions from customs and other officials, so make sure you carry on you at all times documentation from your doctor explaining your need for syringes, insulin and meters.

Before you leave, call the relevant manufacturer to get information on the availability abroad of diabetic supplies like test strips, medication (oral and insulin) and glucose meters. Consumer-friendly meter and pump manufacturers will advise you on repair, replacement and delivery policies if your equipment malfunctions or is lost abroad.

Note that most nations measure blood glucose in mmol/L; the US, however, primarily uses mg/dL. Different meters report glucose readings using either or both of these standards. To convert mmol/L to mg/dL, multiply the glucose reading by 18 (ie 4mmol/L = 72 mg/dL). To convert mg/dL, divide the glucose by 18.

Take two to three times the medical supplies you expect to use (in carry-on, waterproof packs), to protect against loss or damage. On day trips, I carry two half bottles (instead of one or two full bottles) of insulin, so there's backup in case of breakage.

To reduce bulk, try insulin pens over syringes. However, note that manufacturers state that at room temperature some insulin pen cartridges (particularly some slow-acting and premixed insulin) may have shorter lives (as short as seven or 14 days) than vials (which last about a month).

Some diabetic care providers suggest reusing sharps, at your own risk. Consult your physician about reusing, and ask for advice on sterilising syringes and needles if necessary. Always discard needles and lancets appropriately when dull, and never share sharps or meters.

You should be aware that insulin may be sold in different concentrations from country to country. If you have to replenish abroad, use the appropriate syringe with the appropriate concentration. If you mix and match syringes and concentrations (for example if you use U-40 insulin in a syringe marked 'for U-100 insulin only'), you'll be at greater risk of over- or under-injecting insulin. Also, it's a good idea to retain generic-name prescriptions (even if invalid abroad) and medication inserts, as medications may have different brand names in Latin America.

If you find you are running out of supplies in a place with limited resources, be prepared (financially and time-wise) to make a detour to a better-stocked country. For extended travel and for emergencies, consider making preparations before you go for medical supplies to be mailed to you. Packaging is available to insulate insulin from heat and physical damage in the mail.

On the Move

Crossing time zones can be problematic, especially for Type 1 diabetics. Before you leave, take a copy of your itinerary to your diabetic care provider and ask for specific guidance on adjusting your individual protocol en route and as you acclimatise. As a rule, though, keep your watch on home time until the morning after you land.

It's always important to check blood sugars frequently to modify dosages, mealtimes and food choices, and flying presents its own issues. If you make adjustments based on how you feel – a very unreliable indicator whether you're travelling or not – hyper and hypoglycaemic reactions are almost inevitable. Remember that jet lag can further impair your ability to tell highs and lows.

Staying Healthy

Unaccustomed physical activity, erratic sleep and meal times, unfamiliar foods, climate change, altitude sickness and stress are just some of the many variables that can aggravate control while you are away. All the potential effects of unstable blood glucose (like disorientation, headaches and lethargy) are especially unwelcome when you're away from home.

When you're travelling, insulin-dependent diabetics need to take particular care to prevent hyper and hypoglycaemic reactions. Ideally, monitor at least six times daily; if possible, bring two meters as well as visual blood glucose strips as backup. Carry emergency food, foil-wrapped ketone strips and glucagon. In the event of a reaction, wearing a medical bracelet showing that you are a diabetic (see MedicAlert under Useful Organisations earlier in this chapter) can help prevent misdiagnosis (symptoms are often otherwise presumed to be induced by alcohol or illegal substances).

All diabetics should follow basic guidelines to prevent foodborne illness. If you do (or don't) take extra risks and end up ill, know what you need to do to prevent highs and lows related to illness.

Wounds in hot, humid climates get infected easier and faster – always keep your feet dry, clean, and comfortable. Never walk barefoot, even on the beach. In hot or remote regions, take special care to stay hydrated. Pack extra supplies of medication, food and water. Protect your skin from the sun (severe sunburn can elevate blood sugars).

Keep insulin chilled in thermoses or insulated cool packs. Gels that freeze when shaken can protect insulin for a few hours. Make sure you don't freeze insulin, and don't place it directly against ice. Keep insulin out of direct sunlight. And ask hostels, friends etc to refrigerate your supplies when they have the opportunity. Touring with supportive companions is a good idea; if you're travelling solo, check in with contacts. Mobile phones (cell phones) are handy.

HIV-POSITIVE TRAVELLERS

If you are HIV-positive, travelling poses some special problems, although this depends to a certain extent on your CD4 count. It's essential you get specialist advice on this before you travel (from your doctor, specialist physician or travel health clinic).

As a rule, live vaccines (for example oral polio, oral typhoid, measles, mumps and rubella, and yellow fever) are best avoided in HIV-positive travellers. You are generally at greater risk of travel-related illnesses, and if you do get ill, it may have a greater impact on you. It's even more important to take great

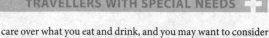
care over what you eat and drink, and you may want to consider taking antibiotics to prevent diarrhoea – discuss this before you go. You are at greater risk than non-HIV-positive travellers of tuberculosis, hepatitis A and leishmaniasis, although you are not at any increased risk of malaria.

Bear in mind that attitudes towards HIV infection may be very different in Latin America from what you are used to. Although some countries in Latin America ask for HIV testing for work permits and long stays, you're unlikely to be asked for this if you're going for a short holiday.

You should be able to get more information on all these issues from your national HIV/AIDS organisation, or you could check out the following web resources: the Special Needs Travel section of **wwwn.cdc.gov/travel**; or **www.aegis.org** (with loads of good links for a variety of HIV-related issues). In the UK, you could contact the Terrence Higgins Trust (☎ 020 7831 0330), 52-54 Grays Inn Rd, London WC1X 8JU, **www.tht.org.uk**.

Climate, Altitude & Action...

The great environmental diversity of Latin America is a major drawcard for travellers to the region. Think of Latin America, and you probably see Andean peaks, volcanoes, deserts where rainfall has never been recorded, high plateaus, picture postcard beaches and humid tropical rainforests. The astonishing diversity of landscape and climate can make travel in Latin America physically challenging, but if you know what to expect and are well prepared, you should be able to have the adventure of your lifetime... and survive to tell the tale.

CLIMATE

Latin America's great geographical diversity is matched by its climate. Travel here can expose you to climatic extremes which, if you're not prepared, can impact both on your health and your enjoyment of the trip. Find out what the climate is likely to be doing at the time of year you're considering travelling, and incorporate that into your travel plans. Remember that the weather can be very fickle, especially in the Andean region and in the extreme south, and always be prepared for the unexpected.

SUN

Don't underestimate the frazzling power of the sun, especially at high altitude and near water. Cover up and use high protective factor sunscreens, including on your lips, and don't forget to take – and wear – UV-blocking sunglasses.

 Natural remedies you might like to try include lavender essential oil applied undiluted to the area, comfrey cream or hypericum oil.

Sunburn

We'd like to think, of course, that after following all the advice about preventing sun damage given earlier in this guide, you won't need to read this section, but just in case...

The trouble with sunburn is that it comes on gradually, unlike burns from other causes, and you often don't notice it until it's too late. Sunburn can vary from just a mild redness with some soreness to more severe swelling with blistering.

With mild sunburn, you can take the heat out of the burn by placing cool, damp cloths on it, or by taking cool or lukewarm baths. Taking simple painkillers or ibuprofen (see p417) can soothe sunburn, and may reduce redness and itching. Creams or ointments containing calamine or aloe vera have traditionally been recommended but there is concern now that these, as well as creams containing anaesthetic agents (such as lignocaine), may cause sensitivity reactions and make itching worse. Avoid greasy preparations as these can trap the heat and make the damage worse. Creams and sprays containing a weak steroid such as hydrocortisone can be very helpful.

 Natural remedies you might like to try on limited areas of sunburn include lavender essential oil (applied undiluted to the area), comfrey cream or hypericum oil.

If the burn is more severe and has blistered, there's a risk of secondary infection. Take steps to avoid this by keeping the area clean and covered. For a smallish area of blistering sunburn, an antibacterial cream like silver sulphadiazine 1% (Flammazine) is useful – spread it on liberally and cover the whole area with a dry sterile dressing. You'll need to reapply the cream and change the dressing daily until it has healed up. For larger blisters, it's best to get medical attention.

Take care not to get burnt again, especially if peeling has left areas of unprotected new skin.

! Note that widespread severe sunburn is a serious condition that needs to be treated like any other extensive burn (see p440) – you will need to get medical help urgently. In the meantime, rest, drink plenty of fluids and try any of the cooling measures suggested for mild sunburn.

Medicines & Sun Exposure

Taking certain medicines can make you hypersensitive to the effects of the sun – you may find you burn more readily and badly than is normal for you. Your doctor or pharmacist should warn you if this is likely to be a side effect. If you take any medicines regularly, check this out with your doctor before you leave. Medicines that can cause problems like this include:

- anti-inflammatory painkillers such as ibuprofen and diclofenac
- ciprofloxacin (antibiotic that may be prescribed for diarrhoea)
- oral contraceptive pill (rarely)
- nalidixic acid (antibiotic often prescribed for bladder infections)
- tetracycline antibiotics, including doxycycline (may be prescribed as a malaria preventive)
- sulphonamide antibiotics, eg co-trimoxazole (unlikely to be prescribed under normal circumstances)
- thiazides (diuretics for blood pressure control and heart problems)

Some medical conditions can make you sensitive to the sun, including lupus and vitiligo. The sun tends to make atopic dermatitis (eczema) worse, although it can improve psoriasis. Sunlight can trigger cold sores, if you get these.

HEAT

Generally, your body is able to adapt to the heat pretty well, although you need to give it time – full acclimatisation can take up to three weeks. The most important change that occurs with acclimatisation is that you sweat more readily and in larger quantities. Sweating helps cool you down, as heat is lost when sweat evaporates off your skin. However, the reason the jungle feels so uncomfortable is that high humidity prevents the sweat from evaporating and cooling you down. If the sweat just pours off you, try fanning yourself as this will encourage the sweat to evaporate, cooling you down.

Some people are more vulnerable to the heat than others. Children are more prone to heat illness than adults. Older travellers who are less fit may be at greater risk of heat illness

(although if you're physically fit, you should cope just as well
as younger adults). People with heart or lung problems are
vulnerable to heat stress because the heart has to work harder
under hot conditions. If you're overweight, you may find it
more difficult to lose heat.

> **!** If you're planning on being active in the heat, trekking or cycling
> perhaps, remember that your body has to work much harder to
> keep cool under these circumstances.

Physical fitness makes you more able to cope with heat stress
and quicker to acclimatise, but you still need to take care to
replace lost fluids.

Sweat contains water and salts, but your main requirement
is to replace water. You can lose an astonishing 2L an hour in
sweat, or more if you're doing strenuous physical activity. You
need to drink a lot more than you would normally in a cool
climate, even when you have acclimatised.

Don't rely on feeling thirsty to prompt you to drink – by the
time your thirst mechanism kicks in, you'll probably already
be dehydrated. How much urine you're passing is a much
better indicator of how dry you are. If you're only passing a
small amount of concentrated (dark yellow) urine, you need
to drink more.

> **!** As a rough guide, an adult needs to drink about 3L of fluid a day in
> a hot climate or 5L and more if you're doing a strenuous physical
> activity such as trekking.

You generally lose more water than salt in sweat, and as you
acclimatise, your body learns to conserve salt better. At first
you can lose more salt than normal, but so long as you're not
on a salt-reduced diet, you should still be able to make it up
from your diet without adding salt or taking salt tablets. The
current thinking is that you don't need to actively replace salt
unless you experience symptoms, usually muscle cramps. As a
rule, salt tablets are best avoided – our diets tend to be relatively
high in salt anyway, and too much salt can cause kidney and
heart problems in the long term.

Heat and dehydration can affect your physical performance and mental judgement, even if you're not ill as such. This is especially important if you are relying on these, such as when you are on a trek or doing other strenuous physical activity.

Heat Cramps

Heavy and prolonged sweating can cause painful cramps in your muscles. This is a sign to rest in a cool environment and drink lots of fluids. If you're not drinking oral rehydration salts, you should add a little extra salt to your food or drinks.

Fainting

This is quite common when you first arrive in a hot climate, and it's more likely to affect older travellers. It occurs because heat causes the blood to pool in your legs when you're standing, meaning that less blood reaches your brain, causing you to feel dizzy and faint.

If you have to deal with a fainting travel companion, lie them down and raise their legs so that their feet are at a higher level than their head. Use fanning and spraying with cool water to help cool them down. When they come to, give them fluids to sip.

Heat Exhaustion & Heatstroke

These two conditions overlap to a certain extent and, for practical purposes, you should treat any heat illness as heatstroke. Both conditions are caused by heavy and prolonged sweating with inadequate fluid replacement and insufficient time for acclimatisation. In heatstroke, sweating stops and you get a dangerous rise in body temperature which can be fatal.

Symptoms to look out for are headache, dizziness, nausea and feeling weak and exhausted. You may notice that you're passing only small quantities of dark urine and you may have muscle aches or cramps. At this stage your temperature may be normal. Treatment is aimed at cooling down and replacing fluids:

- rest in a cool environment (use a fan and cool water sprays)
- drink lots of fluids (water, oral rehydration salts or diluted fruit juice)

DEHYDRATION

This can be caused by any condition that leads to an excessive loss of body fluids, including heat, fever, diarrhoea, vomiting and strenuous physical activity. Signs of dehydration are:

- nausea and dizziness
- headache, and dry eyes and mouth
- weakness and muscle cramps
- passing small quantities of dark urine
- raised temperature

Treatment is to drink lots of fluids: oral rehydration salts if available; otherwise, any fluid will do.

For more guidance on fluid replacement, see the section on treating diarrhoea p156.

If untreated, heat exhaustion can progress to heatstroke. Signs (more likely to be noticed by your travel companions than yourself) include confusion, headache, lack of sweating and flushed and red appearance. The skin feels hot to touch and the person's temperature is raised. In addition, they may show lack of coordination, fits and finally coma (unconsciousness).

Heatstroke can be rapidly fatal, so you need to take immediate action to lower the person's temperature and to get medical help:

- move the person into the shade or a cool environment (get a fan going or use a room with air-con)
- give them cool water to sip (cool fluids are absorbed more rapidly than warm ones); intravenous fluid replacement may be needed once you get medical help
- seek medical help or evacuation urgently

- ice packs, sponging or spraying with cold water and fanning will all help; ice packs are most effective if you put them over the groin and under the arms, but wrap them up first

COLD

Temperature decreases as altitude increases. You may start off in a (relatively) warm valley but the summit is likely to be freezing. Even in tropical America, it can get very cold in highland areas. Daytime temperatures can soar in the hot sun, but as soon as the sun goes down, temperatures plummet. The countries of the Southern Cone basically have a temperate climate, with cold winters. The weather in highland areas can be extremely changeable, so always be prepared for the worst possible conditions.

Your body is fairly limited in what it can do to stay warm – shivering is just about the only thing in the short term – so it's up to you to minimise the dangers by wearing adequate clothing and being prepared for temperature extremes. Food equals heat, so make sure you eat regularly and get sufficient calories in cold climates.

Other problems of cold climates are dehydration (because cold makes you urinate more, you may not feel thirsty, and cold air is very dry), constipation (because of dehydration) and

BUDDY SYSTEM

Many of the signs and symptoms associated with heat, cold and altitude illness are much more likely to be noticed by people you are with than by you. Because of this, it's vital to keep a regular watch on each other if you are in harsh environmental or climatic conditions. Never leave someone on their own if they're showing symptoms. It's also a good idea to self-check for aches, pains, cold areas, numbness and dizziness.

sunburn, especially at altitude, near water or snow. If you're out and about in the cold, the main dangers are hypothermia (general body cooling) or localised cooling, usually affecting your hands and feet, called frostnip or frostbite.

HYPOTHERMIA

This is when your body starts to lose the battle to maintain your body heat in cold conditions and your core body temperature starts to fall (officially, hypothermia is when your temperature, taken by the rectal method, falls below 35°C). You don't need incredibly low temperatures to become hypothermic, just the right combination of circumstances. Windspeed is important in the form of windchill factor.

Because hypothermia can come on gradually and take hold before you realise, it's important to recognise when it might be a risk and to take steps to prevent it. Be aware that you're more at risk of hypothermia if you're thin (less body fat for insulation), tired, wet, or inadequately dressed or equipped (such as not having a sleeping bag). If it's windy, you get colder more easily, as your body heat is removed by convection. You'd be crazy to drink alcohol or do drugs in these harsh environmental conditions – alcohol encourages heat loss and also affects your judgement.

Children and older travellers are more vulnerable to the cold, especially if children are being carried (such as in a backpack child carrier). An added problem is that children may not let you know how they're feeling until it's too late.

! Immersion in cold water, for example if you fall in a mountain stream, can rapidly cause you to become hypothermic.

Check regularly if you're feeling cold or if you have cold hands and toes. Watch for subtle early signs of hypothermia in your travel companions. These are what Rick Curtis of the Princeton Outdoor Program calls the 'umbles' – stumbles, mumbles, fumbles and grumbles – as you get changes in mental function and coordination.

Signs of severe hypothermia are increasing disorientation and a lack of judgement and reasoning, which means that you are unable to make appropriate decisions about survival strategies. Finally, shivering stops, you become unable to walk and lose consciousness.

Prevention

If you think cold might be an issue, take care to prepare well and minimise your risks:

- always be prepared for the worst possible weather, even if there isn't a cloud in the sky when you set out – rain, cold winds and thick mist can descend without warning in the Andes
- wear appropriate clothing – layers are best, as you can adjust them easily to match changing weather conditions throughout the day, and make sure you include windproof and waterproof layers; lightweight polyester fleece clothing is ideal, if a bit sweaty
- a surprising amount of heat is lost through radiation from your head, so wearing a hat can make a big difference
- stay dry – adjust your layers to prevent your clothes getting wet through with sweat, and always carry an umbrella, waterproof layer or large plastic bag on you to keep the rain off, however unlikely rain seems when you set off

While you are out, don't let tiredness get a hold – make sure you have frequent rests.

- Always carry plenty of fluids and carbohydrate-packed goodies, and snack regularly throughout the day.

Treatment

Watch for and treat the early signs of hypothermia:

- remove any cold or wet clothes and replace with warm, dry ones, make sure you cover their head and extremities, and insulate them from the ground (put a blanket or piece of clothing underneath them)
- find shelter for protection from wet, wind and cold
- rewarm by using blankets, sleeping bags and body-to-body contact (zip two sleeping bags together and get in with the cold person to help warm them up)

- you can use hot packs or hot water bottles (or improvise), but remember to wrap these up first to prevent the risk of burns
- drink warm, sweet fluids

'Space blankets' are a popular cold weather survival aid, but there are doubts about their effectiveness in the field, and you're probably better off using a sleeping bag or other thermal layers, depending what you have with you. Carry lots of plastic bags with you – covering yourself up with these prevents further heat loss through evaporation, and can double as protection from rain.

! Severe hypothermia is a very serious condition – get medical help or evacuation immediately. Handle the casualty carefully and don't rewarm them too fast, as this can be dangerous.

CHILBLAINS

These are the most common form of cold injury and the least dangerous. Chilblains can occur if your bare skin is repeatedly exposed to low temperatures (above freezing). They are red, swollen, itchy and tender areas, usually affecting fingers and toes. Chilblains heal up on their own in one to two weeks.

Prevent chilblains by wearing warm mittens (as opposed to gloves) and socks, and suitable footwear. There's no specific treatment, but remember that any open areas on your skin can get infected, so keep them clean and covered.

 Natural remedies that have been recommended include calendula or witch hazel tinctures for unbroken chilblains, or hypericum ointment for broken chilblains. Comfrey ointment is soothing for any skin inflammation.

FROSTBITE

When your tissues get so cold they freeze, this is frostbite. It occurs when you're at temperatures below freezing for prolonged periods of time without adequate gloves or footwear. High winds, high altitude (usually above about 4000m) and badly fitting boots can all make frostbite more likely. Fingers, toes, ears, nose and face can all be affected.

> **!** Prevent frostbite – cover all exposed skin with waterproof and windproof layers in cold conditions and if you notice your hands or feet turning numb, stop immediately and warm them up by body to body contact if necessary.

A frostbitten part looks white and waxy – keep a watch on your companions for this – and it's painless while it's frozen. It's best to seek medical advice as soon as possible. Some effects of frostbite, especially if it's mild, are reversible but you will need expert advice.

What you do immediately depends on your situation. If there is no risk of refreezing (ie you can be evacuated promptly or you are near medical facilities), you should thaw the affected part, although this depends on whether you have appropriate facilities at hand.

> **!** Never rub the affected part to warm it up, as this can cause further damage.

Rewarm the part by immersing it for about half an hour in water heated to 40°C (hotter than hand hot, just bearable). As it starts to warm up, the pain can be pretty severe, and you'll need strong painkillers. The thawed part will swell up, so be sure to remove any rings from fingers. Infection is a significant risk, so make sure you keep the area clean and dry, and cover it with a dry dressing until you reach medical help. If there is a risk of refreezing (ie you are far from help), don't attempt to thaw the part until you reach medical help.

ALTITUDE

Only in Asia do you find mountains as high as the Andes. This great mountain range forms the western margin of South America, extending for some 8000km from northern Venezuela to southern Patagonia. Volcanic Central America also boasts significant peaks. Many popular tourist attractions in the Andean region (including the Inca Trail and Lake Titicaca)

INFORMATION RESOURCES

If you want to find out more about the effects of altitude and other related issues, there are heaps of good sources of information available to you. Some recommended books are listed under Books in the Before You Go chapter, and you might want to check out some of the following web sites:

www.princeton.edu/~oa/altitude.html
Princeton University's Outdoor Action Program has an excellent and comprehensive resource has detailed information on altitude, heat and cold and other wilderness safety issues, as well as lots of links to related sites on a wide variety of outdoor activities, including biking, hiking, caving and mountaineering.

www.thebmc.co.uk
The British Mountaineering Council is another good resource, with information on altitude and related issues. It can also be contacted on ☎ 0161-445 4747, fax 0161-445 4500, email info@thebmc.co.uk, or by post: 177-79 Burton Rd, Manchester M20 2BB.

www.high-altitude-medicine.com
High Altitude Medicine Guide is just that; it also has good information on water treatment and travellers diarrhoea (though mainly aimed at travellers to Nepal), an excellent books section and lots of useful links.

www.wms.org
The Wilderness Medical Society (☎ 800-627-0629, 810 E. 10th Street, PO Box 1897 Lawrence, KS 66044, USA) is an authoritative source of information on all aspects of wilderness safety.

REMEDIES FOR SOROCHE

Given the altitudes many people habitually travel to and live at, it's not surprising that many local remedies are advocated for treating altitude sickness. Probably the best known remedy is *mate de coca* (tea made from coca leaves) or chewing coca leaves, but others include tea made from the leaves of various high altitude plants, Coramina glucosada, Effortil, Micoren or Sorojchi, a blend of Micoren, caffeine and aspirin. These remedies may help alleviate some of the symptoms (although rest, painkillers and oxygen will have the same effect), but they won't affect how quickly you acclimatise.

are at altitudes that are likely to produce symptoms of altitude sickness (known locally as *soroche* or *apunamiento*), especially if you fly straight in from a lowland city (such as Lima in Peru). Make sure you are aware of the altitudes involved and take time to acclimatise before going to higher altitudes.

The problem with altitude is that as you go higher, the air becomes thinner and less oxygen is available. Humans are able to function – and live – at high altitudes through adaptation. At first, the rate and depth of your breathing increases; later you get an increase in heart rate and increase in the number of red blood cells and their ability to use oxygen. Although you can acclimatise sufficiently in a couple of days to a particular altitude, full acclimatisation takes about three weeks.

You're not usually at risk of altitude illness until you reach about 2500m, but it is possible to get symptoms from about 2000m upwards. You're very unlikely to get problems if you stay at altitude for less than about six hours. Going above 3500m, about 50% of trekkers experience symptoms of mild altitude illness, whereas about one in 20 have life-threatening severe altitude illness.

WHO'S AT RISK?

You can experience problems at altitude whatever your age or fitness level. The most important risk factor is how rapidly you ascend. If you fly into Cuzco (in Peru) at over 3000m from Lima at sea level, you will almost certainly experience symptoms due to the altitude.

Some people are naturally more prone to altitude illness than others, and you're much more likely to get problems at altitude if you've had them before (60% likelihood for high altitude pulmonary oedema), so you should get expert advice in this situation.

> **!** If you have any ongoing conditions, particularly heart or lung problems, discuss this with your doctor before you go.

Children & Altitude

Children appear to be at the same risk of altitude sickness as adults, but they are less likely to be able to let you know if they have symptoms, which makes it more risky. It's best to descend promptly if your children show even vague symptoms. Drugs such as Diamox (see later) are best avoided in children.

Oral Contraception & Altitude

Note that there's a theoretical risk that the oral contraceptive pill or hormone replacement therapy will make altitude sickness worse in women taking these, although at altitudes below about 5500m there's little evidence to support this. It probably makes sense to discuss this issue with your doctor in advance if you fall into either of these categories.

PREVENTION

The best way to prevent acute mountain sickness (AMS) is to ascend slowly and gradually, allowing time for acclimatisation to occur. In practice this means:

- having frequent rest days – plan to spend two to three nights at each rise of 1000m
- 'climb high, sleep low' – as far as possible, sleep at a lower altitude than the greatest height you reached during the day

- above 3000m don't increase your sleeping altitude by more than 300m per day
- if you have any symptoms of AMS, stop ascending until the symptoms have gone
- descend immediately if your symptoms persist or worsen in 30 to 60 minutes

If you fly straight to high altitude, you will need to allow at least two to three days to become accustomed to the altitude, and a week is sensible if you are planning on trekking higher.

! Never trek alone at altitude – you may not recognise the symptoms of AMS in yourself and you may not be able to get to safety if you are ill.

Other general measures for preventing illness at altitude include the following:

- if you plan to trek at altitude, make sure you know where the nearest medical facility is
- drink plenty of fluids to prevent dehydration (4L or 5L daily), as the air at high altitude is dry and you lose plenty of moisture through sweating and breathing
- don't overexert yourself, especially in the first week or so at altitude
- eat light, high-carbohydrate meals to give you energy
- avoid alcohol, sedatives or any other mind-altering substances

Another option for preventing AMS is with drugs, but be aware that this is a highly controversial issue, and you will get different advice from different sources. Although there are some situations where drug treatment is useful, the bottom line is that if you follow the rules of gradual safe ascent, you shouldn't need drug treatment.

Currently, the most widely used drug for preventing AMS is acetazolamide (Diamox). This drug works on cellular biochemistry, resulting in increased breathing rates and improved oxygen supply to the body and brain. Diamox can be used to prevent mild AMS as well as to treat it, but it doesn't prevent or treat severe AMS or high altitude pulmonary or cerebral oedema. Side effects are common, usually tingling in the fingers, and it makes you pass more urine.

There is no evidence that Diamox masks the symptoms of AMS. However, if you decide to take it, you should realise that Diamox is not a replacement for acclimatisation – if you ascend too fast, even if you're taking Diamox, you'll get AMS. For more information about Diamox and other drugs used in altitude illness, check out the information sources listed earlier in the boxed text or talk to your doctor. Remember:

- the best treatment for AMS is descent
- you should never use drug treatment as a means of avoiding descent or to enable you to ascend further

MILD AMS

Above about 2000m, it's common to get mild symptoms of AMS, which usually come on gradually. These include:

- headache
- loss of appetite
- nausea and vomiting
- tiredness and irritability

You may also notice that you're a bit unsteady on your feet, and you may feel a little short of breath. Because symptoms of AMS are so nonspecific, it can be difficult to distinguish them from flu, colds or jet lag, if you've recently arrived – if in doubt, assume it's AMS. Having difficulty sleeping is very common at altitude – you may find it hard to get to sleep, have vivid dreams and wake up frequently. Your travel companions may notice you have periodic breathing, when your breathing slows and appears to stop. Periodic breathing can be very scary to witness, but it's not dangerous.

You may notice that your face or limbs are puffy when you wake up. This doesn't mean that you are getting a more severe form of altitude illness, and it usually settles without any treatment over the course of a couple of days.

Symptoms of mild AMS are unpleasant, but they usually disappear after two to three days, as long as you don't go any higher. The main concern with mild AMS is that it can progress to more severe forms if you ignore it or go higher.

SEVERE AMS

About one in 20 people will develop more severe forms of altitude illness, usually at 4000m and above, but sometimes lower. Severe AMS includes high altitude pulmonary oedema and high altitude cerebral oedema.

In high altitude pulmonary oedema (HAPE), fluid accumulates in your lungs, preventing you from breathing properly. It can follow from mild AMS or it can come on suddenly without any warning. The main symptoms are:

- breathlessness at rest or a persistent cough (common early symptoms)
- coughing up pink, frothy sputum
- tiredness and weakness

If fluid collects within your brain, you get high altitude cerebral oedema (HACE). This condition is rare, but it is life-threatening, so you need to know how to recognise it and what to do about it. Symptoms to look out for:

- severe headache, unrelieved by simple painkillers
- change in behaviour, confusion and disorientation
- double vision
- unsteadiness
- drowsiness and coma (unconsciousness)

Early HACE causes a condition called ataxia (a form of incoordination) which can be picked up by the straight line test. To do this test, draw a line on the ground and get the person to walk heel to toe along it. If they can't do it without overbalancing or stepping off the line, assume they have HACE, especially if they have other signs of illness.

TREATMENT

Remember: the best treatment for any form of AMS is descent. Mild symptoms of AMS can be treated with simple measures, but bear in mind some not-to-be-broken rules:

- never ascend with any symptoms of AMS
- always descend promptly if your symptoms are moderate to severe or getting worse, or there's no improvement in mild symptoms after two to three days
- seek medical advice if necessary, but don't let this delay descent
- rest up for a couple of days
- drink plenty of fluids, as dehydration is common at altitude
- take simple painkillers or an anti-inflammatory like ibuprofen for the headache
- try a motion sickness remedy (p70) for nausea and vomiting
- if you have access to oxygen by mask, this can be helpful

Severe AMS, HAPE and HACE are all medical emergencies – you need to act immediately.

- Seek medical advice if possible but don't let this delay descent.
- Descend immediately (even 500m can help).
- Use oxygen by mask, if possible.

Drug treatments are as follows, but remember these are powerful drugs that can be dangerous if used incorrectly. If you are carrying them, make sure you know all about how to use them before you go:

- severe AMS or HACE – dexamethasone 8mg by mouth immediately, followed by 4mg every six hours until you are evacuated
- HAPE – nifedipine 20mg by mouth immediately

If necessary, if you're not sure what the problem is (as is often the case), you can take all treatments together. Note that dexamethasone is a powerful steroid drug that should be used with extreme caution, and ideally only under medical supervision. Side effects include mood changes and an increased risk of indigestion and ulceration. Nifedipine is a drug used in the treatment of high blood pressure and heart problems.

OTHER HEALTH CONCERNS

Sunburn is common at high altitude because less sunlight is filtered out by the atmosphere; if there is snow, this reflects sunlight more than plain ground. Cover up and use a high protection factor sunscreen (don't forget your lips), and wear good sunglasses to protect your eyes. Dehydration is common, so drink plenty of fluids, even if you don't feel thirsty.

You still need to take precautions with your drinking water. Most diarrhoea-causing microorganisms are resistant to cold temperatures, even freezing, and water from streams on popular routes is quite likely to be contaminated with faeces. Water from glacial streams can contain mineral salts, which may have a laxative effect.

Snow blindness is sunburn of the backs of the eyes and is caused by sunlight reflected off snow. Prevent it by wearing goggles or sunglasses with UV protection. It gives you a gritty feeling in your eyes, extreme sensitivity to light, redness and temporary blindness several hours after exposure. There's no specific treatment apart from relieving the pain (for example by putting cold cloths onto your closed eyes), and it usually heals completely in a couple of days. Anaesthetic eye drops are sometimes used but they may slow the healing process and make your eyes more vulnerable to other injuries. Antibiotic eye drops are not necessary. You can make emergency eye protection by cutting slits in cardboard or cloth.

ACTION SAFETY

Latin America provides endless opportunities for adventuring, from trekking in the high Andes to cruising down the mighty

Amazon. However, if you injure yourself or find yourself in an emergency situation in a remote area, you will have to rely on your own resources. Take care to stay in one piece, and make sure you know what to do in an emergency. In this section we've outlined some basic safety rules for outdoors action.

- For advice on keeping feet happy and healthy, see the section on Feet at the end of the Skin chapter.
- Need guidance on fuelling up? See the Food for Action section at the end of the Diet & Nutrition chapter.

TREKKING SAFELY

If you decide to go on a trek of any length, here's a quick health and safety checklist.

Preparation

Always inform someone reliable of your route and estimated arrival date so that if you do run into difficulties, the alarm can be raised. You could consider letting the folks back home know via a brief phone call; alternatively, leave the information with your hotel or other travellers. This system will only work if you let people know when you get back, so that unnecessary rescues aren't initiated.

- Fitness – trekking can be a strenuous activity, particularly if you're not in peak physical condition, so make sure what you are planning is within your capabilities and that there is some flexibility built into your plans in case you find you need to bail out at any stage.
- Training – if you can, some pre-trek fitness training is a good idea, and will reduce the likelihood of sprains, falls and overuse injuries.
- Equipment – make sure you are fully prepared for the environmental conditions you're likely to encounter and take a well stocked medical kit (see the Before You Go chapter earlier in this book).
- Footwear – running shoes and sandals are not much use on a trek in rough terrain, so unless you can get hold of a decent pair of walking boots, consider changing your plans.

- High altitude trekking – make sure you know what to look for and what to do if you develop signs of altitude illness.
- Map and compass – a reasonable map of the area is vital, especially if you are going without a guide (but is a good idea anyway), but it's no good if you can't follow it.
- Insurance – check that your insurance covers you for trekking, and consider joining a local emergency rescue organisation.

On the Trek

Consider hiring porters to carry the heavy equipment (and help the local economy), and a guide if you're unsure of the route.

- Water – don't assume there will be water along the way unless you find out that there is from a reliable source; otherwise, you'll need to carry all your water requirements with you (remember if it's hot, you will need a minimum of 5L of water each per day). Even if there is water along the way, you will need to purify it before using it.
- Food – don't rely on food being available along the way; take plenty of food with you, including energy-giving snacks such as chocolate and dried fruit (see the Food for Action section in the Diet & Nutrition chapter for more suggestions).
- Tiredness – this makes injuries more likely, so eat properly throughout the day, take regular rests and don't push yourself too hard, especially towards the end of the day.
- Blisters – avoid these by wearing well worn-in walking boots and socks that fit snugly with no seams; if you do get one, follow the guidelines given in the section on Feet at the end of the Skin chapter.
- Protect yourself against insect bites and stings (p89), and be aware of the risk of Chagas' disease (p369) if you are staying in local houses. Horse flies, midges, gnats and mosquitoes can be a nuisance when you're out and about, and sometimes the only way to avoid them is by trekking above the treeline.

If you're walking on paths slashed through the forest, beware the cut-off ends of bamboo. These can be extremely sharp and are potentially dangerous if you slip and impale yourself on one.

JUNGLE TRIPS

A trip into the Amazonian jungle is probably high priority for most travellers to tropical Latin America. Rainforests are full of the most interesting and unusual life forms you can imagine. The rainforest or jungle environment maintains a fairly constant temperature with high humidity. This prevents sweat from evaporating and thus cooling you. Make sure you drink plenty of fluids in these conditions, especially if you are trekking or doing other vigorous exercise. Take a water bottle with you, and sip from it regularly.

Although it's hot and steamy, it's very important to cover up with clothes and to use insect repellent to prevent yourself being eaten alive by mosquitoes, sandflies and gnats. Sleep up off the forest floor if possible, under an insecticide-treated net. Sleeping under a net will also protect you from vampire bats.

Leeches are a problem in most rainforest areas, so remember to tuck your trousers into your boots. Sturdy footwear is vital – it will not only protect your feet from cuts and scratches, but also against hazards such as ants, snakes and spiders. See the Bites & Stings chapter for details on these creepy-crawlies.

It can be tempting to cool off by taking a dip in the river, but beware of strong currents and other hazards – see the boxed text on p363 for more details.

Finally, it is not unknown for people to get lost in the jungle, so be prepared to take a guide.

River Crossings

Most river crossings will have bridges, but if you have to cross any fast-flowing rivers, take one arm out of your pack, and unbuckle your pack so if you feel yourself getting swept away, you can slip out of it easily. Use a stick to feel the river bed before putting your feet down, and walk side-on to the direction of flow so that the water can flow more easily round your body. Snowmelt is very cold, so beware of hypothermia and muscle cramps.

Lightning

Beware of lightning if you find yourself out in the open when a storm comes on. Lightning has a penchant for crests, lone trees, gullies, caves and cabin entrances, as well as wet ground. If you are caught out in the open, try to curl up as tight as possible, with your feet together, and a layer of insulation between you and the ground. Make sure you're not sitting next to metal objects like walking poles or metal-frame backpacks – place them a short distance away from you.

Rescue & Evacuation

If one of your group is injured or falls ill, leave someone with them and go for help. If there are only two of you, leave the person in a sheltered position with as much warm clothing, food and water as you can sensibly spare, as well as some means of attracting attention (like a whistle or torch). Mark the position with something conspicuous, such as a brightly coloured bag or a large stone cross on the ground.

Or at least this is the accepted strategy for rescue, but when you're travelling in remote areas, self-evacuation is going to be your best, and probably only, option, especially as rescue may be delayed or difficult due to transport problems and communication difficulties. Note that helicopters don't generally fly above 5000m or so. Make sure you have good insurance that covers evacuation from remote areas.

CYCLING SAFELY

There are plenty of opportunities for some decent cycling trips in Latin America. If you're considering a short or longer cycle tour, here are some basic health and safety tips.

Health & Fitness

It's a good idea to get fit on a bike if you plan on doing more than a couple of days of cycle touring – practise riding an average daily distance two or three days in a row. Before you set off, be sure to warm up and stretch properly. On the ride:

- take regular breaks during the day
- consider having a massage in the evening
- avoid sore hands from gripping the handlebar on rough roads for long periods by changing hand position (if possible), relaxing your grip on the handlebars and taking frequent rests
- be prepared for climatic extremes
- remember to drink plenty of fluids, especially if it's hot, and avoid cycling during the hottest part of the day
- take snack food with you for any ride that's more than about an hour long

Equipment & Cycling Technique

These can make a big difference to your enjoyment and comfort, as well as safety on the ride:

- if you're hiring a bike, check it over carefully – make sure the brakes work and check the wheels and tyres
- wear safety gear – helmet (essential), sunglasses, cycling gloves and two layers of clothing (helps prevent road rash if you come off your bike), and check your bike on a daily basis
- learn the local road rules, ride in single file and ride defensively
- make sure your bike is adjusted for you – check that the seat and handlebar height are comfortable and the seat is parallel to the ground
- take lights with you if you're intending to ride at night
- balance the load on your bike and keep the weight low to the ground, preferably with panniers
- learn to spin the gears (70 to 90 revs per minute) not push them – this way you'll avoid sore knees from pushing big gears

For more information, you could try *The Bicycle Touring Manual* by Rob van der Plas, or check out this recommended website: **www.ctc.org.uk**.

CAVING HAZARDS

Going in caves involves some hazards you should be aware of, although you're unlikely to be at any great risks from these on most standard guided tours. Caves are dark, so you'll want to take a good torch with you, and even in hot climates they can be cold, so be prepared with layers. Flash floods are always a risk.

- Leptospirosis may be a risk as this bacterial disease can be transmitted through rat or bat urine, and you can get infected if you scrape yourself against the cave walls; you can also acquire it by swimming in contaminated water – see p364 for more details.

- You can get a fungal chest infection, histoplasmosis, by inhaling dried bat droppings, but this is a risk mainly in small confined spaces; you get a fever, headache, chest pains and cough about two weeks after you've been exposed – there's no specific treatment, but you should seek medical advice, as it can make some people very ill.

- Rabies can be carried by bats and rats, as well as animals like cats and dogs – although you normally acquire the disease through bites, there have been cases in cavers from inhaling dried bat droppings, so if you are planning on any serious caving, you should make sure you get immunised against rabies before you leave (see p35 for more details).

- Scorpions and snakes live in caves, so be wary of where you put your hands.

- Various insects (including sandflies, mosquitoes, ticks and leeches) live in and around the entrance to caves – cover up and apply insect repellent to prevent bites and the diseases they transmit.

Water...

Safe water for drinking is covered in detail on p83 of the Staying Healthy chapter. In this chapter we discuss potential hazards associated with immersing yourself in water.

➕ For guidelines on the emergency resuscitation of a drowning person, see the inside back cover.

SWIMMING

Relatively few travellers will be in line for many of the tropical diseases described elsewhere in this guide but most travellers are likely to be swimming at some stage on their trip. Accidents at the beach or poolside are common, from cuts and scratches to encounters with marine creatures and even drowning. In fact, drowning is surprisingly common in Latin America (and elsewhere), especially in children and young adults. For some basic swimming safety tips, see p96 in the Staying Healthy chapter.

❗ Swimmers and divers should always watch out for motorboats, as they may not be watching out for you, and many accidents occur in this way.

Make the most of your beach or pool holiday by bearing some of the following in mind:

- the effects of the sun and heat are major risks at the beach or poolside – see the Acclimatisation section of the Staying Healthy chapter for more guidance on this
- swimming at night or after you've had an alcoholic drink or two tends to be especially risky and is best avoided
- eye and ear infections are common in swimmers, especially if the water is none too clean – see the relevant sections in the Ears, Eyes & Teeth chapter for more details; wear goggles and ear plugs if you are in any doubt about the cleanliness of the water
- fungal skin infections are common in hot humid climates – drying yourself off between swims can help prevent these

SURFING SAFETY TIPS

Peter Neely, author of Indo Surf & Lingo, *has the following tips for safe surfing.*

The surfing lifestyle is all about fun and freedom, but you need to take a few simple precautions to avoid unwanted injuries.

Sun Protection
Possibly the most dangerous aspect of surfing is sunburn, which can keep you out of the surf for a few days. In the long term, sunburn can cause potentially fatal skin cancer.

- Use waterproof sunscreen (ideally SPF 30); apply it before you go out, and reapply it regularly.
- Wear a Lycra wetshirt in the surf. A cap protects your eyes in the water too.
- Avoid surfing when the sun is at its most intense, between 11am and 3pm.

Check the Conditions
When you arrive at a new surf spot, it pays to watch the line-up for at least 15 minutes before paddling out.

- What is underneath the water? Any rocks or shallow ledges? If you're surfing over a coral reef, always wear protective rubber boots and maybe a wetsuit.
- Where do the local surfers paddle out from? Where do they exit the surf?
- Are there any rips? If caught in a rip, always paddle across it, not against it.
- How often do the big sets come? Can you handle that size wave?
- Where do the locals end their ride? Is there a dangerous end section they avoid?

Dangerous Creatures

Sharks are universally feared by surfers, but you are unlikely to see one, and attacks are even rarer. Avoid surfing in river mouths and be watchful around sunset. Other hazards include jellyfish, sting rays, blue ringed octopus and stone fish. Be watchful when surfing in on-shore winds which carry these stingers towards shore. For more details, see the section on Marine Life later in this chapter.

Be Prepared

- Travel with a simple first aid kit.
- Drink plenty of water before and after surfing to prevent dehydration
- Practise long swims before your trip to increase stamina.
- Swim between the flags on a patrolled beach where lifesavers are on duty.
- Stretch before and after each surf.
- Never surf alone.

Equipment

Make sure your board has no sharp edges – repair dings smoothly, sand sharp edges off your fins, use a rubber nose guard and most importantly attach a new leg rope before your trip.

Happy surfing!

- cuts and scratches can easily get infected by bathing in unclean water or by not cleaning them thoroughly and promptly at the time
- sand and soil can be contaminated by animal faeces, which can transmit diseases, including a rash known as 'creeping eruption' – sit on a towel, chair or hammock if necessary

Tempting though it is, walking barefoot in or out of the water is probably best avoided, as injury is common and you never know if there might be sharp objects just below the surface of the sand. You can also pick up parasites in this way, including jiggers (chigoes) and hookworm (in rural areas).

WATER POLLUTION

Quite apart from any aesthetic considerations, swimming in polluted waters can cause illness and is best avoided. Water pollution is a worldwide problem, but it is particularly severe around urban centres in Latin America, affecting rivers and the ocean. Disposal of sewage is far from adequate in Latin America, where only 10% of the waste water collected is treated before it is disposed of – often into the ocean or nearby waterways. In Lima (Peru), for example, the daily papers are full of warnings of the dire health consequences of swimming at the city's beaches, although these are rarely heeded. Other ocean and river pollutants include chemical spills, industrial by-products, fertilisers and pesticides. Pollution tends to be worse after torrential rain as surface contaminants get washed away, and sewage channels overflow.

Illnesses you can get from swimming in polluted water (by swallowing small amounts of water) tend to be all the intestinal infections, including diarrhoea and hepatitis. Children often swallow water when they swim, and are especially at risk. Direct contact with chemical pollutants in the water can cause irritation to your skin and eyes, as well as uncertain, possibly carcinogenic, long-term effects.

Chlorinated pools that are well maintained should be safe, although some diarrhoea-causing parasites (such as *Giardia* and cyclospora) are able to survive chlorination. You can't get diseases like HIV from swimming in pools.

Here are some safety tips to bear in mind:

- stick to well maintained chlorinated pools or ocean beaches far from urban settlements and the mouths of rivers, streams and storm-water drains
- never swim in sluggish rivers in urban areas (remember that schistosomiasis is a freshwater hazard in some areas – see Freshwater hazards later in this chapter)

- do a quick check for floating objects before you get in the water, and if in doubt, try not to swallow any water

CRAMPS

These muscle spasms can be extremely painful and may occur for a variety of reasons, including swimming in cold water, tiredness, overexertion or dehydration. It starts as a twinge at first, often in your calf, then the pain builds up and is only relieved by resting the muscle. Massaging and stretching the muscle, for example by pulling on your toes while straightening your leg, can help. Cramps are potentially dangerous if you are in rough seas or you're a weak swimmer. Try to rest the muscle, then use it gently.

Help prevent cramps by warming up well and stretching before starting any activity. Remember to warm down after strenuous activity.

WAVES, TIDES & CURRENTS

If you're not a confident swimmer or you're not used to big waves, it's best to err on the side of caution. Ask around locally about dangerous currents and tides. Many hundreds of people drown each year in coastal waters in Latin America, especially off the Pacific coast.

Be especially wary of rips, as these strong currents are a common cause of beach drownings. A rip is where the water brought to the beach by breaking waves runs back out. It tends to take you out to sea, not down under the water. Rips can be very difficult to spot, even if you're looking for them.

> ! Telltale signs of a rip current include colour (it may be darker than the water on either side), a rippled effect on the surface of the water and a trail of surf extending beyond the surf zone.

Also keep a look out for side shore currents. These flow parallel to the shore and can wash you quite a way down the beach, where conditions may be less safe. Don't stray too far from the shore in this situation, and watch the shoreline to make sure you don't drift too far along. Swim in to the shore before you float too far away from your starting point.

GETTING OUT OF A RIP

If you do get into a rip, you may feel yourself being dragged out to sea, or you may be sucked underwater if it passes through a rocky passage. To avoid getting into serious trouble, do the following:

• don't panic – this will tire you out quicker
• get out of the rip current by swimming parallel to the shore, then catching the waves back in; don't swim against the current, as you'll just exhaust yourself

If you are unsure of your swimming abilities and there are people on the beach, raise an arm above your head to indicate that you are in trouble, and tread water (you can stay afloat for a surprisingly long time) until you are rescued. Alternatively, you could try conserving your energy while you wait for rescue by allowing yourself to float motionless face down in the water, raising your head just when you need to take a breath.

MARINE LIFE

The oceans and reefs around Latin America are home to a variety of fascinating and often beautiful creatures, some of which can be a danger to you. If you are going to be swimming or diving in the sea, learn to recognise and avoid the villains. The risk of encountering a potentially dangerous sea creature is fairly small, so long as you use a bit of common sense:

■ seek out and heed advice on local dangers
■ don't walk along reefs in shallow water
■ don't go diving or snorkelling when the waters are murky (this may attract predators and you won't be able to see them coming)

- unless you're a marine biologist and know what you are doing, don't touch or feed any creature underwater
- it's a good rule never to put your hands or feet somewhere you can't see first
- most marine creatures are not aggressive – if you don't threaten them, most will leave you alone

In this section we outline some of the more noteworthy hazards to be aware of. All things considered, it's probably best to give that midnight skinny dip on a tropical beach a miss.

CORAL
Coral is sharp stuff and if you brush against it, you're very likely to injure yourself (and the coral). Coral wounds are notoriously troublesome, mainly because people don't clean them properly when they occur. Coral is covered in a layer of slime that is full of marine microorganisms, and small particles of coral, including its stinging cells, are often left in the wound.

If you ignore a coral wound, there's a good chance it will get infected and take ages to heal up. Treat any coral cut promptly, however small and insignificant it seems, as follows:

- rinse the wound with plenty of pure water (eg bottled water), perhaps using a small brush or a syringe (with or without the needle) to flush out any small particles
- apply an antiseptic solution such as povidone-iodine
- apply an antibiotic cream or powder (eg mupirocin 2%) to the area
- cover it with a dressing
- watch for signs of infection (p437)

You can cause irreparable damage to the coral when you come into contact with it, so it's mutually beneficial to avoid getting cut by coral in the first place.

- Don't walk or swim over reefs.
- Maintain correct buoyancy and control when you're diving on reefs.
- Always wear shoes in the water – flip flops (thongs) or sports sandals are good.

SHARKS

➕ Treatment of a shark bite (and bites from other fish such as barracuda) is basic first aid for a traumatic injury – see the First Aid appendix, p434.

Although not entirely to blame, the film *Jaws* has ensured that for most people shark attack is their ultimate marine fear. However, only about a hundred or so shark attacks are reported around the world each year – compare that with the number of people who go swimming and diving every year!

Sharks occur in all oceans of the world but are more common in warmer waters. Only a few sharks are known to be a danger to humans. The great white, tiger and bull sharks are thought to be the most dangerous, while mako sharks and the weird-looking hammerhead are also known to attack humans occasionally. Sharks are primarily an ocean hazard, but bull sharks sometimes swim up freshwater rivers, and have been spotted in the Amazon River and Lake Nicaragua.

Ask about sharks (and other marine hazards) locally. Great whites are more common around seal colonies, which swimmers and divers should avoid for this reason. Spearfishing and line fishing may attract sharks. If you decide to swim in an area known to have sharks, here are some tips on avoiding trouble:

■ don't swim or dive where fishermen are cleaning their catches (not an attractive option anyway)

■ avoid swimming in murky waters or with an open wound

■ be careful at dusk, as this is when sharks feed

In the unlikely event that you spot a shark, don't panic – try to move away slowly. The less you look like a frantic seal to the short-sighted shark, the better. Sharks have poor eyesight and are attracted by movement and smell.

SEA SNAKES

These beautiful creatures are found in warm waters on the Pacific coast of Central America, from Mexico to Ecuador. They're often very inquisitive, although not usually aggressive.

However, their venom is extremely toxic, so you should give them a wide berth. Unlike venomous fish bites, sea snake bites are not painful. Bites look like two or more small dots or scratch marks. Although sea snake venom is very poisonous, the quantity of venom injected is rarely enough to cause serious problems. Symptoms of poisoning may not appear for several hours, and include pain and stiffness, weakness, dry mouth, difficulty swallowing or speaking, thirst and respiratory failure.

❗ **Get medical treatment urgently for any sea snake bite.**

First aid treatment in the meantime is as for any snake bite:

- keep the casualty calm
- apply a pressure bandage (see p436)
- immobilise the limb by splinting it (this helps prevent the toxin from spreading)
- be ready to perform emergency resuscitation if necessary

JELLYFISH

Despite their ethereal appearance, jellyfish are carnivorous animals. They are distributed widely, and occur in all tropical and subtropical waters. Jellyfish catch their prey by discharging venom into it from special stinging cells called nematocysts. Most jellyfish stings are just uncomfortable, but a couple of species are capable of causing severe, potentially lethal stings. In general, stings on thick skin like the soles of your feet are less likely to blister and cause other problems. Children are more likely to suffer a severe reaction to stings.

Sea Lice

Sea lice, also called sea bather's eruption, are thought to be the tiny larvae of thimble jellyfish. They can be a problem in any tropical waters. They sting and cause an uncomfortable rash, especially if they get caught in your swimming suit. Shower thoroughly after getting out of the sea. Calamine lotion may relieve the pain.

Deadly Jellyfish

Look out for these in tropical waters.
The Portuguese (or Pacific) man-of-war (right)
looks like a bluish float on the surface of the water.
Underneath the float are long stinging tentacles.
Large numbers of these jellyfish may be blown
ashore. Stings are extremely painful, and can cause
blisters and swelling. Symptoms of poisoning include
fever, chills, muscle cramps and paralysis, sometimes
leading to death.

> ▌ Dead man-of-wars are often washed up on shore and they may
> still be able to sting – don't touch any jellyfish on the beach.

Box jellyfish (below) species are the most deadly jellyfish in
the world. Stings are excruciatingly painful, their long tentacles
leaving multiple whiplash marks. Other effects depend on the
species, but can include breathing difficulties, coma and death.
Antivenin is usually available in affected areas.

Lion's mane and sea nettle jellyfish are found in the Pacific
Ocean and are also hazardous.

> ▌ Avoid contact with jellyfish; if necessary, wear a wetsuit or a lycra
> bodysuit in high-risk box jellyfish areas.

Treatment

> ▌ Don't wash jellyfish stings with water or rub them, as this may
> make the pain worse.

You will need to get medical
help urgently for severe stings,
especially if dangerous species
are known to be in the area. In
the meantime:

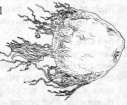

- get the casualty out of the water

- remove any bits of tentacle with
  tweezers or a gloved hand

- pour vinegar on the affected area (this doesn't help the pain, but it prevents stinging cells left in the wound from firing)
- be prepared to start emergency resuscitation if necessary – see inside backcover

For painful stings, ice packs or local anaesthetic sprays, creams or ointments may help, but strong painkilling injections may be needed. Antivenin may be available for some stings (for example box jellyfish).

RAYS

Rays are widespread throughout tropical and subtropical waters and, in South America, freshwater rays are common in some areas. They're not aggressive but because they like to lie half-submerged in mud or sand in the shallows, swimmers often step on them accidentally. If you do, you'll certainly know, as rays whip up their tails in self-defence and can inflict a nasty ragged wound. They also inject venom through special spines, which can sometimes be fatal. Electric rays can deliver a shock of up to 200V.

Sting ray injuries are common, and usually minor; severe poisoning is relatively rare. First aid treatment of a ray injury is as for Dangerous Marine Fish (see following section). You need to clean any sting ray wound very carefully, as for coral wounds, as otherwise infection is common.

❗ Always shuffle your feet when in the shallows to give sting rays, stonefish and other creatures a chance to get out of your way.

DANGEROUS MARINE FISH

Relatively few fish are dangerous to humans, but there are a couple of species that produce venom capable of causing severe poisoning and sometimes death. Of these, stonefish and scorpionfish (including butterfly cod and lionfish) are probably the most dangerous, and occur in most tropical waters. You'll know if you've been stung, as stings from venomous fish are extremely painful.

Stonefish (above) have the dubious distinction of being the deadliest of all venomous fish. Stonefish are as ugly as scorpionfish are beautiful, and they are masters of disguise: they lie half-submerged in sand, mud or coral debris, looking exactly like (you guessed it) a stone. As with sting rays, the danger is stepping on one accidentally.

Stonefish stings are said to be the most devastatingly painful of any marine sting. The pain is immediate, causing the casualty to writhe around in agony. There is usually a puncture mark at the sting site, which develops a characteristic blue discolouration. The whole limb swells up. Severe poisoning may lead to collapse and even death. There is a stonefish antivenin, which should be given as soon as possible after the sting.

Scorpionfish (below) are much easier to avoid, as they are distinctive and easily recognised, and the chances of you being stung by one are pretty remote. No antivenin is available.

Treatment

Hot (nonscalding) water helps to break down the toxins and is surprisingly effective at relieving pain from venomous fish stings. General treatment principles are as follows:

- if any spines are poking out, try to remove them gently (be sure to protect your own hands)

- wash any surface venom off with water
- immerse the wound in hot (nonscalding) water for up to 90 minutes or until the pain has gone, or apply hot packs
- wash the wound thoroughly once the pain is under control and apply a clean dressing
- rest with the limb raised
- seek medical help for antivenin (for a stonefish sting) and pain control if necessary

BLUE-RINGED OCTOPUS

This deadly creature is found in tropical waters. At low tide they can be found in rock pools, and if you don't realise what they are, you may pick them up. They are surprisingly small, varying in size from 2 to 20cm. The ringed marks, normally yellowish brown, turn a bright blue when the octopus is stressed. Bites can cause paralysis and possibly death.

You must get help urgently. While you are waiting:

- wash out the wound with any water or antiseptic available
- apply a pressure bandage (see p436) to the affected limb and immobilise it (to prevent spread of the poison)

CONE SHELL

However pretty a shell looks, it makes sense not to pick it up, especially if you don't know what it is. Fish-eating cones are found in tropical and subtropical waters. They kill their prey by harpooning them with a poisonous barb, which has been known to cause death in humans. The pain from a sting can be excruciating, and may be followed by generalised symptoms, including paralysis. Treatment is as for blue-ringed octopus bite, with pressure bandaging and immobilisation.

CROWN OF THORNS

These impressive reef creatures are a hazard if you tread on them by accident or brush against them while diving. They inject venom from the base of their spines, which can break of and remain embedded in you. If the spines are not removed, they can cause pain, swelling and generally make you feel unwell for several weeks or months.

Remove any spines you can see, making sure not to break them. Immerse the affected area in hot (nonscalding) water, which will help ease the pain, then immobilise the limb. Seek medical advice as soon as possible.

SEA URCHINS

Sea urchins make an unlikely culinary speciality (in Chile, for example) and are best treated with care in their natural environment too. If you step on one with bare feet, their spines can become embedded and are difficult to remove. One species is capable of causing generalised poisoning.

If you step on one, remove any spines you can with tweezers, taking care not to break them off. Run hot (nonscalding) water over the wound to relieve the pain, then apply antiseptic to the wound. Applying meat tenderiser, made from the flesh of the paw paw (papaya) fruit, to the area may be helpful. Keep a careful lookout for breathing difficulties – seek medical help immediately if these develop.

OTHER STINGERS

Various other marine creatures can cause problems if you come into contact with them. Some sponges can cause severe itching, fire coral or feathery stinging hydroid can cause a painful sting and prolonged itching, and anemones can also give you a painful sting, so don't put inquisitive fingers on their tentacles.

SCUBA DIVING

Diving is a prime attraction for many visitors to the Caribbean coast of Latin America. Diving is a fantastic sport, allowing you to enter another world. However, diving accidents do happen, often involving beginners, and can be fatal or cause permanent injury. To dive safely, you need to have done the proper training and have a good understanding of the risks involved and how to minimise them.

DIVING CERTIFICATE

To dive, you will need a diving certificate issued by a major diving organisation (PADI, NAUI etc) – it's a bit like a driving licence when you're hiring a car. To get a certificate, you need to complete a diving course. You can either do this before you go or at a dive centre at your destination. Once you've got your diver's card, you can dive anywhere you want.

> ! Diving is not suitable for everyone; if you intend to go diving, it's a good idea (and sometimes mandatory) to have a diving medical check-up to make sure you are physically fit to dive, especially if you are on any medications or you have a medical condition.

Some dive centres may just want you to fill in a questionnaire, but ideally you should get a proper diving medical check-up before you leave. Age is not a barrier to diving in itself, but conditions that may make diving unsuitable for you are heart or lung disease (including asthma), ear or sinus problems and any fits or dizzy spells.

INSURANCE

This is vital! You will need specific diver insurance that covers evacuation to a hospital or recompression chamber and subsequent treatment, something that will otherwise cost you thousands of dollars. Divers Alert Network (DAN – see the boxed text for details) offers this, as do some other organisations (such as PADI). Note that some dive operators won't let you dive unless you have this insurance.

> ! In an emergency situation, use what services are available at the time but make sure you contact your insurance provider as soon as possible.

DIVERS ALERT NETWORK (DAN)

DAN is an international nonprofit organisation providing expert medical information and advice for the benefit of the diving public. It operates a 24 hour diving emergency hotline in the USA (☎ 919-684-8111); alternatively, ☎ 919-684-4DAN (4326) accepts collect calls in a dive emergency.

DAN does not directly provide medical care, but it does provide advice on early treatment, evacuation and hyperbaric treatment of diving-related injuries.

For general queries and information about diving health and safety, contact DAN in the USA on ☎ 919-684-2948 (or toll-free ☎ 800-446-2671 from within North America) or check out its website (**www.diversalertnetwork.org**).

You should always make sure you know where the nearest hyperbaric chamber is, especially if you are planning on diving in more remote areas – check with your dive operator before you start.

DIVING RESOURCES

As part of the services they provide, DAN has a Medical Information Line (☎ 1-919-684-2948, 9am to 5pm Monday to Friday), or you can email a query (see the boxed text on DAN for contact details).

You'll find lots of good books on all aspects of diving, including health and safety. Some recommended titles include *Encyclopaedia of Recreational Diving*, a basic text produced by PADI; and *The Diver's Handbook* by Alan Mountain, which is a comprehensive, well thought-out guide covering most aspects of diving. Another good book is *Scuba Diving Explained – Questions and Answers on Physiology and Medical Aspects of Diving* by Martin Lawrence. Lonely Planet's *Diving &*

Snorkeling series has specialised diving guides, including Latin American sites.

DIVING & ANTIMALARIALS

If you're taking mefloquine (Lariam) for protection against malaria, you need to be aware that diving isn't recommended while you are taking it. This is because mefloquine can cause dizziness and balance problems, especially in the first few weeks of taking it, and it can make fits more likely in susceptible people. If you are planning on going diving and need to take antimalarials, mention this to your doctor before you leave so you can be prescribed an alternative if necessary.

! If you are taking any medications, check with a diving medicine specialist (such as DAN) that it is safe to dive.

DIVING & FLYING

If you fly too soon after diving – even a single dive – you can get decompression sickness, as the cabin pressure is set to a lower level than the pressure at sea level, which encourages nitrogen bubbles to form. If you are planning to dive before you fly, discuss it with a reliable diving instructor, but basic guidelines are as follows:

- don't fly within 12 hours of a single no-decompression-stop dive (ie you didn't need to stop or descend to relieve pressure effects) and not within 24 hours of multiple no-decompression-stop dives
- wait 24 to 48 hours before flying after any dive which required decompression stops
- if you required recompression therapy, you need a medical certificate to say you are fit to fly

DIVING SAFELY

Basic rules for safe diving are:

- don't dive if you're feeling physically or mentally below par
- avoid going in if you are uncertain about the water or weather conditions
- check rental equipment carefully before using it
- never dive after taking alcohol or mind-altering substances
- always follow your dive leader's instructions – but be aware that there are good and less good divemasters; ask around beforehand
- be aware of your limitations and stick within them
- never dive in murky water – you won't be able to see and avoid hazards
- stop diving if you feel cold or tired, even if it's not the end of the dive
- try not to panic if you find yourself in difficulties – instead, take some slow deep breaths and think through what you need to do
- avoid touching or picking up things underwater – they may be harmful to you and you may cause harm to a fragile environment

DIVING SAFETY TIPS

Although most dive centres are very safety-conscious, fierce competition between dive schools at some popular dive sites (such as Utila in Honduras) can mean that corners are cut and safety standards suffer as a result. Some basic rules for safe diving are as follows.

When you're looking for a dive school, look for:

- small instruction groups – about four to six learners to one instructor is probably the most you'd want
- experienced diving instructors; there should always be a divemaster on board any dive charter
- good, well maintained equipment
- boats should have a two-way radio, oxygen and medical kit, and there should always be someone on board (with diving equipment) while divers are underwater

Before the dive:

- don't dive if you're feeling physically or mentally below par
- avoid going in if you are uncertain about the water or weather conditions
- check rental equipment carefully before using it
- never dive after taking alcohol or doing drugs

On the dive:

- always follow your dive leader's instructions – but be aware that there are good and less good divemasters; ask around beforehand
- be aware of your limitations and stick within them
- never dive in murky water – you won't be able to see and avoid hazards
- keep a watch on your diving companions for signs of difficulty – the 'buddy' system
- stop diving if you feel cold or tired, even if it's not the end of the dive
- try not to panic if you find yourself in difficulties – instead, take some slow deep breaths and think through what you need to do
- avoid touching or picking up things underwater – they may be harmful to you and you may be harmful to them; it's usually illegal to take anything from a marine park

Even if you are an experienced diver, if you haven't been on a dive for a while consider doing a refresher course before you take the plunge, or ask to be taken on a site tour if you're uncertain about conditions or navigation in the area.

DIVING & HEALTH

Described here are some of the main problems that may be associated with diving. Note that these are not the only problems that can occur. A good training course should provide you with more information, or you could consult any of the resources mentioned earlier.

Decompression Sickness

Also known as the 'bends', decompression sickness is one of the most serious hazards of diving – make sure you know what it is and how to avoid it.

Breathing air under pressure (as when you're diving) forces quantities of nitrogen (a major component of air) to dissolve in your blood and body tissues. If the pressure is later released too quickly (for example you ascend too fast), nitrogen can't be eliminated in the usual way and bubbles of gas form in the blood stream and body tissue.

Symptoms depend on where the bubbles are. Bubbles in the bloodstream can block circulation and cause stroke-like symptoms, such as blackouts and weakness of one side of the body. The most common form of decompression sickness is where bubbles form in large joints (joint bends) like the shoulder and elbow, giving you pain that increases to a peak some hours after the dive, then gradually subsides. Skin bends can occur, giving you itches and a rash over your body. In spinal bends, you get back pain that typically circles your abdomen, followed by pins and needles in your legs, unsteadiness and paralysis. Inner ear bends make you dizzy and unable to balance.

Recompression

Treatment of the bends is by recompression in a hyperbaric chamber, which causes any bubbles to dissolve again, followed by slow, controlled decompression. This allows all the dissolved nitrogen to be eliminated without forming bubbles.

> ❗ Recompression treatment is usually effective but you need to get to a recompression chamber as soon as possible, because any delay could result in further damage, which may be irreversible.

Prevention

You can never guarantee that you won't get the bends, but you can do a lot to make it very unlikely. Dive tables are available to give you guidance on safe dives but they obviously don't take your individual condition into account.

> ❗ Never dive if you are feeling unwell in any way, avoid strenuous activity before you dive and drink plenty of fluids to prevent dehydration.

Be particularly careful to avoid diving if you're dehydrated, as this can slow down the rate at which nitrogen is eliminated from the blood. Sea sickness, alcohol the previous evening and heat can all make you dehydrated.

Nitrogen Build-Up

Nitrogen build-up can be a problem if you're on a diving holiday, doing multiple dives a day or diving on consecutive days, and is the most common cause of decompression sickness at diving resorts. Taking a day off can allow any nitrogen that has built up to be eliminated.

Nitrogen Narcosis

Also known as 'rapture of the depths', this occurs below depths of about 30 to 40m, and is due to the build-up of nitrogen in the blood to levels at which it has toxic effects on the brain. Symptoms can be quite frightening, and include a feeling of detachment from reality and apprehension, sometimes leading to panic. In addition, your thought processes slow down and you lose your concentration. Symptoms clear if you ascend 5 to 10m. Nitrogen narcosis is one reason why it is vital for divers to be on the lookout for signs in other members of the team, and to be familiar with an emergency drill for this situation.

Pressure Effects

The increased ambient pressure underwater can cause problems if pressure is not equalised within various air-filled cavities in the body, including the lungs, ears, sinuses, teeth cavities and gut. Lung barotrauma (damage due to pressure) is a very serious condition, often caused by not breathing out on ascent from a dive. Symptoms are variable but include chest pain, dizziness and unconsciousness. Treatment is by recompression in a hyperbaric chamber.

Ear and sinus pain can be quite severe, and you should avoid diving if you have a middle ear infection (see p188), sinus trouble, a cold or hay fever. If you get dental pain while diving, it may be due to cavities in your teeth (for example dental decay), and you should see a dentist as soon as is convenient.

FRESHWATER HAZARDS

CAIMANS & CROCODILES

These prehistoric creatures need to be treated with respect, but don't pose a major hazard to most travellers. They live throughout the region, from southern Mexico to northern Argentina. They can be found in ponds, streams, marshes, rivers and drainage channels. Caimans float half-submerged in the water, looking for prey in the water or on the river banks, and they attack with surprising speed.

Although you are very unlikely to come under attack from one of these, it's as well to be extremely wary of them. Ask around locally for reliable advice on risks, and keep your wits about you if you are walking or camping near waterways or travelling on a river. That log may not be a log after all.

PIRANHAS

The infamous piranha is a flesh-eating freshwater fish found only in the wide, sluggish rivers of South America. They have razor-sharp teeth and strong jaws and are said to be able to bite off a person's finger or toe, although their preferred diet is other fish, dead animals and insects. Piranhas are usually

about 35 to 70cm long. Stories
of the ferocity of this predator
abound and are undoubtedly
somewhat exaggerated – when
a passenger ship capsized at the
port of Obidos in Brazil in 1981,
some 300 people were said to
have been eaten by piranhas!
But to put things in perspective,
piranhas usually leave humans and

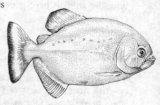

large animals alone, although they are more dangerous at
certain times of the year, usually the dry season. Don't get
between a hungry piranha and its next meal, or your flesh could
become the next meal.

URETHRA FISH

The candiru or urethra
fish, a minute parasitic
catfish that lives in
the deep waters of the

Amazon river, is weird but true. These tiny fishes are normally
parasitic on larger fish but have a particular predilection for
human (male or female) urethras (the tube that leads to the
bladder), presumably because they mistake it for the gills and
passages of fish. Humans are at risk if they swim in the water,
or just urinate into it. The pain, as you can imagine, is said to be
considerable. Local people take good care to avoid this hazard
by covering their genitalia before entering the water. You'd be
wise to do the same.

ELECTRIC EEL

This large, brown-ish freshwater fish, unique to South America,
is capable of emitting powerful electric discharges (up to 550V)
to stun its prey. Depending on the severity of the shock, be
prepared to perform emergency resuscitation on the casualty. A
trick of the local population is reportedly to send their animals
through eel-infested water to use up the eel's discharges. Then

once the animals have gone through, they know it's safe for people to go through.

SCHISTOSOMIASIS

✚ For guidelines on how to avoid this disease, see p92

Also known as bilharzia, in Latin America this parasitic disease is a risk mainly in parts of Brazil and Aragua and Carabobo states in Venezuela (see map p23). Worldwide, it's a common cause of ill health in tropical and subtropical regions, affecting up to 20 million people – the second-most common tropical disease after malaria. Tropical areas with lakes, streams and large rivers are generally worst affected.

Schistosomiasis is caused by tiny parasitic worms that live the first part of their life cycle in a type of freshwater snail, and the second part in humans. You can get schistosomiasis by bathing, swimming or showering in fresh water in which these snails are living. The tiny worms are only just visible to the naked eye. They can burrow their way through your intact skin (you don't need to have an open cut). It takes about 10 minutes or so for the worms to penetrate your skin, so vigorous drying with a towel after you have been exposed to risky water can help prevent infection.

The worms don't multiply once they're inside you, but their eggs can cause damage when they get lodged in your tissues. Schistosomiasis is primarily a disease of poor hygiene, as inadequate sewage disposal systems mean that eggs from infected people passed in urine or faeces find their way back into water, and the life cycle starts again.

There are two main types of the disease, affecting either your bladder or your intestines. In Latin America, you're mostly at risk of the intestinal form.

Signs & Symptoms

Schistosomiasis doesn't generally cause an acute, serious illness, in the way malaria does, but if it is left untreated it can cause serious health problems in the long term. Although chronic

RIVER IDYLL

Although the hazards of swimming in the sea are well known, swimming in rivers is also not without risks. Large rivers can have extremely strong currents, and you can easily get swept out of your depth. Waterfalls are great natural showers but dangerous swirls and eddies may occur in the water below them, and the rocks around them can be treacherously slippery.

Apart from these mechanical hazards to swimming in rivers, remember that schistosomiasis is a problem in some areas. Freshwater sting rays are a risk in some river beds, and the possibility of piranhas and the tiny parasitic catfish make immersion in some rivers in the area uninviting.

Larger hazards include caimans and aquatic snakes such as the notorious anaconda. Out of the water, various biting insects can be a real nuisance, including incredibly persistent swarms of mosquitoes, blackfly and midges. Leeches love damp river banks.

Finally, if you are going on a river trip, make sure there is some protection from the elements. Reflection of the sun off the water makes sunburn a major hazard.

schistosomiasis is a major public health problem in risk areas, it's extremely unlikely that the disease would reach this stage in you.

Most people don't get symptoms at the early stage, although you can get an itchy rash known as 'swimmer's itch' a few hours after you've been in contact with infected water as the worms penetrate your skin. This doesn't last long (a day or two), and you may not even notice it. You may notice a cough or wheezing about a week to 10 days later as the worms pass through your lungs.

Although you can sometimes get an acute illness four weeks or so after infection, with fever, schistosomiasis generally causes symptoms that come on gradually after several months. At this time, you may get abdominal pain and blood in your urine or faeces. Often this is the first indication that there is a problem.

Diagnosis & Treatment

Infection can be diagnosed by a blood test (but not until at least three months after you were infected), or by a urine or faeces test.

! If there's a chance you may have been infected while you were away, be sure to get it checked out when you return home.

Effective treatment is available with a single dose of a drug called praziquantel, which has few side effects.

LEPTOSPIROSIS (WEIL'S DISEASE)

This is another reason to be wary of swimming in fresh water. Leptospirosis is a bacterial disease that you can get from contact with water contaminated by animal urine (for example dogs and rats). It occurs throughout the Latin American region. You're probably at greatest risk of this if you're an 'adventure traveller', especially if you're swimming or doing water sports (canoeing, rafting or caving) in affected water. It's more common after a period of heavy rainfall or flooding. The bacteria enter your body through breaks in your skin or through your nose or eyes.

You can get just mild flu-like symptoms, about 10 days after infection, but sometimes a more severe illness results, with high fever, vomiting, diarrhoea and red, irritated eyes. The illness can occasionally progress to jaundice and severe liver failure, and even death in about one in 100 affected people.

You should seek medical help as soon as possible if you think you may have leptospirosis. After the diagnosis is confirmed, treatment is with antibiotics (penicillin or doxycycline).

Bites & Stings...

Bites and stings from insects and other small critters are probably going to be the main wildlife hazard you face on your travels through Latin America. In contrast, you're much less likely to be at risk from higher profile dangers like jaguars and snakes.

FLYING INSECTS

+ For the complete low-down on preventing insect bites, see p89.

MOSQUITOES

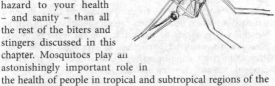

These bloodsuckers are likely to pose more of a hazard to your health – and sanity – than all the rest of the biters and stingers discussed in this chapter. Mosquitoes play an astonishingly important role in the health of people in tropical and subtropical regions of the world, mainly because they are carriers of a number of major diseases, including malaria, dengue fever, yellow fever and filariasis. If there was any justice in this world, mosquitoes would get the diseases they carry.

But it's not just the diseases mosquitoes carry; mosquito bites itch like mad and you run the very real risk of infection developing if you scratch them open. Insects, including mosquitoes, inject a small amount of saliva when they bite and this sets up a reaction around the bite, causing itching and swelling. Some people (often women) are particularly sensitive to bites, which can swell up alarmingly, often with a central blister. Bites are usually more troublesome when you first arrive but, in theory at least, you become desensitised to them (ie they cause less itching and swelling) with time.

SANDFLIES

Sandflies are tiny (2 to 3mm long), hairy flies with long legs which, in Latin America, are found in forested, tropical areas. Female sandflies feed on blood, causing extremely itchy bites in humans. Sandflies are responsible for transmitting leishmaniasis, sandfly fever and bartonellosis.

Sandflies rest in dark, moist habitats (such as the cracks in walls) during the heat of the day, emerging during the hours of darkness. Forest sandflies tend to rest on tree buttresses during daylight hours. Sandflies have a short flight range and don't fly very high, for example they rarely bite people sleeping on the 1st floor of a building.

Because sandflies are so small, they can get through most standard mosquito netting. You can get special sandfly netting but this will probably be too suffocating for most people. A permethrin-treated net is effective at keeping sandflies out. Prevent bites by using insect repellents containing DEET on exposed skin and covering up with clothes.

Leishmaniasis

This parasitic disease occurs in Central and tropical South America (see map p12). There are three main forms of the disease: skin (cutaneous leishmaniasis, or CL), mucocutaneous (or *espundia*), which only occurs in Latin America, and visceral (VL, affecting the internal organs). CL is the most common form of the disease worldwide, with approximately 1.5 million new cases occurring every year. Travellers do occasionally return with the skin form of the disease, usually an ulcer that fails to heal up, but other forms of the disease are very unlikely. Leishmaniasis presents a greater risk for people with reduced immunity, for example due to HIV infection.

Development of a vaccine seems likely in the near future, although one isn't available commercially yet. Recovery from an attack gives lifelong immunity to all forms of the disease.

! The best prevention of all forms of leishmaniasis is to avoid
sandfly bites.

In Latin America, leishmaniasis is generally a disease of rural,
forested areas, although increasing urbanisation has resulted
in outbreaks in urban areas. Clearing of the forest has brought
about a decrease in the number of cases seen, after an initial
increase of the disease in forest workers. Travellers on adventure
trips into the Amazon region may be at risk.

The skin lesions of CL are often called specific local names
in different parts of Latin America. CL usually starts as a small
bump that develops into an ulcer (sore) that heals slowly after
a variable length of time. A *chiclero* ulcer is a type of CL found
in Yucatan, Belize and Guatemala. It usually affects the ear,
and can result in destruction of the ear, but over a long period
of time. Other types of CL are called *pian bois* or bush yaws,
and *uta* (in Peru).

AN ITCH TO SCRATCH

How best you stop the itch from insect bites is one
of those hotly debated questions that every traveller
has an opinion on. It's important not to scratch those
bites because if you break the skin, you're very likely
to get a troublesome infection. You could try one
of the many commercial anti-sting relief sprays,
although antihistamine creams or sprays are probably
best avoided. They are widely available without a
prescription but they may cause an allergic skin
reaction, which makes the problem worse.

Other tried and tested options include calamine
cream, tea tree lotion, lavender oil or hydrocortisone
cream (applied sparingly, and not if the bite looks
infected). If the itching is driving you mad, you could
try taking an antihistamine tablet (see p422).

Mucocutaneous disease usually affects the mucous membranes of the nose and can be extremely destructive. The most severe form is known as *espundia,* which is Portuguese for sponge, a reference to the gross swelling of the nose and upper lip that can occur. Mucocutaneous leishmaniasis usually occurs within about two years of the original skin ulcer.

VL is a rare but more serious form of the disease and can be fatal. It usually develops several months after a bite, and symptoms fever that often comes and goes, weight loss, anaemia and wasting. It may be associated with enlargement of the spleen and liver.

Seek medical advice if you think you may have leishmaniasis, and remember that it can have a long incubation period. Effective drug treatment (usually sodium stibogluconate) is available, and is usually recommended for treatment of American CL.

Sandfly Fever

This viral disease occurs in Central America; it's rarely serious. Symptoms appear three to four days after a bite and include fever, chills, headache, joint pains, backache, nausea and vomiting, and sore throat. It generally clears up spontaneously without any specific treatment, usually within a few days.

Bartonellosis

This bacterial infection is transmitted through the bite of an infected sandfly. It occurs in mountain valleys of southwest Colombia, Ecuador and Peru. There's no risk at altitudes above about 2500m.

Prevention is by staying out of risk areas at sandfly-biting time (between dusk and dawn) and taking measures to avoid insect bites (cover up, use insect repellent). There is no vaccine against this disease.

Symptoms usually occur about two to three weeks after you are bitten, although it can be a couple of months in some cases. There are two different types of the disease, with different symptoms. With Oroya fever, symptoms include fever, headache, general aches and pains, followed by swollen glands and anaemia. It can last anything from two to six weeks, and can rarely be fatal. With veruga peruana, lots of small nodules appear over your face and limbs. These bleed easily and can last up to a year, after which they heal up without any lasting effects.

Treatment is with antibiotics (chloramphenicol or ampicillin usually). If you develop a fever or skin rash after visiting risk areas, you should see a doctor as soon as possible.

TRIATOMINE BUGS

These distinctive bugs are also known as cone-nose, kissing or assassin bugs; they also have many local names, including *chinchas* (Mexico), *barbeiro* (Brazil), *chipo* (Venezuela), and *vinchuna*, (Argentina). Their main claim to fame (apart from their great names) is that they transmit a serious parasitic infection in Latin America called Chagas' disease.

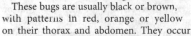

These bugs are usually black or brown, with patterns in red, orange or yellow on their thorax and abdomen. They occur in tropical areas of Latin America, and live on blood from humans and other animals. The traditional adobe houses with palm-thatched roofs that the majority of poorer people live in, especially in rural areas, provide plenty of dark crevices that the bugs like to live in. They tend to hide during the day, only coming out at night to feed. Bites aren't usually itchy unless you become sensitised to them. In heavily infested households, blood loss due to bug bites can be significant.

Chagas' Disease

This disease is named after the Brazilian physician Carlos Chagas, who first described it in 1909. It is unique to the Americas and occurs throughout Latin America. It is also known as American trypanosomiasis, and is caused by a parasite called *Trypanosoma cruzi*, which is related to the parasite that causes

ERADICATING CHAGAS' DISEASE

Intense insect eradication programs (mainly spraying of high-risk houses with insecticide) are making the eradication of Chagas' disease (transmitted through insect bites) a real possibility within the next decade in some countries such as Brazil. However, transmission through infected blood transfusion remains a significant though diminishing problem. Part of the difficulty is that there is no single 100% reliable test for detecting the infection in blood donations. However, better donor screening as well as more sophisticated blood testing is helping to eliminate this problem.

sleeping sickness (African trypanosomiasis) on the other side of the Atlantic in Africa.

Although very rare in travellers, Chagas' disease is a major public health problem in Latin America. It affects about 16 to 18 million people in the region, and the World Health Organization (WHO) estimates that about a quarter of the population of Latin America is at risk of acquiring the disease.

Because the insect that transmits the disease has a predilection for poor quality housing in rural and urban areas, Chagas' disease is directly associated with socio-economic factors. Pets and other domestic animals act as a reservoir of the disease. Although it used to be primarily a rural disease, urban migration in the 1970s and 1980s has transformed it into a disease of the urban poor as well. Chagas' disease can also be passed through blood transfusion, and figures suggest that you're much more at risk of getting Chagas's disease than HIV or hepatitis B in many urban areas.

! You can minimise the risk of getting Chagas' disease by not staying in poor housing and by taking measures to avoid insect bites.

Chagas' disease has two stages, an acute stage that appears soon after you are infected but often goes unnoticed, and a chronic stage that may appear after several years and can be fatal. The acute phase is usually a feverish illness with no particular identifying symptoms, although swelling of the extremities can occur.

The chronic stage involves irreversible damage to internal organs, primarily the heart, gut and nervous system. About 27% of people infected develop serious heart problems that often lead to sudden death, about 6% develop gut problems and about 3% develop damage to the nervous system.

Infection can be diagnosed through blood testing. Specific drug treatment is available for treating Chagas' disease and is effective in the acute phase, but cannot reverse damage done in the chronic phase.

BLACKFLIES

These small flies (1 to 5mm long) live and breed near rivers, and are vicious little biters. When there are lots of them, they can be a real nuisance. Bites can be very itchy. They live and breed near running water – irrigation channels, streams and rivers. Apart from being a nuisance, they transmit an important disease, river blindness. They're yet another reason to cover up and use insect repellent.

River Blindness (Onchocerciasis)

This parasitic disease occurs in tropical areas of Latin America, mainly Mexico, Guatemala, Venezuela, Colombia, Ecuador and Brazil, as well as in Africa. It's very rare in travellers.

Onchocerciasis is caused by infection with a parasitic worm that likes to live in the tissues just beneath the skin. The disease affects the skin, lymph glands and eyes. Infection causes intense itchiness that can lead to suicide in severe cases. Nodules also appear, containing the adult worm. Enlargement of lymph glands is common. With heavy, repeated infections, worms enter the eye, and can cause blindness.

Treatment is with regular doses of a drug called ivermectin, and, commendably, the manufacturer of ivermectin, Merck, has made the drug free to organisations involved in onchocerciasis control programs. Control programs in several Central and South American countries are under way, and have had considerable success.

Preventing insect bites will protect you from this disease, and it's probably sensible to avoid camping close to rivers. You may get a mild infection, with some itchiness, but you're extremely unlikely to get any eye consequences (early symptoms are redness, irritation and watering). If you think you may be infected, seek medical attention.

OTHER BLOODSUCKERS

LEECHES

Leeches are a common hazard in tropical rainforest areas. They don't transmit any diseases but their bites can get infected if you don't keep them clean. However, be warned – there's something about leeches that can reduce even the most tranquil nature lover to a state of blind hysteria.

There are two types of leeches: land leeches and aquatic leeches. Land leeches are found near springs and streams in forested areas. Aquatic leeches are much less common, and live in freshwater ponds in parts of South America. Leeches can vary in size but are usually couple of centimetres long; unfed they look like thin black worms, after feeding they look like black blobs.

Land leeches attach themselves to you as you pass by. The rarer aquatic leeches enter body orifices and can reach the nose, lungs and bladder (don't even think about it), if you swim in or drink infested water.

If you don't want to get grossed out by leeches, take some preventive measures:

- check all over for them if you've been walking in infested areas
- don't swim in rainforest pools or streams
- use insect repellent (containing DEET) on your skin to discourage them
- wear long trousers and closed shoes; tuck your trousers into your socks or wear gaiters to prevent leeches dropping down your boots
- considering soaking your clothes in an insecticide such as permethrin

Once a leech has attached itself to you, it produces a substance which prevents the blood clotting and then it drinks its fill. Once full, it will drop off spontaneously. A leech can suck up to 10 times its weight in blood within half an hour. Leech bites cause only minor irritation and don't spread any disease, but it can take a while for the bleeding to stop and there's a risk of secondary infection.

Although leeches will spontaneously drop off if you leave them, unless you have nerves of steel, you'll probably want to remove them before this. Try not to pull them off in a state of panic. If you do this, they may leave their mouthparts behind, which makes infection of the bite more likely.

Tried and tested methods for getting leeches to drop off include applying alcohol, vinegar or salt to the attached end; alternatively – cruel but possibly the simplest – put a lighted match to the unattached end.

After the leech has dropped off, clean the wound carefully with antiseptic and apply pressure to stop the bleeding. It can take some time – keep applying a steady pressure, raise your limb and try not to keep removing the bandage to see if the bleeding has stopped.

TICKS & MITES

Ticks and mites occur worldwide in woodland, scrub and long grass, where they hang around waiting for a meal to pass through. Although they may attack humans, they are basically parasites of wild and domestic animals and birds. Some ticks may live in the walls of huts in rural areas. In the Americas, mites are popularly known as chiggers, *thalzahuatl* or *bicho colorado*.

You need to take care to prevent contact with these little critters because various species can transmit some fairly nasty diseases, usually through bites, but also by contact with their body fluids. Some tick bites are very painful, for example the bites of a large tick known as *tlaaja* or *pajaroello*.

- Get reliable local advice on likely problem areas (usually scrubland or pastures with long grass).

- Wear long trousers and boots, and tuck your trousers into your boots.

- Use insect repellent (containing DEET) on any exposed areas and consider soaking your clothes in an insecticide (such as permethrin) if you are planning a trek in tick or mite country.

- Check your body regularly all over for ticks and mites if you have been walking in infested areas, as they often go unnoticed until you get undressed.

- Use an insect net at night and sleep as high off the ground as possible.

- Animals, wild or domestic, may be a source of ticks, so avoid close contact with these.

If you find a tick attached to you, resist the impulse to pull it off directly, as its body will just separate from the mouthpiece, which makes infection much more likely. Remember that tick body fluids can transmit infection, so avoid handling it with your bare hands as far as possible. If you do, remember to wash your hands thoroughly soon afterwards.

The idea is to induce the tick to let go – various methods have been advocated in the past, including burning the tick off or applying chemicals to it, but these are no longer recommended, as they can be harmful to you and may make the tick's contents more likely to contaminate you.

> **!** The most effective and safest method to remove a tick is to use a pair of tweezers to grasp the head (not the body, or this will squeeze the contents into the wound and make matters worse) and pull gently, as shown in the illustration.

After the tick has dropped off, clean the wound thoroughly and apply an antiseptic solution like povidone-iodine. If tick parts get left behind, try scraping them out (under sterile conditions as far as possible) or get medical help to do this.

There are many different types of ticks and mites, capable causing a variety of diseases in humans, some more serious than others. In general, you are very unlikely to get any of these diseases, but they are a possibility if you've been trekking or camping in tick-infested areas.

> **!** If you fall ill (eg with a fever or rash) after being in tick or mite country, get yourself checked out by a doctor as soon as possible.

Muscle paralysis is an extremely rare complication of tick bites in some areas.

> **!** If you experience any breathing difficulties after a tick bite, seek medical help immediately.

Chigger Dermatitis

If you have been walking through a chigger-infested area, you may find you develop an itchy rash with pustules and hives about three to six hours later, due to chigger bites. Antihistamine tablets and calamine cream may help. Chiggers are also responsible for transmitting typhus.

Typhus

This disease is extremely rare in travellers. Initially, a swelling appears at the site of the tick bite that enlarges and later forms a black scarred area. A variable time after the bite (four days to two weeks) you get fever develops with headache and swelling of the glands near the bite. You may also notice a skin rash that spreads over your whole body, cough, eye irritation and abdominal pain. In its most severe form it can be fatal, but it is unlikely to reach this stage in you. Get medical advice as soon as possible for appropriate antibiotic treatment (usually a course of tetracycline).

Rocky Mountain Spotted Fever

Also known as Brazilian spotted fever in South America, this rare illness occurs in Mexico, Central America, Colombia, and Brazil, especially in the São Paulo area. It comes on suddenly about a week after the tick bite. A blackened scar may form around the tick bite, followed by fever, severe headache, muscle pains and a dry cough. A couple of days after this, a pink rash develops, most noticeable on the soles of your feet, wrists and forearms. Treatment is with antibiotics (usually chloramphenicol or tetracyclines). The illness can be fatal if treated too late.

FLEAS

These can be a problem in low-budget accommodation wherever you are. Neither human nor animal fleas will live on you but they do like to visit for a meal. Flea bites are small itchy red dots, usually in groups around the ankles or on any exposed skin. Use an insecticide spray to kill fleas, and wash yourself and your clothes. It's probably easiest to move to flea-free lodgings if you can.

Fleas are widespread, but they very rarely cause disease. However, as every self-respecting hypochondriac knows, some fleas can transmit plague. This disease is rare and, in spite of the hype surrounding occasional outbreaks of the disease, no case has ever been reported in travellers.

Plague

Outbreaks of this notorious disease always receive a huge amount of publicity, often associated with considerable scare-mongering by the international media, so it's worth knowing a little bit about it. Cases have been reported from Bolivia, Brazil, Ecuador and Peru.

Plague is caused by a bacterial microorganism that primarily infects rodents. It can be transmitted to humans by the bite of certain species of flea that live on the rodents, as well as by direct contact with infected animals and person-to-person spread from an infected person.

Outbreaks of plague occur in some areas of Peru, but it generally occurs as single cases in the wild. Plague in urban areas is more likely where living conditions are poor, so you are unlikely to be at risk under normal circumstances. You're most at risk if you're a naturalist handling animals, or a hunter or camper in affected areas. A vaccine is available but it's only indicated for people like zoologists who might be at high risk of infection. Sensible precautions in these circumstances are:

- avoid handling live or dead rodents (including rats, rabbits and squirrels)
- use insect repellents to prevent flea bites
- avoid flea-infested hang-outs

The disease occurs quite soon (two to seven days) after the infecting bite or contact, with a sudden onset of high fever, severe headache, chills and muscular pains, with pain in the groin or armpit (from inflamed lymph nodes called bubos, hence the name 'bubonic plague'). Untreated, the illness progresses rapidly, and sufferers are highly contagious. The chance of dying from untreated plague is high (60 to 65%) but it's very unlikely to get to this stage. If caught early, treatment with antibiotics (ideally streptomycin or tetracycline) is very effective. If you think you may have plague, you should seek medical advice as soon as possible.

VENOMOUS STINGS & BITES

BEES, WASPS & ANTS

Most stings are not dangerous but they can be painful. Children often get stung, especially if they're eating outdoors. Bees, wasps, hornets and yellowjackets are widespread. Fire ants are common in tropical Latin America and Argentina. No guesses as to the origin of their name – these ants can inflict painful bites if you get in their way.

Bees leave their stings behind but wasps and ants usually do not. If the sting is still visible, remove it with a pair of tweezers, taking care not to squeeze the venom sacs. You can relieve the pain and swelling with an ice pack or a cloth soaked in cold water. There are plenty of commercial sting relief sprays (such as those containing aluminium sulphate), or you can use calamine lotion, tea tree or lavender oil to soothe the sting.

! If the sting is in the mouth or throat, you will need get medical help; in the meantime, try to remove the sting, and suck on an ice cube.

Rarely, some people are very sensitive to bee, wasp and ant stings and get a severe allergic reaction if they are stung, which is a medical emergency.

! If you know you are allergic to stings, you should carry with you an emergency kit containing antihistamines and adrenaline to be used if you are stung – discuss this with your doctor before you leave.

You should seek medical help for stings in the following situations:

- if you've been stung in the mouth or throat, especially if the area swells rapidly
- if you get rapid swelling from a sting anywhere
- if it's followed by breathing difficulties or signs of shock – rapid pulse, pale clammy skin, breathlessness, sweating, faintness

In an emergency, ie if a severe allergic reaction occurs and no medical help is available, treatment is as follows:

- get the casualty to lie flat, and raise their feet
- give an injection of adrenaline/epinephrine (1 in 1000) 0.3mL into the top of the casualty's arm or thigh
- get medical help urgently

KILLER BEES

In recent years, these have spread throughout the Americas, attracting much publicity, often sensationalist. Killer bees are honey bees that have interbred with imported African varieties. They are much more aggressive than native bees, and can inflict multiple stings, leading to severe poisoning and sometimes death, even in people who are not oversensitive to bee stings. In adults, it takes something like a few hundred bee stings to cause this level of illness, although in children, it can take fewer stings than this. Treatment of multiple stings is as follows:

- remove any stings that are left in the skin, as this will help prevent further injection of poison
- get medical help as soon as possible – antihistamines and steroids may need to be given

SPIDERS

Although many Latin American spiders are harmless, there are a few awe-inspiring varieties. We're talking fangs, hairy legs and impressive size, as well as deadly venom. Having said that, you're hardly likely to find a tarantula under every bed, and the brown recluse spider is so-called because it is so shy! In addition, it's worth bearing in mind that although most spiders are venomous, only a few have powerful enough fangs to penetrate human skin and cause you harm. Orb web spiders, often exquisitely patterned, aren't generally harmful to you.

The black widow is probably the most notorious venomous spider and is found in most warm areas of the world (it's closely related to the Australian redback spider). Only the female bites. The female black widow is black or brown, about 25mm long, and has a distinctive red hourglass shape on the underside of her abdomen. The male black widow is usually too small to bite, and he gets eaten by the female after mating. Black widows tend to live outdoors, hanging from webs under and around dwellings and other buildings such as outhouses.

Black widow spider venom affects the nervous system and can be fatal. Several hours after the bite, which is initially painless, intense pain develops, and you get muscle spasms, abdominal pain, breathing difficulties, nausea and vomiting.

Various members of the brown recluse spider family occur in Latin America. They are yellow-brown, with a dark violin shape on the back. Most bites do not produce a serious reaction, but some bites can cause a severe local reaction, with the formation of a blister and later an ulcer, and very occasionally, bites can cause generalised poisoning. People often get bitten while they are dressing if the spider has crawled into their clothes overnight.

Another spider best avoided is the South American banana spider (*Phoneutria* species), also called the wandering spider, which can be up to 3cm long (body), and may be found in bunches of bananas. It produces a potent venom that acts on the nervous system, causing similar symptoms to the black widow.

Avoid spider bites by being aware of the risk:

- shake your clothes out and check in your boots before putting them on
- check under the seat in outhouse toilets – you don't want to get caught with your trousers down…

- sleep off the ground, in an insect net
- inspect banana bunches carefully
- finally, heed local advice on particular risks

If you get bitten by a potentially venomous spider:

- don't panic!
- immobilise the limb and apply a compression bandage (not a tourniquet – see p436) to prevent the venom from spreading
- get medical help for antivenin (if appropriate) and other hospital treatment

SCORPIONS

These weird lobster lookalikes are found throughout the tropics and subtropics, especially in dry desert areas. Not all

TARANTULAS

A favourite with arachnophobes, these are some of the largest spiders in the world, with the largest varieties living in the South American jungle. The largest tarantulas have a body span of up to 9cm and a leg span of 24cm. They are nocturnal, and live during the day in cavities in the ground, squeezing themselves into abandoned rodent tunnels and other similar places. They eat cockroaches and other insects, even baby mice. Because they are large and hairy, tarantulas have a fearsome reputation, but are said to be docile and are popular as pets. While we suggest you don't test this out in the wild, it's worth remembering that tarantula bites are not dangerous, and are a bit like a bee sting. Some species produce stronger effects, especially if you are sensitive to them. Should you be foolish enough to get this close, tarantula hairs can cause skin irritation.

scorpions are dangerous but, wouldn't you know it, a couple of notably poisonous species live in parts of Latin America. In Mexico, the Durango scorpion is responsible for thousands of poisonings every year. Children and young people are most often stung, and many children die from scorpion stings in affected areas. Scorpions grip their prey with their front pincers, while injecting poison through the tip of their tail (hence the expression 'sting in the tail').

Bites by poisonous scorpions can cause severe pain and swelling, followed later by symptoms of generalised poisoning, including vomiting, sweating, breathing difficulties, muscle spasms and abdominal pain. Antivenins are generally available in risk areas.

Scorpions are nocturnal creatures, so you're very unlikely to see them, but sensible precautions are:

- always check your shoes before putting them on in the morning if you are camping out
- take care when lifting or moving rocks
- if you're camping, clear your camp site of rocks and other debris

Get medical help urgently if you are stung by a scorpion.

SNAKES

Latin America boasts an impressive selection of worrisome snakes. However, these are generally a small risk to you, although snake bites can be an important cause of illness and death in local people, especially plantation workers and hunter-gatherers in rural or forested areas.

In Latin America, venomous snakes include various members of the viper family, such as the bushmaster (reaching 3m in length, this is the largest viper in the world), terciopelo (the common name used to describe four different species, all venomous), fer-de-lance and jararacussu. Other venomous snakes to watch out for include coral snakes and the cascabel or tropical rattlesnake. Most of these snakes are forest dwellers. They generally only bite humans if they are provoked or taken by surprise. Even bites from venomous snakes don't always result in enough venom being injected to be dangerous.

Different types of venom cause different effects, from pain and ulceration around the bite (common with viper bites) to severe generalised poisoning and death. Effective antidotes to snake venom are generally available in high-risk areas. Avoid getting bitten in the first place:

- never handle, threaten or chase after a snake
- wear socks and strong boots if you are walking through grasslands or undergrowth, and give snakes plenty of chance to 'hear' you coming
- use a torch if you are walking at night in rural, snake-infested areas
- be careful if you're climbing foliage-covered rocks or trees or swimming in lakes or rivers surrounded by thick vegetation
- take care if you're collecting firewood or moving logs, boulders or other debris, as these may shelter resting snakes

Treatment

Treat snake bite as follows:

- reassure the casualty and try to keep them calm – they will probably be very frightened, and movement encourages the venom to spread
- immobilise the bitten limb with a sling or splint (see p449 in the First Aid appendix) – this helps prevent the venom from being absorbed
- pressure bandaging, which is useful and safe in Australia for snake bites, is probably best avoided in Latin America, as it may worsen the damage caused by viper bites
- seek medical help urgently for antivenom treatment and other supportive measures
- make a note of what the snake looked like but don't endanger yourself and others by trying to catch it
- watch for signs of shock and breathing difficulty and be prepared to start emergency resuscitation if necessary

ANACONDAS & BOA CONSTRICTORS

Think of a Latin American snake, and you'll probably think of an anaconda first, then perhaps boa constrictors. There are four species of anacondas, all of which live in South America. Anacondas are water boas, and spend most of their time in swamps, marshes, or basking on stream banks or on floating vegetation. They hunt for their prey in the water, usually fish, reptiles, mammals or birds, ambushing animals as they come to drink. When the prey comes within striking distance, the anaconda attacks, bites the prey and then throws loops of its body round the prey, constricting and killing it. Most anacondas grow to about 5m in length. Because anacondas can capture quite large animals, there is a theoretical, but very unlikely, risk to humans.

Boa constrictors are the land version of anacondas. They occur from northern Mexico through Central America to northern Argentina, and live in a wide range of habitats, including rain forests and jungles, rocky semi-deserts and cultivated fields and plantations. They are smaller than anacondas, and don't pose a big threat to humans, although they are worth avoiding.

! Traditional first aid methods like cutting into the bite and sucking the poison out or applying tourniquets are potentially dangerous and you should avoid them, whatever you may be told locally.

Antivenoms are antibodies from horses or sheep. Although they are very effective at preventing the harmful effects of snake venom, Antivenoms can cause severe allergic reactions in some people. This means that they should not be given without medical supervision except in extreme emergency.

ANIMAL BITES

Bites from dogs, bats and rodents may be a risk in some areas. Remember that dogs, especially in rural areas, are not generally kept as pets, and you shouldn't treat them as such. Vampire bats are known to cause rabies cases in Brazil and surrounding countries. Rodents can be a risk in markets as well as in rural areas. Animal bites are important because they carry a high risk of secondary bacterial infection (mouths harbour many bacteria and animals don't brush their teeth) and the risk of rabies.

> Note that human bites are potentially as dangerous as animal bites from an infection point of view – they must be cleaned thoroughly and you'll need antibiotics to prevent infection.

RABIES

Rabies occurs throughout Latin America. This serious viral disease is transmitted through animal saliva. Practically any warm-blooded animal can be infected, although dogs (mostly), rodents and bats (especially vampire bats which drink blood), are probably the greatest risk to you in Latin America. Bites are a major hazards but any contact with animal saliva and an open cut or graze on your skin is risky. You can't get rabies from touching an infected animal. It's possible to get rabies from bats by inhaling infected bat faeces, which can be a risk if you are caving. Domestic pets are less likely to be infected but you can't assume they are risk free.

Before you go, it's a good idea to find out the current status of rabies in the areas you're planning to visit, especially if you're planning to spend time in remote, rural areas. Reliable sources of information include specialist travel health clinics, the US Centers for Disease Control & Prevention, the World Health Organization (see under Information Sources in the Before You Go chapter for contact details) and embassies of the countries you are planning to visit.

VAMPIRE BATS

They really exist, in forested areas of tropical Central and South America, which is about as different as you can get from Transylvania. They don't live up to their fearsome reputation, but they are considered a significant pest as they target cattle and horses. The main risk as far as humans are concerned is that bats are the second most common cause of rabies (dogs are the most common).

Vampire bats are quite small, with bodies are about the size of an adult's thumb and a wingspan of about 20cm. They feed on the blood of domestic animals such as cattle, horses and pigs, as well as large birds and humans if they are in the right place at the wrong time. Vampire bats are killed as pests in cattle-raising areas, and, and, tragically, a great many other harmless bats are needlessly killed in error.

Vampire bats don't suck blood; instead they lap it up after making a small nick in the skin with their sharp teeth. Although they can fly, they are also good at crawling or hopping along the ground. Like leeches, bat's saliva contains a chemical that prevents blood from clotting. It's so good at this that researchers are trying to find a way of using it medicinally.

You may be at risk of bites from these creatures if you are spending the night in rural areas, so always sleep under a mosquito net.

Rabid dogs may not show any signs of illness but if they do, they usually rush around, biting things and people at random and salivating excessively. An infected dog will usually be dead within 10 days.

The rabies virus attacks your central nervous system, causing extremely unpleasant symptoms.

! Once symptoms have appeared, the disease can't be cured and a
painful death is inevitable, but the infection can be stopped at any
stage before symptoms appear, which can be anything from about
five days to a year or more.

Symptoms of rabies infection include fever, headache, sore
throat and nausea. This is followed by pain and burning
around the bite, extreme sensitivity to light and sound, and
anxiety. Hydrophobia, or fear of water, is a classic symptom,
which is a result of painful throat spasms on drinking, and
foaming at the mouth occurs (because of overproduction of
saliva). Convulsions and coma then lead to death.

Treatment

If you are bitten by an animal, immediately clean the bite or
scratch thoroughly. This is important even if the animal is not
rabid because animal teeth harbour all sorts of microorganisms.
If the animal is rabid, cleaning can help to kill the rabies virus
before it has time to enter your body.

- Use lots of soap and water to flush the wound out, then apply an
  antiseptic solution like povidone-iodine directly to the wound.

- Apply strong alcohol to kill the rabies virus (in an emergency you
  can apply spirits directly to the wound).

- Do not attempt to close the wound with stitches.

- Get medical help as soon as possible.

You'll need to get advice on rabies prevention (you can wait
until the next day if necessary). You will also need a course of
antibiotics if it is a deep wound, as well as a tetanus booster if
you're not up to date with this.

! Bites to the head and neck area carry a higher risk of rabies, and
need to be treated immediately.

If no medical help is available, a suitable antibiotic course to
take is co-amoxiclav 250mg three times daily (erythromycin
500mg twice daily if you're allergic to penicillin – see p418 for

more details on antibiotic treatment), while you find reliable advice on rabies prevention.

Anti-Rabies Injections

❗ After a potentially rabid bite, you will need a course of rabies vaccination to prevent the disease, whether or not you were vaccinated before.

In addition, if you weren't vaccinated before, you will need a rabies immunoglobulin injection.

There are a couple of issues to be aware of with post-exposure rabies treatment. For a start, both the vaccine and the immunoglobulin are expensive. Secondly, both are often in short supply, particularly in rural areas. Even when they are available, you need to avoid locally made vaccine and immunoglobulin, as they are usually derived from non-human tissue, and carry a high risk of serious reactions.

You need to find imported human vaccine, which should be available in most major cities.

Unfortunately, even if you wanted to, taking rabies vaccine with you is not an option, partly because it's often in short supply, but mainly because it needs to be kept at fridge temperature to remain effective.

After You Get Back...

Some illnesses can show themselves for the first time when you get back, and illnesses that started while you were away may persist or get worse after you return. Before you rush off to make an appointment, remember that unless you're worried for some reason, you don't need a post-travel health check. In some situations, however, a post-travel health check is advisable:

- if you develop any of the symptoms listed in the following section
- if you have any persistent symptoms (eg diarrhoea, recurrent fevers, generally under the weather, weight loss)
- if you were bitten by an animal, whether or not you received a rabies injection
- if you were on a long trip or you spent some time in rural areas or living rough
- if you're worried you might have something
- if you were ill when you were away (unless it was just a brief episode of travellers diarrhoea)
- if you received medical or dental care while you were away
- if you had unprotected intercourse with a new partner

You can go to your usual doctor, a travel health clinic or, if you're concerned you may have something exotic, a doctor specialising in tropical medicine. The advantage of a travel health or tropical medicine specialist is that they may be more alert to symptoms of tropical diseases. On the other hand, your doctor will be familiar with your health history.

See the section on Post-Travel Blues later in this chapter, but you should consider seeing your doctor or arranging counselling if you experience significant stress, anxiety or depression after you return.

! If you had medical or dental treatment while you were away, remember to claim for it as soon as possible on your travel insurance.

WHAT TO LOOK OUT FOR

You should see your doctor, a specialist travel health expert or tropical medicine specialist if you develop any symptoms in the days or weeks after you get back.

> **!** Remember that doctors at home may not consider tropical diseases as a cause for your symptoms unless you tell them. Be sure to mention that you have been travelling, where you went and any risk situations you were in.

The time between getting infected and symptoms appearing varies with different diseases, but it can be weeks or even months, so if you were on a short trip, they may not appear until after you get back. In addition, some aspects of travelling (such as exposure to the sun) can make conditions like skin cancer more likely in the longer term.

Keep a lookout for any of the following symptoms.

Fever

This is especially important if there's any risk that you may have malaria. You should suspect malaria if you develop any fever or flu-like symptoms after you return, especially in the first four weeks. Although the most serious form of malaria (falciparum) is most likely to occur in the first four weeks after you return, other forms of malaria can occur several months after you were infected. In some circumstances you may need to have a course of primaquine, an antimalarial which clears persistent liver forms of the parasite.

Malaria deaths have occurred in returned travellers because the infection was not suspected by doctors at home, so it's important to tell them if you have been to a malarial area, even if you were taking malaria prevention medication.

> **!** Don't forget that you need to continue taking your antimalarials for four weeks after you leave a malarial area or you will be at higher risk of getting malaria.

There are lots of other causes of fever in returned travellers: dengue fever, hepatitis, typhoid and tuberculosis can all show up in this way.

Diarrhoea

Gastrointestinal problems can persist or appear for the first time after you get back – see the section on Prolonged Diarrhoea in the Digestive System chapter for more details. Bacterial dysenteries, giardiasis and amoebiasis are all possibilities, and even malaria, the great mimic, can cause diarrhoea. You often find that diarrhoea clears up spontaneously once you get back to your usual routines and lifestyle. You need to see your doctor if your symptoms persist for longer than a week after you get back, or if there's any blood or mucus in it.

Worms are often symptom-less, so it's probably a good idea to get a check for these if you've been on a long trip or you've been travelling rough. If you know you ate something dodgy like raw meat or seafood, you may have picked up tapeworm or liver flukes, so you should get this checked out.

Travelling can make you more likely to develop noninfectious conditions like irritable bowel syndrome or milk intolerance (usually temporary), so bear this in mind if you develop any gut disturbances that are not normal for you. Some gut problems may be unrelated to travelling – you may have got them anyway – so get any symptoms checked out.

! Be aware that diarrhoea can be contagious and this may affect whether you can go back to work when you return (eg if you work with young children or in the food industry).

Skin

If you've got any infected cuts, persistent ulcers or rashes, or any weird skin blemish you're not sure about, you should get these checked out as soon as possible. Mention if tick bites were a possibility, and any other nasties. Fungal infections like athlete's foot are common while you're away, but they may clear up once you get back.

SCHISTOSOMIASIS

This disease occurs in a few risk areas of Latin America, and can cause long-term problems if it's not picked up and treated early (see p362). If you have been swimming in freshwater in risk areas, you may have become infected – but bear in mind that infections are regularly picked up in travellers who didn't think they had been at risk.

It can appear as an acute illness with fever and other symptoms a few weeks or months after you were exposed or you may get no symptoms for several months, then you may notice blood in your urine or faeces. Infection can be confirmed by a test on your faeces or by blood test. The blood test needs to be done at least three months after you were exposed to the risk.

Another thing to look out for is any change in a mole or freckle (see p125 for more details), especially if you've been scorching yourself in the tropical sunshine.

Animal Bites

If you were bitten by any animal while you were away and didn't get rabies injections, it's a good idea to discuss with your doctor whether you should take any action now, eg it may be advisable to have a course of rabies injections.

Sexual Health Check-up

This is definitely a good idea if you had unprotected intercourse with a new partner while you were away, or you experience any symptoms. Hepatitis B, HIV and other STIs are all a possibility. STIs can be symptom-less and can cause serious effects on your fertility, so it's worth getting this checked out early if you think it may be a possibility.

Other Symptoms

It's worth reporting any unusual symptoms, such as weight loss, night sweats, recurrent fevers or if you're simply not feeling right and don't know why. Tuberculosis can sometimes appear after you get back, and may be a cause of weight loss, fevers and night sweats. Consider this possibility if you spent several months living with members of the host community. Some more exotic diseases may not show up until after you get back.

POST-TRAVEL BLUES

It's a sad fact that everyone has to go home eventually. You may be glad to get back to familiar faces, culture and your old haunts. On the other hand, you may be reluctant to exchange the exciting, challenging, temporary world of travelling for a return to a life that may at first seem less enjoyable and less meaningful.

If you've been away for a while, you may experience reverse culture shock when you return. Have a read of the section on Culture Shock in the Mental Wellbeing chapter, and see if you recognise any of the feelings described.

Added to this is the big change in lifestyle that coming home usually involves – trying to pick up where you left off, maybe trying to find a job, somewhere to live, coping with dreary weather and a (comparatively) dreary environment can be stressful. Friends and family may be surprisingly uninterested in hearing all about the wonderful and not-so-wonderful experiences you had while you were away (but can you blame them?).

Be prepared for at least some emotional turmoil after you get back, as you try to match up your expectations of life with the realities. Talking through experiences you have had may help, especially if you had any particularly life-altering or traumatic experiences. Try talking to other travellers to find out how they coped with the transition, to sympathetic friends or to a trained counsellor. Activity and a purpose in life can help enormously. On the other hand, if you feel persistently low and lose interest in life, you may be depressed (see the section on Depression in the Mental Wellbeing chapter for more details) and you should seek medical help.

Traditional Medicine...

Misfortune, illness and death are inescapable facts of life that have led societies everywhere to develop ways of explaining and dealing with them. For thousands of years, the original inhabitants of the Americas have relied on the expertise of traditional healers and their knowledge of natural remedies to ward off and cure illness. The colonising Europeans and the religious authorities vilified traditional healing practices, labelling them as 'black magic' and 'witchcraft'. Over the last few decades, however, there has been a dawning international appreciation of the value of this tradition, and a resurgence of interest in remedies derived from rainforest plants. Although it can be difficult for outsiders to appreciate fully the spiritual beliefs and cultural contexts on which traditional healing practices are based, the value of living in harmony with the environment, using the resources available naturally, is self-evident.

This chapter is a necessarily brief overview of a fascinating and wide-ranging topic. If it stimulates your interest, we thoroughly recommend you find out more from one of the many resources available – see Further Information at the end of the chapter for more details.

SHAMANS

'Shaman' has become something of a New-Age buzz word, but what does it actually mean? A shaman is simply a traditional healer-priest, a medicine man or woman. They are not unique to any one society, and are found throughout the world. (The term 'shaman' is thought to come from Siberia, meaning 'the one who knows'). Shamans are also known as witch doctors, *curandero*, *feiticero* and many other names, depending on their society of origin.

In this chapter, we will discuss shamans of the Amazon region, although much of this discussion holds true for shamans everywhere. In Native American societies, shamans usually hold an important position, second only to that of the chief. Shamans are usually (but not exclusively) men and generally undergo lengthy apprenticeships. Anyone can receive the calling to be a shaman, although in practice it tends to be handed down within families.

As well as being responsible for preventing and curing illness, shamans provide guidance on spiritual matters, which is why they are best described as healer-priests. They generally have an extensive knowledge of the healing and toxic properties of a huge variety of plants (and other living things). As with all aspects of traditional Indian culture, this immeasurably valuable knowledge is now under threat. Erosion of traditional culture through contact with outsiders means that the new generation has little interest in acquiring this knowledge, which has traditionally been passed on through the oral tradition. Apart from the efforts of ethnobotanists concerned with the preservation of this information (see later), there are essentially no written records. This knowledge is in real danger of being lost forever.

DISEASE, SPIRITUALISM & HEALING

Modern medicine looks for disease processes within the body, such as cancerous cells, microorganisms, chemical imbalances etc, because this fits in with the world view of most Western societies. In contrast, shamanism looks for influences outside the body as the cause of illness and misfortune. These influences usually arise from the co-existent spirit world, which plays an important part in the world-view of societies in which shamanism is practised.

In shamanistic societies, disease can be a result of breaking a taboo, having a 'spell' cast by an enemy as a result of interpersonal or intertribal hostilities (often by the shaman of a rival tribe), anger of the deities, or a disharmony between the physical and spiritual world. As an illustration of how this belief system works, take malaria. An Indian patient with malaria may blame it on a bite from a malarial mosquito, but will want to know why the malarial mosquito singled them out. In response, the shaman may tell them that it's because the mosquito was sent to bite them by an evil person.

EARLY MEDICINE

Research into attitudes and methodologies concerning disease and illness in pre-Colombian times has been difficult, as most of the manuscripts or codices of the Aztecs and Mayas (and their forebears, the Toltec, Olmec and Moche) were destroyed by their Christian 'saviours'. The Inca had no written language and therefore no manuscripts to burn. Most of what we know comes from those very same destroyers, oral histories, and painstaking research on what codices and hieroglyphs remain.

Diseases such as smallpox, mumps, measles, polio, influenza, rabies and tuberculosis were unknown before the arrival of Europeans. Once these viruses and bacteria were unleashed, they devastated the indigenous populations. In the Antilles, influenza, introduced in 1493, wiped out the entire indigenous community. There are records indicating that many diseases still in existence today were known to the pre-Colombians, including amoebic, parasitic, rickettsial (eg typhus) and treponemal (pinta, yaws and syphilis) infections. Although controversial, if it is true that this is how syphilis was introduced into European populations, it only seems fair!

Aztec public health so astonished the *conquistadors* that they wrote glowingly of public sanitation, closed sewers and public toilets. The Spanish often used traditional healers in preference to their own. Healer, priest, shaman were often the same person. Among the Maya the art of healing was entrusted to the *hemenes*, priests who inherited their knowledge from the gods. The Aztec medical profession was also heritable though less divine. Father passed knowledge to his son, who could not practise until his sire's death.

Many of the plant remedies used then would be familiar to today's pharmacist in the form of drugs such as cocaine, quinine, curare, theophylline and atropine. The Aztecs were fond of purgatives ('bowel clearers') and emetics to induce vomiting. Ulluchu, a member of the papaya family was prized for its effects on bloodclotting, which allowed sacrifice victims to bleed more profusely.

Surgery was often a separate profession, especially in Incan society. Surgeons were proficient in wound repair, bloodletting and trepanning (the process of drilling a large hole into and through the skull) to release evil humours. Recent archaeological evidence has uncovered thousands of skulls upon which this was practised. The majority show healing, indicating that most patients survived their treatment.

Fred Peterson

Some diseases have an easily recognisable set of symptoms for which there are set cures, often with medicinal plants, shamanic dances or the laying of hands. If the disease is not so easily recognised or it fails to resolve with treatment, a different approach to 'diagnosis' is required, which is where the shaman's role as an intermediary between the spirit and physical world becomes all-important. The shaman will usually have to communicate with the spirit world in order to find out what's causing the illness and what the appropriate treatment is.

Communication with the spirit world is through well-established rituals, which have variations within different communities. Typically, the shaman uses a hallucinogenic substance to enter into a trance. Accompanying rituals involve rhythmic beating of a drum, chanting and dancing. In this way the shaman reaches an understanding of the disease process and what the best treatment is likely to be.

HALLUCINOGENS

Hallucinogenic plants are an important part of the traditional culture of many Native American cultures in Latin America, and there are many regional variations. For example, in South America, *ayahuasca* or *yage* (or *caapi*, made from a vine, *Banisteriopsis caapi*) is the most widely used hallucinogenic in the Amazon. The Yanomami use a hallucinogenic herbal powder called *epena*. In Mexico, the Huichol Indian healers eat *peyote*, a hallucinogenic cactus. Much has been written on the use of hallucinogenic substances in Indian cultures; if you are interested you could check out the classic text on hallucinogenic plants, *Plants of the Gods* by RE Schultes and A Hofman, or *Wizard of the Upper Amazon – the Story of Manuel Cordova-Rios* and the sequel *Rio Tigre and Beyond* by F Bruce Lamb.

A word of warning about *ayahuasca*: you will find many people in places like Leticia and Iquitos claiming to be shamans and offering *ayahuasca* for sale. Be extremely wary! If you decide to experience an *ayahuasca* session, do it with someone you know or who has been vouched for by someone you trust.

Treatment is logical, and is based on what is believed to have caused the illness. For example, if the shaman determines that the illness has been caused by angering a spirit, treatment involves appeasement of that spirit through offerings or rituals. In the case of a 'spell', the shaman has to identify the villain and mete out a suitable punishment.

If illness is determined to be a result of possession of a person's body by evil spirits, cure is aimed at expelling the harmful spirit. In this case, the shaman may enlist the help of good spirits against the bad spirits. Exorcism of an evil spirit involves ritual prayers and chanting, often in a place of special significance to the community, and surrounded by witnesses. It represents a confrontation between the shaman and the evil spirit, and can be a powerful and disturbing experience to watch. Loss of soul can also be a cause of disease, and in this case, the healer must negotiate with the spirit world for repossession of the lost soul.

The shaman isn't only a healer, he or she must also provide members of the community with guidance on how to avoid illness. This may involve the 'prescription' of tonics, but more importantly, it involves advice on living in harmony with the spirit world – another of the 'priest' aspects of the shaman's role.

MEDICINAL PLANTS

The forest is the traditional source of food, medicines and shelter for Indian communities, although this reliance on their environment is slowly being eroded by the invasion and destruction of their traditional homelands and culture by outsiders. Through a process of trial and error over thousands of years, indigenous communities have built up a unique and extensive knowledge of forest plants and wildlife.

Some plants are valued as sources of nutrition (for example the ubiquitous cassava, also known as manioc or yuca), for their healing properties (for example, quinine bark from the *Cinchona* tree), or as hallucinogens or stimulants (for example, tobacco and coca). Others are known and used as poisons (for example, curares). These distinctions are often not clearcut, as plants don't usually contain just a single active ingredient and diet and nutrition are inextricably linked with health and fitness. A plant or different parts of the plant may be used for a variety of purposes. A plant remedy may be therapeutic at one dose but poisonous at a higher dose.

The most common way in which healing plants are used is as a tea, made by infusion or decoction. The tea can be drunk or gargled, or rubbed on the affected part if it is to treat aches and pains, skin conditions or bites. Poultices made by crushing parts of the plant are also popular. Some plant remedies are taken as snuff: the plant is dried and powdered and then sniffed up through a hollow tube. The inside of the nose is richly supplied with blood vessels, and the remedy is absorbed into the bloodstream in this way.

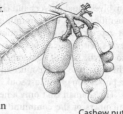

Cashew nut

Many useful plants, medicinal and poisonous, are very bitter to taste. (Just think of the taste of tonic, which is made with quinine from the bark of a rainforest tree.) The bitterness comes from chemicals called alkaloids, contained in most plants but most common in tropical plants. One indication to a shaman that a plant may be useful is if it tastes bitter.

In the following section, we have highlighted a very small selection of the thousands of useful plants known to the Indians. To find out more about useful plants, try some of the resources listed at the end of this chapter. All the plants described here are indigenous to tropical America.

Hevea guianensis (rubber tree)

Quinine

Quinine is one of the most famous remedies to come from the Andean rainforest. It comes from the bark of an evergreen tree called *Cinchona,* which is indigenous to the eastern slopes of the northern Andes. Quinquina, or the 'bark of barks', was known to the Indians as a remedy for fever long before the Spaniards invaded and later malaria was introduced into the New World. Legend has it that the viceroy of Peru used this remedy from the 'fever tree' as a last resort to cure his wife, the Countess of Cinchon, who was suffering from malaria. The tree was named Cinchona in her honour.

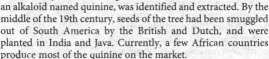

Although malaria is now a disease of the tropics, it used to be much more widespread, affecting much of Western Europe as well as North America. Quinine bark was a popular and much sought after remedy for 'swamp fever' (as malaria was known), and demand soared. In the early 19th century, the active ingredient, an alkaloid named quinine, was identified and extracted. By the middle of the 19th century, seeds of the tree had been smuggled out of South America by the British and Dutch, and were planted in India and Java. Currently, a few African countries produce most of the quinine on the market.

Quinine changed the history of the world. Without quinine, Europeans probably would not have been able to colonise much of the developing world, the Panama Canal could not have been built, and WWII in the South Pacific could not have been fought. Ironically, without quinine, the rainforests might not have been overrun and destroyed.

South American Indians use the *Cinchona* bark for a variety of conditions, including for gastrointestinal disorders, cancers, fever and influenza. Drug-resistant malaria is a huge problem worldwide, but there is some evidence that the natural *Cinchona* bark is effective against these strains.

Cat's Claw

Cat's claw (*una de gato, Uncaria tomentosa* or *guiansis*) is a large woody vine from the coffee family. Named for the hook-like thorns that are said to resemble cat's claws, it has been used by the Indians for thousands of years. Its many uses include dysentery, arthritis and rheumatism, menstrual problems, tumours and inflammation. It is used in herbal medicine throughout the world for its antitumour, anti-inflammatory and antioxidant properties. Alkaloids found in the bark and roots of the plant have been shown to increase immune function significantly, leading to its use in 'conventional' medicine in the treatment of cancer and AIDS.

Coca

Trees and shrubs of the *Coca* family occur naturally mainly in the Andes and the Amazon Basin. Leaves from these trees have been used as a stimulant by South American Indians for centuries, long before the Spanish arrived, and are the source of cocaine. In the northwest Amazon, coca is probably the most important crop, second only to cassava (manioc), for most Indians. It is widely cultivated in the Amazon, especially in Colombia, Peru and Ecuador. As evidence of its long use by Indian tribes, there are many legends as to the origin of the *Coca* tree. In the classic reference text on rainforest plants, *The Healing Forest,* Schultes and Raffauf make the point that coca (and other sacred plants such as tobacco) is cultivated exclusively by men, whereas the food crop, cassava, is cultivated and harvested by women.

Traditional methods of preparing coca for use differ according to the availability of added ingredients, but are essentially the same in principle. The coca leaves are gathered and roasted on a flat oven until they are dry and crisp. They are then pounded in a mortar with a pestle of hardwood until they are reduced to a fine powder. These are mixed with the ashes of the leaves of a plant chosen for its alkaline properties. This coca-ash mixture is finely sifted, and occasionally, a small amount of cassava flour may be added at this stage. A spoonful or two of the powder is put in the mouth and, as it moistens, is placed between the gums and cheek. This is replenished throughout the day, as required.

The general stimulant effect of coca is thought to be of benefit in getting the user through long hunting trips without food (coca is an appetite suppressant), and, it's likely, generally getting through a life of considerable physical hardship. The energy-giving properties of coca may also play a role in some of the exuberant dance rituals of many tribes. As every traveller to the Andes knows, a tea made from coca leaves is used as a remedy for altitude sickness.

Cocaine is well known as a drug of abuse. In conventional medicine, cocaine and similar substances are used as local anaesthetics. If you try coca leaves, you'll notice that one of the first effects is a numb feeling in the inside of your cheeks. Coca is not generally thought to be addictive, and many travellers find *maté de coca* a great cure for altitude sickness.

Yerba Maté

You'll find this refreshing tea all over southern South America, where it is practically the national drink. It's made from the leaves of a holly-like tree (*Ilex paraguariensis*) that grows near streams in the wild, but is now widely cultivated. The wild tree is said to produce a maté with a superior taste and is much sought after. During the harvest season, maté gatherers called *tarrafeiros* or *yerbateros* search the forest for stands of wild trees. Traditionally, yerba maté is used as a tonic to reduce appetite and combat fatigue, as well as medicinally to treat digestive disorders. The active ingredients are primarily caffeine and caffeine-like substances and phytochemicals, which are thought to have a stimulant effect on the immune system. It's also a good source of minerals and amino acids. A possible anti-diabetic effect is being investigated.

Tonka Bean (Cumaru)

These large brown seeds have a vanilla-like smell and were once used as a vanilla substitute until it was found to be toxic in large quantities. The seeds contain a substance called coumarin, which is known to have a blood-thinning effect. It's used locally as a shampoo, and in baths for children to treat fever. In Brazil, the seeds are crushed and used as cough medicine. You may see the seeds worn in necklaces or anklets to ward of illness or as decoration.

Amargo (Quassia)

The bark of the *Quassia amara* tree is used traditionally in a similar way to quinine bark, as a treatment for malaria and fever. The tree grows at lower elevations than *Cinchona*, the source of quinine bark. Other traditional uses include as an insecticide, for intestinal parasites and as a tonic. In herbal medicine, amargo tablets are used for indigestion and other digestive disorders, and as a laxative. Teas of the bark have been found to be a safe and effective remedy for mild digestive problems. Amargo bark extract has also been shown to be effective at treating head lice. The active ingredients in the bark include many quinine-like alkaloids as well as a chemical called quassin, which is even more bitter than quinine. Amargo has been reported to have anti-tumour activity.

Guarana

This shrub is originally from the Brazilian Amazon but is now known worldwide, not least as the main ingredient in the Brazilian soft drink of the same name. As the round red fruit ripens, it splits, allowing the black seed to emerge, making the fruit look like a red eye. The rainforest Indians have used this seed medicinally for many thousands of years. The seeds are dried and roasted, then mixed to a paste with water. This paste, similar to chocolate, is used in foods, drinks and remedies. Medicinally, guarana is used in a variety of ways, but mainly as a stimulant, astringent and in the treatment of diarrhoea. Internationally, there are many guarana products on the market. In herbal medicine, guarana is used as a health tonic, and specifically as a mental stimulant and to combat fatigue. There's been much interest in guarana's ability to thin the blood and its antibacterial properties.

Manaca

The botanical name for this medium-sized tree is *Brunfelsia uniflorus* or *grandiflora*. It produces beautiful fragrant white flowers, and is an important medicinal and sacred plant for many rainforest peoples. Its chemistry is poorly understood, and it's not advisable to ingest it in the wild form. Medicinal uses include as a painkiller, anti-inflammatory, for fever, rheumatism and some sexually transmitted infections such as syphilis. In international herbal medicine, it is used a diuretic, purgative and anti-inflammatory.

RAINFOREST CONSERVATION & ETHNOBOTANY

The jungles of tropical America harbour an incredible diversity of life within their fragile ecosystems. The Amazon, for example, contains a tenth of the planet's plant and animal species, and a quarter of all plant species. The warm, wet conditions of the rainforest provide the perfect environment for many different life forms to flourish in. It is a damning indictment of the shortsightedness of human beings that, through the quest for short term gain, this irreplaceable reservoir of food, medicine and other potentially useful chemicals is being destroyed.

For thousands of years, plants have been the primary source of therapeutic substances for every society. The advent of synthetic compounds has lessened our reliance on plants as a source of medicines but with the increase in resistance of microorganisms to available drugs and the existence of incurable diseases such as AIDS and some cancers, there is a growing recognition of the value of the plant kingdom

CURARE

Curare is an umbrella term, referring to substances used as arrow-tip and blow-dart poisons by South American Indians. They are classified into three major types according to the type of container the Indians traditionally kept them in: tube curare (in bamboo), pot curare (in earthenware jars) and calabash curare (in gourds). Tube curare, used predominantly in the western Amazon, is made from a large canopy liana, *Chondrodendron tomentosum*. The roots and stems are crushed, cooked and mixed with other ingredients to form a sticky resinous liquid in which arrows and darts are dipped. Pot curare, used mainly in the eastern Amazon, is derived from the toxic plant *Strychnos guianensis*. Curares act by preventing nerves from activating muscles, leading to paralysis. Death is due to paralysis of the respiratory muscles.

In modern medicine, a purified form of the principal active ingredient in tube curare, an alkaloid called tubocurarine, is used primarily as a muscle relaxant in general anaesthesia. Tubocurarine is yet another rainforest substance modern medicine is indebted to.

as a reservoir of potentially valuable chemicals. Traditional remedies can act as pointers to discovering plants that may be worth investigating.

Ethnobotanists such as Dr Mark Plotkin, author of *Tales of a Shaman's Apprentice* and president of the Amazon Conservation Team, believe that traditional healers hold the key to the preservation of the forest. (Ethnobotany is a branch of botany dedicated to the study of plants used by traditional societies.) Through their knowledge of the properties and medicinal uses of forest plants (and other forest wildlife), traditional healers can provide evidence of the economic worth of the forest and therefore the rationale for its preservation. Experience has shown that economic arguments command international and local governmental attention more effectively than any other.

One way in which ethnobotanists are helping to preserve this knowledge is through initiatives such as the Shaman's Apprentice Program. In this program, a tribal member is assigned as the trainer, and information gathered and recorded by ethnobotanists is translated back into the local language and is used as the basis for teaching apprentices. Programs in Colombia and Suriname have had considerable success, and other programs are ongoing. For more information about this program, check out the Amazon Conservation Team's website (**http://amazonteam.org**).

USING TRADITIONAL REMEDIES

If you decide to try some of the herbal or other traditional remedies available locally, bear in mind that these aren't necessarily harmless because they are 'natural' or 'herbal'. (See also the warning about *ayahuasca* in the boxed text 'Hallucinogens' earlier.) In particular, if you are taking any regular medication check with a doctor or herbal practitioner about possible interactions. As a general rule, it's best not to stop regular medications suddenly.

Herbal remedies can contain ingredients that may be toxic if you take them inappropriately or in the wrong dose. Some basic guidelines are as follows:

- follow the instructions carefully for any remedies you are prescribed (dose, how often, when to take them, how to make them up)
- stop taking them immediately if you experience any adverse effects
- herbal remedies can be unsafe in pregnancy, so are probably best avoided
- some conditions like kidney or liver disease can make toxic effects more likely
- combination remedies containing traditional herbs and Western medicines are generally best avoided as they have a greater potential for harm

WHO GETS THE MONEY?

The word 'exploitation' hovers like a cloud over the subject of research into rainforest plants. Of all the medicines in use today derived from rainforest plants, none has benefited the rainforest peoples in any measurable way. Quinine is a good example: seeds of the *Cinchona* tree were smuggled out of the Amazonian rainforest and planted in English and Dutch colonies in the tropics. Now most quinine in use medicinally is grown in countries in Africa.

The issue of who is to benefit from discoveries was discussed at the ground-breaking UN Conference on Environment in Rio de Janeiro in 1992, and it was agreed that some legal framework was needed in order to ensure that a proportion of any profits arising from discoveries in the rainforest go to indigenous people of the region.

Try to make sure you are clear about what the remedy is for and whether you really need to take it.

FURTHER INFORMATION

If you're interested in finding out more about traditional Native American medicine, here are some suggestions to get you started.

For an extremely readable account of a decade spent learning about traditional medicines from shamans in the rainforests of the northwestern Amazon, try the fascinating *Tales of a Shaman's Apprentice* by Mark Plotkin. As a plea for conservation of the rainforest's resources, this book is unsurpassed.

To find out more about shamanism, other books you may like to try include *The Shaman and the Jaguar* by G Reichel-Dolmatoff, an intriguing account of shamanism in tribes of the northwest Amazon, *Hallucinogens & Shamanism,* a classic account by Michael Harner, or his book on the Jivaro, *Jivaro – People of the Sacred Waterfall.* Also worth trying is *Sastun* by Rosita Arvigo about her apprenticeship under a Mayan shaman in Belize.

For more details on useful plants of the rainforest, try *The Healing Forest* by RE Schultes and RF Raffauf, a classic reference text, or *A Field Guide to Medicinal & Useful Plants of the Upper Amazon* by JL Castner. *Plants, People and Culture* by M Balick and Paul Cox provides a global overview of ethnobotany, with an emphasis on the tropical American rainforests.

There are some great resources you could check out on the web. For starters you could try either of the following:

- **http://amazonteam.org** – the website of the Amazon Conservation Team, of which Mark Plotkin is president.
- **http://rain-tree.com** – a fantastic resource, with heaps of good information on medicinal plants of the rainforest and how to use them

Buying & Using Medicines...

+ For guidelines on medicines and children see p280.
+ For a discussion of medicines during pregnancy, see p267.

All medicines have side effects, but the trick is to balance up the possible risks of using a medicine against the probable benefits – something most of us are usually happy leaving to our doctors to work out.

When you're travelling, expert advice may not be available and there may be occasions when you may need to self-treat with medicines – either ones you have with you or ones you have bought locally. Travellers medical kits are popular and have the advantage of coming with instructions. In this chapter we give general guidelines on how to use prescribed drugs safely and how to avoid dangerous medications. Although these guidelines are primarily for Western-style medicines, many of the general safety points also apply if you're buying traditional medicines.

DRUG NAMES

This is a confusing issue for everyone, including medics. You need to know that all drugs have two names: the generic (chemical) name and the brand name chosen by the manufacturer.

There can be several different brands containing the same generic substance. You can consider different brands as basically interchangeable (although brands can differ in the way they are absorbed and how convenient they are to take). Some common drugs that have been around for ages are available under the generic name (eg aspirin) as well as various brand names.

To confuse the issue further, some medicines that are made up of a combination of generic substances may be given a new generic name. For example, the painkiller co-codamol is a combination of paracetamol (acetaminophen) and codeine.

Because brand names vary from country to country, we've used generic names for drugs throughout this book – any doctor or pharmacist will recognise the generic name and should be able to suggest brands available locally. If you want to find out the generic name of a drug, look on the packet or leaflet accompanying the drug – the generic name should be there, usually in smaller type just below the brand name – or ask a pharmacist.

BUYING MEDICINES IN LATIN AMERICA

You are probably used to living somewhere with rigorous safety standards for medicines, as well as well-regulated medical and pharmaceutical professions. So you may be surprised to find that in most countries in Latin America, nonprescription remedies, as well as most of the prescription remedies available back home, are sold without prescription and often much more cheaply. Even controlled medicines such as some tranquillisers are often available without prescription. Prescriptions tend to be very strictly controlled in Western countries but in Latin America you will generally find that prescriptions can be dispensed by a wide range of medical, veterinary and related workers. Because medicines tend to be considerably cheaper over the border, many Americans regularly cross the border into Mexico to buy them.

In Latin America (and elsewhere in the developing world), medicines are not seen as something special but as a commodity like any other. The majority of local people self-treat with medicines bought from the pharmacy as a matter of course. Often pharmacists are the main source of treatment advice for the majority of people, especially in rural areas.

Although this set up can seem very convenient for you as a traveller, it's not quite as good as it seems. Pharmacists are not necessarily medically trained, and often recommend totally inappropriate treatment. In malarial areas, for example, potentially toxic antimalarial drugs may be recommended for fever, without a blood test to check the diagnosis. In particular, antibiotics tend to be readily used for many ailments, often inappropriately. People often don't complete a full course of treatment, which contributes to the rise in antibacterial

MEDICINES

CAN YOU HELP ME PLEASE?

What do you do when a local person asks you for treatment? It's a dilemma you'll almost certainly be faced with if you're travelling in a less developed country. In most situations it's probably better to avoid immediately diving for your medical kit – short-term gratitude may well lead to longer-term harm. If the question arises, consider the following: do you know what is wrong with the person and thus the appropriate treatment? Do you know enough about that person to be reasonably confident that they will not react adversely to the treatment? Are they on any other medication that would interact badly with your treatment? Could they be allergic to your treatment? Can you communicate well enough with them to find all this out and explain the dosage regime? Even if you're a doctor, answers to these questions are not always straightforward.

If you're feeling guilty about not helping, a simple explanation that you are not a doctor and do not know how to treat them will usually be met with understanding. It is almost always better to encourage people to seek help from a local health centre.

Don't forget that simple advice may be more helpful than you appreciate. For example, it is common to be shown a dirty open wound. A suggestion to bathe the wound in boiled-and-cooled water regularly and to keep it as clean as possible will hopefully be heeded, and is far more useful than any tablets.

Corinne Else

resistance worldwide – see the section on Antibiotics later in this chapter for more discussion on this.

With less control over medicines, it is easier for counterfeit drugs to be passed off. These are drugs containing inactive or sometimes poisonous substances that are sold as the real thing. In developing areas of the world, counterfeit drugs are big business. In Mexico, counterfeits are estimated to constitute 10% of the market in towns like Tijuana, and the situation is likely to be similar in other countries in the region. In addition, drugs made by local companies may be substandard and therefore less effective.

If you buy medicines while you are away, take some basic precautions:

- if possible, buy from a trustworthy doctor or large pharmacy
- check whether the drugs have been kept in optimal conditions, for example out of direct sunlight or refrigerated if necessary
- check the expiry date – very few drugs (tetracycline is a notable exception) are actually harmful if they are kept too long, but they may well be ineffective
- if possible, look for drugs made by local branches of international drug companies
- look out for fakes (although these can be difficult to spot) – check the label and safety seal

In many Latin American countries, injections are seen as the best and most effective way to administer medicines, and may be given by pharmacists. Unless you are confident of that the equipment used is sterile, it's probably best to avoid injections. There's an increased risk of serious side effects from the drug, as well as the risk of an abscess at the injection site or infection with HIV or hepatitis B. Try asking if a tablet form is available instead.

In less-developed countries, especially those affected by war, conventional medicines may be in short supply and difficult to obtain.

MEDICINES

MEDICINES TO AVOID

Some medicines to be wary of include the following (we've used the generic name unless indicated):

- steroids – these are powerful drugs used in a variety of conditions (eg asthma and dermatitis), usually to suppress inflammation. They have some pretty powerful side effects too, and shouldn't be used except under medical supervision. Combination medications may contain steroids, so look out for them (this is not a complete list) – prednisolone, betamethasone, cortisone, dexamethasone, hydrocortisone, methylprednisolone. Never use eye drops containing steroids except under medical supervision

- chloramphenicol – an antibiotic that may be prescribed for tonsillitis or travellers diarrhoea. It can have a very serious effect on the blood system in some people and should only be used for life-threatening infections (eg sometimes for typhoid fever). Note that this does not apply to chloramphenicol eye and ear drops, which can be used safely

- clioquinol – an antidiarrhoeal drug that should be avoided because it can have serious effects on the nervous system

- opium tincture – may be available in for treatment of diarrhoea and other ailments; best avoided for obvious reasons

- phenylbutazone – an anti-inflammatory painkiller with potentially serious side effects

- sulphonamide antibiotics – these will work if no alternatives are available, but are best avoided if possible because of potential side effects

- Fansidar (brand name) – this antimalarial is no longer used for prevention in most Western countries because of side effects, although it is still used to treat malaria; if you are offered it as a preventive, try to find an alternative

SIDE EFFECTS & ALLERGIES

Any drug may produce unwanted or unexpected effects, so be on the lookout for these when you take any medicine. You may need to stop taking that particular drug and take a different one. If you know you're allergic to a drug, you should avoid it.

Some drugs produce well recognised side effects that your doctor or pharmacist should warn you about. Familiar drugs that have been around for many years are unlikely to have any unexpected effects, although new drugs may still be capable of causing a few surprises. Sometimes it can be difficult to work out if it's the drug or the actual illness process causing the problems, especially when you're treating diarrhoea; all antibiotics can cause stomach upsets.

Allergies are one serious type of side effect, but not all side effects are allergies. Mild symptoms of headache, diarrhoea, nausea and maybe vomiting are not signs of allergy. Signs of allergy usually appear soon after taking the medicine and include:

- a red, raised itchy rash (common)
- breathing difficulties and swelling of the face
- fainting or collapsing

Note that a severe allergic reaction is always a medical emergency, and you will need to seek medical help urgently.

Make sure you record any drug allergies that you know you have, and carry this information on you at all times. Some companies specialise in making engraved bracelets with these details – see the Useful Organisations section in the Before You Go chapter at the start of this book for more details. Always tell anyone treating you of any drug allergies you think you have.

Medicines that commonly cause allergies include aspirin and antibiotics like penicillin and sulpha (sulphonamide) drugs. Remember that if you are allergic to one drug, you should avoid any related drugs too.

DOSES, TIMING & SPECIAL INSTRUCTIONS

Ideally, for any medicine, you should be clear about what dose to take at what interval and follow any special instructions on the label. In practice, you may find that the dosage of the brand available locally may differ from the one we've suggested in this book. This is usually because the drug has been formulated slightly differently, or possibly the dose may have been expressed in different units.

If you're not sure what dose to take, ask either the pharmacist or doctor, read the information leaflet carefully or try to find another brand of the drug that causes less confusion. Remember that a single extra dose of most drugs is unlikely to cause problems.

Note that usually 'every six hours' means in practice to take the dose four times a day during waking hours; 'every eight hours' means take it three times a day.

Alcohol is best avoided because it can affect the absorption of drugs and may have an additive effect on drugs that are sedative (ie make you drowsy), such as some antihistamines. Alcohol should not be taken with metronidazole – an antibiotic that you may take for some types of diarrhoea – as it causes a particularly bad reaction, making you feel stupendously dreadful.

If you're taking several different drugs together, they can interact to make adverse effects more likely or reduce effectiveness. Similarly, medical conditions can affect how well a drug works and how likely it is to cause unwanted effects, eg you should not take the contraceptive pill if you have hepatitis.

COMMONLY USED MEDICINES

We've summarised here details about doses, side effects and cautions for some common medicines that you may find you need to use while you're away. Details about other medicines used for specific conditions are described in the relevant sections:

✚ drugs for treating and preventing malaria p42
✚ drugs for motion sickness p70
✚ ear (p187) and eyedrops p193
✚ drugs for vaginal thrush p255
✚ drugs in pregnancy p267

✚ drugs for altitude illness p331

✚ antifungal creams p208

✚ homoeopathic/naturopathic first aid p60

Where the brand name tends to be better known than the generic name, we've listed some common brands, but be aware that these brands may not be available in Latin America.

PAIN & FEVER

Simple painkillers include aspirin and paracetamol (acetaminophen in the US) and are also good for reducing fever.

Paracetamol has very few side effects, except perhaps nausea, although it can cause liver damage in overdose. Aspirin is more problematic and should be avoided if you are hypersensitive to it, asthmatic or suffer from indigestion or stomach ulcers. It can also cause heartburn and stomach irritation.

Aspirin is not suitable for children under 12 years, but paracetamol is fine in infants and children.

Stronger painkillers include codeine phosphate, which will also stop diarrhoea in an emergency. Side effects include constipation and drowsiness. Some customs officials may be a bit suspicious of codeine, because of its potential for abuse, so it's safest to have a letter from your doctor explaining what it is and why you need it, to keep customs officials happy. Other painkillers include a combination of paracetamol with codeine (eg co-codamol). Codeine can be given to children, but is best avoided if possible.

Ibuprofen (eg Nurofen and other brand names, also in forms suitable for children) is an anti-inflammatory drug that is good for fever, pain (including period pain) and inflammation (eg painful joint). Avoid it if you have had stomach ulcers or a hypersensitivity to aspirin. Stronger anti-inflammatory drugs include naproxen and indomethacin, which are useful for treating strains, sprains, sports injuries and joint pains.

MEDICINES

Drug	Dose – adult	Dose – children
aspirin	one to two 300mg tablets every four to six hours when necessary (maximum 4g in 24 hours)	avoid in children under 12 years
paracetamol (acetaminophen)	one to two 500mg tablets every four to six hours (maximum 4g in 24 hours)	three months to one year: 60 to 120mg; one to five years: 120 to 250mg; six to 12 years: 250 to 500mg; over 12 years: adult dose; (maximum four doses in 24 hours)
codeine phosphate	two to four 15mg tablets every four hours, maximum 240mg in 24 hours	one to 12 years: 1mg/kg every six hours
ibuprofen	two 200mg tablets every six hours, as necessary	suspension (100mg/5mL) available for children; six months to one year: 2.5mL; one to two years: 2.5mL; three to seven years: 5mL; eight to 12 years: 10mL; all doses given three to four times daily

ANTIBIOTICS

Many travel-related illnesses are caused by infections, and you may need to take antibiotics to treat them while you're away. Antibiotics work against bacterial infections but don't have any effect on viral or fungal infections. This means they won't be any good against common viral infections like colds and flu, as well as many throat and gastro infections.

Different antibiotics are effective against different bacteria. We give antibiotic recommendations in this book based on the likeliest cause of infection; however, the best way to find out if an antibiotic will be effective against an infection is to have a laboratory test to identify the bacteria causing it.

Antibiotics should stop most infections within a few days. Because they work to stop the infection and not the symptoms, you may need to treat symptoms (such as pain and fever) with other medications until the antibiotics kick in.

If an antibiotic appears not to be working (it needs at least two days to do its stuff), you may be taking the wrong dose (check) OR it's the wrong antibiotic (the bacteria are resistant or they aren't affected by this particular antibiotic) OR the illness is not what you think it is. In this case, it's always best to seek medical advice (after you've checked that the dose is correct).

Antibiotics can cause problems, which is why they need to be treated with respect. They commonly cause nausea and diarrhoea and, because they disrupt the normal balance of organisms in the body, can make women more likely to develop thrush (vaginal candidiasis). Antibiotics (especially penicillins and cephalosporins) can cause severe allergic reactions, so you should always carry a record of any allergic reactions with you.

! If rashes and swelling of the throat and face occur, stop taking the drug immediately and seek medical advice. Always carry a record of any allergic reactions with you.

Antibiotic Resistance

This is a growing problem worldwide, and is one reason why you should always finish the whole course of an antibiotic (unless you experience severe adverse reactions). Antibiotic resistance is more likely to occur if the infection is not quickly and completely eliminated. In many countries, antibiotics are readily available without prescription and are often taken indiscriminately and perhaps inappropriately. People may not be able to afford to buy a whole course and are often not aware of the importance of doing so anyway. The use of antibiotics in livestock rearing has also been an important factor.

You can help by only using antibiotics if really necessary, choosing the most effective antibiotic and completing the full course of antibiotics – this way there aren't any bacteria left hanging around with nothing better to do than work out ways of fighting back.

MEDICINES

The Details

Suggested lengths of courses of antibiotics are indicated in the relevant sections. Note that all the antibiotics described in this section can cause nausea and stomach upsets.

Co-amoxiclav (Augmentin) is a combination of amoxycillin (a penicillin drug) and clavulanic acid (which makes it more effective against some bacteria than plain amoxycillin). It's a useful 'broad spectrum' antibiotic, and is effective against bladder, ear, chest and sinus infections. It's also good for skin infections and animal bites. Although amoxycillin (Amoxil) is

ANTIBIOTIC GUIDE

Here's a quick guide to which antibiotics are suitable for what. Read the details about the antibiotics to find out if they are suitable for your age group, and avoid any antibiotics (including related antibiotics) you are allergic to:

- diarrhoea – ciprofloxacin (and related antibiotics), co-trimoxazole, metronidazole, tinidazole
- chest infection – co-trimoxazole, amoxycillin, co-amoxiclav, erythromycin/clarithromycin
- throat infection – phenoxymethylpenicillin or co-amoxiclav
- ear infection – amoxycillin, co-amoxiclav or co-trimoxazole
- urinary infection (cystitis) – amoxycillin or co-trimoxazole
- skin infection – phenoxymethylpenicillin, flucloxacillin or co-amoxiclav

Note: clarithromycin/erythromycin can be used if you are allergic to penicillin.

less reliable generally, it is useful if you can't get co-amoxiclav. Both drugs can sometimes cause skin rashes, and should be avoided if you are allergic to penicillin.

Trimethoprim is useful for treating bladder and ear infections, and for diarrhoea in children. There are concerns over its potential to cause serious but rare side effects, including severe skin rash and blood disorders. It should be avoided in pregnancy. Note that co-trimoxazole is a combination drug that contains a sulphonamide antibiotic plus trimethoprim – it's best avoided if possible, as there is a slightly higher risk of serious side effects.

Ciprofloxacin is effective against most bacterial causes of travellers diarrhoea, cystitis (bladder infection) and chest infection. Ciprofloxacin can occasionally cause kidney problems, which is why you should drink plenty of fluids when you take it. Similar drugs that can be used as alternatives include norfloxacin, nalidixic acid and ofloxacin. Ciprofloxacin should be avoided in pregnancy and it is not generally recommended for children under the age of 12 years because of potential side effects. Suitable alternatives for children are suggested in the relevant sections.

Flucloxacillin (eg Floxapen) is a penicillin drug that is effective for skin infections, although co-amoxiclav is usually the first choice. It can cause rashes and allergic reactions, and you should avoid it if you are allergic to penicillin.

Erythromycin (eg Erymax) or clarithromycin can be used as an alternative to penicillin drugs if you are allergic to penicillin. Clarithromycin is less likely to cause side effects such as nausea and vomiting.

Metronidazole (eg Flagyl) is effective against infections causing diarrhoea, especially with a fever and abdominal pain, eg giardiasis and amoebic dysentery. It is also effective against bacterial vaginosis. You should avoid alcohol when you are taking it, as it causes a severe reaction (flushing, headache, palpitations). Tinidazole (eg Fasigyn) is similar and can be used as an alternative.

Drug	Dose– adult	Dose – children
ciprofloxacin	500mg twice daily	not recommended in children under 12 years
amoxycillin	250mg three times daily (double dose if infection is severe)	up to 10 years: 125mg three times daily; 10 years and over: adult dose
co-amoxiclav	250mg three times daily	up to 10 years: 125mg three times daily
trimethoprim	200mg twice daily	two to five months: 25mg; six months to five years: 50mg; six to 12 years: 100mg; all doses twice daily:
flucloxacillin	250mg four times daily (double dose if infection is severe)	under two years: 75mg; two to 10 years: 125mg; all doses four times daily
erythromycin	500mg to 1g twice daily	up to two years: 125mg; two to eight years: 250mg all doses four times daily
metronidazole	500mg three times daily	7.5mg/kg three times daily

ANTIHISTAMINES

These are useful for hay fever, allergies, itchy rashes, insect bites and motion sickness. There are many different ones available, mostly without prescription, and they vary in what side effects they cause (mainly drowsiness).

Antihistamines that are more likely to cause drowsiness include promethazine, chlorpheniramine and cyclizine. Non- (or at least less) sedating ones include astemizole, cetirizine and loratidine. Ask your pharmacist for guidance on brands available to you, and follow the dosing instructions on the packet. They can be given to children.

Side effects include drowsiness, headache, dry mouth and blurred vision. They're more common in children and older people. Because drowsiness can occur, you shouldn't drive, dive or drink alcohol in large quantities after you take antihistamines.

NAUSEA & VOMITING

For details about drugs to prevent and treat motion sickness, see p70. Metoclopramide (eg Maxolon) is useful for nausea and vomiting associated with diarrhoea or food poisoning. The adult dose is 10mg three times daily. It's best avoided in children – if necessary, try an antihistamine instead. Some are available in suppository form (ie you insert it in the rectum), which might sound uninviting, but a it's useful option if you're vomiting, and other forms (such as soluble forms or a patch you put against your cheek) are also available.

ANTIDIARRHOEALS

These drugs are best avoided unless it's an emergency and you have to travel. They include loperamide (eg Imodium and other brand names), probably the most useful; diphenoxylate with atropine (eg Lomotil; less useful because of potential side effects); and bismuth subsalicylate (Pepto-Bismol).

The dose of loperamide is two 2mg tablets initially, followed by one 2mg tablet after each loose motion, to a maximum of eight tablets in 24 hours. It commonly causes constipation; other possible side effects include abdominal cramps, bloating and, rarely, paralysis of the gut. The dose of diphenoxylate is four tablets initially, followed by two tablets every six hours until the diarrhoea is under control. Neither drug is recommended for children, and you should avoid them if you have a fever, or blood in your diarrhoea.

Bismuth subsalicylate is available in tablet or liquid form, but tablets are more convenient if you're travelling: take two tablets four times daily. It's not suitable for children (as it contains aspirin). It can cause blackening of the tongue and faeces, and ringing in the ears. You shouldn't use it for more than three weeks at these doses.

Medical Services...

➕ See the Help... chapter earlier for more guidance on how to go about getting medical help.

In an emergency situation, you'll just have to use whatever services are immediately available, but in less urgent situations you will probably have time to look around for a reliable source of medical advice and care. In some situations, you may need to consider being evacuated back home or to the USA.

AVAILABILITY

Medical care, usually of a reasonable standard, is generally readily available in towns and cities, but is much more limited in rural areas. Public hospitals tend to be free or at least cheaper than private clinics but they are generally less well equipped and often overburdened. Private clinics and doctors often provide medical care of a high standard, and you should have no trouble finding them in most towns and cities. However, they can be quite expensive – an illustration of the two-tier system that exists in many Latin American countries. If you have insurance (strongly advised), you're probably better off sticking to the private sector, if you have the choice. Hospitals affiliated to a university and specialist medical centres are recommended for more serious ailments.

In many countries, immunisations and malaria medication are available free of charge at public health centres called (in Spanish) *unidades sanitarias*. You should be able to get yellow fever vaccination or rabies shots at one of these if you are bitten by a suspect animal. In some cities there may be specific anti-rabies centres – in Spanish, ask for the *centro antirrabico*.

WHAT TO EXPECT

Different cultures have different views about symptoms, treatments, and, perhaps most importantly, the doctor-patient relationship. In Latin America, you will probably find that

IN AN EMERGENCY

Unless you're travelling in one of the more developed countries in the continent, you can't rely on fast-reaction emergency services coming to your rescue, for example in a road traffic accident. If you are in an emergency situation:

- don't wait for emergency services to arrive – if you can, get a taxi or flag down some transport, and ask them to take you to the nearest doctor or hospital
- contact your embassy for advice
- phone your travel insurance hotline as soon as possible

doctors are treated with great respect, and patients would not be expected to question or doubt the diagnosis or any treatment the doctor prescribes. Often multiple anonymous (and often unnecessary) tablets are prescribed (and expected by patients) for any illness.

❗ If you do have to take a medicine while you are away, make sure you know what it is and what it has been prescribed for.

Here are some guidelines for assessing if you have seen a good doctor.

- Willing to listen and spends a reasonable amount of time asking about your problem; doesn't just jump to a diagnosis. In most cases, the doctor should also examine you for at least the basics like pulse rate and temperature.
- Happy to discuss fully the diagnosis and any treatment with you and any companion you would like with you in the consultation.

MEDICAL SERVICES

- If blood tests (or other procedures) are needed, the doctor uses good aseptic techniques ie wears surgical gloves (should put on a new pair for each patient), uses a sterile needle (opens packet in front of you) and a clean dressing.

- Generally, illnesses need one specific treatment (in addition to painkillers, for example); if you are prescribed multiple treatments, ask what they are for and if they are all necessary. If you are not seriously ill, it's always worth trying a few simple measures first, as outlined in the Help... chapter earlier.

- Explains what you need to do if your symptoms get worse.

- You feel confident about the way you were treated – if you have any doubts, see a different doctor and get a second opinion.

Language is an obvious problem although, if necessary, you can communicate much through gestures and miming. It's a good idea to brush up on a few basic words or phrases before you go – see the Language glossary later in this book.

As a rule, standards of nursing and auxiliary care are very different from those you may be used to, eg attitudes towards basic hygiene can be alarmingly casual.

PAYMENT

Unless you are using a free public health service, you will generally be expected to pay upfront for any medical services. Credit cards are not usually accepted, so you can't rely on this as a method of payment. Even if you are covered by insurance, many clinics will still expect you to put the money down upfront, so be prepared. Keep any receipts so you can claim reimbursement later.

DIRECTORY

If you have an embassy and the time to contact it, this should be your first call for information on local doctors and clinics, or you can ring your travel insurance hotline. In most major cities, you can get the number for a hospital or doctor from the telephone book. The services listed here are intended as a guide only, to get you started.

! Although we have done all we can to ensure the accuracy of the information listed, contact details change and places disappear. Note that listing here does not imply any endorsement or recommendation by Lonely Planet of the services provided.

ARGENTINA

Medical care available here is good, especially in major cities.

British Hospital ☎ 011-4304-1081; www.hospitalbritanico.org.ar; Perdriel 74, Buenos Aires

Hospital Municipal Juan Fernández ☎ 011-4808-2650; Cerviño 3356, Palermo, Buenos Aires

BELIZE

Medical facilities are very limited here. For serious illnesses, many Belizeans fly to Chetumal or Mérida in Mexico, or to Houston, Miami or New Orleans in the USA.

Karl Heusner Memorial Hospital ☎ 223 1548; Princess Margaret Dr, Belize City

Lion's Club Medical Clinic ☎ 226 2851; Lion St, Ambergris Caye

San Carlos Medical Clinic ☎ 226 2918; Pescador Dr, Ambergris Caye

BOLIVIA

In large cities, you can get reasonable medical care, but elsewhere standards vary.

Centro Epidemiológico Departamental La Paz (Centro Pilote) ☎ 02-245-0166; Vásquez 122, La Paz

Clínica del Sur ☎ 02-278-4001; Siles 3539, Obrajes, La Paz

Clínica Japonesa ☎ 346-2031; 3rd *anillo*, Santa Cruz

High Altitude Pathology Institute ☎ 224-5394, 222 2617; www.altitudeclinic.com; Saavedra 2302, Miraflores, La Paz (Bolivian member of the International Association for Medical Assistance to Travelers; maintains a hyperoxygen acclimatization chamber at the summit of Chacaltaya.)

BRAZIL

Although you can find excellent medical care in major cities (some private facilities in Rio are on a par with US hospitals), it is limited in rural or remote areas.

Einstein Hospital ☎ 3747 1233; Av Albert Einstein 627, Morumbi, São Paulo

Hospital Ipanema ☎ 3111 2300; Rua Antônio Parreiras 67, Ipanema, Rio de Janeiro

Miguel Couto Hospital ☎ 2274 2121; Av Bartolomeu Mitre 1108, Gávea, Rio de Janeiro

Sírio-Libânes Hospital ☎ 3155 0200; Rua Dona Adma Jafet 91, Bela Vista, São Paulo

CHILE

You can generally get reasonable or good medical care in major cities. If you're travelling to the Antarctic or Easter Island, make sure you have insurance to cover the possibility of evacuation from these regions, otherwise you could be facing a hefty bill (US$50,000 and upwards).

Clínica Alemana de Santiago ☎ 02-2101111; Av Vitacura 5951, Vitacura, Santiago

Hospital Carlos van Buren ☎ 032-204000; Av Colón 2454, Valparaíso

Posta Central ☎ 02-6341650; Portugal 125, Santiago

COLOMBIA

Adequate medical care is available in Bogotá but much more limited elsewhere in the country. If you're insured, it's preferable to use private clinics rather than government-owned institutions, which are cheaper but may not be as well equipped.

Centro de Atención al Viajero ☎ 215 2029, 612 0272; Carrera 7 No 119-14, Bogotá

Clínica de Marly ☎ 343 6600; Calle 50 No 9-67, Bogotá

Hospital San Ignacio ☎ 288 8188; Carrera 7 No 40-62, Bogotá

COSTA RICA

Good medical services are available in major cities but are limited in rural areas. Public hospitals are free to everyone, including foreigners. Private treatment is generally less expensive than you may be used to back home.

Clínica Bíblica ☎ 257 5252; www.clinicabiblica.com; Av 14 btwn Calles Central & 1, San José

Hospital Clínica Católica ☎ 246 3000; www.clinicacatolica.com; Guadalupe, San José

Hospital San Juan de Dios ☎ 257 6282; cnr Paseo Colón & Calle 14, San José

ECUADOR

Medical care is available and of adequate standard in major towns but limited in rural areas. Members of the South American Explorers Club can get a list of doctors and other medical services recommended by members.

Clínica de la Mujer ☎ 02-245-8000; Av Amazonas 4826 at Gaspar de Villarroel, Quito (private clinic specialising in women's health)

Clínica Pichincha ☎ 02-256-2408, 256-2296; General Veintimilla 1259 & U Páez, Quito

Hospital Voz Andes ☎ 02-226-2142; Juan Villalengua 267 near América & 10 de Agosto, Quito

Hospital Metropolitano ☎ 02-226-1520; Av Mariana de Jesús at Occidental, Quito

EL SALVADOR

Medical care is very limited here. Consider evacuation to Mexico or the USA for serious illness.

Hospital de Diagnóstico ☎ 2226 8878; Calle 21 Pte at 2a Diagonal, San Salvador

Hospital Diagnóstico Escalón ☎ 2264 4422; 3a Calle Pte, San Salvador

Hospital Bloom ☎ 2225 4114; Blvd de los Héroes at Av Gustavo Guerrero/25a Av Norte, San Salvador

MEDICAL SERVICES

GUIANAS

Medical care is very limited in French Guiana, Guyana and Suriname, although you should be able to get reasonable care in the private sector in major towns.

Academisch Ziekenhuis (AZ) ☎ 442222; Flustraat, Paramaribo, Suriname

Centre Hospitalier Cayenne ☎ 39-50-50; 3 Av Flamboyants, Cayenne, French Guiana

St Joseph's Mercy Hospital ☎ 227-2072; 130-132 Parade St, Georgetown, Guyana

GUATEMALA

Adequate medical care is available in private hospitals in Guatemala City; public hospitals and clinics provide free consultations but can be very busy and short on equipment.

Clínica Cruz Roja (Red Cross Clinic) ☎ 2381 6565; 3a Calle 8-40, Zona 1, Guatemala City

Hospital Centro Médico ☎ 2332 3555, 334 2157; 6a Av 3-47, Zona 10, Guatemala City

Hospital General San Juan de Dios ☎ 2253 0443/7; 1a Av at 10a Calle, Zona 1, Guatemala City

Hospital Herrera Llerandi ☎ 2334 5959, emergency ☎ 334 5955; 6a Av 8-71, Zona 10, Guatemala City

Hospital Reina de los Ángeles ☎ 7832 2258; Calle Ancha de los Herreros 59, Antigua

HONDURAS

Adequate medical care is available in Tegucigalpa but is very limited elsewhere. Consider evacuation to Mexico or the States for serious illness.

Honduras Medical Center ☎ 216 1201; Av Juan Lindo, Tegucigalpa

MALVINAS/FALKLAND ISLANDS

There's an excellent joint military/civilian hospital in Stanley.

King Edward VII Memorial Hospital ☎ appointments 27328, emergencies 27410; St Mary's Walk, Stanley (fee for service)

MEXICO
Public hospitals are inexpensive for most common ailments and minor treatments. Clinics in smaller towns tend to be overburdened, but are linked by radio to emergency services. Care in remote areas is limited and evacuation to Mexico City or the USA costs thousands of dollars without insurance. For advice on doctors and clinics, call the 24-hour tourist assistance help line in Mexico City, SECTUR (☎ 5212-0260).

Dalinde Centro Médico ☎ 5265-2805, emergency dial 9; Tuxpán 25, Colonia Roma Sur, Mexico City

Hospital ABC (American British Cowdray Hospital) ☎ 5230-8000, emergency 5230-8161; Sur 136 No 16, Colonia Las Américas, Mexico City

Hospital Ángeles Clínica Londres ☎ 5229-8400, emergency 5229-8445; Durango 64, Colonia Roma, Mexico City

Hospital Americano ☎ 884 6133; Viento 15 at Av Tulum, Cancún

General Hospital ☎ 678 0770; Insurgentes, San Cristóbal de Las Casas

NICARAGUA
As you might expect, medical care is very limited here, especially outside Managua.

Hospital Bautista ☎ 249 7070, 249 7277; about 1km east of Crowne Plaza Hotel, Managua

Hospital San Vicente ☎ 311 6990; beyond the bus station, León

PANAMA
Medicine in Panama, especially in Panama City, is of a high standard.

Centro Medico Paitilla ☎ 265 8800, 265 8883; Calle 53 Este & Av Balboa, Panama City

Chiriquí Hospital ☎ 777 8814; Calle Central & Av 3 Oeste, David

PARAGUAY

Medical facilities are very limited. You'll need to fly to a regional centre such as Buenos Aires or Rio, or back home for anything serious.

Hospital Privado Frances ☎ 021-295250; Av Brasilia 1194, Asunción

Hospital Bautista ☎ 021-600 171; Av Rep Argentina, Asunción

PERU

Good medical care is available in major cities, especially Lima, but is variable elsewhere. South American Explorers Club members can get a list of recommended facilities from the club house in Lima.

Clínica Anglo-Americana ☎ 221 3656; Salazar cuadra 3, San Isidro, Lima

Clínica Internacional ☎ 433 4306; cnr Washington 1471 & 9 de Diciembre, Lima Centro, Lima

Clínica Montesur ☎ 436 3630; Av El Polo 505, Monterrico, Lima (specialises in women's health)

Clínica San Borja ☎ 475 4000, 475 3141; Av Guardia Civil 337, San Borja, Lima

URUGUAY

Medical facilities are limited here. You will probably have to pay first and then ask for reimbursement later, if you need medical treatement.

Hospital Británico ☎ 02-280-0020; Italia 2420, Montevideo

Hospital Maciel ☎ 02-915-3000; 25 de Mayo & Maciel, Montevideo

VENEZUELA

Good medical care is available in Caracas, but limited elsewhere. However most minor health problems can be solved in a pharmacy – look for the sign reading 'Turno'. You can even get basic shots right at the counter.

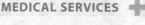

Centro Médico de Caracas ☎ 552-2222, 555-9111; Plaza El Estanque, Av Eraso, San Bernardino, Caracas

Clínica El Ávila ☎ 276-1003, emergency 276-1090; Av San Juan Bosco at 6a Transversal, Altamira, Caracas

Clínica Albarregas ☎ 244-8101, 244-7283; Calle Tovar No 1-26, Mérida

Clínica Mérida ☎ 263-0652, 263-6395; Av Urdaneta No 45-145, Mérida

Hospital Ruiz y Páez ☎ 632-0077; Av Germania, Ciudad Bolívar

First Aid...

Although we give guidance on basic first aid procedures here remember that, unless you're an experienced first aider and confident you know what you're doing, it's possible to do more harm than good. Always seek medical help if it is available, but if you are far from any help, follow the guidelines given in this chapter.

> **!** See the inside back cover for guidelines on responding to an emergency situation, dealing with near drowning and how to perform cardiopulmonary resuscitation.

CUTS & OTHER WOUNDS

This includes any break in the skin – it could be an insect bite you've scratched, sunburn that's blistered, a raw area that your sandals have rubbed, a small graze or cut or a larger open wound from a fall or coming off a motorbike. If you're travelling in areas with poor environmental cleanliness and lack of clean water, there's a high risk of infection, especially in the hot, humid climates of the tropics and subtropics.

Carry a few antiseptic wipes on you to use as an immediate measure, especially if no water is available. A small wound can be cleaned with an antiseptic wipe (but remember to wipe across the wound just once). Deep or dirty wounds need to be cleaned thoroughly, as follows:

- make sure your hands are clean before you start
- wear gloves if you are cleaning somebody else's wound
- use bottled or boiled water (allowed to cool) or an antiseptic solution like povidone-iodine
- use plenty of water – pour it on the wound from a container
- embedded dirt and other particles can be removed with tweezers or flushed out using a syringe to squirt water (you can get more pressure if you use a needle as well)
- dry wounds heal best, so avoid using antiseptic creams which keep the wound moist, but you could apply antiseptic powder or spray

- dry the wound with clean gauze before applying a dressing from your medical kit – alternatively, any clean material will do as long as it's not fluffy (avoid cotton wool) because this will stick

- any break in the skin makes you vulnerable to tetanus infection – if you didn't have a tetanus injection before you left, you'll need one now

A dressing will protect the wound from dirt, dust and flies. Flies can sometimes lay their eggs in wounds, but the main problem is that they carry dirt on their feet. Alternatively, if the wound is small and you are confident you can keep it clean, leave it uncovered.

> **!** Change the dressing regularly (eg once a day to start with), especially if the wound is oozing, and watch for signs of infection (see later in this chapter).

Antibiotic powders are best avoided as a rule (although antiseptic powders are fine) because they can give you sensitivity reactions. Alcohol can be used if you have been bitten by an animal (p387) as it can help kill the rabies virus, but otherwise avoid using it on wounds. In general, it's best to avoid poultices and other local remedies if they seem likely to introduce infection.

If you have any swelling around the wound, raising the affected limb can help the swelling settle and the wound to heal (eg sit with your foot up on your pack, or fashion a sling for your arm).

It's best to seek medical advice for any wound that fails to heal after a week or so. If a wound is taking a long time to heal, consider improving your diet, especially your protein intake, to aid healing – see the Diet & Nutrition section at the end of the Staying Healthy chapter.

DRESSINGS & BANDAGES

If you're wondering how and when to use all those mysterious-looking packages in your first aid kit, here's a quick rundown:

- small adhesive dressings (ie sticking plasters or Band-Aids) are useful for small wounds (although they can cause skin irritation in people who are allergic to them, especially in hot climates because they block sweating)

■ nonadhesive dressings are usually general-purpose plain gauze pads or sterile padded dressings; fix in place with adhesive tape or a crepe bandage

■ use nonstick dressings (eg Melolin or paraffin gauze) for open, oozing wounds

Bear in mind the following if you are bandaging something:

■ remove any rings from fingers (or toes) if your hand or arm is injured in case it swells up

■ keep fresh bandages rolled and unroll them as you put them on – this makes it easier to put them on smoothly and evenly

■ start from the extremity and bandage in (ie for an ankle, start bandaging from the toes upward)

■ don't just bandage the painful bit, you need to bandage from the joint below the injured area to the joint above (ie from toes to knee for an ankle)

■ fix the bandage in place with tape (best), a safety pin or by tying a knot on the opposite side to the wound

■ never put tape all the way around a limb or finger/toe, as it can cut off the circulation

■ make sure the bandage is firm enough to prevent it from slipping, but not tight enough to cut into your flesh or stop the circulation – if your fingers or toes start going numb and cold, it's too tight

PRESSURE IMMOBILISATION BANDAGE

This is used for bites and stings from some venomous creatures: some snakes, blue-ringed octopus, box jellyfish and cone shell. It's not a tourniquet, but applies pressure over a wide area of the limb and delays the rate at which venom enters the circulation. Use a roller bandage, and apply it from the fingers or toes as far up the limb as possible. It should be as firm as for a sprained ankle. Use a splint to immobilise the limb.

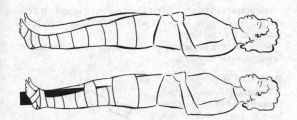

SIGNS OF WOUND INFECTION

Infected wounds take much longer to heal, which is not only a nuisance when you're travelling, it can also be debilitating. When they eventually heal, they're more likely to scar. If a wound gets infected, the infection can spread into your blood to give you blood poisoning, which makes you seriously ill. If you suspect you have an infected wound, it's best to seek medical advice for an appropriate course of antibiotics. However, if medical help is not available, you should self-treat with antibiotics if you have any of the following signs of (mild) infection:

- pain (throbbing)
- redness, heat and swelling in the area around the wound
- pus (thick yellow discharge) in the wound
- red streaks going away from the wound

A more serious infection is indicated by the following signs:

- swelling of the involved limb
- swelling of the nearest glands eg in the armpit for a wound in the hand, or in the groin for a leg or foot wound
- fever and feeling unwell

Start a course of antibiotics and get medical help as soon as possible. Suitable antibiotics are: flucloxacillin 250mg four times daily OR co-amoxiclav 250mg three times daily OR erythromycin (if you're allergic to penicillin) 250mg four times daily. Double these doses for serious infections while you're getting to medical help.

Some bacteria in the tropics cause ulcers (sores) – treatment is with specific antibiotics.

WOUND CLOSURE

If a wound is deep or gaping, it may need to be closed to help it heal better. If you think you need stitches, the sooner it's done the better. However, it's probably best not to close them yourself unless you feel confident and able to do so. An alternative to stitching is to close small clean cuts with a special strip or butterfly dressings.

Wounds that should never be closed include:

- wounds that are dirty and can't be cleaned adequately
- animal or human bites
- infected wounds

For small clean cuts, you can apply wound closure strips or butterfly dressings as follows:

- see if the edges of the cut come together easily – if not, you won't be able to use these
- clean the wound thoroughly, apply antiseptic and dry it with sterile gauze
- make sure any bleeding has stopped and that the area around the wound is clean and dry so that the dressings can stick
- put the dressings across the wound (see diagram) so that the edges of the wound are held together, taking care not to touch the side of the dressing that is to go on the wound

- space the dressings a few millimetres apart, and work from the middle of the wound outwards
- leave the dressings in place for about seven to 10 days, even if they start to look a bit worse for wear

Wound closure dressings can't be applied to hairy skin like the scalp, but scalp wounds can sometimes be closed by tying hair across them.

BLEEDING WOUNDS

Most cuts will stop bleeding on their own, but if a blood vessel of any size has been cut, it may continue bleeding for some time. Head and hand wounds, also wounds at joint creases, tend to be particularly bloody. To stop bleeding from a wound:

- use your fingers or the palm of your hand to apply direct pressure to the wound, preferably over a sterile dressing or clean pad
- wear gloves if you are stopping bleeding on a travel companion
- apply steady pressure for at least five minutes before looking to see if the bleeding has stopped
- raise the injured limb above the level of your heart
- lie down if possible
- put a sterile dressing over the original pad (don't move this) and bandage it in place
- check the bandage regularly in case bleeding restarts

Get medical help urgently if much blood has been lost.

> **!** Never use a tourniquet to stop bleeding as this may cause gangrene – the only situation in which this may be appropriate is if the limb has been completely amputated.

BOILS & ABSCESSES

Don't try to burst these, however tempting it may seem, because this encourages the infection to spread. Instead:

- wash them with an antiseptic and keep them clean and dry as far as possible

- hot (clean) cloths may be soothing on the boil
- antibiotics don't usually help much with boils unless the infection spreads

SPLINTER

Treat as follows:

- wash the area thoroughly with soap and water
- sterilise the tips of a pair of tweezers by boiling them for a couple of seconds
- grasp the splinter as close to the skin as possible and remove it carefully
- squeeze the wound to make it bleed (to flush out any remaining dirt)
- clean the area with antiseptic and cover it with a sticking plaster (Band-Aid)

You should be up to date with your tetanus injections, but if not, you will need a booster.

BURNS & SCALDS

There are two main dangers with burns:

- fluid loss through damage to blood vessels leading to shock – the amount of fluid lost from a burn is directly proportional to the area affected by the burn
- infection because of damage to the skin's natural barrier

Burns are classified according to how deep the damage to the skin is:

- area of redness, painful – mild or first-degree burn, usually heals well
- blisters form later, painful – moderate or second-degree burn, usually heals well
- white or charred area, painless except around the edge – severe or third-degree burn, may result in extensive scarring

You need to seek medical attention for:

- any burn involving the hands, feet, armpits, face, neck or crotch
- any second or third degree burn
- any burn over 1cm to 2cm
- any burn in children

Mild burns or scalds (caused by hot fluid or steam) don't need medical attention unless they are extensive. Treat as follows:

- immediately pour cold water over the burn area for about 10 minutes or immerse it in cold water for about five minutes
- remove any jewellery such as rings, watches or tight clothing from the area before it swells up
- cover with a sterile nonstick dressing or paraffin gauze and bandage loosely in place
- don't burst any blisters, but if they burst anyway, cover with a nonadhesive sterile dressing
- apply antibiotic cream (eg silver sulphadiazine 1%), but avoid any other creams, ointments or greases
- take simple painkillers if necessary

FAINTING

This can occur in many different situations: pain or fright, standing still in the heat, emotional upset, exhaustion or lack of food. It's a brief loss of consciousness due to a temporary reduction in blood flow to the brain. Faints don't usually last long, but you may injure yourself as you fall. If you feel you are about to faint, or you notice someone you are with is about to (usually because they go as white as a sheet and start to sway), lie down before you fall. If someone faints:

- raise their legs (this helps to improve the blood flow to the brain)
- make sure they have plenty of fresh air
- as they recover, allow them to sit up gradually
- check for and treat any injury caused by falling

CONVULSIONS

A convulsion or fit is caused by a disturbance in brain function resulting in involuntary contractions of the muscles of the body and leading to loss of consciousness. Fits can occur for lots of reasons, including head injury, diseases affecting the brain, shortage of oxygen to the brain, some poisons and epilepsy. In babies and children, fits can be caused by a high temperature. If someone has a fit:

- ease their fall if possible
- loosen any clothing round the neck and protect their head (if possible)
- remove any sharp objects or other potential hazards from the vicinity
- don't try to restrain them or put anything in their mouth
- once the convulsions have stopped, put them in the recovery position (see inside back cover)
- get medical help

NOSEBLEED

This can be caused by blowing your nose vigorously or after a particularly earth-shattering sneeze. It's more likely when you have a cold. It occurs when blood vessels on the inner surface of your nose burst. Nosebleeds can look very dramatic, but most will stop quite quickly. If you get a nosebleed, do the following:

- sit down and put your head forward
- pinch your nose firmly just below the bridge (the bony bit) and keep a steady pressure for 10 minutes or until the bleeding has stopped
- rest quietly after it has stopped, and don't blow your nose or pick it for at least three hours or the bleeding may start again

An ice pack over the bridge of the nose can also help. Putting your head back will allow blood to drip down your throat, which can cause irritation to your stomach and possibly vomiting.

> ❗ If you can't stop the bleeding after about half an hour OR the bleeding is torrential and you start to feel dizzy, get medical help.

Note that if you get a nosebleed after a head injury, it may indicate a skull fracture, and you need to seek medical help urgently.

SPRAINS & STRAINS

> ❗ If in doubt, treat as a broken bone.

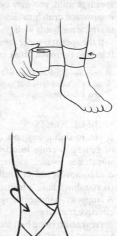

These soft tissue injuries affect ligaments and muscles and are common if you're doing any sort of vigorous activity like walking over rough terrain. They often occur as a result of a sudden wrench or twist. Sprains are injuries to a ligament near a joint, usually the ankle or knee joint. You get pain and swelling, with bruising often appearing 12 to 24 hours later. Strains are damage to the muscle caused by sudden violent movements, and are felt as a sudden sharp pain within the muscle body.

Treatment of any soft tissue injury is with the RICE principles:

- **R**est the injured part
- **I**ce: apply a cold compress (not directly on the skin)
- **C**ompress the injury (use a bandage)
- **E**levate the injured part

All these measures will help to reduce the swelling, bruising and pain, and are best started as early as possible after the injury. Continue with this for 24 to 48 hours or longer if the injury is more severe.

Use an elastic bandage, or a thick layer of padding kept in place with a crepe bandage, to compress the swelling. Check the bandage regularly in case further swelling has made it too tight.

Simple painkillers are useful to ease the discomfort. If the sprain is mild, you may be able to walk on it, perhaps with an improvised crutch to take the weight off it. To prevent further injury, wear boots with good ankle support.

If the sprain is more severe, it's best not to put any weight on it in case there is a break in the bone.

! For severe sprains you will need an X-ray to exclude the possibility of a broken bone, but in the meantime treat as for a broken bone and avoid putting weight on it.

PAINFUL JOINTS

If you're doing any sort of strenuous activity, you're at risk of getting overuse injuries of your joints. Signs are painful, sometimes swollen joints, worse after use. Treat with rest, a cold compress and anti-inflammatory painkillers like ibuprofen (if you don't have a history of stomach ulcers or indigestion). A support bandage may help, although rest is the most effective measure.

Prevention is the best treatment: make sure you are prepared by training well in advance and remember to warm up and down properly.

CHOKING

You choke if your airway is completely or partly blocked, for example as a result of swallowing a small bone, eating too quickly or because of vomit, especially if you're drunk. Children often put things in their mouths, and this may result in choking. Small, hard toys, coins and food such as peanuts or boiled sweets are particular risks. It's usually obvious if a person is choking – they will have difficulty speaking, may gag and usually clutch their throat. A child may make a whistling noise, try to cry but be unable to, or may go blue in the face and collapse.

If an adult or child appears to be choking:

- get them to cough – this may bring up the blockage
- if this doesn't work, give them four sharp blows between the shoulder blades (ask adults to bend forward; children can be up-ended or bent over your knee)

If this doesn't work, try the following techniques:

- child (over one year) – place child on the floor or across your lap and place your hands one on each side of the chest just below the armpits; squeeze the child's chest by giving four sharp thrusts with your hands
- adult – lie the casualty down on the floor on their side; place both your hands on the side of their chest, under their armpit, and give four quick downwards thrusts

Check to see if the blockage is cleared (remove it from the mouth if necessary), if not get medical help URGENTLY.

For babies, you won't be able to get them to cough, so you need to give four sharp slaps between the shoulders to start with – lie the baby face down on your forearm and support their head and shoulders on your hand. If you need to give chest thrusts, lie the baby face down on your lap and give four quick squeezes, as described for a child (but gentler).

MAJOR TRAUMA

INITIAL ASSESSMENT

Accidents can happen anywhere and what you do is determined to some extent by the circumstances you are in and how readily available medical care is. However, remember that emergency services may be very different from what you are used to. They may be very much slower at responding to a call, so you need to be prepared to do at least an initial assessment and to ensure the person comes to no further harm. A basic plan of action is outlined as follows:

- keep calm and think through what you need to do
- carefully look over the injured person in the position you found them (unless this is hazardous for some reason eg on a cliff edge)
- check for heart action (pulses – see diagram), breathing and major blood loss
- if necessary, and you know how, start resuscitation – see inside back cover
- take immediate steps to control any bleeding by applying direct pressure
- check for shock, head injuries, spine and limb injuries, and any other injuries
- make the person as comfortable as possible and reassure them
- keep the person warm if necessary by insulating them from cold or wet ground (use whatever you have to hand eg a sleeping bag)
- don't move the person if a spinal injury is possible
- get medical help urgently

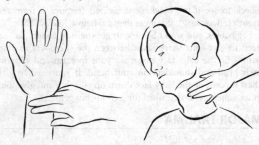

FIRST AID

HEAD INJURY

Your brain is vital to life and you should do everything you can to prevent injury to it – wear a helmet or hard hat if you are going to do any potentially risky activities. You need to seek medical help for any significant head injury.

Scalp wounds need to be treated as for any wound (see earlier). Serious head injury can occur with little or no signs of external injury. If a person has received an injury to the head, you need to assess whether there has been damage to the brain. You can do this by assessing whether they were unconscious at all (how much damage occurred is related to how long unconsciousness lasted), how they are behaving now, and if they show any signs of deterioration in the hours or days following the accident.

- Dazed but didn't lose consciousness – very little risk of brain damage.
- Unconscious (blacked out) for a few minutes, can't remember accident happening – the person is concussed (ie the brain has been shaken and bruised a bit). They may feel dizzy and nauseated, with mild headache, and memory loss can last for a few hours. Concussion generally doesn't cause any permanent damage, but you need to keep an eye on the person for 24 hours in case they deteriorate. Seek medical help.
- Prolonged unconsciousness of more than 10 minutes (coma) – this usually indicates more serious brain damage, and may be associated with a skull fracture. Put the person into the recovery position (see inside back cover) and get medical help immediately. Evacuation may be necessary.

Signs of a skull fracture include:

- blood coming from nose, mouth or throat not due to external injury
- clear, watery fluid dripping from ear or nose
- a depression or dip in the skull

Anyone who has had a head injury causing unconsciousness, however brief, should be observed for signs of deterioration in the 24 to 48 hours following injury. Head injury can sometimes result in compression of the brain because of bleeding from a damaged blood vessel within the head. This causes blood to accumulate gradually within the closed space of the skull, squashing the brain. Signs of cerebral compression or severe brain damage include:

- disorientation and confusion
- vomiting
- severe headache

- drowsiness
- irritability or change in personality
- noisy, slow breathing
- unequal or dilated pupils that may not react to light
- weakness down one side of the body

If someone has a head injury but is conscious:

- staunch any bleeding
- check if they know who they are, where they are, what the date is etc
- check they can move all their limbs and don't have any unusual sensations (eg tingling)
- sit them up gradually and then do a test walk to check balance
- deal with any external wounds
- avoid alcohol and sedatives on the first evening
- rest up for a day or two until you're sure the person is back to normal

If the person is concussed (eg keeps asking the same question), keep a close eye on them for the first 24 hours and be ready to get medical help immediately if there is any deterioration in their condition.

❗ Note that sometimes a head injury can occur when someone has lost consciousness from another cause (eg a faint).

NECK & SPINE INJURY

The main worry with any spinal or neck injury is damage to your spinal cord. Apart from supporting your trunk and head, your backbone (spine) provides a protective covering for nerve fibres (the spinal cord) carrying messages from your brain to all parts of your body. If these fibres are partly or completely cut, the damage caused may be permanent. The most vulnerable parts of the spine are your neck and lower back. Causes of spinal injury include falling from a height, diving into a shallow pool and hitting the bottom, a head-on crash in a motor vehicle, and being thrown from a motorbike.

Severe persistent neck or back pain indicate that you may have injured your spine. If you have also damaged the spinal cord, you may not be able to move your limbs, or you may have abnormal or no feelings in your body below the level of the injury (for example tingling or a feeling of heaviness). If the injury is at a high level, breathing difficulties may occur if the nerves to the chest muscles are affected.

The main priority in someone with a spinal injury is to prevent new or further damage to the spinal cord by immobilisation of the spine and extremely careful handling during any evacuation procedure.

! If in doubt, eg the person is unconscious, assume there is a spinal injury until proven otherwise.

BROKEN BONES

A break or crack in a bone is called a fracture. Bones are generally tough and you need a pretty forceful injury to break one, although old or diseased bones break more easily. In a simple fracture, the bone breaks in one place and the skin isn't torn. An open fracture is where the broken ends of the bone stick through the skin. You should assume that any fracture associated with a wound near it is an open one, even if you can't see the bone protruding, as the broken ends may have come through the skin and gone back.

Any broken bone needs medical attention as it needs to be set properly, and any damage to the surrounding tissues needs to be assessed and treated. Open fractures have the added risk of infection because the bone is exposed, and generally need more urgent treatment.

A broken bone is often obvious because it hurts like hell. Otherwise, indications of a fracture include:

- forceful injury eg a violent blow, a fall or impact with a moving object
- snapping sound as the bone broke
- pain made worse by movement
- tenderness when you press over the bone at the site of injury
- obvious swelling and bruising over the injury site
- pain when you try to use the limb and you can't put your weight on it
- obvious deformity of the limb – twisting, shortening or bending

What you do next will depend to a certain extent on the circumstances you're in and how readily medical help is available. The aim with any type of fracture is to prevent further damage by immobilising the affected part in some way. Unless the person is in immediate danger where they are, don't move them until the fracture has been supported and immobilised. Painkillers are important but if medical help is close at hand, avoid taking anything by mouth in case an operation is needed to fix the fracture.

Some basic guidelines for a simple fracture are as follows:

- if the affected limb is bent or angled, straighten it by pulling firmly in the line of the bone, but if this causes too much pain, it's OK to leave it

- if you are near medical help, immobilise the limb by bandaging it and support the arm in a sling against your body or bandage the uninjured leg to the injured one
- in the field situation, it's worth immobilising the limb in a splint – use plastic air splints or structural aluminium malleable (SAM) splints if you are carrying them, or you can improvise with any piece of equipment you have, but make sure you pad the inside of the splint

Note that simple fractures don't need to be fixed straight away because healing takes several weeks, so if you have a chance to go to a better hospital further away, it would be worthwhile.

With an open fracture, you need to cover the wound and control any bleeding (apply pressure with a clean pad or dressing) before immobilising the limb as for a simple fracture. If no medical help is available within one to two hours, start taking antibiotics (eg cephalexin 500mg four times daily) to prevent infection.

Remember to check that any bandage or splint you've applied is not cutting off the circulation (indicated by numbness, tingling and blue or white colour). Loosen the bandages or splint immediately if necessary.

! In cold conditions, frostbite is a particular risk so you need to protect the hand or foot from cold by covering them appropriately.

DISLOCATIONS

This can occur when a bone is wrenched into an abnormal position or because of violent muscle contractions (eg a fit). This displaces the head of a bone from the joint, most commonly the shoulder, thumb, finger and jaw. There can be an associated fracture and there's often damage to the structures surrounding the joint. Don't attempt to replace a dislocation if a fracture is present.

! As a general rule, don't attempt to replace a dislocated joint if medical help is accessible because you can cause permanent damage.

You need to treat dislocations with immobilisation and pain relief as for a simple fracture.

BROKEN RIBS

Flail chest is when a heavy blow fractures several ribs in more than one place. This is an emergency because you will not be able to breathe properly. On inspection, a section of your chest will be moving in the opposite direction to the rest of your chest during breathing. The broken part needs to be splinted immediately by taping a firm bandage over it and supporting your arm in a sling on the injured side.

Otherwise, broken ribs are painful but don't need any specific treatment. Take strong painkillers, such as co-codamol, at the prescribed intervals. If the pain is very severe, or there are multiple fractures, you may need to strap your chest.

! Get help urgently if you experience breathing difficulties or cough up blood.

INTERNAL INJURIES

Some injuries can cause severe internal damage and bleeding without significant external injury. It's easy to control bleeding from external wounds on the skin by applying pressure but you can't do this for internal bleeding. Internal injuries are generally caused by considerable violence and always need urgent expert medical care and evacuation if you are in a remote area. They may not be obvious to begin with, but you need to suspect internal bleeding if there are signs of shock (pale, dizzy, weak rapid pulse, low blood pressure). Sometimes bleeding in the abdomen can produce a tender, slowly expanding abdomen.

Glossary...

acetaminophen – US name for *paracetamol*

acute – describes an illness of rapid onset and brief duration; compare with *chronic*

adrenaline – hormone that prepares the body for flight or fright; it's given by injection to treat severe allergic reactions (such as to bee sting); US term is *epinephrine*

AIDS – acquired immune deficiency syndrome

AMS – acute mountain sickness

antibiotic – drug used to treat bacterial infections

antidiarrhoeals – refers to drugs used to treat the symptoms of diarrhoea ('blockers' or 'stoppers'); drugs in this category include loperamide (eg Imodium and other brand names), diphenoxylate (with atropine; eg Lomotil) and bismuth subsalicylate (Pepto-Bismol)

bacteria – tiny organisms, some of which can cause diseases which can be treated with *antibiotics*

BCG – stands for bacille Calmette-Guérin; it's the vaccine for tuberculosis

bilharzia – see *schistosomiasis*

booster – dose of vaccine given after a full course to bring protection up to optimal level

bowel – a term for the lower part of the intestinal tract

breakbone fever – old name for dengue fever

CDC – Centers for Disease Control and Prevention (US)

chronic – describes a disease that usually comes on slowly and is prolonged

colic – pain that comes and goes in waves

cutaneous – related to skin

dermatitis – general term for an itchy skin rash

DHF – dengue haemorrhagic fever

diapers – *see* nappies

diuretic – substance (like coffee, alcohol and some therapeutic medicines) that increases the volume of urine lost

drug – any substance used to alleviate symptoms or treat disease; the term 'drug' is used interchangeably with medicine and medication, it's also popularly used to describe illegal substances

dysentery – any diarrhoea with blood

eczema – *dermatitis* due to intrinsic causes

endemic – describes diseases that occur commonly in people in a particular area

enteric fever – another term for typhoid or paratyphoid fever (enteric means related to the intestine)

epidemic – sudden outbreak of an infectious disease that rapidly affects lots of people

epinephrine – see *adrenaline*

fever – when your body temperature is higher than normal (normal is 37°C or 98.6°F); usually caused by a bacterial or viral infection

generic – used in reference to a drug name it means the chemical (eg metronidazole) as opposed to the brand name (eg in this case, Flagyl) of a drug; by convention brand names are always capitalised

glucose – sugar

haemorrhagic – associated with bleeding

HIV – human immunodeficiency virus

immunisation – production of *immunity*, often through injection of a substance (called a *vaccine*), although oral immunisations are also possible

immunity – protection against disease

infectious – describes a disease that is caused by a microorganism (bacteria, virus, fungus etc) and can be transmitted from person to person (ie something you can 'catch'), unlike cancer for example

jaundice – yellowing of the skin and whites of the eyes because of the liver not working properly

Lariam – brand name for *mefloquine*

Malarone – brand name for atovaquone-proguanil combination anti-malarial drug medication – see *drug*

medicine – see *drug*

mefloquine – a drug used in the prevention and treatment of malaria; brand name is *Lariam*

microbe – another term for *microorganism*

microorganism – any organism too small to be visible to the naked eye, includes bacteria, viruses, fungi etc

nappies – called *diapers* in the US

ORS – oral rehydration salts

paracetamol – simple painkiller, also good for lowering fever; US term is *acetaminophen*

prophylaxis – prevention of a disease

parasite – any living thing (eg a tapeworm) that lives in or on another living thing

pressure bandaging – use of a bandage to apply pressure over a wide area of the limb; used in management of some bites and stings (see also *tourniquet*)

prevalent – widespread or current

prophylaxis – prevention of disease

protozoa – single-celled microorganisms; include malaria parasites and *Giardia*

resistance – when antibiotics or other drugs are ineffective against a microorganism

Riamet – brand name of a new malaria treatment drug for adults and children 12 years and older

SARS – (severe acute respiratory syndrome) an infection from bats of a corona virus, that caused an alarming outbreak in Asia in 2003

schistosomiasis – parasitic disease caused by a tiny freshwater worm; also called *bilharzia*

SPF – sun protection factor

STI – sexually transmitted infection

subcutaneous – describes something (eg an injection, a lump) under the skin

subtropics – between tropics and temperate zone

sulpha drugs – a group of antibiotics

TB – tuberculosis

tourniquet – a device used to press on an artery to stop blood flow; use is very restricted, and it's not indicated for treating bites and stings – see *pressure bandaging*

thrush – common name for vaginal candidiasis

topical – term used to describe a treatment that is applied directly to the affected part of the body (such as a cream applied onto a skin rash)

toxin – poison

tropics – region between the tropics of Cancer and Capricorn

ulcer – break in the skin (or mucous membrane like the lining of the stomach)

vaccine – preparation that is used to stimulate immunity

vaccination – not exactly synonomous with immunisation, but in this book we have used the terms interchangeably

virus – minute particle; cause many diseases, including colds, flu, hepatitis, AIDS etc

visceral – related to the viscera, or internal organs

WHO – World Health Organization

Latin American Terms...

BRAZILIAN PORTUGUESE

ESSENTIALS

I need a doctor.	*Preciso de um médico.*
Could you please call a doctor?	*Você pode chamar um médico, por favor?*
Where can I find a good doctor?	*Onde posso encontrar um bom médico?*
I need a dentist.	*Preciso de um dentista.*
Is there a hospital near here?	*Tem um hospital aqui perto?*
I am ill.	*Estou doente.*
My friend (female) is ill.	*Minha amiga está doente.*
My friend (male) is ill.	*Meu amigo está doente.*

AT THE CHEMIST

I need something for a cold.	*Preciso de alguma coisa para o resfriado.*
Do I need a prescription?	*Preciso de uma receita?*

AILMENTS

allergy	*alergia*
anaemia	*anemia*
asthma	*asma*
burn	*queimadura*
constipation	*prisão de ventre*
cough	*tosse*
diarrhoea	*diarréia*
dysentery	*disenteria*
fever	*febre*
headache	*dor de cabeça*
infection	*infecção*
itch	*coceira*
malaria	*maláría*

pain	*dor*
rash	*erupção/irritação na pele*
stomachache	*dor de barriga*
sunburn	*queimadura de sol*
sunstroke	*insolação*
toothache	*dor de dente*
yellow fever	*febre amarela*

PARTS OF THE BODY

arm	*braço*
back	*costas*
blood	*sangue*
bone	*osso*
chest	*peito*
ear	*orelha*
eye	*olho*
foot	*pé*
hand	*mão*
head	*cabeça*
heart	*coração*
knee	*joelho*
leg	*perna*
mouth	*boca*
nose	*nariz*
shoulder	*ombro*
stomach	*estômago*
teeth	*dentes*
throat	*garganta*

SOME USEFUL WORDS

accident	*acidente*
antibiotics	*antibióticos*
antiseptic	*anti-séptico*
aspirin	*aspirinas*
bandage	*atadura*
blood test	*análise de sangue*

broken	*quebrado/a*
condoms	*preservativo*
contraceptive	*anticoncepcional*
faeces	*fezes*
injection	*injeção*
injury	*ferimento*
medicine	*remédio*
nurse	*enfermeira*
tablet	*comprimido*
tampon	*tampão*
urine	*urina*
wound	*ferida*

SPANISH

ESSENTIALS

I need a doctor (who speaks English).	*Necesito un doctor* *(que pueda hablar inglés).*
Could you please call a doctor?	*¿Podría llamar a un* *doctor, por favor?*
Where is the nearest…?	*¿Dónde está… más cercano?*
doctor	*el doctor/el médico*
hospital	*el hospital*
dentist	*el dentista*
I am ill.	*Estoy enfermo/a.*
My friend (female) is ill.	*Mi amiga está enferma.*
My friend (male) is ill.	*Mi amigo está enfermo.*

AT THE CHEMIST

I need something for a cold.	*Necesito algo para gripe.*
Do I need a prescription?	*¿Necesito una receta?*

AILMENTS

allergy	*alergia*
altitude sickness	*soroche/apunamiento*
anaemia	*anemia*

asthma	*asma*
burn	*quemadura*
constipation	*estreñimiento*
cough	*tos*
diarrhoea	*diarrea*
dysentery	*disentería*
fever	*fiebre/calentura*
headache	*dolor de cabeza*
infection	*una infección*
itch	*comezón/escozor/rasquiña*
malaria	*malaria*
nausea	*náusea*
pain	*dolor*
rash	*erupción*
stomachache	*dolor de estómago*
sunburn	*una quemadura de sol*
sunstroke	*insolado*
toothache	*dolor de muelas*
yellow fever	*fiebre amarilla*

PARTS OF THE BODY

arm	*brazo*
back	*espalda*
blood	*sangre*
bone	*hueso*
chest	*pecho*
ear	*oreja*
eye	*ojo*
foot	*pie*
hand	*mano*
head	*cabeza*
heart	*corazón*
knee	*rodilla*
leg	*pierna*
mouth	*boca*
nose	*nariz*

shoulder	*hombro*
stomach	*estómago*
teeth	*dientes*
throat	*garganta*

SOME USEFUL WORDS

accident	*accidente*
antibiotics	*antibióticos*
antiseptic	*antiséptico*
aspirin	*aspirina*
bandage	*vendaje, cura*
blood test	*análisis de sangre*
contraceptive	*anticonceptivo*
dizzy	*mareado/a*
faeces	*excremento, materia fecal*
injection	*inyección*
injury	*daño*
medicine	*medicamentos, drogas*
ointment	*ungüento*
sleeping pill	*somnífero*
urine	*orina*
wound	*herida*

A

abdominal pain 147, 165, 166, 173, 174, 181
  types 124, 128
abscess
  amoebic 166
  tooth 199
accidents
  children and 286
  prevention 93-6
acclimatisation 71-6
  altitude 324-6
  cold 320-1
  heat 71-2
  sun 73-6
acetazolamide 328-9
acute mountain sickness (AMS)
  mild symptoms 329-30
  prevention 327-9
  severe AMS 330-1
  treatment 331-2
AIDS 216-22
  facts 216-17
  in Latin America 220-2
  risks 217
air pollution 176, 182-3, 184
air travel
  dehydration and 65
  ear pain 186-7
  fear of flying 66
  fitness for 65
alcohol 245
  withdrawal 241, 244
allergic reaction
  bee sting 289, 378
  immunisations 39
  medicines 414-15
  skin 205-8, 287

alternative first aid 60-1
alternative travel kits 62
altitude 324-32, *see also* acute
  mountain sickness
  children and 289
  HRT and 252
  information sources 325
  older travellers and 308
  oral contraception and 262
amargo 404
amoebic dysentery 166
amoebic liver abscess 166
anacondas 384
anaemia 123
anal fissure 172
anal itching 173
animal bites 385-8
  first aid treatment 387
antibiotics 418-22
  diarrhoea and 161-3
  doses 422
  guide 420
  oral contraception and 262
  resistance 419
antidiarrhoeals 160-3, 423
antihistamines 422-3
anti-inflammatory drug 417
antimalarials, *see* malaria
  prevention drugs
ants 377-8
anxiety 239-41
appendicitis 174-5
aromatherapy, travel and 66
aspirin 417
asthma 177, 184-5
athlete's foot 209

B

babies, *see* children
back pain 254, 358, 449
bacterial skin infections 209-10
bacterial vaginosis 257

Colour indicates symptoms
Bold indicates maps

INDEX

bandages 435-6
  ankle 443
  pressure immobilisation 436-7
bartonellosis 368-9
bedbugs 212-13
bee sting 377-9
bends, see decompression sickness
bilharzia, see schistosomiasis
bismuth subsalicylate 57, 82-3,
  161, 423
bites, see also specific creatures
  animal 385-8
  human 385
  insects 89-90
  marine creatures 344-5
blackflies 371
bladder infection 253-4
bleeding 148, 439
  dengue fever and 139
  trauma and 447-8
  vaginal 124
  yellow fever and 141
blindness 371-2
blister
  feet 98-9, 334
  skin 204, 205, 206, 207, 210
blister beetles 206
bloating 164, 165
blood, see also illness, danger signs
  in faeces 148, 166, 364
  in spit 184
  in urine 124, 148, 364
  in vomit 124
Blood Care Foundation 106
blood clots 66-7, 252, see also DVT
blood group 106
blood transfusion 103-6
blue-ringed octopus 351
blues, see depression
blurred vision 195
boils 439-40
books 62-4

breakbone fever, see dengue fever
breathing rate 123
breathlessness 179, 183, 184, 330
broken bones 449-51
broken ribs 452
bronchitis 184, see also cough
brucellosis 232-3
buddy system 320
burns 440-1

C

caffeine 242-3
caimans 360
candiru, see urethra fish
Cat's claw 401-2
Centers for Disease Control &
  Prevention (CDC) 27
Chagas' disease 369-71
chancroid 226
checkup
  pretravel 51-3
  post-travel 389
chest infection 179
chest pain 179, 184
chigger dermatitis 375
chiggers, see mites
chigoe, see jigger flea
chilblains 323
children 275-96
  altitude and 289
  immunisations 277-8
  signs of illness 290
chillies 108-9
chlamydia 224
chlorine 87
chloroquine 45-7
  eyes and 190
choking 444-5
cholera 166-8
  immunisation 34
cleanliness 83
climatic extremes 314-20

clothing
  cold climates 320
  hot climates 72
  insect bites and 90
coca 402-3
cold (climate) 320-4
cold (illness) 176
cold sores 181-3
concussion 447
condoms 219, 221, 225, 271
cone shell 351
cone-nose bugs, *see* triatomine
  bugs
constipation 165, 171
contact lens wearers 190
contraception (women) 258-65
  availability 259
  emergency 263-4
contraception (men) 271
convulsion 124, 387, 442, *see also*
  febrile convulsion
coral cuts 345
cough 131, 146, 179, 184-5, 295,
  330, 338, 363, 376
cracked heels 98
cramps, heat 318
creeping eruption 213
crocodiles 360
cruise 307
culture shock 238-9
curare 406
cuts 434-5
cyclospora 154
cystitis, *see* bladder
  infection

D
dark urine 147
deafness 189
decompression sickness 358-9
DEET (diethyltoluamide) 91

dehydration
  children and 288
  diarrhoea and 156-8
  heat and 318
  kidney stone and 173
  signs 319
delirium
dengue fever 137-40, **21**
dental kit 197
dental problems, *see* teeth
dental treatment 201-2
dentures 303
depression 241-3
dermatitis 205-8
de-stressing 237
dexamethasone 331, 332
diabetic travellers 308-12
  information sources 309
  insulin 310-11
  time zones 311
dialysis centres 299
Diamox, *see* acetazolamide
diaper rash 295
diarrhoea 124, 147, 150-68, 240
  antibiotics 161-3
  children and 293-4
  eating and 158-60
  fluid replacement 156-8
  oral contraceptives and 259
  prevention (remedies) 82-3
  persistent 163-6
  treatment 155-63
  types 152-5
diet, *see* nutrition
diphtheria 233
  immunisation 34
dislocation 451-2
Divers Alert Network (DAN) 354
dizziness 240, 318, 319, 320
documents 52
donovanosis 227
double vision 195

doxycycline 48
dressings, see bandages
drinking water 83-9
    boiling 86
    bottled water 86
    chemical disinfectants 87-8
    filters & purifiers 88-9
drugs 246-7, see also medicines
    deliberate drugging 246
DVT (deep-venous thrombosis)
    66-7, 306
dysentery 153

E

ear infection, see earache
earache 187-9
    air travel and 186-7
    diving and 353
eardrops 188
eardrum, burst 186-7
ears 186-9
earthquakes 94
eczema 205
electric eel 361-2
elephantiasis, see filariasis
emergency, what to do 425
    assessment 445-6
    rescue 336
    resuscitation 472
encephalitis 228
espundia, see leishmaniasis
ethnobotany 405-7
expeditions 54-5
eyes 189-96
    black eye 194
    eyedrops 193
    eye wash 191
    foreign body in 191-2
    infection 192-3
    injuries 194-5
    irritation 376
    pain 195-6
    red eye 192-4

F

face pain 177
facial swelling 235
fainting 441
    heat and 318-20
falciparum malaria 130
febrile convulsion 292
feet 97-9
    blisters 98-9
    hygiene 98
fever 124, 125-8, 131, 138, 141,
    142, 143, 146, 147, 153, 166, 173,
    177, 181, 184, 188, 200, 218,
    228, 233, 255, 364, 368, 371, 375,
    376, 387,
    after you get back 390
    causes 126-8
    children and 291
    dehydration and 126
    measures to lower it 125-6
filariasis 228-9, 24
first aid courses 54
fit, see convulsion
fleas 376-7
flu 178-9
fluid replacement
    children and 293-4
    diarrhoea and 156-8
    heat and 319
folliculitis 210
food, see also nutrition
    children and 285
    precautions 77-82
food poisoning 153-5
footwear 97
formula feed 280
fracture, see broken bones
freshwater hazards 360-4
frostbite 323-4
fungal infection
    skin 208-9, 270
    vaginal 255-7

G

gastrointestinal upset, *see* diarrhoea

gay men, health tips 272-4

genital ulcers 225-6

genital warts 226

geography worm, *see* creeping eruption

giardiasis 164

glands, swollen 181, 217-18, 225, 229, 369

glandular fever 181

gonorrhoea 181, 224

guarana 404-5

H

haemorrhage, *see* bleeding

haemorrhagic fevers 231-2

haemorrhoids, *see* piles

hallucinogenic plants 398

halofantrine 135

Hansen's disease 230

hantavirus pulmonary syndrome 231

hay fever 177-8

head injury 446-8

headache 124, 125-6, 129, 131, 138, 141, 142, 143, 147, 177, 179, 196, 240, 318, 319, 329, 447

healer, *see* shaman

heartburn 174

heat 316-20

acclimatisation 316-17

cramps 318

exhaustion 318-19

older travellers and 306

heatstroke

treatment 318-20

hepatitis 146-9

immunisation 34-5

oral contraceptive pill and 149

prevention 149

symptoms 147-8

treatment 148-9

herpes, genital 225-6, *see also* cold sores

histoplasmosis 338

HIV, *see* AIDS

hot flushes 251

HRT, travelling and 252

hydatid disease 170

hypothermia 321-3

I

IAMAT 29

illness

danger signs 124-5

general treatment measures 120-2

immunisations 31-9, *see also* specific immunisations

certificate 31

children and 277-8

older travellers and 301

side effects 37-9

special considerations 31-2

timing 32

impetigo 210

indigestion 164, 174

information sources 25-30

altitude 325

inhalation (steam) 177

injections, infection risk 102-3

injury, *see also* accidents

eye 194-5

major trauma 445-52

prevention 93-6

teeth 201

insect bites 365

prevention 90-1

insect repellents 91

insects, diseases caused by 89-90

insurance 50-1

internal injuries 452

International Association for Medical Assistance to Travelers, see IAMAT
internet resources 28-9, see also information sources
intestinal parasites
  prevention 170-1
  treatment 168-9
intrauterine devices 263
iodine 87
irritable bowel syndrome 165
itching 205, 210, 352, 371
  bites 212, 367
  causes 205
  eyes 177, 191
  rash 205-8, 213, 363
  treatment 207-8

J

jaundice 131, 141, 144, 146-9, 181
  oral contraception and 262
jellyfish stings 347-8
  treatment 348-9
jet lag 67-9
  children 283
jigger flea 214-15
jock itch 270
joint pain 138, 444
jungle hazards 335

K

kidney infection 173, 254, see also bladder infection
  kidney stone 173

L

landmines, see mines
Lariam, see mefloquine
Latin American Bureau 30
lead poisoning 104
leeches 372-3
leishmaniasis 366-8

leprosy, see Hansen's disease
leptospirosis 338, 364
lesbians, health tips 256-7
lethargy 148, 181
lice 211-12
light-coloured faeces 147
lightning 336
loperamide 160
loss of vision 195-6
lymphogranuloma venerum 226-7

M

maggot boils 214
malaria 130-7, 390, 20
  children and 279, 292
  diagnosis 132
  drug resistance 134
  emergency treatment 49, 133
  information sources 40-2
  pregnant travellers and 267
  prevention 42-9
  risk 42
  symptoms 131-2
malaria prevention drugs 42-9
  doses & timing 44-5
  long-haul travellers 45
  scuba diving and 355
  side effects 45-8
malaria treatment drugs 133-7
  doses 136
manaca 405
marine life 344-52, see also specific marine creatures
measles 235
medical conditions, travel and 300-1
medical help 119-20
medical kit 55-9
  children 280-2
medical services, payment 426
MedicAlert Foundation
  International 29-30

medicinal plants 399-405
medicines
    buying 410-13
    children and 280-2
    customs and 55-6
    generic vs brand names 56
    side effects 414-15
mefloquine 46, 47-8, 267, 279
melatonin 69
meningococcal meningitis 141-3
    immunisation 35
menopausal symptoms 251
menstruation 248-51
    absent periods 250
    heavy periods 250-1
    practicalities 248
migraine 196
milk 80
mines 100
mites 373-5
morning-after pill 263-4
mosquito nets 92
mosquitoes 365
motion sickness 69-70
    children and 283
mouth ulcers 183-4
mumps 234
muscle strain 443-4

N
nappies 280
nappy rash 295
natural remedies
    chilblains 323
    colds 61, 176
    constipation 60
    diarrhoea 60, 161
    first aid 60
    immune boosters 84-5
    insect bites 61, 91
    jet lag 69
    menopausal symptoms 251

motion sickness 60, 70
premenstrual syndrome 249
skin rashes 61, 207
stress 61
sunburn 61, 315
travel kits 62
nausea 131, 138, 142, 147, 152,
    318, see also vomiting
neck injury 448-9
neck stiffness 142
night sweats 146
nitrogen build-up 359
nitrogen narcosis 359
nosebleed 442-3
nutrition 106-17
    activity and 116-17
    children and 284-5

O
older travellers 300-8
onchocerciasis, see river
    blindness
oral contraception 259-62
    altitude and 327
    missed pill 262
oral sex 181
Oropouche fever 231
Oroya fever 368-9
over-breathing 240
Overseas Citizen's Service (US) 27
ozone hole 74

P
painkillers 417-18
palpitations 240
panic attacks 241
paracetamol 417
paranoia 247
permethrin 91-2
piles 172-3
pinta 231
piranhas 360-1

plague 376-7
poisoning, accidental 286
polio 234
post-travel blues 393
pregnancy test 264
pregnancy, accidental 264-5
pregnant travellers 265-9
    air travel and 266
    immunisations and 267-8
    malaria and 267-8
premenstrual syndrome 249
prickly heat 204
prostate problems 272
pubic lice 212
pulse 122

Q

quassia, see amargo
quinine bark 400-1

R

rabies 338, 385-8
    immunisation 35-6
    prevention, post-bite 387-8
rash 129, 138, 142, 144, 203, 205,
    213, 218, 233, 235, 363, 369, 375
    diseases and 203
recompression treatment 358-9
red eyes 364
rehydration, see fluid
    replacement
rescue procedure 336
rigors 126
ringworm, see fungal infections
rip current 343-4
river blindness 371-2
river crossings 335-6
river hazards 363
road safety 95-6
Rocky Mountain spotted
    fever 376
rubella 235

S

safer sex 219
safety tips
    caving 338
    cycling 336-7
    trekking 333-6
sandflies 366
sandfly fever 368
scabies 210-11
scalds 440-1
schistosomiasis 362-4, 23
    prevention 92-3
scorpionfish 350-1
scorpions 338, 381-2
scuba diving 352-60
    information sources 354
    insurance 353
    medical problems 358-60
    safety tips 356-8
sea currents 343
sea lice, see jellyfish stings
sea snakes 346-7
sea urchins 352
sex, travel and 99-102
sexually transmitted
    infections 222-7
shaman 394-5
sharks 346
shigella 154
sinusitis 176-7
skin cancer 288, 340
skin lesions 208
skin nodules 369
skin ulcer 366
skull fracture 447
sling 450
snakes 382-4
    snake bite 383
sneezing 177
snow blindness 332
sore throat 179-81, 233, 368
    causes 180

South American Explorers Club 30
spectacles 190
spiders 379-81
spine injury 448-9
spiritualism 395-9
splint 450
splinter 440
sprain 443-4
steroid cream 207
sting rays 349
stomach cramps 152, 153, 155, 159, 161, 164, 166
stonefish 350-1
street food 82
stress 236-7
stye 197
sun 314-16
    skin cancer and 288, 340
sunburn 314-16
sunglasses 190-1
sunscreen 73
survival skills 54
sweating 126, 131, 146, 204, 251, 288, 306, 308, 316
swimmer's ear 187
swimmer's itch 363
swimming safety tips 96, 339-43
swollen face 200
syphilis 224

T
tapeworms 169-71
tarantulas 381
teeth 196-202
temperature
    how to take it 121-2
    normal 123
termination of pregnancy 265
testicle
    lump 271
    pain 270
tetanus 235

thermometer 121-2
thrush, see vaginal candidiasis
ticks 373-6
    removal 375
tinea, see fungal infections
tooth abscess 199, 200
toothache 199- 200
trachoma 193-4
traditional medicine 394-409, see also natural remedies
trauma 445-52
travel health clinics, see information sources
travel insurance, see insurance
travellers diarrhoea, see diarrhoea
travellers with special needs 297-313
    diabetic travellers 308-12
    HIV-positive travellers 312-13
    information sources 299-300
    older travellers 300-8
triatomine bugs 369-71
trichomoniasis 258
tropical ear, see swimmer's ear
tropical sprue 164
trypanosomiasis, see Chagas' disease
tuberculosis 144-6
    immunisation 36
tummy ache 294-5, see also abdominal pain
tunnel vision 196
typhoid fever 143-4
    immunisation 37
typhus 375-6

U
ulcer
    skin 233, 366, 367, 368
    stomach 174
unconsciousness 441, 442, 447-8
urethra fish 361

urinary tract infection, *see* bladder infection
useful organisations 29-30

V

vaginal bleeding, heavy 250-1
vaginal candidiasis 255-7
vaginal discharge 254-8
vampire bats 385, 386
vegetarian diet and 113-16
veruga peruana 369
vitamins 110-11
vomiting 124, 128-9, 153-5, 168, 174, 175, 319, 329
    medicines for 423
    oral contraception and 259

W

wasps 377-8
water pollution 342-3

water purifiers, *see* drinking water
water sports, safety tips 340-1
web sites, *see* internet resources
weight loss 124, 126, 146, 164, 169
nutrition and 112-13
Weil's disease, *see* leptospirosis
World Health Organization 28
worms, intestinal 168-71
wounds 434-5
    cleaning 434
    closure 438-9
    infection 437-8

Y

yellow fever 140-1, **22**
    immunisation 37
yellow skin, *see* jaundice
yerba maté 403

Remember Dr ABC:

- **D**anger
- **R**esponse

- **A**irway
- **B**reathing
- **C**ompressions

D) ASSESS THE DANGER

Ensure the scene is safe so you or others or the patient do not get injured. Remove risks and hazards. Call for emergency assistance.

R) RESPONSE

Shout and gently shake the patient.

- If responsive, place in recovery position (see above illustration) and be supportive till help arrives.
- If no response, check airway and breathing.

A) AIRWAY

Check the airway is not obstructed. Tilt head back a little and lift jaw forward. Remove any dentures, food or vomit if necessary.

B) BREATHING

Look, listen and feel for normal breathing.

- Is the chest rising and falling? Can you hear the casualty breathing? Can you feel the breath on your cheek? (wait for up to 10 seconds) If yes: place casualty in recovery position.
- If no, you need to breathe for the casualty, see Recovery Breaths, and commence chest compressions, see C.

Recovery Breaths

Turn the casualty on to their back.

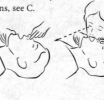

- Use one hand to gently tilt head back.
- Pinch nose closed using thumb and index finger of other hand.
- Open mouth, keeping chin raised.
- Take a full breath and place your lips on the casualty's mouth.
- Blow steadily into the casualty's mouth for about two seconds.
- Watch for chest to rise.
- Repeat so that you give two effective breaths.